PHL

54060000155753

D1348949

WORLD OF
Myths

THE
PAUL HAMLYN
LIBRARY

DONATED BY
THE PAUL HAMLYN
FOUNDATION
TO THE
BRITISH MUSEUM

opened December 2000

THE · LEGENDARY · PAST

WORLD OF Myths

Introduced by
MARINA WARNER

THE BRITISH MUSEUM PRESS

The five titles included in this compilation volume
are also available in individual paperback editions:
Greek Myths Lucilla Burn
Roman Myths Jane F. Gardner
Norse Myths R. I. Page
Egyptian Myths George Hart
Celtic Myths Miranda Green

Other titles in The Legendary Past series:
Aztec and Maya Myths Karl Taube
Chinese Myths Anne Birrell
Inca Myths Gary Urton
Mesopotamian Myths Henrietta McCall
Persian Myths Vesta Sarkhosh Curtis
Russian Myths Elizabeth Warner

© 2003 The Trustees of The British Museum
Introduction © 2003 Marina Warner

First published in 2003 by The British Museum Press
A division of The British Museum Company Ltd
46 Bloomsbury Street, London WC1B 3QQ

A catalogue record for this book is available from
the British Library

ISBN 0 7141 2783 3

Designed by Gill Mouqué and Martin Richards
Jacket design by Slatter-Anderson

Typeset in Sabon and printed in Great Britain by
The Bath Press, Avon

398.2
WAR

THE BRITISH MUSEUM
WITHDRAWN
THE PAUL HAMLYN LIBRARY

Contents

Introduction

Marina Warner

M aps may be coloured to show many things: the ebb and flow of empires; density of populations; volcanoes, tundra and moraine; ruined castles and the sites of battles; standing stones; waterfalls. I suppose an atlas might exist – though I have never seen one – which charted the presence of myths over time and showed Baldur the Beautiful in Scandinavia, Harpocrates with his finger to his lips in Egypt, Persephone swallowed up by the earth in Sicily, and Atlas shouldering his burden in present-day Morocco. Yet because the telling of stories is inextricably bound up with the presence of cultures, mythical geographies can track civilisations as surely as the rise and fall of cities. When the British Museum unfolds the character of a people over time it assembles traces and artefacts from daily life and artistic production, but even the most humdrum tool or cooking pot will probably offer some evidence of the imaginary cosmos inhabited by that people through its myths. A Grecian urn, with satyrs pursuing nymphs around the brim, introduces you to the stories that civilisation told, as religious belief or entertainment.

A myth is a story – a certain kind of story – about gods and goddesses, questing heroes and not a few persecuted maidens, about the origins of creation and natural phenomena, about deep time past and the ultimate possible destiny of this moment in which we find ourselves now. Frequently the stories puzzle at the meaning and purpose of it all, and they show quite extraordinary inventiveness in their responses. The word 'story' comes from the Greek *istoria*, inquiry, and myths are indeed stories that inquire into everyday realities, projected on to an eternal and supernatural horizon. They offer family trees of divinities; these divine powers embody the elements and every kind of natural phenomenon, and their immortal adventures provide explanatory stories for the origins of things and their interconnections. For example, myths observe the diurnal cycle of the earth from our human vantage point on its surface as we look up at the skies in wonder, and speculate on the relationship between the sun, moon and stars. They are consequently intertwined with the establishment of the calendar by which we still plant, work and enjoy ourselves even after the brilliance of electricity has shone light into the darkness. The months of the year and the days of the week are called, in English and Romance languages, after a mixture of Roman, Norse, Celtic and Christian divinities. Myths form a deep substratum to knowledge held in common, often (as in the case of the calendar) so deep as to be forgotten. Roland Barthes commented in 'Myth Today', his 1957 polemic against the ideological thrust of myth, that the stories that myths tell seem to describe the way things just are, not the way things have been made to be: '[Myth] transforms history into nature', he writes. And later, 'things lose the memory that once they were made.' He is stressing that myths do not present themselves as fabulous creations but as fixed eternal verities. He wanted to warn his readers against accepting invisible moralities encoded in the handed-down stories. For myths are made-up stories, and they belong to the order of human cultural artefacts as surely as a wheeled chariot or a tragedy on the stage.

If a myth is a kind of made-up story, then, what kind of stories do myths tell? According to the anthropologist Georges Dumézil, myths arise from inquiring into the three dominant spheres that constitute societies: sovereignty (or kingly political and military power), wisdom (knowledge systems involving scholars, magi, priests), and fertility (sex and reproduction). While journeying into fantastic realms, myths continually engage with questions about due order in politics and human relationships. In an oblique, inaccessible fashion, myths encipher the story of the past for a certain group. Virgil's *Aeneid* follows the Homeric character Aeneas from the fall of Troy to the foundation of Rome in order to glorify the history of the Latin empire under Augustus. The myth of Cú Chulainn and Gráinne and others from Celtic legend became crucial to the identity of Young Ireland during the Celtic revival in the battle for Irish independence, for example. 'Tell all the Truth – and Tell it slant', as Emily Dickinson writes, becomes an inevitable principle of mythic testimony. Historians are increasingly alert to the ambiguities of evidence and try to register the pressure of fabulist interests in the reconstruction of the past: I'm thinking of Noel Malcolm's writings on the Balkans, R. F. Foster's studies of Ireland. The spheres of political power and priestly power contend over controlling the slant on the story as it is told.

With regard to power in the sphere of fertility, societies are so different in their ways that even a law that might seem axiomatic to human beings, such as the prohibition against incest, undergoes different kinds of regulation in different groups. Stories reproduce these twists and turns. Gods and goddesses in many different cosmologies show a decided tendency to intermarry even when they are brother and sister. Isis and Osiris' union warranted the brother-sister marriage of the Pharaohs in Egypt, but in Greece the permissiveness of the gods remained an exclusively immortal prerogative. Zeus in Greek mythology loves several of his sisters while remaining unhappily married to another, Hera. His adventures define both rape and incest as off limits for mortals. Meanwhile, after God's vengeance on human iniquity has destroyed all other men in Sodom and Gomorrah, Lot's daughters in the Bible make him drunk in order to seduce their father and conceive by him. By contrast, medieval Catholics responded with profound anxiety to original incest between Cain and Abel and their sisters and even banned unions between couples who shared the same godparent, regardless of blood ties.

The stories that mythologies develop establish borders between decorum and transgression, and this carries them into highly charged sexual territory.

Though for a long time mythology was relegated to the nursery in influential compilations such as Nathaniel Hawthorne's *Tanglewood Tales*, Charles Kingsley's *The Heroes* and Andrew Lang's series of *Fairy Books*, its characteristic content does not on the face of it make soothing or improving reading. The fantastic fate of Horus, vividly recounted in this anthology by George Hart, reveals the many strange adventures of divine body parts in Egyptian myths. A principle of inversion often applies and myths tell of 'heavenly crimes', for to a god all things are possible, and gods can do things that human beings expressly cannot: their very boundlessness helps to set out the boundaries of mortal conduct. The mythic structure of permission and prohibition, the valences of consent and recoil, conjure the nature of outsiders, of monsters and malignant forces; as noted on early maps, at the edges of the known world: 'Here Be Dragons'. Such monsters vary from one body of stories to another: a dog's head may mark out a supreme embodiment of power and knowledge in one group's mythology (Anubis the jackal is the ferryman of the dead for the Egyptians), whereas in an Homeric and Ovidian story of metamorphosis, the beautiful nymph Scylla is turned into an horrendous sea monster and finds twelve dogs' heads snapping and barking round her waist.

One sphere these stories explore, however, lies within every human being's earthly experience, for myths almost always deal with the reality of death. They travel to the land of the dead and bring back news of its arrangements. They dramatise the passage from life to afterlife for the individual and inquire into the justice or otherwise meted out to mortals by those in supreme authority over them. When Christopher Columbus left a Christian monk – Fra Ramón Pané – on the island of Hispaniola in the New World on his second transatlantic voyage in 1493, and ordered him to discover what the local Taino Indians believed about the gods and what they thought happened to the dead, he was in effect going to the very heart of myth.

How are myths different from religious belief? In one obvious way the answer to this question lies in history. Mythologies are other peoples' faiths when those other peoples existed in the distant past, as in the case of the five cultures represented in this anthology, or when, as in traveller's reports and Victorian anthropological studies, the peoples may still be surviving but are somehow conceptually placed on the other side of the perimeter wire of Western thought: Australian aboriginals represent the most vigorous living example of this effect. Their complex body of stories, developing their relations with one another, with territory, with the dead, and with cosmological forces, would be quite ordinarily termed 'myths' rather than 'religion' in almost any contemporary context. But myths also differ profoundly from the theological tradition in one respect quite distinct from the question of belief: in our time they are not told by priests and their integrity is not zealously guarded by designated scholars (this is a separate question from history and memory). While they communicate all manner of values about sex and love and honour and mourning, they do not form a moral code that can be or would be appealed to by authorities. Victorian anthropologists argued that myth was narrated ritual, and indeed many of the most powerful we know were re-enacted in religious mysteries. The abduction of Persephone into the Underworld, the grieving of her mother Demeter, and the subsequent bargain that Demeter struck with Hades in order to restore her daughter to life and bring back spring on earth, shaped the secret rituals at Eleusis. The second-century fabulist Apuleius, in *The Metamorphosis of Lucius or the Golden Ass*, concludes with the hero's initiation as a priest of Isis and an account of her deeds and wonders. The Catholic Mass also recapitulates in symbolic and ritual form the sacred Christian story of Christ's sacrifice. But today the ritual embodiment of divine myths has fallen away along with the cultures that performed them, while the stories endure.

Of course, some objections to my broad distinction between a living religion and the mythologies of different cultures instantly spring to mind: scholars do ponder problems in the texts, and they refine and define authorship and corrupt and incorrupt manuscripts; while, with Sigmund Freud triumphantly leading the way, therapists of the soul today most definitely invoke the stories of Oedipus, Orestes, Electra, Narcissus or Psyche to illuminate emotional and psychological states of mind. But the stories themselves fly free of these tethers: they are themselves polymorphic and can be told and retold and shaped and reshaped over and over again. Euripides wrote a play, *Helen*, in which Helen never goes to Troy at all. In his version, the Greeks fight a bitter ten-year war and destroy a great city for an illusion. Rather more recently, Christa Wolf from the former East Germany returned to the story of Medea, the witch who is most notorious for murdering her children in revenge on Jason after he abandons her. In Wolf's impassioned vindication, Medea is blameless and the whole story a political witch-hunt, a tabloid conspiracy, a lie. The structuralist anthropologist Claude Lévi-Strauss declared that every retelling of a myth is another myth. In this sense, no revealed scripture of mythology exists analogous to the Bible or the Koran: as this anthology shows, there are only fragments of papyri, crumbling inscriptions, vase paintings, late variations and word of mouth moving down the traffic lanes and sea roads of the centuries. The process of transmission continues unabated through writings and rewritings in a myriad languages by generations of authors telling stories in oral, visual and verbal forms. Film, television and video have largely inherited the role of the *griot* of West Africa, the balladseller of eighteenth-century Britain, and the storyteller of the bazaars of the Ottoman empire. What we are making of this inheritance through our new narrative media remains a hugely difficult and troubling issue.

The continuous exchange of voices as the stories are told implies that the nucleus of the myth is held in common: variations on a theme can only be heard if the theme is first established for its audience, and so the force of Euripides' anti-war challenge to Homer's story about Helen of Troy depends on the audience knowing the earlier version. We can appreciate the irony if we know the Greeks thought Paris had abducted King Menelaus's wife from Sparta to Troy. The hidden connection to an original reveals a fundamental characteristic of myths: they are publicly known stories which circulate through a culture and beyond, through authored works (Ovid of the *Metamorphoses*, Snorri Sturluson of the Norse sagas). But they do not only remain uniquely embedded in these writings. Shakespeare read Ovid's *Metamorphoses* in the richly encrusted Elizabethan translation of Arthur Golding, and he did not stick to its version. He performed many acts of metamorphosis himself; his freedom to do so conveys not just his own imaginative daring and brilliance, but the very relation that writing bears to myths: it refashions them. As the French classicist Jean-Pierre Vernant has pointed out, the Greek word *muthos* (myth) stands in close affinity with the concept of the Word (*logos*), as public declaratory speech conveyed and understood in common. But whereas *logos* or the Word strives to a condition of permanence and law (speech as edict or pronouncement), *muthos* or myth remains more closely tuned to the fluidity and instability of conversation (speech as communication); the first institutes truth above and beyond individuals and their personal sympathies and feelings; it does not truck with pleasure if it does its duty properly. By contrast, myth shares publicly all manner of pleasures; the stories of mythology contain truths, perhaps, but fantastic wild delightful plots and characters, and they address with amoral festivity the audience's whole sensory and emotional being: these are materials that provoke passions and sympathy, wonder, pity and fear, that invite identification even if the events described seem so extremely outlandish and far-fetched. It is also the case that the split between official worship and mythology places mythic stories in the private memory palaces of individuals, rather than in the archives of a state priesthood.

This collection of stories from five different cultures reveals that, even while myths bore in the past a close relation to each people's metaphysics, to tribal memories and the life of their language, and to their imagined history and self-portraiture, myths' rich multiplicity does not institute a series of discrete fortified enclaves of ethnic purity. The stories meld and merge with one another across time and place in an organic process of compost and sediment. As the Sanskrit scholar Wendy Doniger explores in *Splitting the Difference* and *The Bedtrick*, many of the motifs of the monumental Indian epics the *Mahabharata* and the *Ramayana* twist and turn through the body of Greek and Roman myths, and then return in the best-loved themes of popular cinema such as *Some Like It Hot*, *Psycho* and *Dead Ringers*.

Two opposed theories offer explanations of this phenomenon: the theory of archetypes advocated by Carl Jung argues that certain concepts are embodied in figures such as the Nymph and the Crone and have an independent life of their own. They take up occupation of the human mind and structure its imaginative and psychological inquiries, providing the very building blocks of stories. In contrast to this universalising vision of mythological unity across time, the diffusionist argument proposes that stories migrate along with peoples and follow trade routes and caravans and shipping lanes, just as now e-mail transmits 'urban myths' all over the globe on the instant.

The two arguments need not be seen as mutually exclusive if you accept that certain fundamental questions – about the metamorphoses of a person over a lifetime, about sexual desire and love, about the state of the dead – are indeed universal and will inspire every body of mythological story. But I am of the view that the profound differences between cultures cancel any idea of consistency or stability of such universal figures, while the values ascribed to them also mutate across cultures. In Chinese mythology, the highest and wisest divinities can be very aged, all bent and bald and halt, whereas in Greek myths the gods are prized for their youth and beauty and athleticism as zealously as in any contemporary gym.

Shakespeare presents a model of the mythological process in action: he decocted mythical ingredients from many sources. He sailed on the sea of stories ranging from North to East and as far West as the New World, and he picked up cargo on the way from different cultures, languages and peoples with a blithe disregard for originality or fidelity to his source. He drew on Celtic faery lore, early world travellers' tales, and Mediterranean myths and legends as well as the classical corpus. Ovid and Apuleius number among his most closely read writers. Myths offered him raw material and his procedure was eclectic. He transmuted the figure of Circe the enchantress (Sycorax/Prospero in *The Tempest*), Lucius the ass (Bottom in *A Midsummer Night's Dream*), and Pygmalion and Galatea (Hermione as a statue in *The Winter's Tale*), and he blended and mingled official documents, ancient and contemporary poetry, broad groundling comedy, orature (oral narrative) and learned literature. As he recast these elements, he exemplifies the organic life of myths. He produced in turn new polyglot and motley myths for his own time, and they have since themselves metamorphosed into many other more recent myths about England (*Henry V, Richard III*) and the beginnings of empire (*The Tempest*), and even the popular myth of the original creative genius sparked by passion (*Romeo and Juliet/Shakespeare in Love*).

Myths' associations with fantasy banished them for a long time from higher consideration and branded them as proper to the minds of heathens, barbarians and children. Real adults would grow out of them just as they would mature beyond childish things and acquire morality and decorum – aspects of the logos. But many changes in ideas about culture and about the role of fantasy itself have transmuted this prejudice: few poets today would repeat Philip Larkin's scathing remark that there should be no more 'dipping in the myth-kitty'. Instead we see Seamus Heaney translating *Beowulf*, Ted Hughes revisiting the *Metamorphoses* of Ovid, the Canadian poet Anne Carson reassembling some sherds of a little-known Greek poem about the monster Geryon to write a fully-imagined verse novel (*Autobiography of Red*) about a gay love affair in the here and now. A younger poet, Alice Oswald, has returned to the haunted terrain of the River Dart in Devon and evokes its local legends and stories. Meanwhile, the success of reconfigured epic mythologies has never been surpassed (J. R. R. Tolkien, Philip Pullman). J. K. Rowling's Harry Potter series relocates the combat myth of ancient Babylon in a kind of Malory Towers British boarding school.

The bardic relationship between spoken and written forms of mythological storytelling has come back through recordings – both Heaney and Hughes recite their own work superbly – and through mass marketing of film versions and offshoots such as figures and cards with which children can play make-believe games and invent new dramas. *Dungeons & Dragons* and *Pokémon* teem with extravagant populations of mythical beasts and characters: their devisers have combined and recombined hybrids, heroes and demons into a syncretic world mythology. Personal growth gurus and anger management consultants are also turning to myth and fairy tales, as in the best-selling *Women Who Run With the Wolves* by Clarissa Pinkola Estes and John Gray's *Men Are from Mars, Women Are from Venus*. It would be a truism to say that contemporary culture is being leached of lifeblood at the same time: global mass media tend to standardise and homogenise, and by needing to be understood anywhere a myth loses particularity, thins out, deprived of local oxygen. Forgetting has become a constant danger. Like the amnesiac who, in Gabriel García Márquez's *One Hundred Years of Solitude*, writes labels for this and that in order not to forget what they are, we have to reinvigorate failing cultural memories: this anthology brings back stories behind so many of the objects and images in the British Museum collections.

Yet the very word 'myth' still casts a shadow of fraud: it is used in common parlance to describe not just an illusion but a falsehood, intended to deceive or at best inadvertently constructed to delude its receivers. If I refer to 'the myth of male superiority', few people will think I'm talking about the fabulous exploits of a Hercules or an Achilles: the phrase means a lie peddled about in a culture. The contradictory meanings of the word 'myth' persist: myths are stories which illuminate and explore transcendent and urgent questions in a gripping series of plots but at the same time they perpetuate false consciousness and dupe the public through the spell they cast over impressionable minds. This last stance derives from Enlightenment dislike of fabulation: Jean-Jacques Rousseau, as a Utopian educationalist, wanted his model child Emile to study beetles and rock formation and other sensible empirical data to hand. Anything else, he warned, would over-excite a child's reprehensibly over-excitable imagination.

Apart from the overheated extremes of their narratives, mythical stories have also come under attack for their relations with ideology – as in Barthes's critique already quoted. The historical record includes recent malignant examples of an unholy alliance of political dictatorship with ethnic myth and folklore. In Italy and in Germany, the regimes of Mussolini and Hitler invoked imperial might through a revived body of stories: the Third Reich in particular annexed the legends of Teutonic and Northern heroes that had been recovered through the popular nationalist revivals of the nineteenth century, and co-opted them to serve their racist tyranny.

Can a case be made for myths in the face of this justifiable anxiety about the sick delirium of the imagination (as deplored by Rousseau) and the damning record of use in dangerous propaganda?

An answer can be broadly given: it depends who tells the story, who listens and how they listen. The fault does not lie so much in the tale as in the tellers, and the trouble starts when the tales are held to enclose some inalienable truth that serves the purposes of the narrators.

A story will possess certain intrinsic aspects: Medusa's head turns to stone anyone who looks upon her and the story would no longer be the story if her head lost its fatal power. But the meanings such stories communicate extend to limitless possibilities, and some of the most familiar interpretations in circulation begin to look odd when you pause to give them a second thought. For example, Freud cast the Gorgon's head as the chief protagonist in his castration theory. He argued that the petrifying sight of the bristling snakes on her head recapitulated in symbolic form the sight of a mother's genitals and induced the same terror a male child feels when he first realises that his mother does not have a penis, and becomes alarmed that such a fate might befall him. This highly ingenious reading forms a foundational step in the discipline of psychoanalysis – with huge repercussions on ideas about sexuality and about male and female difference.

Accepting and confronting myths' polyvalence seems to me the strongest line of defence against the problem of atavistic ideological use. We can watch how the Nazis applied the legend of the Ring and take lessons from it. Interpretations like Freud's are attaining their own mythic status and floating away on the ocean of stories. The excesses of nationalist drum-beating mythologies, however tragically damaging they still continue to be, can be set against the inspiration offered in other contexts and historical times: in Auschwitz Primo Levi pieced together from memory the magnificent speech of Ulysses from Dante's *Divine Comedy*. Summoning an ideal of human striving, as dramatised in one of the highest literary achievements of the imagination, gave him courage to endure the camp. Today the memory of myths sustains many persecuted peoples over many continents where conditions still necessitate – unfortunately – that concepts of identity and belonging be kept alive against destruction through stories shared across time.

Imagination is necessary to thought and stories exercise its energies. Every culture on earth has created myths to inquire into life and death and to try to explain their mysteries. It seems that myth-making marks out human beings in the same way as language does: we are a speculative and fantasticating species and our consciousness and storytelling are bound up together in a defining cognitive process. The complexity and infinite variety of the stories in this book inspire awe, and however many hermeneutical tools are applied to prising open their meanings, the peculiarity of their inventions will always place them beyond reason's reach. There is no need to make excuses for the sheer enjoyability of myths: the fascination of the stories is reason enough for exploring them. However, 'the reason of myth' – to use the title of a celebrated essay by Jean-Pierre Vernant – lies in myths' deep relation to our social and human concerns; they communicate what people have seen, over the millennia, when they looked through the charm'd magic casements at themselves and their existence.

Suggestions for further reading

Jean-Pierre Vernant is the leading exponent of the historical approach to mythology that takes account of psychology and politics as well. His 1974 essays, *Myth and Society in Ancient Greece* (London, 1980), include his inspiring position statement, 'The Reason of Myth'. Marcel Detienne (*The Gardens of Adonis*, 1994), Nicole Loraux (*The Children of Athens*, 1981) and Pierre Vidal-Naquet (*The Black Hunter*, 1981), colleagues of Vernant in France, also examine myths fruitfully in a socio-historical light. Roland Barthes' classic, *Mythologies* (1957), concluding with the polemical essay 'Myth Today', exposes the ideological thrust of contemporary symbols and stories. The Sanskritist Wendy Doniger looks at worldwide plots and stories in her brilliant and entertaining companion volumes, *Splitting the Difference: Gender and Myth in Ancient Greece and India* (1999) and *The Bedtrick: Tales of Sex and Masquerade* (2000). Mircea Eliade ranges far and wide in studies such as *Patterns in Comparative Religion* (1958); Claude Lévi-Strauss, who studied Native American myths (*Myth and Meaning*, 1978), represents the structural anthropological approach. Robert Graves, with his *Greek Myths* (1955), provides one of the richest collections (if somewhat eccentrically interpreted) of classical mythology; Ken Dowden, *The Uses of Greek Mythology* (1992), presents its theme with helpful lucidity. For the psychoanalytic tradition, Sigmund Freud, *Totem and Taboo* (1912–13, first published in English 1950), gives a strong flavour of his interpretations, while C. G. Jung's autobiography, *Memories, Dreams, Reflections* (1961), reveals the Jungian approach to myth. For the current twists and turns of mythological interpretation, Ted Hughes, *Shakespeare and the Goddess of Complete Being* (1992) contains powerful acts of mythical imagination; Jonathan Bate's *Shakespeare and Ovid* (1993) reveals how profoundly classical myths inspired Shakespeare's plays and poetry. In the realm of politics, Noel Malcolm, in *Kosovo* (1998), discloses how nations erect their totemic histories; R. F. Foster, *The Story of Ireland* (2001), throws clear light on this process at work today; any novel of Salman Rushdie explodes with mythological references and repercussions; Philip Pullman's trilogy *His Dark Materials* (1995–2000) tackles the Judaeo-Christian mythical tradition with dazzling verve and defiance. My own *Managing Monsters* (the 1994 Reith Lectures) and a study of fairy tale, *From the Beast to the Blonde* (1994), address popular contemporary tales we live by; Laurence Coupe's *Myth* (1997) offers a lively and clear introduction to different approaches.

Greek

Myths

LUCILLA BURN

Acknowledgements

Help with various aspects of this book has been received from many friends and colleagues. For the photographs I am indebted to all those in museums abroad who responded to my requests, and to Christi Graham and P.E. Nicholls of the British Museum Photographic Service. Sue Goddard and Sue Bird produced the map and Sue Goddard and Michael Strand the line drawings; Brian Cook, Emma Cox, Lesley Fitton and Susan Woodford were kind enough to read early drafts of the text. I am most grateful to them for their helpful comments, especially Susan Woodford, who tactfully mingled encouragement with painstaking and enlightening correction of numerous embarrassing errors of fact and judgement; I am of course solely responsible for those that remain. Finally, without the practical assistance and moral support of my husband, Roger Bland, this book would not have been written, and it is dedicated to him, with affectionate thanks.

Author's note

It would have been impossible to include the entire corpus of Greek mythology in a book of this size. The myths selected for discussion are of course a personal choice, but they do include some of the most important and interesting; those who feel the need for more may refer to the suggestions for further reading on p. 77. It may be felt that references to the ancient sources are uneven in their occurrence: where it has seemed useful and appropriate, the ancient sources have been closely and extensively followed, but in cases where the sources are numerous, contradictory, late and of little intrinsic interest, it has not seemed desirable to detract from the story by close reference to texts. The same motive, that of putting the myths themselves across as clearly as possible, lies behind the obvious inconsistencies in the transliteration of Greek names. In general, Greek forms have been preferred, so that Herakles and Antaios are used rather than Heracles and Antaeus, but where an accurate transliteration might appear strange and jarring, familiar 'English' forms have been used, so that Oedipus and Circe replace the more 'Greek' versions of Oidipous and Kirke.

Picture credits

p. 7: BM GR Vase E140; *p. 10: (top left)* BM GR Vase B248; *(top right)* Providence, R.I., 25.078; *(bottom)* BM GR Vase D2; *p. 11:* BM GR Vase B424; *p. 12:* BM GR Vase E256; *p. 13: (left)* BM GR 1980.10-19.1; *(right)* BM GR Vase B215; *p. 15: (top)* BM GR Vase F149; *(bottom)* BM GR Bronze 544; *p. 16:* BM GR Vase B213; *p. 17:* BM GR Vase B163; *p. 18: (left)* BM GR Bronze 642; *(right)* BM GR 1814.7-4.1652; *p. 19:* BM GR Vase B194; *p. 20: (top)* Paris, Musée du Louvre E701 (photo M. Chuzeville); *(bottom)* BM GR Vase E224; *p. 21: (top)* BM GR Vase E38; *(bottom left)* BM CM BMC *Alexandria* 1054; *(bottom right)* BM GR Vase E458; *p. 24:* BM GR Terracotta D594; *p. 26:* BM GR Vase E84; *p. 27:* BM Parthenon South Metope 27; *p. 30: (top)* BM GR Vase B215; *(bottom)* Karlsrühe, Badisches Landesmuseum 259; *p. 34:* BM GR Vase F157; *p. 35:* New York, The Metropolitan Museum of Art, Rogers Fund, 1931 (31.11.13); *p. 37: (top)* BM GR Vase B210; *(bottom)* Mykonos Museum 70 (photo DAI Athens); *p. 40:* Boston, Museum of Fine Arts 63.1246. William Francis Warden Fund; *p. 42: (left)* BM GR Vase B687; *(right)* Eleusis Museum 544 (photo DAI Athens); *p. 43:* BM GR Vase E804; *p. 45:* Boston, Museum of Fine Arts 99.515. H.L. Pierce Fund; *p. 47:* BM GR Bronze 882; *pp. 51, 54:* Chiusi, Museo Archeologico 1831 (after A. Furtwängler and K. Reichhold, *Griechische Vasenmalerei*, Munich 1904-32, pl. 142); *p. 58:* BM GR Terracotta D603; *p. 60:* BM GR Vase E163; *p. 62: (top)* Boston, Museum of Fine Arts 13.200. Francis Bartlett Fund; *(bottom)* BM GR Vase B471; *p. 63:* BM GR Vase E169; *p. 65:* ex-Berlin, Staatliche Museen (Antikensammlung) 2634; *p. 68:* London, Freud Museum 3117; *p. 75: (top)* Manchester City Art Galleries; *(bottom left)* Ferens Art Gallery: Hull City Museums and Art Galleries (UK); *(bottom right)* London, Freud Museum 4387.

Contents

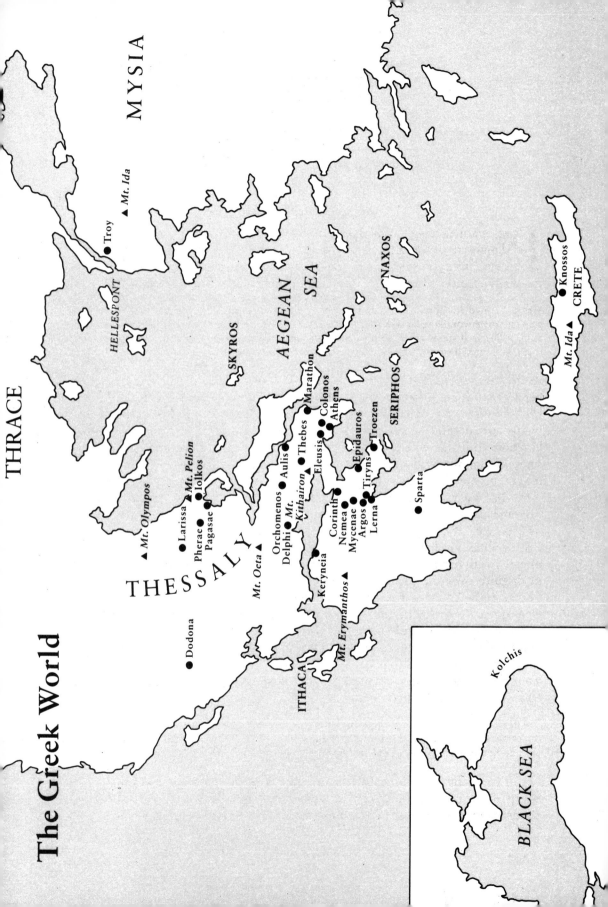

The Greek World

THRACE

MYSIA

Troy ●

▲ Mt. Ida

HELLESPONT

▲ Mt. Olympos

Larissa ●

Pherae ●   ▲ Mt. Pelion
         Iolkos ●
Pagasae ●

THESSALY

SKYROS

AEGEAN

SEA

Marathon
Thebes ●   Colonos ●
Orchomenos ●   Athens ●
Aulis ●
         Eleusis ●
Delphi ● Mt.   Epidauros ●
         Kithairon   Tiryns ● Troezen ●
▲ Mt. Oeta   Corinth ●   Lerna ●
         Nemea ●
Keryneia ●   Mycenae ●
         Argos ●
▲ Mt. Erymanthos   Sparta ●

NAXOS

SERIPHOS

CRETE
Knossos ●
▲ Mt. Ida

Dodona ●

ITHACA

BLACK SEA

Kolchis

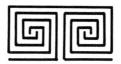

Introduction

Persephone, daughter of Demeter the goddess of grain, was with the daughters of Ocean in a grassy meadow picking flowers. There were roses, lilies, saffron plants, violets, irises and hyacinths, but most beautiful of all, according to the Homeric *Hymn to Demeter*, was a narcissus,

a trap planted for the blossoming maiden by Earth in accord with Zeus's plans ... it was radiantly wonderful, inspiring awe in all who saw it, whether immortal god or mortal man; a hundred stems grew from its root; and the whole wide heaven above, the whole earth, and the salt surge of the sea smiled for joy at its fragrance.

As Persephone reached out to the irresistible flower, the earth fell from under her feet, and out from the chasm rushed the chariot of Hades, king of the Underworld and brother of Persephone's father Zeus. He snatched up Persephone and, despite her cries and screams, carried her off to his underground kingdom to be his wife. Only one goddess, Hekate, heard her, and only the sun-god Helios saw the rape; but as Persephone passed out of the light, the mountains and the rocks sent back echoes of her cries to her mother Demeter.

Distraught with grief and worry, Demeter cast a veil over her head and for nine days searched the earth for her daughter, never stopping to rest or even eat. Then Helios told her what had happened and that it was the will of Zeus for Persephone to marry her uncle. Demeter's grief was now mingled with fury; leaving Mount Olympos and the other gods, she wandered in disguise over the earth among mortal men until she arrived at Eleusis. There, in the house of Keleos, she became nursemaid to Keleos's infant son Demophon. She tried to make Demophon immortal by placing him at night in the flames of the fire. One night his mother stayed awake to watch, but when she saw her son in the hearth she cried out in terror and the wrathful Demeter was provoked to reveal her true identity. The people of Eleusis built a temple for the goddess and there she remained, totally neglecting her duties, and mourning for her lovely daughter:

She made the most terrible, most oppressive year for men upon the nourishing land, and the earth sent up no seed, as fair-garlanded Demeter hid it. Cattle drew the many curved ploughs in vain over the fields, and much white barley seed fell useless on the earth ...

Eventually Zeus, king of all the gods, took notice and summoned Demeter to his presence. But she utterly refused to return to Olympos, or to allow the crops to grow, until she saw her daughter again. So Zeus sent his messenger

Hermes to fetch Persephone home. The cunning Hades obeyed his brother's command to release Persephone into the upper world, but before he let her go he made her eat a pomegranate seed, which meant that she would have to return to him again. Persephone was therefore only temporarily reunited with Demeter and Zeus ordained that she should spend two-thirds of the year above ground with her mother and one-third in the misty darkness as the wife of Hades.

Demeter had to be content with this arrangement. Now, as she sped over the earth, the barley sprang up and ripened below her feet. Returning to Eleusis, she explained to the leaders of the people the rites that were to be performed there in her honour and in honour of Persephone. These rites were to be the Eleusinian Mysteries, whose contents were a closely kept secret: all the *Hymn to Demeter* will reveal of them is that

Blessed of earthbound men is he who has seen these things, but he who dies without fulfilling the holy things, and he who is without a share of them, has no claim ever on such blessings, even when departed down to the mouldy darkness.

Myths have recently been defined as 'traditional tales relevant to society', and although this definition may seem a little colourless, its two propositions clearly do apply to the myth of Demeter and Persephone. Like most other Greek myths, it is so 'traditional' that it is scarcely possible to say when it arose. The *Hymn to Demeter* is the earliest extant version of the story, and in its present form it is generally thought to date to the seventh century BC. But like the slightly earlier epic poems, the *Iliad* and the *Odyssey*, the *Hymn* probably existed for several centuries before this in the form of oral poetry handed down through the generations. Very few Greek myths appear to have been invented in historical times: the vast majority seem as old as Greek civilisation itself.

The myth of Demeter and Persephone is also highly 'relevant to society'. Not only is the division of Persephone's year between the upper and the under worlds a vivid image of the division of the year into its different seasons; the myth also encompasses some of the most fundamental issues of human existence. In the first place it is concerned with the provision of food, necessary to sustain life. In the Greek world the most basic food was bread. When Demeter ceases to look after the crops and the grain fails to grow, man faces starvation. The Eleusinian Mysteries, it is thought, were in part concerned with propitiating Demeter in order to ensure the fruitfulness of the fields. But at the same time the myth of Persephone is an allegory of the natural social requirements for girls to grow up and leave home. In the end Demeter does not get her daughter back on a permanent basis, for Persephone must be reconciled with fulfilling her function as a wife. In Greek literature of the fifth century and later it is clear that the rape of Persephone is seen as the paradigm for all weddings; all girls weep as they are dragged from their mothers' sides, and again and again the imagery of marriage is that of rape and death. Like Persephone's descent to the world of the dead, from which

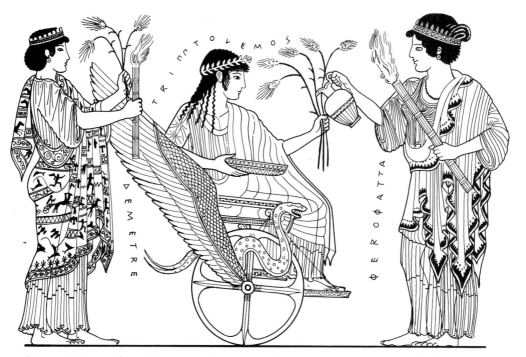

Demeter (left), goddess of the harvest, often holds stalks of wheat or barley; the torches she and her daughter Persephone both hold suggest their connections with the Underworld. Here they are sending the hero Triptolemos to take the gift of corn to mankind.

she emerges as a wife, Greek marriage was a rite of passage, involving a girl's separation from her own family, her initiation into the duties of a wife, then her reintegration into society, where she may again mix with her own relations, but with a different status.

Greek myths permeated Greek life, private and public. In the well-documented society of Athens in the fifth century BC, for example, it is clear that a major part of education was learning and reciting epic poems on heroic subjects. Guests at drinking parties might entertain each other by reciting stories from myths, or they might listen to a professional performer, who would sing of the deeds of heroes while accompanying himself on the lyre. Private homes contained pottery vessels decorated with scenes from the adventures of the gods and heroes; these same vessels accompanied their owners to the grave. Scenes of myth could also be woven into fine textiles.

Moving outside the home, most of the great public religious festivals were linked with specific mythological incidents, and these were commemorated in the rites which marked such occasions. At the spring festival of the Anthesteria, for instance, there was both a re-enactment of the sacred marriage of Dionysos and Ariadne and a silent drinking competition which commemorated the occasion on which Orestes, polluted by matricide, sought sanctuary at Athens. To comply with the laws of hospitality and yet avoid contaminating anyone who shared a table with him, Orestes was put to sit on his own, and he ate and drank in silence. At the Anthesteria, therefore, each participant in the drinking contest sat silently at his own table and drank from his own jug. The Homeric *Hymn to Demeter*, interweaving its mythological narrative with allusions to the great Mysteries of Eleusis, provides another typical example of the way Greek myth and cult were inextricably blended.

Greek myths inspired great art and great poetry. The large-scale mythological paintings which decorated the walls of such important fifth-century Athenian buildings as the Theseion (the Shrine of Theseus) do not survive, and we are left to imagine from ancient descriptions how impressive they must have been; occasional survivals, such as the painting of the Rape of Persephone in a fourth-century tomb at Vergina in Macedonia, are a tantalising reminder of what we have lost. Much more architectural sculpture survives from all periods of Greek art. In the sculptured metopes of the Parthenon, for example, we can see episodes from the battle between men and centaurs; the sculptural programme of the Great Altar at Pergamon in Asia Minor, built in the second century BC to honour the gods and glorify a ruling dynasty, provides not only an extremely vivid representation of the battle between gods and giants, but also a rare and invaluable record of a lesser myth, that of the local hero Telephos. Not just for painters and sculptors, but for poets too, the great corpus of Greek myths was their basic raw material and source of inspiration. Each year at the great dramatic festivals of classical Athens, versions of the familiar myths, either freshly worked or in popular old revivals, were brought before the public; and at the festivals of the gods hymns of praise and commemoration, both new and old, were sung; the *Hymn to Demeter* may well have been composed for such an occasion. Were it not for the remarkable poetic qualities of these reworkings of the old stories, and the lasting appeal of their beauty, both our present knowledge of Greek myths and their fascination would be far less.

The principal characters of the *Hymn to Demeter* are gods and goddesses, but in most Greek myths heroes (and heroines) play a more prominent part. The Greeks of the historical period liked to think that the Age of the Heroes had preceded their own times. As the poet Hesiod explained in the late eighth century BC, Zeus, the king of the gods, had created five successive races of men. The race of Gold had been the first to inhabit the earth: these fortunate people had lived a carefree existence like the gods, with the earth producing food for them of its own accord. They were succeeded by an inferior Silver race of people weak in both body and mind; and in their turn the men of Silver were replaced by those of Bronze. The men of Bronze lived principally for war; they were great and terrible warriors, and in time they destroyed themselves entirely.

To replace them Zeus created a new and glorious breed, 'a godlike race of heroes, who are called demi-gods – the race before our own'. These were the men whose deeds and characters inform Greek myth: they routed fabulous monsters, crossed the sea in search of Helen, died on the plain of Troy or ringed the seven-gated citadel of Thebes; after death they enjoyed a god-like existence in the Islands of the Blessed at the ends of the earth. To the fifth and last race of men the pessimistic Hesiod himself belonged. His was the race of Iron, in which unceasing work was relieved only by death: 'I wish I were not of this race, that I had died before, or had not yet been born.' Hesiod's feelings were echoed by many later Greeks, who looked back with regretful nostalgia to the lost Age of the Heroes as a not far-distant time when life had been both more noble and more glorious.

Nobility and glory were fundamental to the Greek concept of the hero. While many heroes had a divine father or mother – the father of Herakles was Zeus and the sea-nymph Thetis was the mother of Achilles – all were of noble birth; they were kings or princes, rulers of countries or cities, commanders of armies, possessors of fabulous wealth. They were invariably good-looking, athletic and brave. They adhered to strict standards of behaviour: they were respectful towards women and others in need of protection – the laws of hospitality, for example, were sacred, and no hero worthy of the name would drive a beggar from his hearth. Most important, however, was the heroes' obsession with fame and glory. Like the knights of medieval chivalry they rose eagerly to every challenge, whether it were the sacking of a city or the slaying of a Minotaur.

The world of the heroes was not distinctly segregated from that of the gods; the gods came and went among them, helping their sons or particular favourites and laying traps for those with whom they were displeased. Both gods and heroes, however, were subject to the higher authority of fate. Again and again we come across characters who are aware of their destiny, like Achilles and his parents, who knew that if Achilles went to Troy he would die there. Fate might be revealed through oracles, such as that of Apollo at Delphi, or through such intermediary agents as prophets, dreams and omens. But very often heroes had only a partial understanding of what was fated, and their inability to recognise and accept their destiny might well lead to tragedy, as in the case of Oedipus.

In the chapters which follow we shall be more concerned with heroes than with gods, but the gods are always present in the background: their relationships, passions, jealousies and spheres of influence and responsibility formed the backcloth against which the heroes played out their dramas. Before looking at the myths themselves, therefore, we will first look briefly at the gods.

The principal gods of the Greeks are often referred to as 'the twelve Olympians', after their home on Mount Olympos. There were actually at least thirteen important deities and numerous lesser figures besides. Chief among the gods was **Zeus**, whose grandfather was **Uranos**, personification of the sky; Uranos lay over **Gaia**, the earth, and she produced countless children, the youngest of whom was **Kronos**. Growing weary of child-bearing, Gaia enlisted the aid of Kronos, who cut off his father's genitals with a sickle and threw them into the sea. Kronos went on to marry his own sister **Rhea**, but since he knew that he in his turn was destined to be overthrown by

Poseidon (below), *the sea-god, generally bears a trident; here he is riding on a hippocamp, a creature part fish and part horse.*
Hera (right), *like Aphrodite, has no special attributes beyond her sceptre and her beauty.*

one of his own sons, he swallowed his first three daughters and two sons as soon as each was born. When she was pregnant with Zeus, Rhea escaped to Crete and gave birth in a cave on Mount Ida. Leaving the infant there in the care of the nymphs, she returned to Kronos and presented him with a large stone wrapped up in swaddling clothes, which he duly swallowed, thinking it was his newborn child. When Zeus grew up, he forced his father to regurgitate all his older brothers and sisters; they then declared war on Kronos, overcame him and confined him forever in the depths of Tartarus, below the surface of the earth.

Next, Zeus and his brothers drew lots to determine how their power should be divided. **Poseidon** was given control of the seas and **Hades** power

Aphrodite, goddess of love, is here shown riding on one of her sacred birds, the goose. She has no special attributes beyond her beauty, but her association with the fertility of nature may be suggested as here by flowers or tendrils of vegetation.

over the underworld and the dead, while Zeus won overall sovereignty, ruling over the earth and the sky. Their three sisters were **Hestia**, goddess of the hearth, **Demeter**, goddess of crops and grain, and **Hera**, wife of Zeus.

These six were the older generation of the Olympians, but many of the children of Zeus became equally important. Some were born to Hera, the rest to a variety of mothers. Hera gave birth to **Ares**, the god of war, and the lame smith-god **Hephaistos**, as well as **Hebe**, goddess of youth, and **Eileithyia**, goddess of childbirth. There are differing accounts of the parentage of **Aphrodite**, the goddess of love: either she was the daughter of Zeus and Dione, or else she was born from the foam which arose when Kronos threw the genitals of Uranos into the sea. **Athena**, goddess of wisdom and of war, was the daughter of Zeus and **Metis**, the personification of counsel; her birth was unusual, for when Metis was already pregnant, Zeus learnt of a prophecy that if she gave birth to a daughter, she would go on to produce a son who would rule the universe. So Zeus swallowed Metis, and in due course Athena sprang fully grown and fully armed from her father's head, helpfully split open by Hephaistos. The daughter of Zeus and Demeter was, as we have

*Zeus, leader of the gods, is always bearded and often brandishes a thunderbolt, as here. The smith-god **Hephaistos** (right) usually wears a short tunic, as here, and he may carry an axe. Here he has just used the axe to split open Zeus's head, from which emerges **Athena**, goddess of wisdom and of war, brandishing her shield.*

*Apollo (left) usually plays the lyre; his sister **Artemis** is generally armed with a bow and quiver, and frequently accompanied by wild animals.*

seen, **Persephone**, goddess of the Underworld. Leto bore Zeus the twins **Apollo**, the god of music and poetry, and **Artemis** the huntress; Semele bore **Dionysos**, god of wine; and Maia was the mother of **Hermes**, the messenger god.

It is not possible here even to attempt to answer the question of how the Greeks saw their gods. Undoubtedly they regarded them in different ways at different times, their views changing with the progress of their civilisation, and the development of their scientific knowledge and moral philosophies. For the present it must suffice to take the gods as we find them in the myths. In the Homeric poems, for example, the gods are at their most anthropomorphic, resembling nothing so much as a large, powerful, talented and extremely quarrelsome human family. The story of Ares and Aphrodite, as recounted in the *Odyssey*, serves as a useful example of their behaviour and may conclude this introduction.

The beautiful Aphrodite, goddess of love, was married to Hephaistos, god of fire and metal-working, but conceived a passion for Ares, god of war. Hephaistos, though a consummate smith and craftsman, was lame and ugly, while Ares was handsome and virile. Aphrodite and her lover used to meet secretly in Hephaistos's palace, until one day the Sun saw them and told the smith-god what was going on. Hephaistos was furious, and immediately contrived a wonderful net, light as gossamer but strong as iron, invisible to the naked eye; this he fastened around Aphrodite's bed before departing on a well-publicised trip to the island of Lemnos. Ares was quick to seize the opportunity and went straight to Aphrodite. But as the pair lay entwined in each other's arms, the net fell around them and caught them up so that they could not move. Hephaistos, warned again by the Sun, hurried home and gave vent to his rage; standing in the doorway he shouted to all the other gods to come and look at the shameless couple. Poseidon, Apollo and Hermes all turned up, though the goddesses stayed modestly at home. When they saw Hephaistos's clever trick, 'a fit of uncontrollable laughter seized these happy gods'; there were suggestions that Ares would have to pay Hephaistos the fine paid to husbands by adulterers, and Apollo asked Hermes if he would care to take Ares's place; Hermes replied that even if the chains were three times as strong and even if all the gods and goddesses were looking on, he wouldn't give up such a chance of sleeping at Aphrodite's side. The respectable Poseidon, however, was rather embarrassed by the affair and urged Hephaistos to set them free. Eventually, when Poseidon offered to guarantee any recompense that Ares promised to pay, Hephaistos relented and released the chains. The luckless pair fled in disgrace, Ares to Thrace and the discomfited Aphrodite to her sanctuary of Paphos in Cyprus, where the Graces bathed and anointed her and dressed her in fine clothing, so that she was once more a marvel to behold.

Dionysos (left), the wine-god, wears a wreath of vine or ivy leaves in his hair; here he carries a spray of vine leaves in his hand.

Hermes (right), messenger of the gods, wears winged boots to speed him over land and sea; he usually has a petasos, the broad-brimmed travellers' hat, and he carries a caduceus, a special form of staff.

13

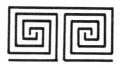

The labours of Herakles

Herakles, the greatest of all the Greek heroes, was the son of Zeus and Alkmene. Alkmene was the virtuous wife of Amphitryon, and in order to seduce her Zeus assumed the form of Amphitryon while the latter was absent from home. When her husband returned and found out what had happened, he was so angry that he built a great pyre and would have burnt Alkmene alive, had Zeus not sent the clouds to extinguish the flames and so forced Amphitryon to accept the situation. Once born, the infant Herakles was quick to reveal his heroic potential. While still in his cradle, he strangled two snakes which Zeus's jealous wife Hera had sent to attack him and his half-brother Iphikles; while still a boy, he killed a savage lion on Mount Kithairon. In adult life the adventures of Herakles were both more extensive and more spectacular than those of any other hero. Throughout antiquity he was hugely popular, the subject of numerous stories and countless works of art. Although the most coherent literary sources for his exploits date only from the third century BC, scattered references and the evidence of the artistic sources make it very clear that most if not all of his adventures were well known from the earliest times.

Herakles performed his famous twelve labours at the command of Eurystheus, king of Argos or Mycenae. There are several explanations as to why Herakles found himself obliged to carry out all Eurystheus's tiresome and seemingly impossible requests. One source suggests that the labours were a penance imposed upon the hero by the Delphic oracle when, in a fit of madness, he had killed all the children of his first marriage. While the first six labours are all set in the Peloponnese, the later labours took Herakles to various places on the fringes of the Greek world and beyond. Throughout the labours Herakles was pursued by the hatred of the goddess Hera, who was always jealous of Zeus's children by other women. The goddess Athena, on the other hand, was an enthusiastic supporter of Herakles; he also enjoyed the company and occasional assistance of his nephew, Iolaos.

The first labour of Herakles was the killing of the Nemean Lion. Since this enormous beast was invulnerable to any weapon, Herakles wrestled with it and eventually choked it to death with his bare hands. Afterwards he removed the skin with the aid of one of its claws, and wore it ever after as a cloak, with the paws knotted round his neck, the jaws gaping above his head and the tail swinging out behind. The second labour required the destruction of the Lernaean Hydra, a many-headed water-snake which was

Alkmene on the pyre *Alkmene, the mother of Herakles, sits on a pyre built of logs, her right hand raised imploring mercy; her husband Amphitryon holds torches to the pyre, but Zeus sends two Clouds who pour water on to the flames and so save Alkmene's (and Herakles's) life. Paestan red-figured bell-krater (wine-bowl), about 330 BC.*

Herakles and the Hydra *Neither Herakles, nor the winged Athena who accompanies him, appear to have noticed the Hydra coiled behind the goddess, three forked tongues hissing from three ferocious mouths. Etruscan bronze mirror, fifth century BC.*

Herakles and the Boar *Herakles offers the Boar to Eurystheus, who cowers terrified inside a large storage-jar partly sunk in the ground. Herakles wields the huge animal as though it weighs nothing. Athenian black-figured amphora (wine-jar), about 530 BC.*

Herakles and the Stymphalian Birds (opposite) *The beautifully patterned and coloured birds fly or perch before Herakles, their wings and long necks stretched in a variety of graceful attitudes. Herakles takes aim with his sling. Athenian black-figured amphora (wine-jar), about 530 BC.*

plaguing the swamps around Lerna. Every time Herakles cut off a head, two more grew in its place, and as if this were not bad enough, Hera sent a giant crab to nip Herakles in the foot. This mean trick was too much for the hero, who decided to enlist the aid of Iolaos; while Herakles cut off the heads, Iolaos cauterised the stumps with a blazing torch so that no more could grow, and finally they got the better of the monster. Afterwards Herakles dipped his arrows in the Hydra's blood or venom and so made them poisonous.

On Mount Erymanthos, a fierce wild boar was rampaging and laying waste the countryside. Eurystheus rather rashly asked Herakles to bring it back to him alive, but the ancient illustrations of this episode, which mostly show the cowardly Eurystheus taking refuge in a storage jar, suggest that he came to regret his request. It took Herakles a whole year to accomplish his next labour, which was to capture the Keryneian Hind. This animal seems to have been more shy than dangerous. It was sacred to the goddess Artemis, and, though female, possessed most wonderful antlers. According to the legend, when Herakles had finally caught the Hind and was taking it to Eurystheus, he encountered Artemis, who was most displeased and threatened to kill Herakles for his impudence in capturing her animal; but when she learned about the labours, she agreed to let Herakles take the Hind on condition that Eurystheus released it as soon as he had seen it.

The Stymphalian Birds were so numerous that they were destroying all the crops in the neighbourhood of Lake Stymphalos in Arcadia; various sources claim that they were man-eating, or at the very least able to shoot their feathers out like arrows. It is not altogether clear how Herakles met the challenge: one vase painter shows him attacking with a sling, but other sources suggest he shot them with arrows from his bow or scared them away with a bronze rattle specially made for the job by the god Hephaistos. The

last of the six Peloponnesian labours was the cleansing of the Augean Stables. King Augeias of Elis owned vast herds of cattle, whose stables had never been cleared out, so that the dung was several metres deep. Eurystheus must have thought that the task of cleansing the stables in a single day really would prove impossible, but Herakles once more rose to the occasion, diverting the course of a river so that its waters did the whole job for him.

Eurystheus now asked Herakles to capture the wild, ferocious Cretan Bull, the first labour to take him outside the Peloponnese. Once Eurystheus had seen it, Herakles released the Bull, and it survived to be killed by Theseus at Marathon. Next, Eurystheus sent Herakles to Thrace to bring back the man-eating horses of Diomedes. Herakles tamed these animals by feeding them their brutal master, and brought them safely home to Eurystheus. He was immediately sent off again, this time to the shores of the Black Sea, to fetch the girdle of the queen of the Amazons. Herakles took an army with him on this occasion, but he would not have needed it if Hera had not stirred up trouble. When he arrived at the Amazon city of Themiskyra, the Amazon queen was quite happy for him to take her girdle; Hera, feeling this was too easy, started a rumour that Herakles was trying to carry off the queen herself, and a bloody battle ensued. Herakles did of course escape with the girdle, but only after heavy fighting and much loss of life.

In order to accomplish his last three labours, Herakles passed entirely beyond the boundaries of the Greek world. First he was sent beyond the edge of the Ocean, to distant Erytheia in the farthest west, to fetch the Cattle

Herakles and the Horses of Diomedes
Herakles stands nonchalantly between the two rearing horses, one hand on the neck of each. Etruscan bronze group, fourth or third century BC.

Herakles and the Bull *The prancing Bull is not totally subdued; the hero braces his body against the Bull's flanks, both hands restraining its head. Roman ivory group, first or second century AD.*

Herakles and Geryon *The herdsman and the savage dog having been dealt with, Herakles here turns his attention to Geryon himself. One of the three heads falls back, perhaps already wounded. Athenian black-figured amphora (wine-jar), about 540 BC.*

of Geryon. Geryon was a formidable challenge; not only was he triple-bodied, but to help him guard his wonderful red cattle he also employed a ferocious herdsman named Eurytion and a two-headed, snake-tailed dog named Orthos. Orthos was the brother of Cerberus, the dog who guarded the entrance to the Underworld, and Herakles's encounter with Geryon is sometimes interpreted as his first meeting with death. Although Herakles disposed of Eurytion and Orthos without too much difficulty, Geryon, with his three fully armed bodies, proved a more formidable adversary, and only after a terrible struggle did Herakles succeed in slaying him. When he arrived back in Greece, Eurystheus sent him out on a still more desperate errand, to descend to the Underworld and fetch Cerberus, the hound of Hell himself. Guided by the messenger-god Hermes, Herakles descended to the gloomy realm of the dead, and with the consent of Hades and Persephone he borrowed the fearsome, triple-headed monster to show to the terrified Eurystheus; this done, he politely returned the dog to its rightful owners.

Even then Eurystheus demanded one last labour: that Herakles should bring him the Golden Apples of the Hesperides. These apples, the source of the gods' eternal youth, grew in a garden at the end of the earth; they had been a wedding present from Gaia, the Earth, to Zeus and Hera. The tree which bore the golden fruit was tended by nymphs called Hesperides and guarded by a serpent. Accounts vary as to how Herakles tackled this final labour. Those sources which locate the garden below the Atlas Mountains, where the mighty Atlas held up the sky on his shoulders, say that

Herakles and Cerberus (*left*)
*Eurystheus takes cover in his
storage-jar again, as Herakles
lets Cerberus bound forward to
greet him, snakes hissing from
his three mouths and writhing
around his six front paws.
Caeretan hydria (water-jar),
about 520 BC.*

***Herakles in the Garden of the
Hesperides*** (*below*) *Herakles
rests at the end of his final
labour. The Hesperides prepare
to hand over their apples, while
the guardian snake coils
languidly around his tree.
Athenian red-figured hydria
(water-jar), about 420–400 BC.*

Herakles persuaded Atlas to fetch the apples for him; while he went off on
this errand, Herakles shouldered the sky himself, and when Atlas returned
Herakles had some difficulty in persuading him to resume his burden. Other
versions of the story suggest that Herakles went to the garden himself and
either fought and killed the serpent or else persuaded the Hesperides to hand
the apples over to him. The apples of the Hesperides symbolised immortality,
and this final labour meant that eventually Herakles would ascend to Olympos
and take his place among the gods.

In addition to the twelve labours, many other heroic deeds and adventures
were ascribed to Herakles. In his quest for the garden of the Hesperides,
he had to wrestle with the sea-god Nereus to compel the god to give him

Herakles and Busiris (below) Having escaped sacrifice at the hands of the Egyptian king, Herakles sets about punishing his oppressors. One Egyptian is about to be battered to death by Herakles's club; the others flee, scattering musical instruments and implements of sacrifice. Athenian red-figured kylix (drinking-cup), about 520–500 BC.

Herakles and the Delphic tripod (below right) Herakles and Apollo, the god of Delphi, enact a tug of war over the Delphic tripod. Apollo's sacred animal, the deer, appears to be pulling on his side. Athenian red-figured calyx-krater (wine-bowl), about 500–480 BC.

Herakles and Antaios (above) Herakles lifts the giant Antaios away from the Earth, his mother Gaia, in order to deprive him of his source of strength. Bronze coin of the Roman Emperor Antoninus Pius, AD 142–3.

the directions he required; on another occasion he confronted another marine deity, Triton. Traditionally it was in Libya that Herakles encountered the giant Antaios: Antaios was a son of Gaia, the Earth, and he was invulnerable so long as he retained physical contact with his mother. Herakles wrestled with him and lifted him off his feet; deprived of maternal support, he became quite powerless in the hero's mighty arms. In Egypt Herakles had a narrow escape from sacrifice at the hands of King Busiris. A seer had once advised Busiris that sacrificing foreigners was a sure method of alleviating droughts. Since the seer was himself a Cypriot, he became the first victim of his own advice; when the method proved gratifyingly effective, Busiris ruled that all foreigners misguided enough to enter his kingdom should be sacrificed. When it was Herakles's turn, he let himself be bound and led to the place of sacrifice before turning the tables on his assailants and butchering the lot of them.

Herakles was not infrequently involved in conflicts with the gods. On one occasion, when he failed to receive a response he had hoped for from the Delphic priestess, he tried to make off with the sacred tripod, saying he would found a better oracle of his own. When Apollo tried to stop him, a fierce quarrel broke out, which was only resolved when Zeus hurled a thunderbolt between them.

Herakles was very loyal to his friends; more than once he risked his own life to help them, most spectacularly in the case of Alkestis. Admetus, king of Pherae in Thessaly, had made an arrangement with Apollo that when the time came for him to die, he would be allowed to live on provided that he found someone else who was willing to die in his place. However, when Admetus was later on the verge of death, it proved harder than he had anticipated to find a substitute; after his elderly parents had selfishly refused to sacrifice themselves, his wife Alkestis insisted that she should be the one to die. When Herakles arrived she had already descended to the Underworld, and he instantly set off after her. He then wrestled with Death and won, bringing her back in triumph to the world of the living.

Herakles was the Greek Superman, and many of the stories of his deeds are simply gripping tales of superhuman achievements and fabulous monsters. At the same time Herakles, like Odysseus, stands for the average man, and his adventures are exaggerated parables of human experience. Quick-tempered, not terribly bright, fond of wine, food and women (his amorous adventures are too numerous to detail here), he was an eminently sympathetic figure; and on the whole his example was to be emulated, for he destroyed evil and championed good, rising above all the blows that fortune showered on him. Above all, he offered some hope of defeating man's ultimate and crucial challenge, death.

Herakles's end was characteristically dramatic. Once, when he and his new bride Deianeira were crossing a river, the centaur Nessos offered to carry Deianeira over, and in midstream tried to rape her. Herakles shot him dead with one of his poisonous arrows, and as he expired, Nessos, simulating repentance, urged Deianeira to take some of the blood from his wound and keep it safe; if Herakles ever seemed to be tiring of her, she should soak a garment in the blood and give it to him to wear; after that he would never look at another woman. Years later Deianeira remembered this advice when Herakles, on his way home from a distant campaign, sent on ahead of him a beautiful captive princess with whom he was evidently in love. Deianeira sent her husband a robe dyed in the blood; as he put it on, the poison of the Hydra ate into his skin and he collapsed in frightful agony. His eldest son Hyllos took him to Mount Oeta and laid his mangled but still breathing body on a funeral pyre, which was eventually kindled by the hero Philoktetes. However, the labours of Herakles had ensured his immortality, and so he ascended to Olympos and took his place among the gods who live for ever.

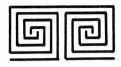

Theseus of Athens

Theseus was the quintessential Athenian hero, the embodiment of all that the Athenians thought was best and most distinctive about themselves. He was endowed with most of the same superhuman characteristics as Herakles, and his deeds were almost as impressive. But he was more refined and civilised than Herakles, a consummate statesman who could number among his achievements not merely the establishment of such religious and social institutions as the great Panathenaic festival of Athens, but also the political consolidation of Attica and the foundation of the Athenian democracy.

Theseus's mother was Aithra, the daughter of Pittheus, king of Troezen in the Argolid. His father was either Aigeus, king of Athens, or the sea-god Poseidon; Aigeus was thought to be sterile, and Aithra had lain with both on the night that Theseus was conceived. Aigeus was worried that his nephews, the fifty sons of Pallas, would try to murder their cousin if they knew of his existence, and so the boy was brought up at Troezen by his mother and grandfather. Beneath a great rock at Troezen, Aigeus concealed a sword and a pair of sandals, giving instructions that when Theseus was strong enough to lift the rock, he should be allowed to travel to Athens in search of his father. When Theseus had passed this test, his mother told him that it was time for him to set out for Athens. However, both she and Pittheus were most anxious that Theseus should not go by land, for the road from Troezen to Athens lay across the isthmus of Corinth, which was plagued by villains and ruffians of all description. But Theseus was determined not to avoid the danger; he hoped to emulate the deeds of Herakles and win renown by overcoming the hazards of the road.

The deeds accomplished by Theseus on his journey from Troezen to Athens seem to have been designed to rival those of Herakles. They were almost certainly the subject of an epic poem, which no longer survives. Tradition says that Theseus met his first challenge at Epidauros, where he came upon Periphetes, a lame brigand who wielded a huge, knotted club; Theseus wrested it from him, killed his opponent and took the weapon along to help in the rest of his adventures. All the way across the isthmus Theseus played the brigands at their own murderous games and won.

His second adversary, Sinis, specialised in tearing travellers limb from limb: he would bend two pine trees to the ground, tie one arm and one leg of his victim to the top of one tree and the other arm and leg to another,

Theseus lifting the rock *Watched by his mother Aithra, Theseus exerts all his strength to push away the huge rock and reveal the sword and sandals left there by his father. In a variation on the usual story, there is a quiver with the other objects. Roman terracotta relief ('Campana plaque'), first century* BC *or* AD.

then let go of the trees so that they sprang up and tore the wretched man apart. When Theseus drew near, Sinis asked him to test his strength by helping him to bend down a pine tree. Theseus agreed, but cunningly ensured that it was he rather than Sinis who first let go of the tree, and Sinis rather than he who ended up flying through the air. Surveying the sad remains of earlier travellers suspended around him, Theseus then bent down two trees and tied Sinis between them, so that he met the same painful death he had enjoyed inflicting on others. Theseus next encountered the Krommyonian Sow, a fierce wild pig which was ravaging the land; this creature too he killed.

The bandit Skiron had positioned himself where the isthmus was at its narrowest, with a sheer drop down to the sea on either side of the road. As Theseus approached, Skiron commanded him to kneel down and wash his feet. Theseus warily obeyed, kneeling as far from the edge as he could. As he did so, Skiron shouted that he should go and feed Skiron's turtle and tried to kick him over the cliff. But Theseus was too quick for him, and Skiron ended up in the sea. At Eleusis, the wrestler Kerkyon challenged Theseus to a bout, but he too found that he had met his match.

Drawing nearer to Athens, Theseus was urged by the infamous Prokrustes to spend the night on his wonderful bed, a couch guaranteed to provide the perfect fit for all comers. Prokrustes would invite travellers to lie down and then set to work to make them fit the bed: if they were too short, he pounded them with a mallet in order to stretch them out, and if they were too long, he lopped off their feet and heads. Theseus was to be Prokrustes's last visitor, and Prokrustes's own mutilated body was the final occupant of his terrible bed.

When Theseus finally arrived at Athens, he found his father Aigeus under the spell of the sorceress Medea, who had promised to cure him of his supposed sterility and give him numerous sons. Theseus did not reveal his identity to Aigeus, but Medea knew at once who he was. Since his arrival on the scene had rather spoiled her plans, she tried hard to get him out of the way. First she suggested to Aigeus that he should ask the young stranger, who claimed to have dealt with so many villains, to get rid of the Bull of Marathon; brought from Crete by Herakles, this creature was then ravaging the Athenian countryside. Despite its enormous size and the fire it breathed from its nostrils, Theseus managed to subdue the beast and bring it back to Athens, where he sacrificed it to the city's patron goddess, Athena.

Foiled in her first attempt to get rid of Theseus, Medea now tried to poison him. According to tradition, her attempt took place at the public banquet which accompanied the sacrifice of the Bull of Marathon. Just as Medea set a cup of poison on the table, Theseus drew the sword he had brought with him from Troezen as though to cut the meat of the sacrifice. Aigeus, recognising the weapon, sprang up in surprise and delight and upset the cup, whose contents spilt over the floor, hissing and eating their way into the marble. Father and son were reunited, and the discredited Medea was forced to flee for her life.

Theseus proceeded to get rid of the challenge to his father and himself from his cousins, the sons of Pallas, whom he ambushed and completely routed. But now there was another ordeal he had to face – the Minotaur. Every nine years Minos, king of Crete, demanded from Athens a tribute of seven girls and seven youths, whose fate was to be sacrificed to the beast. The Minotaur, a monstrous creature with the body of a man and the head of a bull, was the child of Minos's wife Pasiphae and a bull sent from the sea by Poseidon. Its home was the Labyrinth, a dark maze of endlessly winding corridors, blocked exits and confusing turns, built for Minos by the master-craftsman Daidalos.

The legend of the human tribute may reflect an era when the Minoan civilisation exercised control over Athens, but the Theseus story refers to a more specific incident: Aigeus had earlier sent Minos's son Androgeos to fight the Bull of Marathon, and he had been killed, so it was in compensation for his death that the tribute was exacted. At any rate, soon after the defeat of the sons of Pallas, the time for the tribute approached, and when Theseus found out about it, he was determined to be one of the party. Aigeus was overcome by grief, and tried hard to dissuade him, but Theseus would not change his mind, promising Aigeus that he would slay the Minotaur and return safely home.

Aigeus was convinced that he would never see his son again. However, he made sure that the ship which carried the youths and girls to Crete was equipped with two sets of sails, one black and the other white. They set sail with the black ones, as suited the melancholy nature of the expedition, but Aigeus requested that if they returned in triumph they should hoist the white set as a signal he could see from the Acropolis. Upon the ship's arrival in Crete the Athenian party was hospitably entertained by Minos and the Cretan court; during a display of athletics Minos's daughter Ariadne saw and fell instantly in love with Theseus. When the time came for the victims to enter the Labyrinth, Theseus, who had asked to go first, was secretly supplied with a ball of thread by Ariadne; he made one end fast to a point near the entrance and unwound the ball as he travelled through the maze. Finally he came to the centre and found himself face to face with the Minotaur,

The deeds of Theseus *In the centre, Theseus drags the defeated Minotaur from the Labyrinth, suggested by the meander-and-chequer border. Round about, Theseus is shown with Sinis, the Krommyonian Sow, the wrestler Kerkyon, Prokrustes, Skiron, and the Bull of Marathon. Athenian red-figured kylix (drinking-cup), about 440–420 BC.*

The Centauromachy The Centaur gropes at a wound in his back, his powerful torso arched in pain; the youthful Lapith arrests his adversary with his left hand, lifting his right to deliver a decisive blow. The two figures strain away from each other, but are formally reunited by the backcloth of the Lapith's heavy cloak. Marble metope (relief panel) from the Parthenon, Athens, 445–440 BC.

a far more terrifying creature than any he had before encountered. Theseus had no weapon, but with his bare hands he fought off the monster's attack and eventually wore down its strength to the point where he was able to break its neck. Thoroughly exhausted but unharmed, with the aid of the thread he retraced his steps to the exit, where Ariadne was anxiously awaiting him. Together they collected the rest of the Athenians, fled to their ship and instantly set sail for the mainland.

For neither Theseus nor Ariadne did the story have an entirely happy ending. Ariadne had made Theseus promise to take her with him back to Greece, but he abandoned her on the island of Naxos, in circumstances not altogether clear. The popular and romantic version of the story is that the gods made Theseus forget all about Ariadne, so that he left her sleeping in a secluded spot where she was later discovered by Dionysos. However, more prosaic sources, anxious to explain and excuse such unheroic conduct on the part of Theseus, suggest that he put her ashore on Naxos because she was pregnant and badly seasick; then he and his ship were swept out to sea by a storm and she was left to die in labour. In this version of the story, Theseus had the black sails hoisted on the ship as he approached Athens because he was still mourning the loss of Ariadne; the more usual account is that in his eagerness to return home he simply did not remember to change them for the white ones. So Aigeus, anxiously scanning the horizon, was greeted by the sight of the black sails; believing that his son had perished, he threw himself to his death from the rocks of the Acropolis.

After the death of Aigeus, Theseus became king of Athens, but his involvement in heroic adventures did not cease. Invited to the wedding of his close friend Peirithoos, king of the Lapiths, Theseus found himself in the thick of a great battle with the centaurs, creatures part-man and part-horse.

Peirithoos had invited the centaurs to his wedding feast because they were his neighbours, but they had drunk too much wine and tried to carry off the Lapith women, including the bride. Only with heavy losses did Theseus and the others manage to beat off the attack.

Theseus was frequently involved in amorous affairs. His abduction of the Amazon Antiope led to the Amazon invasion of Attica, only repulsed after fierce fighting. In their old age Theseus and Peirithoos joined forces to abduct two daughters of Zeus, Helen and Persephone. They managed to kidnap Helen (this was before she became the wife of Menelaos), but when they descended to the Underworld in search of Persephone things started to go badly wrong. Persephone's consort Hades, god of the Underworld, invited the pair to sit down to a meal with him; when they tried to rise, they found they were stuck to their seats. Eventually Herakles managed to rescue Theseus, but Peirithoos was compelled to remain in the Underworld forever. Theseus's own death was strangely unheroic: he was pushed over a cliff on the island of Skyros by Lykomedes, its king.

The principal source for the story of Theseus is Plutarch, a Greek philosopher, priest and moralist who lived in the later first and earlier second centuries AD. Amongst his works is a series of parallel *Lives* of various famous Greeks and Romans, some historical, others legendary. In the *Lives* Theseus is paired with Romulus, an indication of the political significance which tradition attached to him: if Romulus was the founder of Rome, Theseus was the father of Athenian democracy. This idea seems to have originated in the last years of the sixth century BC, when democratic reforms were initiated by the Athenian statesman Kleisthenes. Many reforms are ascribed both to Theseus and to Kleisthenes; both are said to have organised the unification of Attica and to have divided the people into the three classes which were to be the basis of the political divisions of Athens in the historical period. Theseus, like Kleisthenes, is held to have established various civil and judicial councils and assemblies; to have founded festivals; and to have initiated such economic reforms as the minting of coins. It is thought that a new epic poem on the subject of Theseus may have been commissioned by Kleisthenes or by the new democracy, and it is certainly true that from the late sixth to the mid-fifth century, the popularity of Theseus rivals that of Herakles in Athenian art and thought. He appears on the sculptural decoration of temples and on the painted vases which people used in daily life and took with them to the grave. In 490 BC, when the Athenians were hard pressed by the Persians at the Battle of Marathon, it was Theseus, founder of the way of life which they were fighting to preserve, who was said to have appeared at the head of the army and inspired the soldiers with new strength.

Around 475–470 BC huge bones were found in a tomb on Skyros; they were identified as belonging to Theseus and ceremonially brought home to Athens, where a special shrine, the Theseion, was built to house them. At this time Theseus was not merely a figure of mythology for the Athenians, but a political symbol too, the image of their democracy.

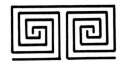

The Trojan War

Did the Trojan War take place? The extent of the appeal which the story of Troy has exercised over successive generations is demonstrated by the efforts of countless historians, archaeologists and romantic enthusiasts to establish the historical basis of the Trojan War and to discover the site of Troy. Today it is generally agreed that the site was correctly identified in the late nineteenth century by Heinrich Schliemann as the mound of Hissarlik on the plain by the Dardanelles, on the north-west coast of Turkey. However, Schliemann's claim to have discovered the Troy of the Trojan War is now largely discredited. The mound of Hissarlik contains numerous successive habitation levels, and it was in one of the earliest that Schliemann claimed to have discovered wonderful treasure: this settlement is now thought to be about a thousand years too early to have been destroyed by Greeks from the Mycenaean palaces of the Greek mainland. They might, though, have been instrumental in the destruction of one of the later settlements of Hissarlik, which seems to have been burnt to the ground, possibly after a siege, at about the right time (around 1200 BC). This later Troy was a relatively humble settlement, but in its destruction may lie the kernel of historical reality around which the legend grew. However, the development of the legend remains a mystery unlikely to be solved by archaeology, and so there is no danger that the romantic enigma of Troy will ever be destroyed.

Whatever its basis in historical fact, the Trojan War is the single most important episode, or complex of episodes, to have survived from Greek mythology and legend. The events which led up to the actual war and those which followed are combined in the group of stories known as the Trojan Cycle; some are known from the two great Homeric poems, the *Iliad* and the *Odyssey*, but other sections of the story have to be pieced together from numerous later sources, ranging from the Greek tragedians of the fifth century BC to much later Roman authors. The story as a whole may be compared to a Wagnerian opera in the richness and complexity of its interweaving of characters and themes; it is hugely romantic and of great human appeal, for like all Greek myths it is fundamentally the story of man and of his struggle to exist in the face of fate and the gods.

One of the first links in the chain of events which formed the prelude to the Trojan War was forged by Prometheus, the great benefactor of mankind. Prometheus, a cousin of Zeus, had given man fire, an element whose benefits had previously been enjoyed solely by the gods. He had also instructed men

Peleus and Thetis (right) Peleus grasps Thetis firmly in a wrestling hold. The panther on Peleus's back and the wolf-head with snake attachments to the right of Thetis's head suggest her transformations into a variety of animals in her attempt to make Peleus release his hold. Athenian black-figured amphora (wine-jar), about 500 BC.

The Judgement of Paris (below) As Hera and Athena approach from the left, Paris turns to the Eros at his shoulder and looks across at Aphrodite, seated on the right. Hermes stands between her and Paris. Emerging from behind a hillock above him is Eris, personification of Strife and a presentiment of the abduction of Helen and the ten-year struggle for Troy. Athenian red-figured hydria (water-jar), about 420–400 BC.

to offer to the gods only the fat and bones of meat sacrifices, and to keep the best bits for themselves. To punish Prometheus, Zeus chained him to a rock high in the mountains and daily sent an eagle to eat his liver, which grew again by night.

According to some sources, Prometheus was eventually set free by Herakles, but others state that he was released by Zeus when he finally agreed to tell him an important secret. This secret concerned the sea-nymph Thetis, who was so beautiful that she counted several gods among her suitors, including Poseidon and Zeus himself; however, a prophecy known only to Prometheus foretold that the son of Thetis was destined to be greater than his father. On learning this, Zeus rapidly abandoned the idea of fathering a son by Thetis himself, and decided that she should marry the mortal Peleus instead; their son would be Achilles, the greatest of the Greek heroes at Troy.

Thetis at first resisted the advances of Peleus, changing into fire, serpents, monsters and other forms, but he held tightly on to her through all her transformations and eventually she had to submit. All the gods and goddesses of Olympos save one were invited to the magnificent wedding of Peleus and Thetis; and in the middle of the feast Eris (Strife), the only goddess who had been left out, burst in and threw among the guests the apple of discord, inscribed (though we hear of this only from very late sources) 'for the fairest'. This apple was claimed by three goddesses, Hera, Athena and Aphrodite. Because they were unable to reach an agreement, and Zeus was understandably reluctant to decide the issue himself, he sent the goddesses to have their beauty judged by the herdsman Paris on Mount Ida, outside the city of Troy on the eastern shore of the Mediterranean.

Paris was a son of Priam, king of Troy, but when Priam's wife Hecuba was pregnant with him, she dreamed she was giving birth to a torch from which streamed hissing serpents, so when the baby was born, he was handed over to a servant with orders to take him out to Mount Ida and kill him. The servant, however, instead of killing him, simply left him on the mountain to die; he was rescued by shepherds or herdsmen, and brought up to be one himself. As Paris was minding his flocks on the mountain, Hermes led the three goddesses to him for judgement. Each offered him a reward if he would choose her; Hera wealth and power, Athena military prowess and wisdom, and Aphrodite the love of the most beautiful woman in the world. Awarding victory to Aphrodite, he incurred the undying wrath of the other two, who became henceforward implacable enemies of Troy. Shortly afterwards Paris returned by chance to Troy, where his prowess in athletic contests and his amazingly handsome appearance aroused the interest of his parents, who soon established his identity and received him back with rapture.

The most beautiful woman in the world was Helen, the daughter of Zeus and Leda. Many kings and noblemen had wished to marry her, and before her mortal father, Tyndareus, announced the name of the successful suitor, he made them all swear an oath to abide by Helen's choice and to come to the aid of her husband if she should ever be abducted. Helen married

Menelaos, king of Sparta, and by the time that Paris came to visit them they had a daughter, Hermione. Menelaos welcomed Paris into his home, but Paris repaid his hospitality by stealing Helen and escaping with her back to Troy. Helen's part in this was explained in different ways by various sources: either she was abducted against her will, or Aphrodite drove her mad with desire for Paris, or, most elaborate of all, she never went to Troy at all, and it was for the sake of a phantom that the Greeks spent ten long years at war.

The expedition sets sail

Menelaos summoned all Helen's former suitors, and all the other kings and noblemen of Greece, to help him mount an expedition against Troy to recover his wife. The leader of the Greek force was Agamemnon, king of Mycenae and elder brother of Menelaos. The Greek heroes came from all over the mainland and the islands to the port of Aulis, the assembly point from which they planned to sail across the Aegean to Troy. Their origins and the names of their leaders are listed in the great Catalogue of Ships near the beginning of the *Iliad*:

The tribes (of warriors) came out like the countless flocks of birds – cranes or long-necked swans – that gather in the Asian meadow by the streams of Cayster, and wheel about with harsh cries as they come to ground on an advancing front. So tribe after tribe streamed out from the ships and huts ... innumerable as the leaves and flowers in their season.

Some of the heroes came to Aulis more willingly than others. Odysseus, king of Ithaca, knew it had been prophesied that if he went to Troy he would not return for twenty years, and so he feigned madness when the herald Palamedes came to summon him, yoking two mules to a plough and driving them up and down the beach; but his ploy was revealed when Palamedes put Odysseus's infant son Telemachos in the way of the mules, and Odysseus immediately reined in his team. Achilles's parents, Peleus and Thetis, were reluctant to let their young son join the expedition, since they knew it was fated that if he went he would die at Troy. In an attempt to evade his destiny they sent him to Skyros, where, disguised as a girl, he mingled with the daughters of the king, Lykomedes. During his stay he married one of the daughters, Deidameia, who bore him a son, Neoptolemos.

Odysseus, however, discovered that the Greeks would never capture Troy without the assistance of Achilles, and so he went to Skyros to fetch him. According to one version of the story, Odysseus disguised himself as a pedlar, gained entrance to the court and spread out his wares before the women; among the jewels and textiles were weapons in which the young Achilles displayed a revealing interest. Another source describes how Odysseus arranged for the sound of a trumpet to be heard in the women's quarters: while the genuine daughters scattered in confusion, Achilles stood his ground and called for arms. His disguise abandoned, Achilles was easily persuaded to accompany Odysseus back to Aulis, where the fleet was preparing to sail.

The huge Greek force, whose greatest heroes were Agamemnon, Menelaos, Odysseus, Aias, Diomedes and Achilles, was ready to sail, but the wind held stubbornly against them. Eventually the prophet Kalchas revealed that the goddess Artemis demanded the sacrifice of Agamemnon's daughter, Iphigeneia, before the wind could turn. Agamemnon was horrified by this, but public opinion forced him to comply: Iphigeneia, summoned on the pretext that she was to marry Achilles, was instead slain upon the altar. Some sources say that Artemis took pity on her and substituted a deer at the last moment; at all events the wind veered round, and the ships set sail.

The wrath of Achilles

It is sometimes assumed that the *Iliad* is the story of the Trojan War. In fact, although it ranges widely over the whole story, its ostensible subject, as announced in its first lines, is rather more restricted:

Sing of wrath, goddess, the destructive wrath of Achilles, son of Peleus, that brought countless sorrows to the Achaeans, and sent many valiant souls of heroes to Hades, while their bodies made carrion for dogs and birds, and the will of Zeus was fulfilled...

The story of the *Iliad* is, then, the story of Achilles, and of his quarrel with Agamemnon. At the opening of the *Iliad* the Greeks had already been at Troy for nine years. They had sacked much of the surrounding countryside and skirmished sporadically with any Trojans who had emerged from behind their massive fortifications. The Greeks were wearying of the campaign and irritated by their inability to score a decisive victory over Troy itself, when Achilles fell out with Agamemnon over a matter of honour.

Agamemnon, as his share of the booty from a raid in which Achilles had played the leading part, had been allotted a girl named Chryseis, daughter of Chryses, priest of Apollo. Chryses offered Agamemnon a fine ransom for her release but Agamemnon refused to give her up. So Chryses prayed to Apollo, who sent a plague upon the Greek camp, and the prophet Kalchas revealed that it would be lifted only if Agamemnon gave Chryseis back. Achilles was all in favour of him doing this, but Agamemnon was reluctant. They quarrelled, and Agamemnon eventually agreed to do as he was told, but in order to reassert his authority over Achilles in the most insulting way he could, and simultaneously compensate himself for the loss of Chryseis (whom he claimed to prefer to his own wife Clytemnestra), he took away from Achilles *his* slave-girl, Briseis. Achilles was justifiably enraged. Not only was it an insult to his honour, but it was grossly unfair, as he, Achilles, had done most of the fighting necessary to procure all the treasure and booty that Agamemnon felt he had a right to enjoy. Accordingly, Achilles withdrew to his tent, and took no more part in the fighting or the council meetings. The fighting grew fiercer, with more direct attacks made on Troy and the Trojans. But the Greeks were hard pressed without their greatest fighter, and even Agamemnon was eventually forced to make overtures to Achilles, offering

Odysseus, Diomedes and Dolon *The Greek heroes Odysseus and Diomedes surprise the Trojan spy Dolon in the dark. The painter has treated the subject as a burlesque, with the facial features of the three and their stealthy movements between the trees grotesquely caricatured. Lucanian red-figured calyx-krater (wine-bowl), about 410–400 BC.*

him riches of all description, along with the return of Briseis. Achilles, however, rejected all appeals, declaring that even if Agamemnon's gifts were 'as many as the grains of sand or the particles of dust' he would never be won over.

At this point, Odysseus and Diomedes went out on a night expedition to see what the Trojans were up to. Unknown to them, a Trojan named Dolon was setting out on a similar errand: the Greeks surprised him, and forced him to tell them the dispositions of the Trojan camp. On his recommendation they ended their night excursion with an attack on the encampment of Rhesus, king of Thrace, with whose beautiful horses they escaped back to the Greek camp.

Despite the success of this daring raid, in the overall fighting the Greeks were being driven back to their ships by the Trojans and were in desperate straits, when Achilles's friend Patroklos came to him and begged to be allowed to lead Achilles's troops, the Myrmidons, into battle. He also asked if he could borrow Achilles's armour in order to strike terror into the ranks of the Trojans, who would mistake him for Achilles. Achilles agreed, and Patroklos went out and fought long and gloriously, before, predictably, he was slain by Hector, son of Priam and the best fighter on the Trojan side.

Achilles was overcome by grief. His mother, the sea-nymph Thetis, came to him, and promised him new armour to replace that which had been lost with Patroklos. The new armour, made by the smith-god Hephaistos, included a beautiful shield covered with figured scenes, cities at peace and war, scenes of rural life with flocks, herds and rustic dances, and round the rim of the shield ran the River of Ocean. Achilles and Agamemnon were reconciled, and Achilles returned to the field of battle, where he slaughtered Trojan after Trojan with his spear, 'like a driving wind that whirls the flames this way and that when a conflagration rages in the gullies on a sun-baked mountainside and the high forest is consumed'. After killing many Trojans and surviving even the attack of the River Scamander, which tried to drown him in its mountainous waves, Achilles was at last able to meet his chief adversary, Hector.

The rest of the Trojans had fled from the onslaught of Achilles and taken refuge within their walls, but Hector remained outside the gates, deliberately awaiting the duel which he knew he must fight. Yet when Achilles finally appeared, Hector was overcome by understandable terror and turned to flee. Three times they ran the circuit of the walls of Troy before Hector stopped and bravely faced his great opponent. Achilles's spear lodged in Hector's throat and he fell to the ground. Barely able to speak, Hector begged that Achilles should allow his body to be ransomed after his death, but Achilles, furious with the man who had killed Patroklos, spurned his appeal and proceeded to subject the body to great indignities. First he dragged it by the heels behind his chariot round the walls of the city, for all of Troy to see. Then he took the body back to the Greek camp, where it lay untended in his huts.

Achilles then arranged an elaborate funeral for Patroklos. A huge pyre was built; over it many sheep and cattle were slaughtered and their carcasses

New armour for Achilles *The sea-nymph Thetis and her sisters, riding on dolphins, bring the new armour made by Hephaistos to replace that which was lost with Patroklos. Thetis herself carries a shield, emblazoned with a springing lion. Athenian red-figured and white-ground lekythos (oil-flask), about 440–420 BC.*

35

piled around the body of the dead hero. Jars of honey and oil were added to the pyre, and then four horses and two of Patroklos's dogs. Twelve Trojan prisoners were slaughtered over the pyre, which was then set alight. It burned all night, and all night Achilles poured libations of wine and mourned aloud for Patroklos. The next day the bones of Patroklos were collected and laid in a golden urn, and a great mound was raised where the pyre had been. Funeral games with magnificent prizes were held, with competitions for chariot racing, boxing, wrestling, running, armed fighting, throwing the discus and archery. And every day at dawn, for twelve days, Achilles dragged the body of Hector three times round the mound, until even the gods, who had foreseen and arranged all this, were shocked, and Zeus sent Iris, messenger of the gods, into Troy to visit Priam and instruct him to go secretly to the Greek camp with a fine ransom, which Achilles would accept in return for relinquishing the body of Priam's son.

So Priam, escorted by a single herald, set out for the Greek camp, and was met in the dusk as he drew near to the Greek ships by Hermes, disguised as a follower of Achilles. Hermes guided Priam through the Greek camp, so that he arrived unseen at the hut of Achilles. Priam went straight in and threw himself at Achilles's feet: he asked the hero to think of his own father Peleus, and to show mercy on the father who had lost so many of his fine sons at the hands of the Greeks; he asked to be allowed to take the body of his greatest son back to Troy with him in order that he should be properly mourned and buried by his kinsmen. Achilles was moved by his appeal; they wept together, and Priam's request was granted. So Hector's body was returned to Troy, where he was mourned and buried with appropriate rites.

Here the *Iliad* ends, but it is by no means the end of the story of Troy. The rest of the story is recounted partly in the *Odyssey* and partly by the tragedians, but also by later Roman authors, principally Virgil in the *Aeneid* and a miscellany of later poets such as Quintus of Smyrna. After the death of Hector, a series of allies came to the assistance of the Trojans, including the Amazons under their queen, Penthesileia, and the Ethiopians led by Memnon, a son of Eos, goddess of the dawn. Both Penthesileia and Memnon were killed by Achilles. But Achilles had always known that he himself was fated to die in Troy, far from his native land, and eventually he was killed by an arrow, shot from the bow of Paris. Achilles's mother, Thetis, had wanted to make her son immortal, and when he was a baby she had taken him down into the Underworld and dipped him into the waters of the River Styx; this made his body impervious to injury, except for the heel by which she held him, and it was here that the arrow struck.

The sack of Troy

After the death of their greatest champion, the Greeks resorted to guile in their efforts to capture Troy, which had withstood their siege for ten long years. The Wooden Horse was said to have been the idea of Odysseus, while

The death of Penthesileia *Achilles has forced the Amazon Queen to the ground and, as she looks up at him, he drives his spear into her throat. The brutality of the action is emphasised by the way her face and throat are shown naked and defenceless, while only Achilles's eye is visible through his helmet. According to one tradition, their eyes met in this instant and, belatedly, they fell in love. Athenian black-figured amphora (wine-jar), about 540 BC.*

The Wooden Horse *This is the earliest known representation of the Horse: the artist has given it wheels, and there are port-holes in the sides for the warriors to look out. Some brandish weapons through the port-holes, while others have already emerged from the Horse. Relief pithos (large storage-jar) from Mykonos, 650–600 BC.*

37

the craftsman responsible for its manufacture was Epeios. When it was built, a party of the boldest Greeks climbed into it, including Odysseus himself and Neoptolemos, son of Achilles. The rest of the Greek force burnt their huts and set sail, but they went only as far as the island of Tenedos, where they beached their ships and waited. The Trojans, scarcely daring to believe that the Greeks had sailed for home, scattered over the plain, marvelling at the Horse and reminding each other of where the Greek camp had been. Soon some shepherds came across a single Greek who had been left behind, Sinon, who told them that his compatriots had wanted to sacrifice him in order to acquire a favourable breeze for their journey; he had with difficulty escaped his chains. This story aroused the compassion of the Trojans, so that they were well disposed to believe the rest of his account. He said that the Greeks, believing that Athena had turned against them, had decided to sail home and attempt to regain the divine favour that their expedition had originally enjoyed. They had made the Horse to propitiate Athena, and they had deliberately made it large in order that the Trojans would not be able to take it within their walls. If the Horse did enter Troy, the city could never be taken; if it stayed outside, the Greeks would definitely return and raze the city to the ground.

A few of the Trojans mistrusted the Horse and were reluctant to bring it within their walls. Priam's prophetic daughter Cassandra, whose fate it was never to have her prophecies believed, warned of the death and destruction its entry into Troy would bring. And Laokoon, the priest of Poseidon, cast his spear against the flanks of the Horse, which resounded with the clang of armed men, and declared that he feared the Greeks, even when they brought gifts. But as he was preparing a sacrifice to the god he served, two great serpents came up from the sea and strangled first his two young sons and then Laokoon himself, before gliding on to take refuge under the altar of Athena. Upon this omen the Trojans hesitated no more, but proceeded to drag the great Horse within their walls, pulling down their fortifications in order to do so. Even then, the hiding place of the Greek heroes might have been discovered, for Helen took it into her head to come down to the Horse, and, walking round it, to call out the names of the Greek heroes, mimicking the voice of each man's wife. Some were tempted to reply, and only Odysseus had the presence of mind to stifle their voices.

When darkness fell, the treacherous Sinon signalled to the fleet at Tenedos, which returned silently to its old anchorage; Sinon also released the heroes from their confinement in the Horse, and the scene was set for the sack of Troy. As the Greeks from the Horse were joined by their comrades from the ships, the Trojans awoke from sleep to find their city going up in flames. The men fought desperately, resolved at least to sell their lives dear, appalled by the sight of their wives and children being dragged from their places of refuge to be either slaughtered or taken prisoner. Most pitiable was the death of Priam, murdered at the altar in his courtyard by Neoptolemos, son of the man who had killed his son Hector. Among the few to escape from Troy was Aeneas, son of Anchises and the goddess Aphrodite. Warned by his mother, he left the city with his little son Ascanios and his elderly father, carrying with him the gods of Troy; his wife followed behind them, but was lost in the confusion, the darkness and the wreckage of the dying city. Aeneas himself was fated after much wandering to reach Italy, where he founded a new and greater Troy, the forerunner of Rome.

The adventures of the Greek heroes on their way home from Troy, and the various homecomings they enjoyed, were enshrined in a number of epic poems known as *Nostoi* (Returns). Of these poems the *Odyssey*, which describes the return of Odysseus to his homeland of Ithaca, is the only one to survive; the returns of the other heroes must be pieced together from a variety of later sources. We shall come to Odysseus shortly, but first we will deal with the homecoming of the leader of the Greeks, Agamemnon, king of Mycenae.

The return of Agamemnon

Agamemnon and Menelaos were the sons of Atreus, who committed a terrible crime when, in a family quarrel, he served his own brother Thyestes with a dish concocted from the severed limbs of Thyestes's children. This act brought a curse upon the house of Atreus, and the fate which met Agamemnon on his return from Troy was in part just retribution for his father's original crime. In Agamemnon's ten-year absence from Mycenae, the government was in the hands of his wife Clytemnestra, assisted by her lover Aigisthos, the one surviving child of Thyestes. A chain of beacons lit against the sky had relayed the news of the great victory at Troy back to mainland Greece, and by the time Agamemnon arrived at his palace, Clytemnestra's plans were well advanced.

Meeting her husband in front of the entrance, she insisted that he should trample over the purple textiles she spread out before him, in a triumphal entrance into his hall. Agamemnon was reluctant to commit such an act of insolence and impiety, but eventually he gave in, and so ensured his doom. Following him indoors, Clytemnestra attacked him as he lay defenceless in the bath, first ensnaring him in a net, before murdering him most brutally with an axe. Her motives for this savage killing were complex, but it would seem that it was not so much her guilty passion for Aigisthos and her desire to see him avenged for the wrong done to his father and brothers, as her hatred of Agamemnon that drove her to his murder. He had brutally murdered her first husband and child before her eyes; he had sacrificed their daughter Iphigeneia at Aulis. She wanted vengeance.

The curse of Atreus did not die with Agamemnon, for he and Clytemnestra had two more children eager to avenge their father's death, Orestes and Elektra. Orestes, when a baby, had been sent away from Mycenae to the safety of Phokis by his sister, anxious to preserve him from their scheming mother. Elektra herself remained at home and was very badly treated by

Clytemnestra and Aigisthos; according to some versions of the story they married her off to a peasant so that the royal line would end in ignominy. When he grew up, Orestes secretly returned home, accompanied by his friend Pylades. Arriving at the tomb of his father, he laid locks of his hair on the mound, where they were recognised by Elektra, who approached to offer a placatory sacrifice on behalf of her mother; Clytemnestra had had a dream of ill-omen, that she had given birth to a snake which had suckled at her breast and drained away her blood. Orestes quite reasonably saw this as auspicious for himself, and after much agonised discussion of the horrors of matricide, Elektra persuaded Orestes to murder both his mother and Aigisthos. For this terrible deed he was driven insane by the Furies, who pursued him until, at a special trial of the Areopagos at Athens, he was acquitted on the grounds that the murder of a mother is a lesser crime than the murder of a husband. In this way the curse of the house of Atreus was worked out.

Death of Agamemnon *Agamemnon has been trapped in a shroud-like garment in which he is powerless to defend himself. Blood is already spurting from a wound in his chest as he falls backwards against Clytemnestra, while Aigisthos prepares to deliver the final blow. Athenian red-figured calyx-krater (wine-bowl), about 500–480 BC.*

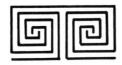

The story of Odysseus

Odysseus had known before he ever went to Troy that it would be twenty years before he returned home to his rocky island of Ithaca, his son Telemachos and his wife Penelope. He was at Troy for ten years, and for ten more he travelled across the oceans, shipwrecked, eventually deprived of all his companions, frequently within an inch of his life, until in the twentieth year he landed once more on the shores of his island home.

The Cyclops

On leaving Troy, Odysseus and his companions first encountered the Cicones, whose city they sacked, but at whose hands they suffered heavy losses. They were in danger of losing more of their number to the Lotus Eaters, hedonists who did nothing but sit around and eat the luscious fruit which made them forget all cares and responsibilities. Odysseus had to drag those of his men who had tasted the lotus back to the ships by force, and scarcely had they recovered from this adventure than they landed in the next, their encounter with the Cyclops Polyphemos.

The Cyclopes were a race of huge, one-eyed giants who occupied a fertile country where the soil bore bountiful crops of its own accord and provided rich pasturage for fat sheep and goats with shaggy fleeces. Eager to meet the inhabitants of such a land, Odysseus took one ship into the harbour and, disembarking, walked up with his crew to the cave of the Cyclops Polyphemos, a son of Poseidon. Polyphemos was out tending his sheep, so Odysseus and his crew made themselves at home until he returned with his flocks at dusk. The Cyclops was huge, monstrous and terrible, and after a few perfunctory inquiries into the origins and business of his unexpected guests, he picked up a couple of them and dashed their brains out on the floor before devouring them whole. The Cyclops then fell heavily asleep; Odysseus contemplated stabbing him to death, but gave up the idea when he realised that escape would then be impossible, since the mouth of the cave was blocked with a vast rock, which the Cyclops could lift with one hand, but which the combined strength of Odysseus and his companions was unable to shift. The Cyclops had two more of Odysseus's men for breakfast and then went out, taking care to replace the huge stone at the cave entrance. The resourceful Odysseus was not slow to think up a plan of action. He sharpened a great wooden stake which lay in the cave and hardened its tip in the fire.

Odysseus escaping from the Cyclops' cave (above left) Odysseus, sword in hand, clings upside-down beneath a large ram, the leader of Polyphemos's flock; he thereby passes safely through the doorway of the cave. Athenian 'Six Technique' lekythos (oil-flask), about 500–480 BC.

Odysseus and the Cyclops (above right) The gigantic Cyclops sits holding the wine-cup with which Odysseus has made him drunk; his mouth opens in pain, as Odysseus and his men drive the sharpened stake into his eye. Proto-Attic amphora (wine-jar), about 700 BC.

When evening came and Polyphemos returned home, Odysseus offered him a bowl of strong wine to wash down his ration of Greek sailors. The Cyclops swallowed the wine with enthusiasm and asked for three refills. Then, in a drunken stupor, he lay down to sleep. Before he nodded off, he asked to know the name of his guest, and Odysseus replied that it was 'Outis', the Greek for 'Nobody'; the Cyclops promised that in return for the wine he would eat 'Nobody' last. As the monster lay asleep, Odysseus heated the tip of the stake in the fire; when it was red-hot he and four of his best men drove the point straight into the Cyclops's one eye. The eye hissed and sizzled, like 'the loud hiss that comes from a great axe or adze when a smith plunges it into cold water to temper it and give strength to the iron'. The Cyclops, rudely awakened by the terrible pain, bellowed and raged, calling out for his neighbours, the other Cyclopes, to come and help. But when they gathered outside his cave and asked who was disturbing him, who had hurt him, he could only reply that Nobody was disturbing him, Nobody was hurting him, upon which they lost interest and went away.

At dawn Odysseus and his men prepared to make their escape from the cave; each man was tied beneath three big woolly sheep, while Odysseus himself clung under the leader of the flock, a huge ram with a magnificent fleece. The blinded Cyclops rolled aside the stone and sat at the door of his cave, trying to catch Odysseus's crew slipping out with the sheep, but they passed safely beneath his hands, Odysseus last of all. Driving the sheep down to their ship, they quickly set sail, although Odysseus was unable to resist taunting the Cyclops, who responded by hurling bits of cliff in the direction of his voice, some coming rather too close to the vessel for comfort. So Odysseus rejoined the rest of the fleet, and while the crews mourned their lost companions, they consoled themselves by feasting on the very sheep that had assisted their escape from the cave.

Aiolia

From the island of the Cyclops, Odysseus sailed on till he reached the floating island of Aiolia, whose king, Aiolos, had been entrusted by Zeus with power over all the winds. Aiolos and his large family received Odysseus and his crew hospitably, and when the time came for them to leave, Aiolos gave Odysseus a leather pouch in which he had imprisoned all the boisterous winds; he then summoned up a gentle westerly breeze which would blow the ships safely home to Ithaca. They sailed on course for ten days and were within sight of Ithaca when disaster overtook them. Odysseus, who had stayed awake to steer the ship for the whole journey, fell into an exhausted sleep, and his crew, who did not know what was in the leather pouch, began to suspect

Aiolos The male figure may represent Aiolos, King of the Winds, marshalling the dance of the Clouds or Breezes. Athenian red-figured 'knucklebone vase' (of uncertain function), about 460–440 BC.

43

that it contained valuable treasure given to Odysseus by Aiolos. They were jealous, feeling that as they had shared Odysseus's hardships, so they should share his rewards: they opened up the bag and accidentally let loose the winds. Odysseus awoke to a raging tempest, which buffeted the ship right back to Aiolia. This time the reception of Odysseus and his comrades was very different. They begged Aiolos to give them another chance, but he, declaring that Odysseus must be a man hated by the gods, declined absolutely to help, and drove him and his shipmates from the door.

Circe

At their next landfall, Laistrygonia, all the ships except Odysseus's own were lost in a calamitous encounter with the monstrous inhabitants, so it was in a state of considerable grief and depression that Odysseus and his surviving comrades found themselves at the island of Aeaea. Disembarking, they lay for two days and nights on the beach, utterly exhausted by their exertions and demoralised by the horrors they had been through. On the third day Odysseus roused himself to explore the island, and from a hilltop he saw smoke rising from a habitation in the woods. Prudently deciding not to reconnoitre at once, he returned to the ship to tell his companions the news. They were predictably dismayed, remembering the Laistrygonians and the Cyclops, but since Odysseus was determined to explore, he divided his company into two groups, one commanded by himself and the other by a man called Eurylochos. The two parties drew lots and the task of exploration fell to Eurylochos, while Odysseus remained at the ship. In due course Eurylochos's party arrived at the house in the woods. Outside were wolves and lions, who gambolled and fawned upon the men; they were in fact human beings who had been given animal shape by the sorceress Circe, whose beautiful singing could be heard inside the house. When the sailors shouted to attract her attention, she came out and invited them to enter; only Eurylochos, suspecting a trick, remained outside. Circe offered the men food, but with it she mixed a drug which caused them to forget their native land; and when they had finished, she struck them with her wand and drove them off into the pig-sties, for they were now to outward appearances swine, though unhappily for them they still remembered who they really were.

The panic-stricken Eurylochos rushed back to the ship to report the disappearance of his companions. Odysseus commanded the man to take him back to Circe's home, and when he refused, set off alone to the rescue. On his way across the island he met Hermes, disguised as a youth; the god gave him a plant called Moly which, mixed with Circe's food, would provide an antidote to her drug; he also instructed him as to how he could get the better of the sorceress: when Circe struck him with her wand, he should rush at her as though to kill her; she would then shrink back in fear and invite him to share her bed. To this he should agree, but he must first extract from her a solemn oath not to try any tricks while he was vulnerable.

Everything happened just as Hermes had predicted. After they had been to bed together, Circe bathed and dressed Odysseus in fine clothes and had a sumptuous banquet prepared for him, but he sat in silent abstraction, refusing all attention. Eventually Circe asked him what was wrong, and he pointed out that she could hardly expect him to be the life and soul of the party while half his crew were languishing outside in the pig-sties. So Circe released the new pigs from their confinement and smeared a magic ointment over them; their bristles fell away, and they became men again, but younger and more handsome than they had ever been before. Odysseus and his men wept for relief and happiness, and only broke off when Circe suggested they should summon the rest of their company to join in the celebrations. They all stayed with Circe for an entire year, eating and drinking and enjoying themselves, forgetting the trials through which they had passed.

The Underworld

Eventually Odysseus was reminded by some of his companions that perhaps it was time to think of Ithaca. Circe warned him that before he could set sail for home he must first visit the Underworld to consult the Theban prophet Teiresias: only Teiresias could give him instructions for his return. So Odysseus sailed across the River of Ocean and moored his ship by Persephone's poplar grove. There on the shore he dug a trench, around which he poured libations to the dead of honey, water, milk and wine; over the trench he cut the throats of a ram and a black sheep. Attracted by the smell of blood, the souls of the dead thronged up to drink, but Odysseus drew his sword and kept them back, waiting for the soul of Teiresias to appear. First to approach was one of his crew, Elpenor, who had fallen off the roof of Circe's house where he had been sleeping on the morning of the departure, and whom in their haste to depart they had left unburied and unwept; this state of affairs

Circe *Circe stands in the centre, stirring the cup she has just taken from one of Odysseus's men, who now has the head of a boar. Four of his companions are shown, with the heads of a boar, ram, lion and wolf. On the far left Odysseus is approaching with drawn sword. Athenian black-figured 'Merrythought' cup, about 550–530 BC.*

45

Odysseus promised to rectify as soon as he could. When Teiresias appeared, Odysseus let him drink the blood, and the prophet then told him that he had a good chance of returning home safely, but that he must be sure not to plunder the Cattle of the Sun on the island of Thrinakie; he also warned him of the situation he would find on Ithaca, where rapacious suitors were wooing his faithful wife Penelope.

After he had heard all that Teiresias could tell him, Odysseus let other ghosts approach and drink the blood which enabled them to converse with him. The first to come was his ancient mother, who relayed to him the manner of her death, and a sad account of the wretched state of his father Laertes and of Penelope's brave efforts to fend off her suitors. Odysseus, overcome by grief and desiring to comfort both himself and his mother, tried three times to embrace her, but three times she slipped wraith-like through his hands and left him holding the air. Other heroines approached and conversed, and after them came Agamemnon, who told Odysseus of his bloody death, comforting him with the thought that Penelope would never act as Clytemnestra had done. Achilles also approached, and Odysseus hailed him as the most fortunate man who ever lived, a mighty prince among the living and the dead. Achilles replied that he would rather be a slave and alive than king among the dead, but Odysseus was able to cheer him up with news of the prowess of his son Neoptolemos, and he departed happy.

During his visit Odysseus saw some of the famous sights of the Underworld: Sisyphus endlessly pushing his great boulder up a mountain, with it always slipping back just as it reached the top; and Tantalus, standing up to his neck in a pool of water which vanished as he bent to drink, with branches of fruits dangling above his head that blew away as he reached to grasp them. Odysseus was keen to see more, and he did meet the ghost of the mighty Herakles, but before he could encounter other heroes of earlier generations he was overwhelmed by a great wave of the dead who came up in their thousands and raised around him their mournful, haunting cry; panic-stricken, he returned to his ship, loosened the moorings and crossed back to the world of the living.

The Sirens and Skylla and Charybdis

Odysseus returned to Circe's island and, once Elpenor was properly buried, Circe was able to give Odysseus further instructions for his journey and to prepare him for some of the evils to come. The ship sailed first by the island of the Sirens, terrible creatures with the heads and voices of women and the bodies of birds, who existed for the purpose of luring mariners on to the rocks of their island with their sweet songs. As the ship approached, a dead calm fell upon the sea, and the crew took to their oars. On Circe's instructions Odysseus plugged the ears of the crew with wax while he had himself bound to the mast, so that they would carry him safely past the danger yet let him listen to the song. 'Draw near, Odysseus,' sang the Sirens:

Skylla With her left arm Skylla reaches over to pull one of Odysseus's men out of the ship; the dogs at her waist are mauling two others, while a fourth is caught in the grip of a powerful fish-tail. Roman bronze bowl, first century AD.

No seaman ever sailed his black ship past this spot without listening to the sweet tones that flow from our lips ... we know all that the Argives and Trojans suffered on the broad plain of Troy by the will of the gods, and we have foreknowledge of all that is going to happen on this fruitful earth ...

Odysseus shouted to his men to release him, but they rowed resolutely on, and eventually the danger was passed.

Their next task was to navigate the twin hazards of Skylla and Charybdis. Charybdis was a terrifying whirlpool, alternately sucking down and throwing up the heaving water; the cautious mariner who chose to avoid her was forced instead to encounter the equally horrific Skylla. Skylla lurked in a cavern set high up in a rock, concealed by spray and mist from the breakers below; she had twelve feet which dangled in the air and six necks, each equipped with a monstrous head with triple rows of teeth. From her cavern she exacted a toll of human victims from the ships which passed beneath. Odysseus, forewarned by Circe, chose not to tell his sailors about Skylla; giving Charybdis as wide a berth as possible, they passed directly under Skylla's rock, and although Odysseus was armed and prepared to do battle with her for the lives of his crew, she managed to evade his watch and succeeded in snatching up six shrieking victims.

The Cattle of the Sun

Next the ship came within sight of the island of Thrinakie, a place of rich pasturage where Apollo kept his herds of fat cattle. Odysseus had been warned by both Circe and Teiresias that if he hoped to reach Ithaca alive he should avoid this place and must not at any cost lay a hand upon the cattle. He explained this to his men, but they, weary and depressed by the loss of six more comrades, insisted on making anchor and spending the night on the beach. Faced with a mutiny, Odysseus had little option but to comply, but he made them swear to leave the cattle strictly alone. That night a storm set in, and for a full month the wind blew from the south, making it impossible for them to continue their journey.

So long as they still had the provisions Circe had given them, the men kept to their oath and did not touch the cattle. But eventually their food ran out and, driven by hunger, they seized the opportunity presented by Odysseus's temporary absence from the ship to round up some of the best of the herd; they reasoned that if they slaughtered them in honour of the gods, the gods could hardly be angry. Odysseus returned to the smell of roasting meat; rebuke was useless for the deed was done, and the gods were determined to avenge the crime. When the meat was finished, the wind dropped, so the ship could set sail; but no sooner was she fairly out to sea than a terrible gale sprung up and the ship was first smashed by the force of the waves, then rent asunder by a lightning flash. All hands were lost save Odysseus himself, who managed to cling on to the wreckage of the mast and keel, which he rode for ten days until he was washed up on the shores of the island of Ogygia, home of the beautiful nymph Calypso.

Calypso

Calypso made Odysseus her lover and he stayed with her for seven years as he had no means of escape. Eventually the goddess Athena sent Hermes, messenger of the gods, to explain to the nymph that the time had come for her to send her visitor on his way. Calypso, though reluctant to lose him, knew she must obey, so she provided Odysseus with the materials for a raft, gave him food and drink, and summoned up a favourable wind to speed him towards Ithaca. Without incident, he came within sight of the land of the Phaiacians, great seafarers who were destined to carry him on the last lap of his journey. But then Poseidon intervened; he hated Odysseus for what he had done to his son, the Cyclops Polyphemos, and now he was outraged to see him so near to the end of his journey. So he sent up yet another storm, which broke the mast off the raft and left it to be flung around by the winds.

As the north wind at harvest-time tosses about the fields a ball of thistles that have stuck together, so did the gusts drive his craft hither and thither over the sea. Now the South Wind would toss it to the North to play with, and now the East would leave it for the West to chase.

Odysseus was saved from certain death by the intervention of the sea-nymph Ino. She gave him her veil, instructing him to wrap it round his waist and then abandon ship and strike out for the shore. As a huge wave snapped his raft into matchwood, Odysseus did as he was told. For two days and nights he swam onwards, but on the third day he reached the shores of Phaiacia and eventually managed to land on the rocky coast at the mouth of a river. He threw Ino's veil back into the water and lay down in a thicket to sleep.

Odysseus in Phaiacia

Inspired by Athena, the Phaiacian princess Nausikaa had chosen that very day to make an expedition to the mouth of the river to wash clothes in the deep pools there. When she and her maids had finished the washing and spread it out on the shingle, they bathed, ate and then amused themselves singing and playing with a ball as they waited for the clothes to dry. As Nausikaa threw the ball to one of the maids, the maid missed and the ball fell in the river; all the girls shrieked loudly and Odysseus awoke from sleep, wondering what savage land he had arrived at now. Breaking off a branch with which to conceal his nakedness, he emerged from his thicket to find Nausikaa standing her ground bravely while the other girls fled in panic. He addressed Nausikaa as a suppliant, begging her to show him the way to the city and give him some rag to wear. Nausikaa answered him with dignity and kindness, and after he had washed, anointed himself with oil and dressed himself in some of their fine clean clothing, she gave him food and drink, and then he accompanied the girls back to the outskirts of the city. To avoid gossip Nausikaa left Odysseus there to finish the journey into the centre alone. She suggested he should make straight for the house of her father Alkinous, and fall as a suppliant at the knees of her mother Arete.

Guided by Athena herself in the guise of another local girl, Odysseus arrived at Alkinous's splendid palace. There were walls of bronze and gates of gold, guarded by gold and silver watchdogs. Inside the hall, light was provided by solid gold statues of youths holding torches. Outside the courtyard was a beautiful garden and orchard, with fruit trees, vines and a well-watered vegetable patch. After he had admired all this, Odysseus, wrapped in a cloud of mist provided by Athena, passed inside and walked straight up to Queen Arete, around whose knees he flung his arms in supplication. As the concealing mist rolled away, the Phaiacians listened in amazement to his petition: he asked for shelter and to be conveyed home to his native land.

When he had overcome his initial astonishment, Alkinous was generous in his reaction. Politely forbearing to question his guest at once, he arranged for his immediate refreshment, promising that in the morning steps would be taken to restore him to his homeland. When the other Phaiacians went home and Odysseus was alone with Alkinous and his wife, Arete asked him who he was and how he had acquired his clothes, which she had not been slow to recognise. So Odysseus told them the story of his adventures since leaving the island of Ogygia, explaining how he had met Nausikaa at the river mouth. Meanwhile Arete arranged for a bed to be made up, and Odysseus was grateful to retire.

The next day a ship was made ready to convey Odysseus home, but before he could set out, the hospitable Alkinous insisted on feasting his guest and regaling him with sports and other entertainment. First the bard Demodokos performed for the assembled company, singing of an episode in the Trojan War, a quarrel which had taken place between the illustrious Achilles and the cunning Odysseus. As he listened, Odysseus wept and drew his mantle over his head to conceal his misery. Only Alkinous noticed, and to cheer his guest up he proposed some athletic contests. Odysseus was at first content to watch the young noblemen, but when taunted he threw the discus a record-breaking length. Dancing followed, and then Demodokos sang again, the story of the amorous adventures of Aphrodite and Ares. The Phaiacian noblemen now vied with one another to shower presents on Odysseus. At the evening meal Demodokos sang again, and at Odysseus's suggestion his theme was the Wooden Horse of Troy. Odysseus wept again as he listened, and again Alkinous alone observed him. At the end of the story, Alkinous asked Odysseus to tell them who he was, where he came from and where he wished to be conveyed; and why he wept at Demodokos's songs. Thus invited, Odysseus told them who he was and described all the adventures he had been through: he spoke of the Cicones and the Lotus Eaters, of the Cyclops, Aiolos, the Laistrygonians, Circe, his visit to the Underworld, the Sirens, Skylla and Charybdis and the Cattle of the Sun, ending with his stay with Calypso, the escape from whose island had brought him to the land of the Phaiacians.

The following evening Odysseus at last said goodbye to his hosts and a swift Phaiacian ship bore him smoothly over the sea to Ithaca. Odysseus slept as the ship surged forward, and was still asleep when the morning star arose and the crew deposited him along with the gifts the Phaiacians had given him on the shores of Ithaca, beside a beautiful cave, home of the nymphs. When Odysseus awoke he failed to recognise the spot, largely because Athena had cast a mist over the island, to give herself time to meet Odysseus and arrange a suitable disguise for him. As he was dismally wondering where the treacherous Phaiacians had landed him, Athena appeared to him in the guise of a shepherd and, in response to his enquiries, told him that he was indeed in Ithaca. The wary Odysseus spun the goddess a story about being a Cretan exile; she smiled at his cunning, and in reply revealed her true identity, reassured him that he really was in Ithaca, and counselled him on how he should proceed in order to regain his wife and kingdom.

Odysseus in Ithaca

In the twenty years that Odysseus had been absent from home most people on Ithaca, apart from his wife Penelope, his son Telemachos and a few faithful retainers, had come to believe that he was dead, that he had perished either at Troy or on the voyage home. Since Penelope was not only beautiful and accomplished but also rich and powerful, and the man who married her would succeed to Odysseus's wealth and status, she was besieged by suitors, young noblemen who lounged around in her husband's palace, eating and drinking his provisions and forcing their unwelcome attentions upon her. For as long as she could Penelope played for time, persuading each that he had grounds for hope but saying nothing definite to any of them. For three years she tricked them into waiting, by announcing that she was weaving a winding-shroud for Odysseus's old father Laertes; it would be unseemly were he to die with no shroud ready for him, and they must wait for her decision until she had finished her work. Every day she worked away at the loom, but when night fell she undid her work by torch-light. As the fourth year began, however,

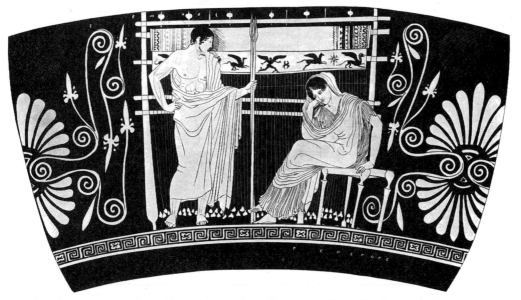

Penelope at her loom *One of her suitors confronts Penelope in front of her loom. Her dejected attitude suggests that her trick of weaving by day and undoing the work by night has been discovered. Athenian red-figured skyphos (drinking-cup), about 460–440 BC.*

she was betrayed by one of her maids, who helped the suitors catch her at her scheme, and reluctantly she was forced to finish her web.

Shortly before Odysseus's arrival in Ithaca, Athena had inspired Telemachos, now of an age to play an active part in his father's return, to set out on a journey with the aim of discovering what had happened to him. Telemachos travelled first to Pylos, where he consulted the ancient Nestor; Nestor had no news, but sent him on to the magnificent palace of Menelaos at Sparta. Menelaos and Helen treated him with great kindness, and Menelaos explained how he had heard from the Old Man of the Sea that Odysseus was marooned on the island of the beautiful nymph Calypso. When Odysseus himself landed on Ithaca, Telemachos was on his way home; the suitors, irritated and somewhat alarmed by Telemachos's grown-up behaviour, were planning to ambush his ship on its return journey, but with the aid of Athena Telemachos successfully evaded their trap and arrived safely in Ithaca.

Athena had advised Odysseus not to go straight into the town but instead to seek shelter with the swineherd Eumaios, who lived with his pigs on a farm some distance outside. Disguised as a tramp, Odysseus did as his patroness suggested, and was very kindly received by Eumaios, whose explanation of the situation in the town was interspersed with much praise of his absent master and prayers for his safe return. In response to Eumaios's questions, Odysseus told him a long story about his origins, saying he was the illegitimate son of a wealthy Cretan; after numerous adventures he had ended up in Thesprotia, where he heard of Odysseus, who had lately passed that way. The king of Thesprotia put him on a ship bound for Dulichium, but the rascally crew had stripped and bound him, intending to sell him as a slave. When they disembarked on Ithaca, he had managed to slip his ropes and swim ashore, so arriving at the homestead of Eumaios.

Eumaios swallowed all of this story except the reference to Odysseus, which he refused to accept, even when his guest swore that Odysseus would be home that very month and offered to let Eumaios's men throw him from a precipice if he were proved wrong. Eumaios served Odysseus a meal of roast pork and spread him a comfortable bed by the fire; he himself spent the night outside, watching over his absent master's property.

The next evening, over supper in the swineherd's hut, Odysseus announced his intention of travelling into the town to beg at the palace; but Eumaios, anxious for the safety of his guest, insisted that he await the return of Telemachos. That evening it was Eumaios's turn to recount his life story, and he told how he had been born of noble parentage but kidnapped by some Phoenician traders when a child, to be sold into slavery on Ithaca. Early the next morning Telemachos landed on the island and, guided by Athena, went straight to the swineherd's hut. While Eumajos walked to the town to tell Penelope that Telemachos was back, Athena dissolved Odysseus's disguise and prompted him to reveal his identity to his son. Telemachos was at first reluctant to accept that the beggar by the swineherd's hearth was really his father, but eventually he was convinced and the two wept together for joy and relief. Recovering, they laid their plans: Odysseus would follow Telemachos back to the town and go to beg in his own palace. There he would assess the situation and wait for the right time to attack; when that time arrived he would signal to Telemachos and the two of them, with the help of Zeus and Athena, would set about the destruction of the miserable suitors.

Odysseus travelled to the town in the company of the swineherd. On the way they met the goatherd Melantheus, a scoundrel completely in the pay of the suitors, who levelled a number of insults and blows at the old beggar. Outside the palace on a dung heap lay an ancient hound, mangy and diseased. When he heard Odysseus's voice he lowered his ears and feebly wagged his tail. Odysseus recognised him at once and, much affected by his appearance, quietly brushed aside a tear. As he commented on the dog's dilapidated appearance to Eumaios, the latter replied that twenty years ago no dog could have outrun Argos or picked up a scent faster, but in his master's absence he had grown old and neglected. As the two passed into the building, Argos quietly expired, happy to have seen his master again after twenty long years.

Predictably, Odysseus was abused and insulted by the suitors when he tried to beg from them in his own hall. They jeered at his rags, threatened him, and one even threw a stool at him. But once he had defeated the resident beggar in a wrestling match, they thought more highly of him. At this point Penelope was suddenly inspired to show herself to her suitors. So she descended to the hall, where her beauty filled them all with desire; she chided Telemachos for allowing them to insult a beggar in her house, and then she turned to the suitors and suggested that instead of eating her out of house and home it would be more seemly for them to bring her presents. They agreed and, much to Odysseus's delight, produced fine gifts of cloth and jewellery. As the evening drew on, it became time for another banquet and Odysseus made himself useful tending the lights and the fires. The suitors again taunted the beggar in their midst, and another stool was thrown, only to be adroitly avoided by its target. When the suitors finally withdrew to their own homes for the night, Telemachos and Odysseus removed all the weapons from the hall and put them away in a storeroom. Penelope then came down again to speak to the beggar, whose presence had aroused her interest. She asked him where he had come from and explained her own miserable situation: the suitors were pressing her to choose between them, while she longed only for the return of Odysseus. He told her he was a Cretan of royal descent, and that he had met Odysseus in Crete. To test the truth of his story she asked him what clothes Odysseus had been wearing, and he described a purple cloak and a gold brooch with a device of a hound gripping a fawn. Penelope wept when she recognised these details. To cheer her up, Odysseus promised her that her husband was alive and well and very close; in fact, he would be back in Ithaca that very month.

Penelope now suggested that the beggar would enjoy a bath and a com-

Odysseus and Eurykleia *As Eurykleia washes the beggar's feet, she feels the scar on his leg and recognises him as Odysseus. Athenian red-figured skyphos (drinking-cup), about 460–440 BC.*

fortable bed. The cautious Odysseus, however, would only allow his feet to be washed by an elderly maid, and so the old nurse Eurykleia was summoned for the task. Eurykleia immediately commented on how the beggar reminded her of Odysseus; Odysseus replied that everyone said so. As she started to wash his feet, Odysseus suddenly remembered the scar on his leg, acquired when he was just a boy and had joined an expedition to hunt wild boar on Mount Parnassus with his grandfather Autolykos and his uncles. He turned into the shadows, but sure enough Eurykleia felt and recognised the scar; in her excitement she dropped the bowl of water and would have shouted aloud to alert Penelope had not Odysseus grasped her firmly by the throat and instructed her not to tell a soul who he was until he had got rid of the suitors. All this time Penelope had been sitting absorbed in her own thoughts. But when Eurykleia had fetched more water and finished her task and Odysseus was once more seated by the fire, she turned to him again, and again explained her quandary: should she marry and so rid Telemachos of the burden of her presence and that of the suitors, or continue to hold out for Odysseus's return? She asked if the beggar could tell her the meaning of a recent dream in which a great eagle had swooped down from the hills and fallen upon her twenty pet geese, killing them all; then, perching on a roofbeam, the bird had told her that the geese were the suitors and he himself was Odysseus.

The beggar Odysseus assured her that the dream would come true and that the suitors were all doomed, but the cautious Penelope replied that dreams were confusing things; those which issued through the gate of horn came true, but those from the gate of ivory came only to deceive. Before she retired to her quarters for the night, to weep for Odysseus until she slept, she told the beggar that she intended to announce a competition for the suitors. She would set up twelve axe-heads in a line and invite the suitors to string the great bow of Odysseus and shoot an arrow straight through all the twelve. She would marry whoever proved himself able to accomplish this feat, which Odysseus himself had frequently performed.

The next day Penelope brought out the great bow of Odysseus and announced the competition to the suitors, each of whom hoped that he would be the only one to string the bow and shoot through the axe-heads. Telemachos prepared the hall for the contest and then tried to string the huge bow himself, bending it across his knee. It required all his strength, yet he would have managed it had he not been stopped by a nod from Odysseus. So he abandoned the attempt and one by one the suitors took their turn, but none could string the bow, let alone shoot an arrow straight through the axe-heads. While they were trying their strength, Odysseus slipped out of the hall and revealed his true identity to the swineherd Eumaios and the equally trustworthy oxherd, Philoetius, instructing them to come to his assistance when he gave them the sign. When one of the two leaders of the suitors, Eurymachos, had tried and failed the test, the other leader, Antinous, suggested they should put it aside for the day, since it was a feast day and they should be banqueting and sacrificing to the archer-god Apollo: his suggestion met with general approval. After they had all drunk their first toast, Odysseus asked if he might be allowed to try the bow. Antinous objected, but Penelope, who had been watching, insisted he should be allowed to have a go; Telemachos then intervened, sending his mother back to her chamber. In the general hubbub the swineherd Eumaios quietly took the bow up to Odysseus and placed it in his hands. He turned the familiar weapon this way and that, checking that it was whole and undamaged by its long rest; then, 'as easily as a musician who knows his lyre strings the cord on a new peg after looping the twisted sheep-gut at both ends', he strung the bow and twanged the cord, which sang under his hands like the call of a swallow. Quietly, without fuss, he fitted an arrow to the string and shot through the entire line of axes.

The suitors, dumbfounded, were still more shocked by the sequel. For as Telemachos stepped up to take his place beside his father, Odysseus aimed a second arrow, this time at the throat of Antinous. Not realising what was happening and thinking it had been an accident, the suitors rounded on Odysseus in a fury, but when he told them who he was and that his intention was to slay the lot of them, they became properly aware of their predicament and turned to attack him. Backed up by the faithful swineherd and oxherd, Odysseus and Telemachos might still have been overpowered by the sheer numbers of the suitors had not Athena herself intervened on their side. As suitor after suitor fell to the floor, only the minstrel and the herald, pressed into the suitors' service against their will, were spared. The suitors 'lay in heaps in the blood and dust, like fish that the fishermen have dragged out of the grey surf in the meshes of their net on to a bend of the beach, to lie in masses on the sand gasping for the salt sea water till the bright sun ends their lives'. Then Odysseus, 'spattered with blood and filth, like a lion when he comes from feeding on some farmer's bullock', summoned the aged nurse Eurykleia. She set those maidservants who had disgraced themselves through consorting with the suitors to clean and tidy up the hall; that done, they were hanged in a row in the yard.

Penelope, under Athena's influence, had slept soundly through the noise of the great battle in the hall and the subsequent cleaning-up operations. Now she was aroused by Eurykleia and told the news of her husband's return. Numbed by shock, she could not be entirely sure that the stranger really was Odysseus, or what she should say to him. Cautious as her husband himself, she put him to one final test by instructing Eurykleia to move out of their bedroom the big bed that Odysseus had built. Odysseus knew that the bed was impossible to move, for it was built around a living olive tree. Only when, exasperated by her obstinacy, he had described the construction of the bed was Penelope convinced that he was indeed her long-lost husband; then she threw herself into his arms and wept. So they went together to their marriage bed and lay at last in each other's arms again; Odysseus told Penelope all his adventures, and the night went on and on, as the goddess Athena kept the dawn lingering by the shores of Ocean.

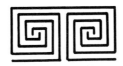

Jason, Medea and the Golden Fleece

The Golden Fleece had originally belonged to the ram which had saved the children of Athamas, Phrixos and Helle from being sacrificed to Zeus at the command of their wicked stepmother Ino. According to the legend, the ram collected the children from their home in Orchomenos and then flew east with them clinging to its back. As they crossed the narrow channel which divides Europe from Asia, Helle fell from the ram's back, giving her name to the sea below, the Hellespont. But Phrixos flew on over the Black Sea until the ram set him down in Kolchis, at the court of King Aeetes. Aeetes received Phrixos kindly, and when the boy had sacrificed the ram to Zeus, he gave its miraculous fleece to the king. Aeetes dedicated the fleece to Ares and hung it in a grove sacred to the war-god, where it was guarded by a fearsome serpent.

Why did Jason want the Golden Fleece? It was not that he coveted it for himself; like other heroes he was required to attempt what was thought to be an impossible deed to satisfy the demands of a hard-hearted taskmaster, in this case Pelias, king of Iolkos. Jason was the son of Aison, the rightful king of Iolkos; Pelias was Aison's half-brother, and in some versions of the story Pelias was supposed to rule only until Jason was old enough to take over. In these circumstances it was hardly surprising that when Jason grew up and demanded his rightful inheritance, Pelias sent him off to bring back the Golden Fleece. The quest for the Fleece is the story of the voyage of the *Argo* and the adventures of her crew, the Argonauts. The legend is probably older than the *Iliad* and the *Odyssey*, but it comes down to us chiefly through a much later epic poem, the *Argonautica* of the Alexandrian poet Apollonios of Rhodes.

There were about fifty Argonauts, and although the sources differ on some of their names, the main characters are clear. Apart from Jason himself, there was Argos, builder of the *Argo*; Tiphys the helmsman; the musician Orpheus; Zetes and Kalais, sons of the North Wind; Helen's brothers, Kastor and Polydeukes; Peleus, father of Achilles; Meleager of Calydonian boar-hunt fame; Laertes and Autolykos, father and grandfather of Odysseus; Admetus, who was later to let his wife die in his place; the prophet Amphiaraos and, for the first part of the journey, Herakles himself; besides these famous names there were a host of other heroes. Their ship, the *Argo*, whose name means

The building of the Argo One of the Argonauts is working on the vessel's prow, while another adjusts the sail on the yard-arm, assisted by the goddess Athena. Roman terracotta relief ('Campana plaque'), first century BC or AD.

'swift', was the fastest ever built. She was constructed in the port of Pagasai in Thessaly and was made entirely of timber from Mount Pelion, except for the prow, which was a piece of a sacred oak tree brought by the goddess Athena from the sanctuary of Zeus at Dodona. This piece of oak was prophetic, and could on occasion give tongue.

The *Argo* set sail with favourable omens and travelled north towards the Black Sea. On the journey to Kolchis her crew met with numerous adventures. In Mysia they lost Herakles, when another member of the crew, a beautiful youth named Hylas, went off in search of fresh water for a feast and failed to return to the ship. The nymphs of the spring that he found, falling in love with his beauty, had abducted and drowned him; but Herakles refused to give up searching, and so the *Argo* had to sail without him.

On the Greek shore of the Bosporos the Argonauts found Phineus, a blind seer and son of Poseidon, on whom the gods had inflicted a terrible curse. Whenever he sat down to eat, he was visited by a plague of Harpies, terrible creatures part-woman and part-bird, who seized some of the food in their beaks and talons and defiled the rest with their excrement. The Argonauts set a trap for these monsters. They invited Phineus to share their table, and when the Harpies duly appeared, the winged sons of the North Wind drew their swords and pursued them until, exhausted, they promised to desist. Phineus then revealed to them as much as he was able concerning their journey: chief among the hazards they would face were the clashing rocks; when they reached these they should send a dove through first. If the dove found the passage between the rocks, so too would the *Argo*, but if the dove failed, they should turn the ship around, for their mission was doomed to failure.

The dove they sent out did pass safely through the clashing rocks, leaving only its longest tail feather in their grip; *Argo* too sped through the narrow channel, suffering only slight damage to her stern timbers, and without any more significant adventures the Argonauts arrived safely at Kolchis.

When Jason explained why he had come, King Aeetes stipulated that before Jason could remove the Golden Fleece he must first yoke two bronze-footed, fire-breathing bulls, a gift of the god Hephaistos, to a plough; he must then sow some of the teeth of the dragon Kadmos had slain in Thebes (Athena had given these teeth to Aeetes), and when armed men sprang up he must destroy them. Jason rather rashly agreed to all these conditions, but was fortunate enough to receive the help of the king's sorceress daughter Medea in carrying them out. Medea, who first made Jason promise that he would take her back to Iolkos as his wife, gave him a magic ointment to rub over his body and his shield; this made him impervious to all attack, whether of fire or iron. She further instructed him on what to do with the crop of armed men: he should throw stones into their midst so that they would attack each other rather than Jason himself. Thus armed and warned, Jason succeeded in all his tasks.

Aeetes, somewhat surprised at his visitor's prowess, was still reluctant to hand over the Fleece, and even attempted to set fire to the *Argo* and kill her crew. So while Medea drugged the guardian serpent, Jason quickly removed the Golden Fleece from the sacred grove, and with the rest of the Argonauts they slipped quietly away to sea. When Aeetes found both his Fleece and his daughter missing, he gave chase in another ship, but even this had been foreseen by Medea. She had brought along her young brother Apsyrtos, and she now proceeded to murder him and cut him up into small pieces which she threw over the side of the ship. As she had anticipated, Aeetes stopped to pick up the pieces, and so the *Argo* made good her escape.

The route of the homeward journey of the *Argo* has baffled many scholars. Instead of returning through the Hellespont, Jason left the Black Sea via the Danube, which miraculously allowed him to emerge into the Adriatic; not content with this achievement, the *Argo* went on to sail up both the Po and the Rhine before somehow finding her way back into the more familiar waters of the Mediterranean. And everywhere they went the Argonauts met with fantastic adventures. On Crete, for example, they encountered the bronze giant Talos, a creature designed by Hephaistos to operate as a sort of mechanical coastal defence system for Minos, king of Crete. Talos would walk around Crete three times each day, keeping ships away by breaking off portions of the cliffs and hurling them at any vessel that tried to come too close. He was completely invulnerable except for a vein in his foot; if this were damaged, his life-force would leak away. Medea was able to drug him so that he became insane and threw himself about on the rocks, eventually damaging his vein and so bringing about his death.

Medea and the ram *Medea demonstrates her magic recipe for rejuvenation by boiling up a ram; surprisingly, the elderly man watching the experiment is not Pelias but Jason himself. Athenian red-figured hydria (water-jar), about 480 BC.*

When Jason finally arrived back in Iolkos, he married Medea and gave the Golden Fleece to Pelias. There are various accounts of what happened next. One version of the story is that Medea tricked the daughters of Pelias into murdering their father. She first demonstrated her powers of rejuvenation by mixing various potions in a cauldron of boiling water, then slaughtering and chopping up an aged ram and dropping in the pieces: immediately a fresh young lamb emerged. Fired with enthusiasm and with the best of intentions, Pelias's daughters hurried to cut up their old father and boil his pieces in the cauldron; unfortunately they succeeded only in hastening his end.

In the ensuing scandal Jason and Medea fled to Corinth, where they lived happily for at least ten years and had two children of their own. Eventually, however, Jason grew tired of his wife and tried to leave her for Glauke, the young daughter of the king of Corinth. Medea, furious with jealousy, sent Glauke a gift of a robe which, when she put it on, clung to her skin and tore it off; as her father tried to help his tortured daughter he too became entangled and they both perished miserably. To punish Jason still further, Medea went on to murder their own children, before escaping into the sky in a fiery chariot. Jason eventually returned to rule in Iolkos.

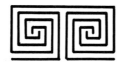

Perseus and Medusa

According to the Alexandrian scholar Apollodoros, Perseus, the legendary founder of Mycenae, would never have been born at all if his grandfather had had his way. Akrisios, king of Argos, was the father of a beautiful daughter, Danae, but he was disappointed to have no son. When he consulted an oracle about his lack of a male heir, he was told that he would produce no son himself, but that in the course of time he would have a grandson, whose destiny it was to kill his grandfather. Akrisios took strenuous steps to evade his fate. He shut Danae up in a tower of bronze, and there she languished in total seclusion until the day when she was visited by Zeus in the form of a shower of gold; subsequently she gave birth to Perseus. Akrisios was furious, but still thought his destiny could be avoided. He made his carpenter construct a large chest into which Danae was forced to climb along with her baby and they were then pushed out to sea. However, they survived the waves, and after a tiresome journey the chest was washed up on the shores of Seriphos, one of the islands of the Cyclades. Here Danae and Perseus were found and looked after by an honest fisherman, Dictys, brother of the less scrupulous king of Seriphos, Polydektes.

In time Polydektes fell in love with Danae, but as he grew up Perseus protected his mother jealously from the king's unwelcome advances. One day at a banquet Polydektes asked his guests what gift each was prepared to offer him. The others all promised horses, but Perseus volunteered to fetch him the gorgon's head. When Polydektes took him at his word, Perseus was forced to make his offer good. There were three gorgons, monstrous winged creatures with snaky hair; two were immortal but the third, Medusa, was mortal and so potentially vulnerable; the difficulty was that anyone who looked at her was turned to stone. Fortunately, Hermes came to the rescue, and showed Perseus the way to the Graiai, three ancient sisters who shared one eye and one tooth between them. Instructed by Hermes, Perseus managed to get hold of the eye and the tooth and refused to return them until the Graiai showed him the way to the Nymphs who would provide him with the equipment he needed to deal with Medusa. The Nymphs obligingly provided a cap of darkness which would enable Perseus to take Medusa by surprise, winged boots to help him make his escape and a special bag to put the head in once he had sawn it off. Hermes produced a sickle-shaped knife, and so Perseus set off fully equipped to find Medusa. With the help of Athena, who held up a bronze mirror in which he could see the gorgon's reflection

Danae, Perseus and Akrisios *Akrisios directs his carpenter to put the final touches to the chest in which he proposes to push Danae and Perseus out to sea. Danae and the nurse holding the child remonstrate with Akrisios, but Perseus himself seems more interested in the carpenter's actions. Athenian red-figured hydria (water-jar), about 490 BC.*

Perseus and the gorgon *Perseus stabs the gorgon Medusa in the throat. He looks away, because any mortal who saw her face would turn to stone. The god Hermes stands watching on the right. Athenian black-figured oinochoe (wine-jug), about 540 BC.*

Andromeda The Ethiopian princess, supported by two slaves, watches the preparation of the stakes to which she will be tied to await the arrival of the sea-monster. Her father sits beyond the stakes, his head in his hands; off the picture to the right is Perseus, coming to the rescue. Athenian red-figured hydria (water-jar), about 450 BC.

rather than looking on her terrible face, he finally managed to despatch her. Packing the head safely into his satchel, he sped off back towards Seriphos, assisted by his winged boots.

As he flew over the coast of Ethiopia, Perseus saw below him a beautiful princess tied to a rock. This was Andromeda, whose foolish mother Cassiopia had incurred the wrath of Poseidon by boasting that she was more beautiful than the daughters of the sea-god Nereus. To punish her Poseidon sent a sea-monster to ravage the kingdom; it would be appeased only if offered the king's daughter, Andromeda, who was duly placed on the shore to wait a terrible fate. Perseus fell in love at once, killed the sea-monster and freed the princess. Her joyful parents offered him Andromeda as a wife, and the two left together to continue the journey to Seriphos. Polydektes had not believed Perseus would ever return, and so it must have been rather gratifying for Perseus to watch the tyrant slowly petrify under the gaze of the gorgon's head. Perseus then gave the head to Athena, who fixed it as an emblem in the centre of her breast-plate.

Perseus, Danae and Andromeda now set off together for Argos, where they hoped to be reconciled with the old king Akrisios. But when Akrisios heard they were coming, he fled from the threat of his grandson's presence into Thessaly where, unknown to each other, both Perseus and Akrisios found themselves at the funeral games of the king of Larissa. Here the oracle that Akrisios had feared came true, for as Perseus threw a discus, it swerved off course and fell upon Akrisios's foot as he stood among the onlookers, killing him outright.

Perseus sensibly decided it would not be a very popular move to return home to Argos and claim Akrisios's throne when he had just killed him, so instead he exchanged kingdoms with his cousin Megapenthes. Megapenthes went to Argos while Perseus ruled in Tiryns, where he is said to have been responsible for the fortifications of Midea and Mycenae.

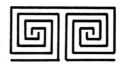

Oedipus and the Theban Cycle

The cycle of myths concerned with the fortunes of the city of Thebes and its royal family is certainly as old as the stories which make up the *Iliad* and the *Odyssey*, but it comes to us largely through much later sources. While the foundation of Thebes is chiefly known from Roman authors such as the poet Ovid, the stories of Pentheus and Oedipus are told by the tragedians of fifth-century Athens, Aeschylus, Sophocles and Euripides.

Kadmos and the foundation of Thebes

Kadmos was one of three sons of Agenor, king of Tyre on the eastern shore of the Mediterranean. Their sister, the beautiful Europa, was playing on the seashore when she was carried off across the sea to Crete by Zeus in the form of a bull. Agenor told his sons to find their sister and not to return home without her. In the course of his wanderings Kadmos arrived at Delphi, where the oracle advised him that a cow would meet him as he left the sanctuary; he was instructed to found a city at the place where the cow finally lay down. The animal led him to the site of the future Thebes. When she lay down to rest, Kadmos recognised that this was the place for his city and he decided to sacrifice the cow to the gods. Needing fresh water, he sent his attendants to fetch it from a nearby spring, the fountain of Ares. The fountain pool, however, was guarded by a dreadful serpent, which attacked and devoured all Kadmos's men. When Kadmos came in search of them, he found only fragments of limbs and the huge monster lying sated. Single-handed and lightly armed as he was, he managed to slay the snake, and then, on the advice of Athena, he sowed its teeth in the ground. Up sprang a crop of warriors, fully armed with swords and spears. They would have turned on Kadmos, had he not had the idea of throwing a great boulder in their midst; at this they began to hack each other to pieces, continuing until only five were left; these five joined Kadmos and became the founders of the five great families of Thebes.

Kadmos's city rapidly became rich and powerful; and its founder prospered with it. He married Harmonia, the daughter of Ares and Aphrodite, and they had four daughters, Ino, Autonoe, Agave and Semele, and one son, Polydoros. These in turn produced children of their own. Autonoe was the mother of Aktaion, the great hunter torn to death by his own hounds after Artemis had turned him into a stag as a punishment for seeing her naked.

Kadmos and the Serpent *Kadmos (left) advances on the rearing Serpent with drawn sword; among those watching him are the goddess Athena and the personification of his future city of Thebes. Athenian red-figured hydria (water-jar), about 430–410 BC.*

65

The beautiful Semele was seduced by Zeus and became pregnant with his child, the wine-god Dionysos. Zeus's divine wife Hera was jealous and cleverly suggested to Semele that she should ask Zeus to appear to her in the form in which he appeared to Hera. Because Semele had made Zeus promise to grant any request she made, he was obliged to reveal himself as a flash of lightning, which burnt her alive. Zeus snatched the child from her womb and implanted him in his own thigh, from which he was in due time born.

Semele's family refused to believe that Zeus was responsible for their sister's condition, or her death. And as the worship of Dionysos spread throughout Greece, it met with much enthusiasm and little resistance save in Thebes, where Dionysos's cousin Pentheus, Agave's son, refused to accept it.

Pentheus

A major feature of the worship of Dionysos in classical times was the formation of bands of women known as maenads; these would wander for days at a time in an ecstatic trance or frenzy over the mountainsides, drinking wine, suckling young animals or tearing them to pieces and eating them, charming snakes and generally running wild. Because of this orgiastic aspect and because its devotees were principally women, the worship of Dionysos was regarded with suspicion by the male authorities who liked to keep women in the house and under their control. Euripides's tragedy *The Bacchai* depicts an extreme case of Dionysiac revelry and male suspicion. In the play Dionysos himself comes to Thebes, determined to punish his mother's family for their lack of faith in both their sister and himself. The women of Thebes, including Semele's sisters, are all carried away by enthusiasm for the god; caught up in the revelry, they roam wild on Mount Kithairon for much of the play. Pentheus, the ruler of Thebes, regards his long-haired, effeminate cousin Dionysos with considerable suspicion, but as the god gradually drives him mad, he is brought to confess his desire to go out on to the mountain and spy upon the maenads. So Dionysos takes him up there, and when they come upon the women, the god bends down a tall pine tree so that Pentheus can perch on the top and see as much as he wants. Predictably he becomes an easy target for the maenads, who uproot the tree and tear him to pieces with their bare hands. Foremost among them is Pentheus's own mother, Agave, who returns triumphantly to Thebes bearing her son's head, believing it to be the head of a young lion. As the play ends, she is brought to realise what she has done, and all admit the power of the god.

The House of Oedipus

Oedipus, the great-great grandson of Kadmos, is today perhaps the best known of the Greek heroes after Herakles; he is famous for solving the riddle of the Sphinx, but still more notorious for his incestuous relationship with his mother. In ancient Greece he was renowned for both these episodes, but he was also more generally significant as the archetypical tragic hero, whose history embodied the universal human predicament of ignorance – man's lack of understanding of who he is and his blindness in the face of destiny.

Oedipus was born in Thebes, the son of Laios, its king, and his wife Jocasta. Because an oracle foretold that Laios would meet his death at the hands of his son, the infant Oedipus was given to a shepherd to expose on Mount Kithairon, his ankles pierced so that he could not crawl away. This was the origin of his name, which means 'swollen foot'. However, the kindly shepherd could not bring himself to abandon the child, and so handed him to another shepherd from the opposite side of the mountain. This shepherd in turn brought the child to Polybus, king of Corinth, who, being childless, was glad to raise the boy as his own. While Oedipus was growing up, he was taunted by remarks to the effect that he was not Polybus's own son; although Polybus assured him that he was, Oedipus at last resolved to travel to Delphi and consult the oracle. The oracle did not reveal his true parentage, but it did tell him that he was destined to murder his father and marry his mother. Utterly horrified, and so shocked that he completely forgot his own doubts about his parentage, he left Delphi resolved never to return to Corinth while Polybus and his wife were alive.

Unknown to Oedipus, his real father Laios was also travelling in the neighbourhood of Delphi. At a place where three roads met Oedipus came alongside Laios's chariot; a member of Laios's escort roughly ordered Oedipus out of the way, and he, in no mood to comply, lashed out. As the chariot passed, Laios himself struck Oedipus with a staff and Oedipus retaliated by dragging him out of the chariot and killing him. He then put the incident out of his mind and continued on his way.

Turning his back on Corinth, he eventually arrived at Laios's city of Thebes, which was being terrorised by the Sphinx, a monster part-winged lion, part-woman, who asked a puzzling question: 'What is it that walks upon four legs, two legs and three legs?' Those who tried and failed to solve the riddle she cast over a precipice, the foot of which was thickly littered with the bones of her victims. When the death of Laios became known in Thebes, the kingship and the hand of Laios's queen were offered to the man who could solve the riddle and free the land from the pestilent Sphinx. To Oedipus the riddle posed no problem; he was quick to identify its subject as man, who as a baby crawls upon all fours, in his prime walks upright on two legs and in old age needs the support of a third leg, a walking-stick. When the Sphinx heard his reply, she was so enraged and mortified that she flung herself from the precipice to her doom.

The citizens of Thebes received Oedipus with rapture and made him their king; he married Jocasta and for many years they lived in perfect happiness and harmony. Oedipus proved a wise and benevolent ruler, and Jocasta bore him two sons, Eteokles and Polyneikes, and two daughters, Antigone and Ismene. Eventually, however, another plague came over the land of Thebes, and it is at this point in the story that Sophocles's great tragedy

Oedipus and the Sphinx *Oedipus sits on his mantle gesturing conversationally towards the Sphinx, who sits bolt upright on a rock in front of him. Athenian red-figured hydria (water-jar), about 380–360 BC, in the collection of Sigmund Freud.*

Oedipus Tyrannos begins. The crops are dying in the fields and orchards, the animals are barren, children falling sick and unborn babies withering in their mothers' wombs, while the gods are deaf to all appeals. Jocasta's brother Kreon returns from consulting the Delphic oracle, which ordains that the pollution will be lifted only when the killer of Laios is brought to justice. Oedipus immediately and energetically undertakes to seek him out, and as a first step consults the blind prophet Teiresias. Teiresias is reluctant to reveal the identity of the killer, but is gradually goaded to fury by Oedipus's insinuations that he himself must have had something to do with the murder. Eventually he announces that Oedipus himself is the sinner who has brought pollution upon the city; he also prophesies that Oedipus, who thinks himself so wise and so far-sighted, will refuse to accept the truth of his words, refuse to recognise who he is or what he has done.

Oedipus, enraged, suspects that his brother-in-law Kreon is plotting with Teiresias to take over the throne; nor can Kreon say anything to reassure him. Jocasta tries to smooth things over: it is impossible that Oedipus killed Laios, she says, for Laios was killed at a place where three roads meet. Suddenly Oedipus remembers his chance encounter with the old man near Delphi; questioning Jocasta about Laios's appearance (oddly enough, he looked rather like Oedipus himself) and the number of his escort, he realises that Laios was probably his victim. As he waits for confirmation to arrive from the one member of the escort who returned to Thebes, a messenger arrives from Corinth with the reassuring news that Polybus has died a natural death; Oedipus, not yet suspecting the full extent of his crime, is thankful that he seems to have evaded at least part of the oracle, but resolves to be cautious still lest he find himself marrying his mother.

The well-meaning messenger, anxious to put his mind at rest, assures him that Polybus and his wife were not his real parents; the messenger himself had received Oedipus, when a baby, from one of Laios's shepherds on Mount Kithairon, and given him to Polybus. Even now Oedipus fails to make the proper connection, and while the terrified Jocasta tries in vain to persuade him to halt his investigation, he persists in his efforts to get to the bottom of the mystery and demands that Laios's shepherd, now an old man, be brought before him. By a trick of fate this man is also the sole surviving witness to the murder of Laios. When he finally appears, the full horror of the situation is at last brought home to Oedipus; the man admits that he took Laios's son and out of pity gave him to Polybus's shepherd instead of leaving him to die. This child was Oedipus, who has now succeeded to his father's throne and bed.

Jocasta has not waited for the dénouement; she has gone ahead of Oedipus into the palace, and when he follows her with what seems like murderous intent, he finds that she has hanged herself. Tearing the golden brooches from her dress, he plunges them again and again into his eyes until blood runs down his face in streams. How can he bear to look upon the world, now that he sees the truth? The chorus in the play is left to point the moral of the story: however secure a man may feel, however rich, powerful and outwardly fortunate he may appear, no one can be confident of escaping disaster; it is not safe to call anyone happy this side of the grave.

Although he begged Kreon for immediate banishment, Oedipus was not allowed to leave Thebes for several years, until this punishment had been ratified by an oracle. By the time he was sent away, he was much less anxious to go. Now an old man, he was condemned to wander from place to place begging for food and refuge, his blind footsteps guided by his daughters Antigone and Ismene. While they brought him comfort and even some happiness, his sons, Polyneikes and Eteokles, were increasingly estranged from him, from their uncle Kreon and from each other. It had been arranged that they would take it in turns to rule for a year at a time, but when Eteokles's first year was up he refused to hand over the throne to his brother. Polyneikes took refuge in Argos, where he gathered around him a band of six other champions with whom he proposed to lay siege to his native city. Such is the state of affairs at the beginning of Sophocles's *Oedipus at Colonos*, when Oedipus, drawing near to the end of his life, arrives in the olive groves of Colonos, a district on the outskirts of Athens.

Supported by Antigone, Oedipus takes refuge at an altar to await the arrival of Theseus, king of Athens, when Ismene arrives with news from Thebes. The rival factions of the brothers are growing daily more heated, and an oracle has pronounced that the side which can gain possession of Oedipus will emerge the winner. Oedipus, equally irritated with Kreon and both his sons, is adamant that he will not support either side; they can fight it out between themselves, and he hopes that they will destroy each other in the process. When Theseus arrives, therefore, Oedipus asks to be allowed to end his days in Athens. Theseus listens with favour to his request and offers to take Oedipus somewhere more comfortable, but Oedipus wishes to remain where he is. Then Kreon appears, determined to get Oedipus to accompany him back not to Thebes, but to the city's frontier, so that while avoiding the pollution of having Oedipus actually on Theban soil, his faction might be protected by his close proximity. When Oedipus spurns Kreon's pretence at friendship and rejects his offer out of hand, Kreon becomes violent and threatens to take Oedipus by force; he has already captured Ismene, and now his soldiers drag Antigone too away from her helpless father.

Theseus, returning just in time to stop Oedipus being dragged from the altar, is highly critical of Kreon's actions and promises to restore Oedipus's daughters to him; he orders Kreon back to Thebes. Polyneikes then arrives, also with a political reason for desiring the protection of the father whom he helped eject from Thebes; he too is sent packing, as Oedipus announces his intention of remaining at Colonos to the end of his days. The play ends dramatically: after Oedipus disappears into the sacred grove, a messenger emerges to recount his miraculous end, witnessed only by Theseus. Oedipus, it is pronounced, has transferred the blessings he could have given Kreon or Polyneikes to Athens, which will hereafter be protected by his presence.

The attack made on Thebes by Polyneikes and his allies is the subject of Aeschylus's *Seven Against Thebes*. Seven champions lead the attack at the seven gates of Thebes, and it falls to Polyneikes to take the gate defended by his brother Eteokles. Although the Thebans finally repulse the attack upon their city, the two brothers die by each other's swords, thus fulfilling their father's curse and continuing the unhappy saga of the house of Oedipus.

The dramatic action of Sophocles's *Antigone* begins at this point in the story. With Oedipus's male heirs both dead, Kreon assumes the title of king of Thebes. He decrees that while Eteokles should be buried with all ceremony, the traitor Polyneikes must be left where he fell, to have his corpse destroyed by dogs and birds of prey. Kreon sets a guard over the corpse to ensure that his edict is obeyed, and soon his soldiers return with Antigone, who has been caught throwing handfuls of soil over her brother's mangled remains in an effort to provide him with a symbolic burial. When challenged with her disobedience, she replies that the laws of the gods, which require that kinsmen be buried, are irrevocable and immutable and must take precedence over the laws of man. In his *Antigone*, Sophocles uses the myth to explore this conflict between human and divine law: what is the ordinary person supposed to do when the two sets of laws conflict? Although ultimately the answer seems to be that the divine law must be obeyed at whatever cost, the issue is by no means clear-cut from the start. While Antigone is portrayed as a headstrong, unfeminine woman who is not content to remain in the traditional female realm of the home but ventures out to defy the laws of her male guardian, Kreon comes across initially as a man doing his best to govern his city by the rule of law.

When Antigone shows no remorse for her crime, Kreon orders her to be entombed alive, a cruel method of execution calculated to absolve him from direct responsibility for her death. At this point Antigone's fiancé, Kreon's son Haimon, comes to Kreon to plead for her life, pointing out that the punishment is both barbarous and politically unwise, for Antigone is well on the way to becoming a heroine among the people of Thebes. Kreon, how-ever, remains obdurate, like the trees that will not bend to the torrent on the margins of a flooded river, or the sailor who will not slacken his sheets before the gale; and so he gives instructions for the entombment to go ahead. Only when the prophet Teiresias appears, and reveals the anger of the gods and the terrible punishment that will fall upon Kreon if he persists in this course of action, does Kreon at last take the advice of the chorus and set off to release Antigone from her prison. Foolishly, as it turns out, he stops on the way to bury the remains of Eteokles and only arrives at the tomb to find Haimon holding the body of Antigone – she has hanged herself with her girdle. Haimon then turns his sword upon himself. Kreon returns home to the news that his wife Eurydice has killed herself, too, cursing her husband with her dying breath. Utterly crushed by the tragedy that has so suddenly befallen him, Kreon is led away, and the chorus is left to reflect that the greater part of happiness is wisdom, coupled with due reverence for the gods.

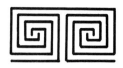

The imaginative legacy

T here would have been no market for a book on myths in fifth-century Athens, since the Greeks did not relegate them to a separate section of their lives. The characters and episodes of mythology were, rather, integrated into Greek society, reflected in all social activities from the cradle to the grave. To ask whether the average fifth-century Athenian 'believed' in all these stories is probably anachronistic. If the question is about accepting them as historical fact, it becomes part of a larger discussion of how the Greeks saw history, while if we are equating 'belief' with 'religious faith', a similar problem of definition arises.

The surviving evidence suggests that mythology was a natural and accepted part of life, which operated simultaneously on several different levels. The stories provided popular entertainment, their expression inspiring those excursions into music, poetry and the visual arts for which the Greek world is justly famous. At the same time, myths provided an inexhaustible stock of examples, not merely of good and bad behaviour for instructing the young, but also of the workings of fate, destiny and character, and the mystery of life, for older people to ponder. Moreover, the complex patterns of mythology, the functions and interrelationships of gods and heroes and their associations with particular places, formed the basis of the intricate network of cults whose observance was so important to the Greek social structure.

All civilisations need mythologies, and many invent their own. But because Greek civilisation is the foundation of Western society, and the study of Greek culture has been so important in the education systems of the Western world until relatively recently, many Western societies have adopted Greek myths and used them alongside their own contemporary or historic legends. The Romans led the way, adapting the Greek pantheon only very slightly in order to accommodate a few local Italic deities, and endlessly reproducing Greek myths in their literature and their art. For Romans of both the Republic and the Empire, Greece represented culture and civilisation; those who wished to demonstrate their taste and erudition decorated the walls of their houses with paintings of Greek myths, and after they died they had themselves placed in marble coffins bearing sculptured panels depicting the battles of the Greeks and the Amazons, or the wine-god Dionysos with his entourage. The subject matter of Roman poetry, too, was basically Greek; many Greek myths are preserved only thanks to the Augustan poet Ovid, while his contemporary Virgil legitimised and glorified the origins and growth of Rome in his epic poem of the *Aeneid*, whose story starts in the Sack of Troy, the greatest of all Greek myths.

The widespread adoption of Christianity did nothing to curb the popularity of the characters and stories of the myths and their continual recycling in art, music and literature. With the rediscovery of classical antiquity in the Renaissance, the poetry of Ovid became a major influence on the imagination of poets and artists. His were among the first classical texts to benefit from the invention of printing in the late fifteenth century; they were widely and enthusiastically translated, and remained a fundamental influence on the diffusion and perception of Greek myths through subsequent centuries. From the early years of the Renaissance, artists were happy to portray the pagan subjects of Greek mythology alongside more conventional Christian themes: so today in the Uffizi Gallery in Florence, Botticelli's 'Birth of Venus' or 'Pallas and the Centaur' rub shoulders with the same artist's Annunciations and Madonnas. Italy, and Rome in particular, became an important focus for artists interested in the classical past, from the early Renaissance until well into the eighteenth century. Artists of all nationalities were attracted there, including, in the seventeenth century, the Frenchmen Nicolas Poussin and Claude Lorrain; for them the classical world provided as much inspiration as the Christian, the two traditions happily fused in Rome.

In northern Europe, classical mythology never took the same hold of the visual arts, but its effect was very obvious in literature: in Elizabethan England, for example, classical texts both Latin and Greek were translated with enthusiasm, so that the stories of mythology became easily available to contemporary poets. In seventeenth-century France, too, Greek tragedy found contemporary relevance at the hands of such masters as Racine, who reworked the ancient myths – including those of Phaidra, Andromache, Oedipus and Iphigeneia – to new purpose.

The eighteenth century saw the philosophical revolution of the Enlightenment spread throughout Europe, accompanied by a certain reaction against Greek myth. In this age of reason some poured scorn on the frivolous nature of the myths, and there was a tendency to dwell rather on the scientific and philosophical achievements of Greece and Rome; typical of this attitude is Jacques-Louis David's painting of the 'Death of Socrates'. It was, however, impossible for the myths to be entirely overlooked, and they continued to provide an important source of raw material for dramatists, including those who wrote the libretti for Handel's operas *Admeto* and *Semele*, Mozart's *Idomeneo* and Gluck's *Iphigénie en Aulide*.

By the end of the century, Romanticism was regaining the upper hand, and there was an enormous surge of enthusiasm for all things Greek. This was partly because Greece was joining Italy as an important destination on the Grand Tour. The more practical among the wealthy youth of Europe who had visited the shores of the Aegean, such as the architects James ('Athenian') Stuart and Nicholas Revett, returned home to recreate in northern landscapes the proportions and styles of the ruined buildings they had seen.

The more imaginative would revisit in their mind's eye the scenes they had left and then re-invent the classical past itself in the great new surge of 'Greek' literature and art.

In Britain at least, the popularity of Greek myth reached its climax in the nineteenth century. It was a great period for new translations of Greek tragedies and of Homer, and these in turn inspired contemporary poets. Keats, Byron and Shelley were all indebted to the classics; indeed, it is hard to think of a nineteenth-century poet who was not. The Hellenism of Queen Victoria's poet laureate, Alfred Lord Tennyson, was such that even his portraits of the quintessentially English court of King Arthur are suffused with echoes of the Homeric epics. Several of his poems were directly inspired by classical mythology, such as his 'Lotos Eaters' – a deeply romantic vision, at once exotic and deeply depressing, of an episode touched upon very briefly in the *Odyssey*; his Odysseus (in *Ulysses*) is a strange mixture of Greek hero and restless Victorian gentleman. The visual arts kept pace, stimulated to new 'Greek' heights by the purchase for the nation of the Elgin marbles in 1816; today, many of the 'Greek' paintings of such artists as Lord Leighton or Lawrence Alma-Tadema seem comically romantic, but in their time they were seriously accepted as part of the transmission of the Hellenic ideal.

The comfortable Victorian vision of Hellenism was shattered by the First World War. Many of the young men who sailed through the Dardanelles to die at Gallipoli saw themselves, or were seen by their friends, as reincarnations of the Greek heroes who fought and died at Troy. But in the end the War broke this illusion; as one survivor, Ronald Knox, wrote later:

The great god Pan is dead, and the world of which he is the symbol; we can never recapture it. And I knew that when I saw the Hellespont. It did not remind me of the ship *Argo*, nor of the agony of Troy ... It was peopled for me instead by those who fought and died there fifteen years ago, men of my own country and of my own speech.

However, Western Europe's interest in Greek mythology did not altogether die in 1918. One of the most intriguing twentieth-century obsessions with Greek mythology is that of Sigmund Freud, the father of psychoanalysis. Greek myths, along with other aspects of the classical past, were intensely important to Freud, who recognised that they embodied universal human themes. He saw in them both anticipation and confirmation of his theories, and his published writings are full of allusions to the myths. He compared, for example, his technique of extracting the supposedly indestructible unconscious wishes of his patients to the way in which Odysseus induced the ghosts he met in the Underworld to speak by letting them drink the sacrificial blood. It was Freud who made Oedipus a household name by calling after him a complex that he claimed to have identified in the majority of little boys, their tendency to fall deeply in love with their mothers and consequently to become intensely jealous of their fathers. Freud certainly believed this had happened to him, and in other respects, too, he identified himself with Oedipus, the solver of riddles. He was a passionate collector of Greek, Roman and Egyptian

Captive Andromache, by Frederic Leighton *(above) The wife of Hector was condemned to slavery by the fall of Troy; here she stands, isolated and tragic, at the fountain. About 1888.*

Electra at the tomb of Agamemnon, by Frederic Leighton *(left) Standing beside her father's tomb, Electra's demeanour is despairing, her grief emphasised by the darkness of her clothing. About 1869.*

Terracotta Sphinx *(below) This is from the ancient art collection of Sigmund Freud, who was fascinated by the Oedipus legend. South-Italian Greek, about 400 BC.*

antiquities, and his friends and patients seem to have lost no opportunity of presenting him with any representation of Oedipus or the Sphinx that they could find. On his fiftieth birthday Freud's colleagues presented him with a medallion bearing his own portrait on one side and Oedipus and the Sphinx on the other, along with a line from Sophocles's *Oedipus Tyrannos*: 'he who solved the famous riddle, and was most powerful of men'.

Throughout the twentieth century Greek myths have continued to inspire poets and writers. In 1922, for example, James Joyce published *Ulysses*, a modern epic which compresses Odysseus's ten-year homeward journey to Ithaca into one day in the life of an Irish Jew in Dublin; here Aiolos, king of the Winds, becomes a newspaper editor controlling the currents of popular opinion, the Sirens are a pair of barmaids, and Circe, who turned men into swine, is the madam of a brothel. Greek myths were also important to T. S. Eliot: the central figure of *The Waste Land*, for example, is the blind Theban prophet Teiresias. Translations and adaptations, too, have flourished. In 1944 a new version of Sophocles's *Antigone* by the French dramatist Jean Anouilh showed that its central theme, of individual conscience versus the law of the state, could be of immediate and compelling relevance to contemporary political situations. But surely the most poetic of all translations is W. B. Yeats's free adaptation of the opening chorus of Sophocles's *Oedipus at Colonos*. The third stanza is an outstandingly vivid and beautiful evocation of the story of Demeter and Persephone, the myth with which this survey began:

Who comes into this country, and has come
Where golden crocus and narcissus bloom,
Where the Great Mother, mourning for her daughter
And beauty-drunken by the water
Glittering among grey-leaved olive trees,
Has plucked a flower and sung her loss;
Who finds abounding Cephisus
Has found the loveliest spectacle there is.

Even at the end of the twentieth century, Greek myths retain their appeal. Although the old stories may appear in strange new guises – Herakles is today's Superman, the modern Odyssey is the voyage of the starship *Enterprise* in 'Startrek' – the fact that they continue to be reworked shows the enduring strength of their imaginative legacy.

Suggestions for further reading

The most direct and also the most enjoyable way to approach Greek myths is to read them as they were told by the Greeks and the Romans themselves. Most Greek and Latin literature is available in translation. The Loeb Classical Library offers parallel texts in the original language and in English. Many of the translations were written some time ago, and their language is at times archaic; they are still, however, very useful to anyone with a little Greek or Latin who wishes to know from time to time what the original version says. For most people, the Penguin Classics offer a cheaper and more up-to-date alternative. They cover most of the important texts and are easy to obtain, carry around and read. They vary in style, and the translations of the *Iliad* and the *Odyssey* are generally reckoned to be more successful than those of the Greek tragedies. Rather more poetic translations of these are offered by D. Grene and R. Lattimore in *The Complete Greek Tragedies* (Chicago, 1959). Apart from the *Iliad*, the *Odyssey* and the tragedies, the most important ancient source for Greek myths is probably Ovid's *Metamorphoses*, the most easily accessible translation of which is again the Loeb edition. Greek myths may also be approached via Greek art; a valuable guide here is T. H. Carpenter's *Art and Myth in Ancient Greece* (London, 1989).

There are several dictionaries of Greek mythology. The *Oxford Classical Dictionary* (3rd edn, Oxford, 1999) provides short entries on mythological characters, alongside ancient authors and characters of history. Less dry, however, and a great deal more informative is P. Grimal's *The Dictionary of Classical Mythology* (English translation, Oxford, 1986), which provides detailed accounts of all major and minor myths, a series of useful family trees and numerous well-chosen illustrations. The *Lexicon Iconographicum Mythologiae Classicae* (*LIMC*), produced by a massive international team of art historians and archaeologists, collects together all known artistic representations of all the characters of Greek and Roman mythology; it also summarises literary sources.

A great many general books, designed to appeal to various age groups, tell the stories of Greek myths; these can be found in any bookshop or library and selection amongst them is a matter of personal preference. In the interpretation of myth, the French currently lead the field: good introductions to current ways of thinking may be found in two recent collections of essays: R. L. Gordon (ed.), *Myth, Religion and Society* (Cambridge, 1981) and J. Bremmer (ed.), *Interpretations of Greek Mythology* (London, 1988); see also R. Buxton, *From Myth to Reason* (Oxford, 2001). For a stimulating introduction to women's role in myth, see M. Lefkowicz, *Women in Greek Myth* (Bristol Classical Press, 1995).

Roman

Myths

JANE F. GARDNER

Acknowledgements

The author wishes to thank in particular Dr Susan Walker of the British Museum Department of Greek and Roman Antiquities, and Dr Dora Thornton of the Department of Medieval and Later Antiquities, for bibliographical and other help in selecting items from the British Museum collections for the illustrations.

Picture credits

Abbreviations

BMCRR = *Coins of the Roman Republic in the British Museum* (1910)
BMCRE = *Coins of the Roman Empire in the British Museum*, I (1923)
PCR = *Principal Coins of the Romans*, I (1978)
p. 82: Serge Ransford; p. 85: BM *BMCRR* (Rome) 3891; p. 86: BM CM 1931-5-4-29, *PCR* 23; p.87: BM GR Bronze 1523; p. 88: *(top)* BM GR 1946.4-23.1; *(bottom)* by courtesy of the Allard Pierson Museum, Amsterdam, 1606; p. 91: BM GR Terracotta D690; p. 93: BM CM *BMCRR* (East) 31; p. 94: Copenhagen, Ny Carlsberg Glyptothek 494a; p. 95: BM PD 00.8.269.H.303; p.97: BM CM *BMCRE* (Tiberius) 16; p. 98: BM PD 00.7.240.H.310; p. 101: Cologne, Römisch-Germanisches Museum, Inv. 70.3; p. 104: BM MLA 66,12-29,21; p. 106: BM GR Silver 73; p. 108: BM CM *BMCRR* (Rome) 926; p. 109: BM GR Vase H1; p. 110: BM CM *BMCRR* (Rome) 2322; p. 111: Paris, Musée du Louvre 188 (photo Réunion des Musées Nationaux, Paris); p. 113: BM CM *BMCRE* (Augustus) 76; p. 118: BM GR 1983.12-29.1; p. 120: Paris, Musée du Louvre 189 (photo Réunion des Musées Nationaux, Paris); p. 123: BM MLA 1878,12-30,408; p. 126: BM MLA 1855,12-1,74; p. 130: BM CM *BMCRE* (Augustus) 30; p. 132: *(top left)* BM CM *BMCRR* (Rome) 3652; *(right)* BM GR 1979.11-8.1; p. 136: BM PD 1868.8-22.38; p. 140: BM GR Sculpture 2310, Townley Collection; p. 143: BM GR Sculpture D69; p. 145: *(top right)* Drawing of BM GR Bronze 633; *(lower left)* BM GR Bronze 604; p. 146: *(top right)* BM GR Bronze 1574; *(below)* BM GR Silver 136; p. 148: BM GR 1899.2-18.46; p. 149: BM GR Painting 24; p. 150: BM PRB OA 248; p. 153: BM CM *BMCRR* (Rome) 3415; p. 154: BM PD 1947.1-10.1. Chapter openers by Sue Bird.

Contents

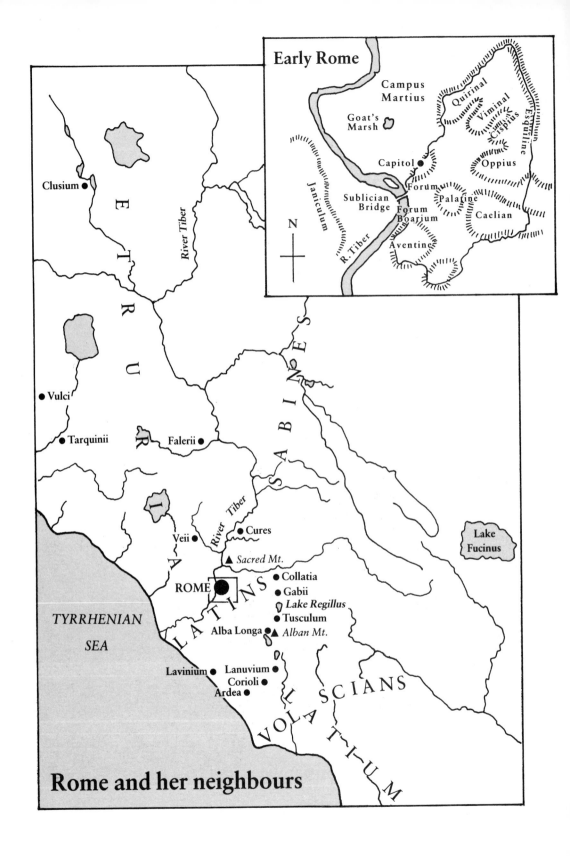

Early Rome

Campus
Martius

Goat's
Marsh

Quirinal

Viminal

Capitol

Cispius

Esquiline

Janiculum

Forum

Oppius

Sublician
Bridge

Palatine

Forum
Boarium

Caelian

N

R. Tiber

Aventine

Clusium

ETRURIA

River Tiber

Vulci

Tarquinii

Falerii

SABINES

Lake
Fucinus

Veii

Cures

River Tiber

▲ *Sacred Mt.*

ROME

Collatia

Gabii

Lake Regillus

TYRRHENIAN

SEA

Tusculum

Alba Longa

▲ *Alban Mt.*

LATINS

Lavinium

Lanuvium

Corioli

Ardea

VOLSCIANS

LATIUM

Rome and her neighbours

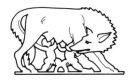

Introduction

The Romans, it has been said, had no myths, only legends. The *Oxford English Dictionary* describes myth as 'fictitious narrative usually involving supernatural persons, actions, or events, and embodying some popular idea concerning natural or historical phenomena'. Most Roman myths do not fit this definition at all well. They are presented in ancient writers not as fiction, but as the early history of the Roman people – even though we can observe their content changing before our very eyes. Many myths do not involve the gods at all, or only to a small extent, and these are not myths *about* the Roman gods themselves.

In the first century BC a speaker in Cicero's philosophical dialogue *On the Nature of the Gods* distinguishes between mythological stories about the gods, which he regards as something Greek, and Roman expectations of religion; Roman religion is made up of (1) ritual, (2) taking auspices, and (3) prophetic warnings issued by interpreters of Sibylline oracles, or of the entrails of sacrificed animals, on the basis of portents and omens. 'I am quite certain that Romulus by instituting auspices, and Numa ritual, laid the foundations of our state, which would never have been able to be so great had not the immortal gods been placated to the utmost extent.'

In other words, *stories* about the gods were unimportant; religion's function was to maintain a stable relationship between the gods and the state, and Rome's past success was its justification. A generation later a Greek writer, Dionysius of Halicarnassus, spoke approvingly of Rome's lack of myths (especially of the morally discreditable kind) about the gods. This he ascribes to the foresight of Romulus, who saw that what was paramount was maintaining the favour of the gods, through suitable ritual practice, and the encouragement of civic virtues.

Two other factors that certainly play a part in determining the character of Roman myth are, firstly, the ancient view, common both to Greeks and to Romans, of what history was for and how it should be written, and, secondly, the fact that the earliest detailed accounts available to us come in writers from the first centuries BC and AD. By that time Rome had already developed into a highly sophisticated, urban society, whose culture, literature and thought were deeply permeated by centuries of influence from Greek literature and culture; the 'myths' are preserved in writings that are the product of highly refined and self-conscious literary techniques. Authors felt free to reshape and even make additions to the traditional stories.

Our main sources

Livy (*c.* 59 BC–AD 17) wrote a history of Rome in 142 books, from the foundation of Rome to 9 BC. Book 1, after briefly outlining the events from Aeneas' departure from Troy to the birth of Romulus and Remus, contains the story of the foundation of Rome and the reigns of its seven kings. Book 2 deals with the establishment of the Roman Republic and its earliest struggles.

The greatest work of **Virgil** (70–19 BC) was the *Aeneid*, an epic poem in twelve books, recounting the adventures of Aeneas after his departure from Troy until his arrival in Italy and the union of Trojans and Italians. There are several prophetic looks ahead to the future greatness of Rome, culminating in the destined appearance of the emperor Augustus (whose family claimed descent from Aeneas' divine mother, Venus).

Ovid (43 BC–AD 17/18) makes occasional use of Roman myth in several of his published poetical works. One, the *Fasti*, was an account of the Roman calendar, month by month, including descriptions and purported explanations of the origins of the sacred rites and festivals of the Roman religious year. Unfortunately only the first six books, January to June, survive. *Metamorphoses* includes some Roman tales, culminating in the deification of Julius Caesar, and ends with an encomium of Augustus.

Dionysius of Halicarnassus came to Rome as a teacher of rhetoric at about the time of Augustus Caesar's achieving sole leadership (30/29 BC) and stayed there for twenty-two years. He wrote *Roman Antiquities*, a romantic and rhetorical history of Rome from earliest times to the beginning of the first Punic War (264 BC). It was a panegyric of early Rome, aimed at reconciling Greeks to being ruled by Romans.

Ancient Latin scholarship also preserved some information, even although in abbreviated and often scrappy form. Marcus Terentius **Varro** (116–27 BC) devoted twenty years after his retirement from public life to research and writing, and he had a prodigious output. A later writer credited him with having edited 490 books by the time he was seventy-seven. Among his lost works was *Divine and Human Antiquities*, in forty-one books. Besides a treatise on agriculture, all of his work that survives is about a quarter of *The Latin Language*, which contains many antiquarian snippets. We also have part of the epitome by Sextus Pompeius **Festus** (second century AD) of a similar work by a learned freedman, Verrius Flaccus, the teacher of Augustus' grandsons.

Plutarch (*c.* AD 46–after 120), a Greek who travelled widely in the Roman world on public business, was also prolific. His best known work is the *Parallel Lives of Greeks and Romans*, of which twenty-two pairs and four separate biographies survive. For early Rome, we have his *Lives* of the kings Romulus and Numa, of Publius Valerius Publicola, one of the first consuls, and of Coriolanus. His *Roman Questions* discusses Roman customs and religious rituals.

None of these works is earlier than the first century BC, that is seven centuries after the traditional date of the foundation of Rome. What sources did these writers have?

A coin issued by the Roman moneyer L. Marcius Philippus in 55 BC: on one side, king Ancus Marcius, legendary builder of Rome's first aqueduct, on the other the Aqua Marcia (144 BC), with the equestrian statue of its builder Q. Marcius Rex.

Mainly they relied on earlier writers. The first known Roman historian (of whom only a few fragments survive) was Quintus Fabius Pictor, who wrote, at the end of the third century BC, a history of Rome from the origins to the middle of the third century. Like Rome's earliest known poets, he wrote in Greek; the first to write a historical account in Latin was the elder Cato, half a century later. Later writers, such as Livy, based their accounts, not on original research (for which there were virtually no materials) but on those of their predecessors, sometimes consciously trying to assess the value of conflicting versions, but more often than not picking the one that made the best story or the most suitable for their particular purposes. The two things that were of main importance for most ancient writers of history were the literary quality of the work, and its didactic value. 'What makes the study of history particularly beneficial and profitable,' wrote Livy, 'is that you have lessons from all manner of experience set out in full view as if on a memorial, and from there you may choose both for yourself and for your country examples of what to imitate and what things (bad begun and worse ended) to avoid.' This meant, amongst other things, that writers would interpret the past in terms of the issues of their own time.

The period from the supposed origins of Rome down to the end of the monarchy and establishment of the Republic (traditionally 509 BC) cannot be called 'historical' in our sense of the word; neither can much of what appears in literary accounts of the first generation or two of the Republic. Modern scholars argue about whether any historical truth can be said to exist at all in the stories about the period of the kings (and if there is, how to identify it), and the traditional accounts of the early days of the Republic are also agreed to be full of invention and contamination from later sources. For anyone interested in myth-making, however, these traditions are a treasure-house, for in them, and in the way they change and develop right down through the historical period, we see the Romans defining themselves through the stories they tell about their past – that is, through their 'myths'. They use a variety of materials, such as ideas and motifs copied from Greek mythology and history, motifs of a traditional 'folk-tale' type, and stories from the family traditions of some of the great Roman families. Republican moneyers issued coin types referring to their supposed ancestors in the legendary past. Historians disseminated the family traditions;

the prominence of the Fabii, the Valerii and the Claudii in the history of the early Republic probably owes something to Fabius Pictor, and to Valerius Antias and Claudius Quadrigarius, who wrote their own histories of Rome round about 80 BC.

These family legends appealed particularly to historical writers and also to orators like Cicero (even though they might sometimes express scepticism about them) because of their value as what the Romans called *exempla*, illustrations of a particular moral truth ('what to imitate and what things to avoid'). The early books of Livy, like the historical 'flash-forwards' in Virgil, have many of these patriotic legends exemplifying the 'Roman' virtues.

The Romans, like the Greeks, were also particularly interested in aetiology, i.e. accounting for beginnings, the beginning of rituals, of place-names, of institutions, of cities, of the whole Roman people and its history. This does not mean that they wanted actually to find out how they began, simply to tell a satisfactory story about them.

So, for instance, the beginnings of the main political religious and civic institutions of historical Rome are allocated among the seven kings (themselves mainly imaginary): Romulus – the senate, the 'curiate' assembly and the 'centuries' of cavalry; Numa – the calendar and the major priesthoods; Hostilius – treason trials, and religious procedures for making peace; Ancus Marcius – procedures for declaring war, Rome's first prison, bridge and aqueduct; Tarquinius Priscus ('the First') – the first stone wall round the city, the annual Roman games; Servius Tullius – the census, the tribal system and the hierarchical 'centuriate' assembly. Even the main sewer was attributed to a king, Tarquinius Superbus ('the Proud'), though the parts of it that survive go back no earlier than the fourth century BC.

Roman gods and Greek myths

The Romans, it seems, had a native god, or gods, for almost every important object or activity. For instance, Consus ('storage' – though Varro thought the name came from 'counsel'), Pales (goddess of flocks and herds) and Robigo /–us (blight) were agricultural; Janus looked after doorways, Faunus was the god of wild things, Silvanus the god of woodlands and untilled land; and there were

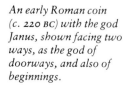

An early Roman coin (c. 220 BC) with the god Janus, shown facing two ways, as the god of doorways, and also of beginnings.

*The woodland god Silvanus,
wearing an animal skin and
bearing a tree in one hand; the
other originally held something,
perhaps a pruning-hook.*

In the early Empire freedman families liked to be portrayed on their tombs in the guise of gods. From the neck down, this young woman is Venus; her hairstyle closely resembles that worn by Hadrian's mother-in-law.

Terracotta lamp showing the Capitoline triad – Jupiter, between Juno and Minerva.

many others who appear merely to have been personified functions – but to us, and to Romans of the classical period, they are only names. They have *numen* (divine power) but no individual personalities. Though Roman religious observance was elaborate and detailed, and the calendar, all through the year, was full of sacrifices and rituals, administered by boards of priests, few have stories attached to them, and few of these, even when they purport to explain the particular cult or functional title of a god, involve the gods themselves. If there ever was a Roman mythology about their gods, it has vanished irretrievably. Roman gods lack personal adventures, and family relationships: for the great gods, these were simply taken over from the Greeks, Olympian and Roman deities being matched up in a very rough and ready way.

The principal Greek gods were **Kronos**, father of Zeus, who overthrew him; **Zeus**, king and weather god; his brother **Poseidon**, god of waters and earthquakes; **Hera**, queen goddess, wife (and sister) of Zeus, deity of marriage and women; and Zeus' other sisters **Demeter** (grain and crops) and **Hestia** (the household hearth). To these must be added the children of Hera, **Ares** (war), and **Hephaistos** (smith-craftsman), who was married to **Aphrodite**. She was the goddess of love, and variously said to be 'foam-born' from Kronos' father Uranos, or Zeus' daughter by a Titaness. **Athena**, goddess of wisdom, was daughter of Zeus and Metis (a personification of counsel). Other children of Zeus, by various lovers, were the twins **Apollo** (music – also medicine, archery, flocks and herds) and **Artemis**, associated with wild animals, hunting and virginity; and also **Hermes**, messenger of the gods, and patron of merchants and thieves, and a late-comer to Olympus, **Dionysos** (also called Bacchus), god of wine.

Some of these, though not all, the Romans simply identified with gods of their own, not always very appropriately. **Jupiter** (also known as 'Jove'), **Neptune**, **Mars**, **Venus** and **Vesta** are more or less good fits for Zeus, Poseidon, Ares, Aphrodite and Hestia. **Vulcan**, the Roman fire-god, is equated with Hephaistos. Artemis was identified with **Diana**, a goddess of woodlands, but also probably of the moon, women and child birth. **Juno**, though appearing historically in functions very like those of Hera, and especially as a goddess of women, may originally have been a deity associated with the vigour of young warriors. Kronos is ill-matched with the Roman **Saturnus**, originally perhaps a god of sown crops, who became associated, like Kronos, with a primitive Golden Age, before agriculture was necessary.

Minerva is also rather surprising as a match for Athena. **Minerva** was an Italian goddess of handicrafts. For the Romans, she was one of their chief triad of gods, Jupiter, Juno and Minerva, with a temple on the Capitol. The temple and its triad came to symbolise being Roman, and were reduplicated all over the Roman empire. The Romans themselves believed that it had been instituted, *c.* 509 BC, by Rome's last king, Tarquin the Proud. His father had come from Etruria, which may tell us something about Minerva's origins, while her elevation to a senior position, like Athena, perhaps reflects the influence of Greek culture on the Etruscans already at that period.

Mercury, the analogue of Hermes, was probably not originally Roman at all, but merely a renaming of a Greek god taken over by the Romans, along with a group of others, in the first decade of the fifth century BC. About the same time, Demeter and Dionysus were introduced to Rome as **Ceres** and **Liber**. This was done on the advice of the so-called *Sibylline Books*, a collection of oracles kept in the temple of Jupiter Capitolinus and consulted in times of crisis (particularly natural disaster, such as plague or famine) to discover how to make peace with the gods; the response was usually the introduction of a new god, or a new religious rite. Dionysius tells (following, he says, Varro) how the Romans came to possess them:

A certain woman who was not a native of the country came to the tyrant [Tarquin the Proud] wanting to sell him nine books full of Sibylline oracles. When Tarquin refused to buy them at the price asked, she went away and burned three of them; then soon after she came back and asked the same price for the remaining six. She was thought mad, and was laughed at for asking the same price for the smaller number of books as she had failed to get even for the larger number, and she went away again and burned half the remaining books. Then she came back and asked the same price for the three that were left. Surprised at her determination, Tarquin sent for the augurs and asked them what to do. Certain signs told them that he had rejected a blessing sent by the gods. They declared that it was a great misfortune that he had not bought all the books, and told him to give the old woman as much money as she wanted, and take the remaining oracles.

He did, and the woman disappeared. Tarquin appointed keepers of the oracles, a post, says Dionysius, which existed to his day. When the oracles were destroyed by fire in 83 BC, a fresh collection was made by transcribing oracles from various parts of the known world; some of these were found to be fakes.

Rome was generally receptive to new gods and goddesses. Among the first to be admitted to Rome were **Apollo** (for whom no Roman equivalent was found), as healing god, and the deified hero **Heracles** (whom the Romans called Hercules). One of the most famous introductions was the Great Mother Goddess, **Cybele**, or Mater Magna, brought, in the form of a black stone, to Rome in 204 BC during the war against Hannibal; her temple was inaugurated in 191 BC, and an annual festival of theatrical performances and games, the Megalesia, established. The cult came from the 'Greek' end of the Mediterranean, from Phrygia in Asia Minor. The festival, at least, was highly popular among the Romans, though no Romans were allowed to participate in her cult, which did not conform to their ideas of decorum. It involved noisy street processions of ecstatic priests who leapt and danced, accompanied by horns, drums and cymbals, and begged from the passers-by. Abandoned dancing, specially in public, was disapproved of anyway by the Romans, and matters were made worse in their eyes by the fact that the priests were eunuchs.

What the Romans really thought about their Hellenised gods is all the more difficult for us to perceive because in surviving writings the stories have become little more than literary motifs or devices. Ovid in *The Art of Love* simply took over from Homer the story of how Vulcan (Hephaistos) caught his wife Venus and Mars (Aphrodite and Ares) in bed together, trapped them with an invisible net and fetched the other gods to laugh at them. Ovid uses it to illustrate some tongue-in-cheek advice to suspicious lovers: if you suspect she's cheating, don't try to catch her out – you'll lose in the long run. He hastily adds, '*Of course*, this isn't about real married ladies.' This was cautious: Augustus had introduced a law with stern penalties for adultery. He exiled Ovid in AD 8, for reasons which are unknown, but the erotic amorality of much of his poetry cannot have helped.

However, Virgil found it convenient in the *Aeneid* to ignore Venus' infidelity. She persuades Vulcan to make weapons for Aeneas (her son by a mortal, Anchises) by the simple use of marital seduction:

He hesitated, but she put her snowy arms about him and clasped him in a warm and tender embrace. And he suddenly took flame – as usual – and the familiar heat entered his marrow and raced through his trembling bones, just as when thunder cracks apart the storm-clouds and the fiery flash darts out, sparkling. The goddess was aware of it, pleased with her cunning and conscious of her beauty. The old god answered, bound in the toils of undying love.

He consents, conjugal relations (it is hinted) follow, and he falls asleep.

The seduction scene is almost a parody of one in the *Iliad*, in which Hera diverts Zeus' attention from what is happening on the Trojan battlefield. Virgil uses it for the purpose of introducing a description of the arms, particularly of the shield. This also is an idea lifted from Homer's *Iliad*, in which Hephaistos makes a shield for Achilles. Virgil wants to use the decoration on the shield for a sort of picture-show of famous events in Roman history, culminating, in the middle, with a splendid set-piece in which the future Emperor Augustus, Virgil's patron, and (as his publicity kept reminding Romans) descendant of Venus and Aeneas, is shown defeating Antony and Cleopatra at the battle of Actium (31 BC), with Apollo helping him – another myth in the making – and holding a triumph in Rome over conquered peoples from all ends of the world.

This terracotta architectural ornament represents Augustus' triumph. Victory carries a trophy of weapons, and stands on a globe flanked by Capricorns, Augustus' lucky sign.

Aeneas and the destiny of Rome

Aeneas is best known to the later world through the epic poem of Virgil, in which the hero's travels and travails are explicitly presented as a nationalist myth about the origins and divine destiny of Rome. In Homer's *Iliad*, Aeneas the Trojan already had a great future ahead of him; the god Poseidon rescued him from the battlefield, prophesying that he and his descendants would be kings. After the fall of Troy, Greek traditions took him, with his father Anchises and son Ascanius and some Trojan companions, to the West, like many other Trojan War veterans from both sides – so providing foundation legends for many places in Sicily and South Italy, where Greeks had been settling from the eighth century BC onwards.

Early history of the Aeneas legend

Already in the late sixth century BC, the story of Aeneas' flight from Troy was known in Etruria; it is depicted on a number of Athenian black-figure vases found there. The motif also appears on votive statuettes found at the Etruscan town Veii and on Etruscan gems. He is first associated with Rome by Hellanicus, a Greek historian in the fifth century BC, who wrote that Aeneas founded Rome and called it Rhome (Greek for 'strength') after one of the Trojan women accompanying him. Some Greek writers, however, ascribe the foundation not to Aeneas but to other Trojans and Greeks; in one version, Rome was founded by a son of Odysseus and Circe. Later Aeneas reappears, as father or grandfather of the founder of Rome.

It is not really surprising to find Romans willing to accept that their founders were foreigners. These stories enabled the Romans to claim their own place in the tradition, regarded as in a sense 'historical', of the Greek heroic past. As descendants of Aeneas the Trojan, in particular, they could still remain separate from the Greeks; better still, Aeneas in Italy appears as a friend and collaborator of Greeks, not their enemy.

There was an alternative tradition, that Rome was founded, not by Aeneas or any Trojan or Greek founder, but by Romulus and Remus. Some early Roman historians said that they were Aeneas' sons, or grandsons. However, it came to be realised that Aeneas, or even his grandchildren, really would not do as founders of Rome. When a Greek scholar, Eratosthenes of Cyrene (275–194 BC), constructing his universal chronology, *Chronographia*, fixed a date of 1184 BC for the Fall of Troy, the length of the gap between Aeneas and

Aeneas carrying his father Anchises and the Palladium (an image of the goddess Athena); coin issued by Julius Caesar, 49 and 47 BC.

Romulus became obvious. Various dates, ranging from 814 to 728 BC, were proposed for the foundation of Rome; the one which eventually became accepted was 753 BC. In the early second century BC, the elder Cato filled the gap ingeniously with what became in its main outlines the standard version.

Aeneas, arriving in Latium, at a spot called 'Troia', founded a city called Lavinium on land given him by the local king, Latinus, and ruled there with his wife Lavinia, the daughter of Latinus, over their united people, now called Latins. After Aeneas' death in a war with a local prince, Turnus, and the Rutulians (who, in Virgil, fight Aeneas *before* his marriage), his son Ascanius founded Alba Longa, which he later handed over to his brother (or, in some versions, son) Silvius, who was the first of a line of kings who conveniently filled the gap until the birth of Romulus and Remus, and, some years later, the foundation of Rome.

Following the prophetic trail

Every good foundation legend has to have portents and prophecies. In Virgil's story, following correct procedure for a Greek city-founder, Aeneas sailed first to Delos to receive a prophecy from the god Apollo, who told him, in typically obscure fashion: 'O descendants of Dardanus [mythical founder of Troy], the land which bore your first ancestors shall welcome you in its fertile bosom on your return. Seek out your ancient mother.'

Ascanius remembered that Teucer, an ancestor of the kings of Troy, had come from Crete, and there Aeneas and his Trojans sailed. In Crete he had a vision of the Trojan Gods, carrying a message from Apollo, who found it necessary to make his meaning plainer. The 'ancient mother' was Italy, for Dardanus had originally come from there. Sailing through the Ionian sea, the Trojans landed on the islands called Strophades. They slaughtered some cattle and prepared a meal, but were immediately attacked by the Harpies, monstrous bird-women, who fouled the food. The Harpies were beaten off, but their leader uttered a prophecy: 'You will go to Italy and be permitted to enter harbour; but you will not be granted a city, and gird it with walls, until, for the wrong you have done us, dire hunger forces you to gnaw and devour your tables.'

In Epirus they found a fellow Trojan, Priam's son Helenus, now ruling as king over a city created in Troy's image. He gave Aeneas detailed instructions for the voyage, and prophesied:

'I shall give you a sign; keep it stored in your mind. When, anxious and troubled, you shall find by the waters of a secluded river lying on the bank under holm-oak trees a huge sow, which has just farrowed, with her thirty young, a white sow, with her white offspring about her udders, that will be the spot. There you will find rest from your labours. And do not worry about the eating of the tables; the fates will find a way, and Apollo will be at hand if invoked.'

The sow and her litter represented the Latins. Originally, the thirty piglets appear to have been identified as the thirty peoples which traditionally made up the original Latin League, finally conquered by the Romans in 338 BC; the interpretation of the thirty piglets as thirty years appears to have been the contribution of Fabius Pictor, possibly motivated by the fact that the loyalty of some of the Latin communities to Rome faltered during the war against Hannibal. Virgil gives the developed Roman version of the myth of the sow and her piglets, in which the spot where the white (*alba* in Latin) sow farrows is Alba Longa. There had also been a rival claimant to the position of mother-city of the Latins. The town of Lavinium claimed to have been founded by Aeneas himself, who had brought there the sacred objects, the Penates (domestic gods) of the Roman People, to which Rome's senior magistrates paid a ceremonial visit once a year. Around 300 BC, according to the Greek historian Timaeus, there was a bronze image of the sow and her litter in the market-place of Lavinium; how long it had been there is unknown, but there were still traces of it left in Varro's day. For the Romans, however, the sow showed Aeneas the way to *their* mother-city, Alba Longa – and also helped justify their claim to traditional hegemony over the rest of Latium.

Both prophecies, about the sow and the eating of the tables, were duly fulfilled. After a visit to the Sibyl at Cumae in south Italy, the Trojans sailed

The 'Laurentine Sow' and her litter, a marble group (2nd century AD) from Lavinium, commemorating its legendary foundation by Aeneas.

The moment of Aeneas' arrival at the future site of Rome (Virgil, Aeneid, *Book 8), as imagined in 1675 by Claude Lorrain, who illustrated many incidents from the* Aeneid.

north and into the mouth of the Tiber, and landed to picnic on the bank. They were so hungry that, having finished all the food that was available, they began to eat the thin cakes of bread that (inspired by Jupiter) they were using as platters. 'What, are we even eating our tables?' said Aeneas' son.

Any Roman would recognize that as an omen. Aeneas realised that the prophecy was fulfilled. He and his men made their way to the local king Latinus, who, having just received a prophecy from his father, the god Faunus, that his daughter was to marry a stranger, welcomed Aeneas as his destined son-in-law. However, this brought about the wars and troubles that had also been prophesied for Aeneas, because the Rutulian prince Turnus had already claimed Lavinia, and had the support of Latinus' queen. Juno also interfered, sending a Fury to stir the queen to arouse Turnus and also the Latins against Aeneas. War broke out.

Aeneas had a dream vision of father Tiber, who told him: 'This is your assured home, this is where your gods belong,' and repeated the omen of the sow and her piglets, adding that within thirty years Ascanius would found a city, Alba. Meanwhile, to get out of his present troubles, he must go and ask help from King Evander, a Greek from Arcadia now settled in Italy.

Aeneas manned two ships and, as they were about to leave, they saw the omen of the white sow. Aeneas sacrificed her and her litter to Juno, then the

Trojans rowed upstream to the Tiber until they came upon Evander, his son Pallas, and the leading Arcadians sacrificing to Hercules. He received Aeneas kindly, remembering, Virgil tells us, how Anchises had visited Arcadia once with Priam. And so – for Evander's home was on what the Romans knew as the Palatine hill – Aeneas had arrived at the site of Rome.

Rome before Aeneas

Evander was the son of a Greek nymph Themis, called by the Romans Carmenta, because, it was said, 'Thespiodis' is Greek for 'prophetic singer', and *carmina* is Latin for 'songs'. He and his companions emigrated from Greece about sixty years before the Trojan War. The town he founded was called Pallantium, after his mother-city in Arcadia, but the Romans corrupted it to Palatium. He was said to have founded the festival of the Lupercalia, as well as that of Hercules.

Although he lived on the site of the future Rome, Evander was not the founder of Rome, only of a settlement on Rome's citadel, the Palatine (which is ignored in the legend of Romulus' foundation). On the way to his city he showed Aeneas various points of interest, such as the Carmental gate and shrine, the rock of Tarpeia, the Capitol (still rough woodland then, but felt to be the home of a god), the Lupercal, the Janiculum and Saturnia (citadels founded respectively by Janus and Saturn) and the Argiletum – all places whose names would have resonance for a Roman.

The Argiletum, in historical Rome, was the booksellers' quarter (so perhaps Virgil is making a sly joke). The name means simply 'clay-field', but there had to be a legend, so it was 'where Argos died'. Tarpeia and her rock we shall meet again: she came to a bad end. The Lupercal, 'Wolf's Cave', Evander explains is called after the Arcadian god Lycaean Pan (there was a Mount Lykaios in Arcadia). Mention of Lycaean Pan gives the game away. King Evander himself is no more than a literary invention by writers trying to find links between Rome and Greek traditions. Evander was the name of a minor deity worshipped in association with Pan in Arcadia. According to Livy and Tacitus, he introduced writing to Italy (after all, someone had to, and he was an immigrant among the aboriginal Italians).

Carmenta is an equally shadowy figure. Although she had a priest of her own, a shrine near one of the gates of Rome (called after her), and a festival on two days in January, like most Roman deities she had no story. Because of her name, writers called her a prophet, and say that she foretold the future greatness of Rome, fitting her in either as Evander's mother or his wife. Ovid, however, also cheerfully invents a different story out of a bogus etymology, to suit her cult, which had to do with childbirth. Varro said there were *two* Carmentes, Postverta (Backward) and Prorsa (Forward), in reference to the position in which the baby presented itself. Here is Ovid's story:

Once upon a time married women used to ride in *carpenta*, carriages, which I think also got their names from Evander's mother. Later the honour was taken from them, and every woman determined, since their men were ungrateful, not to carry on the line for them by having more offspring. Recklessly, to avoid giving birth, they secretly thrust out the swelling burden from the womb. They say that the city fathers reproved their wives for having dared such cruel acts. All the same, they restored the right that had been taken away. They ordered that now two sets of rites in honour of the Tegean mother [Tegea is in Arcadia] be held for both boys and girls alike. It is not allowed to bring leather into the shrine, lest the sacred hearths be defiled by dead things. If you have any love of ancient rites, be present at the prayers; you will learn names you never knew before. Porrima is placated and Postverta – either your sisters, or the companions of your flight, Maenalian goddess [another Arcadian reference]. One is thought to have sung of what happened in the past [porro], the other of what will come hereafter [postmodo].

There is actually a little bit of 'history' in all this, though it is nothing to do with Carmenta. In 394 BC, it is said, the city matrons contributed their gold ornaments towards a thank-offering to Apollo at Delphi after the capture of Veii, and were given the privilege of using *carpenta* at all times, as a reward. During

A carpentum drawn by mules; the coin commemorates the grant of this honour to Julia Augusta (the name given to Augustus' wife Livia after his death) in AD 22.

the Hannibalic War an emergency sumptuary law (215 BC) forbade the use of such carriages except on religious occasions; this law was repealed twenty years later, though the women did nothing more drastic than demonstrate in the streets in support of the proposed repeal. Much later, Julius Caesar tried to ease Rome's traffic problems by banning the use of *carpenta* to everyone except the Vestal Virgins and the most important priests.

Aeneas and Carthage

In the first six books of the *Aeneid*, before finally reaching Italy, Aeneas travels around in the Mediterranean world – allowing Virgil both to give him weird and wonderful adventures like those in Homer's *Odyssey* and to incorporate various references to Greek myth – and is repeatedly moved on by oracles, prophecies and dream visions. Though it is made clear by Virgil at the outset

Venus, disguised as a huntress, meets Aeneas *near Carthage (*Aeneid Book 1*), drawn by Claude Lorrain (1678).*

that Aeneas *will* reach Italy, and start the chain of events leading to the foundation of Alba Longa and later of Rome itself, the tension is maintained by having him harassed and hampered by the goddess Juno, and not only during his sea travels. As we saw, even after he reaches Italy, and is betrothed to the daughter of King Latinus, local peoples are roused to warfare against him.

Juno's implacable hatred against the Trojans is given two motivations. One is resentment that Aeneas' mother, Venus, not she, was awarded the prize in a beauty contest of the goddesses by the Trojan prince Paris. Virgil adds another, drawn from Roman history: Juno's partiality to Carthage, with whom Rome fought three major wars (the 'Punic Wars') between 264 and 146 BC. Carthage, of course, was founded by the Phoenicians not at the supposed time of the Trojan War, but over four centuries later, like Rome itself. Virgil, however, has the first building of the city actually taking place at the time when Aeneas was shipwrecked on the Tunisian coast. His mother Venus, disguised as a young huntress, met him and told him about the new city and its queen.

Her name was Dido, and her husband Sychaeus had been killed by her brother Pygmalion, prince of Tyre. In a dream, her husband's spectre told her what had happened, urging her to escape, and also told her where to find a buried treasure to take with her. She assembled a group of people opposed to the tyrant, loaded the treasure on to some ships that were in harbour, and sailed to

Africa, where they were engaged, at the time of Aeneas' arrival, in founding their new city, Carthage.

To ensure her son's safety, Venus made Dido fall in love with him. Juno acquiesced, hoping that Aeneas would stay in Carthage and so not fulfil the destiny that would lead to the foundation of Rome. Destiny, however, must not be thwarted. Jupiter sent his messenger Mercury to remind Aeneas of his obligations to posterity and warn him that he must leave. There was a terrible scene between Aeneas and Dido, in which she heaped reproaches upon him. Nevertheless he left, and Dido, before killing herself, uttered a prophetic curse, both on Aeneas himself and on his descendants:

'Thenceforth, Phoenicians, harry with acts of hate his stock, and all the race that will be; render this service to my ashes. Let there be no love nor treaties between our peoples. May some avenger arise from our bones to pursue the Trojan settlers with fire and sword, now or later, whenever the strength presents itself. Let shores be opposed to shores, I pray, waves to waves, weapons to weapons. May they battle, they and their sons' sons.'

Did Virgil also intend, it has sometimes been asked, to remind his contemporaries of another foreign queen who had recently been at war with Rome, Cleopatra of Egypt, the mistress of Mark Antony? She is depicted only briefly and unsympathetically in the *Aeneid*, on the shield made by Vulcan, at the moment of flight from the battle of Actium, surrounded by the outlandish gods of her country. Actium was an easy victory.

Whatever Virgil may have intended, what most people know or remember from the *Aeneid* is not the message of the divinely-directed destiny of Rome, culminating in Augustus, but the tragic love of Dido. In Ovid's poetry Dido recurs frequently, typifying the deserted lover; in his *Heroides*, imaginary letters from famous heroines, number 7 is from Dido to Aeneas. Chaucer includes her in his *Legend of Good Women*, calling her 'Dido the Martyr', and taking, he says, Virgil and Ovid as his sources. He ends by quoting Ovid's poem:

'Right so,' quod she, 'as that the whyte swan
Against his death beginneth for to singe,
Right so to yow make I my compleyninge,
Nat that I trowe to getten yow again,
For weel I woot that it is all in vain,
Since that the goddess been contraire to me.
But since my name is lost through yow,' quod she,
'I may well lose a word on yow, or letter,
Albeit that I shall never be the better;
For thilke wind that blew your ship away,
The same wind hath blowe away your fey [faith].'

If anyone wants the rest of the letter, he adds: 'Rede Ovide, and in him he shall hit finde.'

Christopher Marlowe wrote a somewhat stilted play about her, Henry Purcell an opera, or rather operatic and balletic entertainment. Three of the five acts of the grand opera by Hector Berlioz, *Les Troyens*, which he called 'Virgil Shakespeareanised', are about Dido and Aeneas.

How much of it was Virgil's invention we cannot tell. Timaeus says that Dido, still grieving for her dead husband, killed herself to avoid being forced to marry a Libyan king. Naevius, who wrote in the third century BC a Latin epic on the first Punic War, included Aeneas, but it is impossible to tell from the fragments that remain whether he had him visit Carthage. Varro, in his lost *Antiquities*, had Dido's sister Anna, not Dido herself, commit suicide for love of Aeneas. Nonetheless, it was Virgil's powerful telling of Dido's tragic love story that conquered the world's heart.

The *Aeneid* and Augustus: the legend brought up to date

However, the patriotic myth is uppermost. At the start of the epic, with echoes of Homer's *Odyssey*, Virgil presents Aeneas as a man with a mission:

Arma virumque cano – arms and the man I sing. Made an exile by fate, he was first to come from Troy to Italy, to the coast by Lavinium. He suffered many hardships both by land and by sea, through the might of the gods above, because of the grudge borne by cruel Juno, and he underwent much suffering also in war, until he should found a city, and bring his gods into Latium. Thence arose the Latin race, the fathers of Alba and the lofty walls of Rome.

Three times in the *Aeneid* Virgil introduces a reminder of the future destined for Rome. In Book 1 Jupiter utters a prophecy to allay Venus' fears. Aeneas shall die three years after fighting a successful war in Latium and settling his warriors.

'But the boy Ascanius, to whom now the additional name Iulus is given – he was Ilus, while the royal power of Ilium [i.e. Troy] survived – shall complete thirty full years of circling months in power, and will transfer the seat of power from Lavinium and fortify Alba Longa. Then there shall be three hundred years of rule by the kin of Hector [a Trojan prince] until Ilia, a royal priestess, pregnant by Mars, shall bear twins. Then Romulus, happy to be covered by the tawny coat of the wolf, his nurse, shall take over the people, build walls of Mars, and call his people Roman, from his own name. To them I set no bounds in time or space. I have given them empire without limit ... An age shall come when the house of Assaracus [Aeneas' mythical great-grandfather] shall crush to subjection even Phthia and illustrious Mycenae, and conquer Argos, and hold mastery there [i.e. the Trojans' descendants shall conquer the Greeks]. There shall be born a Trojan Caesar, of noble origin, who shall bound his rule with Oceanus, his fame with the stars, Julius, a name handed down from great Iulus. Some day you will receive him in heaven, laden with the spoils of the East; he also will be invoked in prayers. Then shall the harsh ages lay aside wars and grow gentle. White-haired Faithfulness and Vesta, Remus and his brother Quirinus shall make the laws. The dread gates of war, with their tight iron bolts, shall be shut; evil Frenzy seated within on a pile of cruel weapons, bound with a hundred chains of bronze knotted behind him, shall rave with bloody mouth.'

Another reminder, already mentioned, is the description of the shield in Book 8. Before that, the essence of Jupiter's prophecy is repeated in Book 6. After leaving Dido, Aeneas went first to Sicily, and then at last landed in Italy, near Cumae, where there was an entrance to the underworld. Guided by the Sibyl of Cumae, he went down to visit his dead father, who showed him a pageant of Rome's future greatness. At the beginning are the kings of Alba Longa, founded by a son of Aeneas; towards the end, famous heroes of Rome's Republican past. In between are Rome's founder, Romulus, and its 'second founder' Augustus.

A cameo with the head of the deified Augustus.

Thanks to Romulus' initial foundation, Rome shall grow great and populous. Next to Romulus is Augustus Caesar.

'Here, here is the man whom you have often heard foretold, Augustus Caesar, son of the Deified, who shall reestablish the golden age in Latium, where once Saturn ruled; he shall extend the bounds of the empire even past the Garamantes and the Indians, in land that lies beyond the yearly path of the sun and the constellations, where sky-bearing Atlas turns on his shoulder the sphere studded with blazing stars; even now the Caspian realms and Maeotic land shudder at the prophecies of the gods foretelling his coming, and the sevenfold mouth of the Nile is distraught and panic-stricken. Even Hercules, though he transfixed the brazen hind, pacified the Erymanthian woods and made Lerna tremble at his bow, did not visit so much of the world, nor victorious Bacchus, driving with reins of vines his yoked panthers from the high crest of Nysa.'

Augustus is compared with two gods, both of them late-comers among the Olympians and both, as it happened, the offspring of Zeus by mortal women (Romulus also had a divine father). In addition Heracles, in Greek myth, was deified as a benefactor to mankind, for having rid the world of so many monsters. Similar comparisons were made by other contemporary poets, such as Horace. The implication is that Augustus – if not actually a god already – deserves to be one.

Poetic flattery, perhaps, but overlapping with official propaganda. Augustus is called 'son of the Deified'. Julius Caesar's family traditionally claimed descent from Venus and Iulus, son of Aeneas. Augustus, who was actually only Julius' great-nephew (on his mother's side), inherited Caesar's property after his assassination. He took his name – from being C. Octavius, he became C. Julius Caesar ('Augustus' was an honorific name given him later) – and called himself his son. After the appearance of a comet during commemorative games, Julius Caesar was declared deified, and his 'son' henceforth called himself 'son of the Deified'. As we shall see later, Romulus also, according to one story, was taken up into heaven. After the deification, images of Julius Caesar had a crown with rays like the sun. When Augustus himself died in AD 14, a senior senator took an oath that after the cremation he had seen the form of the emperor ascending into heaven. He was officially declared a god, and his images acquired the radiate crown.

Founding fathers: Romulus and the kings of Rome

Just as Virgil's is the most famous of the stories of Aeneas and his arrival in Italy, so the best known account of the foundation of Rome is the one told by Livy. By his time this had long been accepted, in its essentials, as the 'canonical' story, though Greek and Roman writers in the past had produced many others. Of these nothing survives except what was said about the names and lineage of the founders. The most ingenious is that the Palatine was originally called Valentia because of the physical strength (*valere* is Latin for 'to be hale and hearty') of its aboriginal inhabitants; then when Evander and Aeneas arrived, the name was simply translated into Greek as 'Rhome'.

In earlier versions the founder is Aeneas himself, and if not him, then Rhomus or Rhome (the feminine form), occasionally Romulus (without Remus), and Rhomus/Rhome/Romulus is said to be the son of Zeus, or the companion, wife, daughter or granddaughter of Aeneas, or son of Odysseus or of Latinus, or of 'Italus'. Romulus and Remus (or Romus) start off as sons or grandsons of Aeneas, and are first mentioned in literary sources in the fourth century BC; it is very likely that oral traditions existed much earlier.

Romulus, Remus and the foundation of Rome

Aeneas' son founded Alba Longa, and the hereditary dynasty of its kings, all bearing the additional name 'Silvius', after his son Silvius. The eleventh in the line was Proca. He had two sons, Numitor and Amulius. Amulius usurped the throne from his elder brother, murdering his sons. He then forced Numitor's daughter, Rhea Silvia, to become a Vestal Virgin, so that Numitor might have no male descendant. Rhea Silvia was raped, and bore twin boys. She said Mars was their father, either because she really thought so, or because it seemed more respectable if a god were responsible for her lapse. Cruel Amulius had her imprisoned in chains, and ordered the boys to be thrown into the river.

The job was sloppily done, the boys being left in slow-moving floodwater in a basket which went aground, under the Ruminal fig-tree (two different trees in ancient Rome were said to be *the* tree). A she-wolf found them and suckled them. Then a shepherd Faustulus took them home for his wife Larentia to nurse. Some say that she was actually a common prostitute (*lupa*, in Latin slang; it also means 'wolf'), and that that was how the wolf got into the story.

Plutarch knew a different story. The house of Tarchetius, king of the Albans, a most lawless and cruel man, was visited by a supernatural apparition. A phallus rose out of the hearth and remained for many days. He consulted an oracle of Tethys in Etruria, which gave the reply that a virgin must have intercourse with the apparition, for from her would be born a son who would be most renowned for his valour and surpassing in good fortune and in strength. Tarchetius told the prophecy to one of his daughters and ordered her to have intercourse with the apparition; but she thought it beneath her dignity, and sent a maidservant instead. Tarchetius was furious and arrested both the women, intending to put them to death, but the goddess of the hearth appeared to him in his sleep and forbade the murder. He kept them in prison and set them to weave a piece of cloth, telling them that when they finished they were to be given in marriage. So they spent the days weaving, but at night, on Tarchetius' orders, other women undid their work. When the maidservant, who was pregnant by the phallus, bore twins, Tarchetius gave them to a certain Teratius with orders to kill them, but he took them to the riverside and left them there. A she-wolf visited them and suckled them, and all sorts of birds came and put food into their mouths. At last a cowherd found them and took them to his home, and when they grew up, they overthrew the wicked king.

When they grew up (in Livy's version), Numitor's grandsons formed a gang and took to robbing robbers, and sharing their spoils among the shepherds. The robbers took exception to this, captured Remus in an ambush during the festival of the Lupercalia, and told Amulius that he and Romulus were to blame for the cattle raiding that had occurred on Numitor's land. Remus was handed over to Numitor to be punished.

Matters were desperate. Faustulus revealed the circumstances of his finding the babies; Numitor began to put two and two together, and the young men were acknowledged. With the other herdsmen they raided the palace and killed Amulius, while Numitor seized the citadel, and was reinstated as king.

Alba was becoming overcrowded, so the brothers decided to found a new city, near the spot where they had been left to drown. With the same sibling rivalry that had caused trouble in their grandfather's generation, they quarrelled over who should be the official founder, and give his name to the city. They asked the local gods to declare by augury (that is, to give a sign by the observed flight of birds). Romulus took up position on the Palatine hill, Remus on the Aventine. Remus had a sign first, six vultures; then twice the number appeared to Romulus. Their respective followers claimed each of them as king, Remus because he saw them first, Romulus because he saw more birds. A fight broke out, in which Remus was killed.

Another story is told however, a more common one. Remus made fun of his brother and jumped over the partly-built walls. Romulus lost his temper and killed him, saying, 'So perish anyone else who shall jump over my walls.'

OPPOSITE *The personification of Rome; a furniture ornament of silver, with gilding (4th century AD).*

Mars descends to Rhea Silvia, accompanied by cupids; handle of a silver patera.

The history of the tradition

Clearly, there were two traditions about the founding of Rome, one the 'Greek' tradition involving Aeneas, the other a 'Latin' one, of Romulus and Remus (with an 'Etruscan' variant). Eventually, the two were combined, and in due course inventions, significantly lacking in detail, were added to fill the gap that chronological likelihood was discovered to require. Archaeology belies the story that Rome was a colony founded in the fifteenth generation from Alba Longa; earliest remains at both sites are from the same period. The 'Greek' tradition, as we have seen, goes back at least to the fifth century BC. The 'canonical' version combining the two and with expanded chronology appeared towards the end of the third century in Fabius Pictor, and before him in a Greek writer, Diocles of Peparethus.

However, there is still debate about when the homegrown version with the twins arose, and why. Was it a traditional tale, or a late, literary invention?

That is harder to answer than it looks, for many of the elements in the story that look like traditional mythical components are known to us best through Greek myths, and so could be, in the Roman story, the products of Greek literary invention – the rape of a virgin by a god; the attempt by a king to forestall a threat to his rule, involving danger to the child; the rescue and rearing in humble circumstances; even, perhaps, the twins, and the fratricide.

This does not mean that the kernel of the story, the identity of the founder, is not genuinely local and ancient. The connection with Aeneas is found in the archaeology of Etruria and in the writings of the Greeks, and he is also linked with Lavinium. The 'Roman' tradition, however, links itself with Alba Longa which in historical times was still, in an indirect way, a kind of 'religious capital' for the whole of Latium. One of the annual duties of Roman consuls was to hold the Latin festival on the Alban Mount, part of its former territory. Rome regarded itself as a Latin city; the takeover by kings from Etruria was a transitory, and regrettable, episode in its early history, and in due course Rome conquered Etruria.

Romulus, then, was a 'Latin' founder, from Alba Longa. When and why did he acquire a twin? One founder is enough. Various modern explanations have been offered: the twins are said to have originated in Indo-European creation myth; or the dual consulship in Rome; or two separate communities thought to have existed in early times on the Palatine and the Quirinal; they have even been compared with Cain and Abel. A recent suggestion is that Remus came into the story quite late, and because of Roman politics.

The invention of the twins

The earliest surviving representation of the wolf suckling the twins is carved on the back of a bronze mirror made in the late fourth century BC. In 296 BC the city of Rome itself acquired a public monument. The plebeian brothers Gnaeus and Quintus Ogulnius, magistrates in that year, secured the conviction of several

Faustulus, the wolf, the twins and the figtree: coin of 140 BC (the moneyer's name was Sex. Pompeius Fostlus).

moneylenders, and used the treasury's share of their confiscated property to embellish Jupiter's shrine on the Capitol and improve the approach to Mars' temple. They also set up, beside the famous fig-tree near the Palatine, the Ficus Ruminalis, a statue-group of the infants being suckled by the wolf. About a quarter of a century later, that image began to appear on Roman coins.

Now, between 367 and 296 BC Roman government had undergone a conversion, in which the Ogulnii had played a part, resulting in power-sharing between the two groups making up the Roman citizen body, the patricians (the old nobility) and the plebeians. Remus, whose name in Latin is associated with slowness, came into the story, it is suggested, during this period, to symbolise the late entry of the Roman plebeians into political power. But why kill him?

Archaeology may help. In 295 BC the Romans won a victory at Sentinum against two of their fiercest opponents, the Samnites and the Gauls. The plebeian consul Publius Decius Mus secured victory by deliberately dedicating himself to the gods, and being killed by the enemy. On the Palatine was a temple of Victory, dedicated a year after the battle. Under the foundations of the temple was a recent grave – possibly a human sacrifice. The death of Remus can be seen as combining, in legend, both these sacrifices for the safety of the city. Just one year later a temple was dedicated to Romulus, deified as Quirinus (a title also attached to Janus, Mars, Jupiter and Hercules).

Remus dies and the survivor becomes a god; in that way both are taken out of politics. Perhaps myth-making was at work, cementing reconciliation between patricians and plebeians.

All this, of course, is modern speculation about how the Roman founding myth developed, but there might just be something in it. 'Quirites' was what the Romans called themselves in their civilian role, so Romulus – Quirinus could be thought of as protector of the whole Roman people at peace. The elder Pliny (first century AD) wrote that outside the temple of Quirinus there were once two myrtle trees, one plebeian and one patrician. The patrician tree flourished while the Senate dominated Roman government, but then it withered and the plebeian tree flourished, 'about the time of the Marsic War', that is, 91–90 BC. The sixty years after that war, until the battle of Actium, saw a long series of political conflicts, erupting more than once into civil war.

The sites of the legend

Whatever its ancestry, Romans of the classical period 'knew' that the true story was the one about the twins and the wolf; they had the landmarks to prove it. There was the Wolf's Cave (Lupercal) on the side of the Palatine. The Greek story was that it was the shrine of Arcadian Pan Lycaeus ('Wolfish' Pan); for the Romans, it was named after their famous wolf, and that was where the priest sacrificed at the festival of the Lupercalia.

Near it was the fig-tree, the Ficus Ruminalis. *Ruma* or *rumis* was said to be an old Latin word for a breast, and there was a goddess of nursing mothers, Rumina, so, naturally, the fig-tree with its milky juice had sheltered the wolf foster-mother and the twins. Only vestiges of the tree on the Palatine survived when Ovid wrote. Inconveniently, there was another Ficus Ruminalis near the Roman Forum (which in AD 59 withered and then resprouted), but that was easily explained. It grew alongside a large boulder (probably a meteorite), which was regarded as sacred, and its correct name was 'Navius' Fig-tree'. Rome's fifth king, Tarquin the First, after a victory against the Sabines, decided to change Romulus' original organisation of the cavalry by adding extra units bearing his own name. A famous augur, Attius Navius, objected that this must not be done without first ascertaining divine will by taking the auguries. Tarquin was annoyed and jeered, 'Come on then, seer, divine whether what I am thinking of now can be done.' Attius took the auspices and declared that it certainly could.

'Ah,' said Tarquin, 'but what I had in mind was that you would cut through a whetstone with a razor. Take these, and do what your birds foretell can be done.' Without more ado, Attius did it. A statue of Attius was set up on the spot, beside the steps of the Senate-house, and the whetstone was put there

Some idea of the appearance of the 'hut of Romulus' can be got from this terracotta funerary urn (8th–7th century BC) from Monte Albano in the shape of a rustic hut.

too. Tarquin dropped the idea of the reorganisation (though he did increase the cavalry in numbers), and ever afterwards the Romans never did anything of importance to the state without first taking the auguries, and abandoned their intentions if the birds refused consent. As for the fig-tree, some said that it *was* the Ficus Ruminalis, which Attius by his special skills had transplanted to the Forum.

In Augustus' day there still stood on the Palatine hill a 'hut of Romulus' said to be the very hut of Faustulus, in which Romulus spent his youth, and the spot from which he took his augury. It was made of sticks and reeds, with reed thatch, and its remarkable survival over the centuries was because the Romans constantly made good the ravages of time and weather with new materials.

Romulus gets brides for the Romans

Romulus had founded a city, making the perimeter large to allow for expansion. Next he had to find enough population. He opened a sanctuary offering asylum and attracted a large number of refugees from neighbouring peoples. However, that solved the problem only for one generation; there was posterity to think of. He sent envoys around to all the neighbouring cities asking for alliances and intermarriage between their peoples, but they all refused, telling the envoys to set up a refugee sanctuary for women too if they wanted them. Something had to be done, because Rome's young men were growing restless and angry, so Romulus made a plan.

He arranged a festival in honour of the god Consus and invited the neighbours. They came flocking in their curiosity to see the new town, and the Sabines, in particular, turned out en masse, with their womenfolk and children. They were entertained in local houses and given a tour of the town, and then the show started. When the visitors' attention was absorbed, the signal was given, and the young Romans grabbed the young women and carried them off. Mostly it was first come, first served, but the aristocrats, naturally, had previously booked the prettiest girls, and their subordinates went and fetched them.

One of the best-looking was snatched for an aristocrat called Thalassius, and since people kept asking for whom she was being taken, her captors shouted, to keep people off, 'For Thalassius', and that is why the Romans shout 'Talassio' at weddings. Or, Plutarch the Greek remarks, it may have been from the Greek word for spinning (that is, if the Romans used the word), because

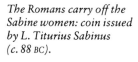

The Romans carry off the Sabine women: coin issued by L. Titurius Sabinus (c. 88 BC).

The intervention of the Sabine women, painted in 1799 by Jacques Louis David.

once the Romans and the Sabines were friends again, it was agreed that their wives should do no work for their husbands except spinning. (Later on it was a joke, as if that was all a wife was for.) And brides are still carried over the threshold because the Sabine women *had* to be; they did not go of their own accord.

The Romans, however, behaved like gentlemen. Romulus reassured the young women that they would be properly married, and honourably treated. What really won them over, though, was when the young men insisted that they had acted out of passionate love. The parents, however, were not happy. The Sabines, under their king Titus Tatius, laid siege to Rome, and the treachery of a Roman girl, Tarpeia, allowed them to capture the citadel. Romans and Sabines began to slog it out in the marshy ground between the Capitol and the Palatine hill.

Then the Sabine women rushed between the two armies, appealing to them. 'If you resent being related by marriage, turn your anger against us. We are to blame, we are the cause of injury and death to our fathers and husbands, and we would rather not live, than be widows and orphans.'

It worked. The two sides were reconciled, and Tatius and his Sabines were incorporated into Rome. If this story seems familiar, it is because the plot was used for the musical *Seven Brides for Seven Brothers*.

Livy's version emphasises the politics, the establishing of a stable community, and plays down the sexual violence. Ovid's approach is typically frivolous. In *The Art of Love*, Book I ('How to make it with Girls'), he recommends the gathering at the games as a good hunting-ground. It has been a hallowed custom, he says, ever since Romulus started it with the Rape of the Sabines.

The end of Romulus

Romulus ruled for nearly forty years, though he was more popular with the common people and the solders than with the Senate (or so said those later annalists who took the 'popular' side in politics). One day Romulus was reviewing his troops in the Campus Martius (near where the Pantheon is now). There was a sudden storm, with thunderclaps, a thick cloud hid him from everyone's sight, and no one ever saw him again. Some of the Senators standing nearby said that he had been swept away by the tempest, though there were some who secretly said that he had been torn to pieces by the Senators. The soldiers hailed him as father of his country, and as a god, Quirinus. One man did what was needed to secure belief in the deification and to calm people's panic and hostility to the Senate. A farmer from Alba, Julius Proculus (so the Julian family gets into the story again), who was in Rome for the day spoke to the people.

'Quirites,' he said, 'at first light this morning Romulus, father of this city, suddenly came down from the sky and presented himself before me. I was awestruck and stood there reverently. "Go," said he, "and tell the Romans that it is the wish of those in heaven that my Rome shall lead the world; tell them to perfect their military skill, and know and teach their children that there is no human power that can withstand the might of Rome." Then he departed aloft.' And so Romulus was declared to be a god.

Quirinus had an ancient shrine on the Quirinal hill, and a *flamen*, a special priest, but no temple until the end of the fourth century BC. Romans of the classical period thought (because the Sabines had a town called Cures) that Quirinus was a Sabine god, that the Quirinal hill took its name from an ancient Sabine settlement there and that 'Quirites' as an epithet for the Roman people came from the Sabine element incorporated into the citizen body.

The kings of Rome

Rome's next king was a Sabine, appointed by the people on the Senate's recommendation. His name was Numa Pompilius, and he was famous for his piety and knowledge of religious ritual. Later Romans thought of him as a philosopher king and some Greeks said (against chronological probability, even if he had been a real person) that he had studied under Pythagoras. He diverted the Romans from thoughts of war to the institutions of peace by establishing priesthoods, the religious calendar, and the proper ritual of religious observance. These he learned, or so he said, from a goddess, Egeria, his wife and adviser, who used to meet him at night and instruct him in religious lore. In order to *elicit* from the gods what portents from visible signs such as lightning were to be acted upon, and how, he dedicated an altar on the Aventine to Jupiter Elicius and consulted him by augury.

Numa found out from Jupiter the correct sacrifice to expiate a lightning strike. Getting a god to yield up his knowledge was not an easy matter, but Numa was his match in cunning. Ovid tells us that the tops of the trees on the Aventine quivered, and the earth subsided under the weight of Jupiter. The king's heart fluttered, the blood receded all over his body and his hair stood on end. When he recovered himself, he said, 'King and father of the gods on high, tell the sure method of expiating thunderbolts, if with pure hands we have touched your offerings, and if it is a pious tongue that asks now for this.' The god granted his prayer, but spoke with alarming ambiguity.

'Cut off a head,' said he. The king said, 'We shall obey. We must cut an onion, dug up in my garden.'

Then Jupiter added, 'A man's.' 'You will have,' said Numa, 'his hair.' Then Jupiter demanded a life, and Numa said, 'Of a fish.'

So, Numa, as befitted a king of peace, had outwitted Jupiter who, apparently, expected human sacrifice. However, the god was not offended. He laughed and said, 'You, man who are not to be scared off from talking with the gods, see to it that you expiate my thunderbolts with these things. But to you, when tomorrow's sun god shall have brought forth his full orb, I shall give sure pledges of empire.' Then he vanished in a thunderclap.

The Romans did not entirely believe Numa when he told them this, but they assembled the next day, and when the sun was fully up, Numa prayed to Jupiter and asked for fulfilment of his promise. Thunder came from a clear sky and a strangely shaped shield, indented in a curve on either side, fell from the sky.

Since this shield was the fortune of Rome, for security's sake Numa had eleven others made exactly like it, to deceive a thief. Only one craftsman, Veturius Mamurius, proved equal to the task. Numa also appointed a priesthood, the Salii, or Leaping Priests, to look after the shields. They were priests of Mars, and every year at the beginning of March, before the campaigning season, they paraded through Rome, performing a curious dance, and chanting a song of such antiquity that no one in Rome understood it any more, though

A coin showing two of the sacred shields; between them is a flamen's hat.

the priests continued to perform it year after year. We have the words, more or less garbled, as they were carved on marble recording the celebration of the ritual in Rome in AD 218, and there is still no certainty about the meaning, except that Mars is invoked.

Rome's next king, the warrior Tullus Hostilius, who incorporated Alba into Rome, was less fortunate in his dealings with Jupiter. The divine displeasure with his constant warfare was shown by a hail of stones, followed by a plague, and when Tullus secretly tried to use Numa's expiation ritual, he got the procedure wrong, and he and the palace were consumed by lightning.

The next king, Ancus Marcius, whose maternal grandfather was Numa, combined the interests of his two predecessors, and, it is said, introduced the concept of the 'just war'. In a ritual which was still practised in a modified fashion in the second century AD, war was formally declared on another country only after a Roman priest had visited its territory, calling each person he met, and Jupiter himself, to witness that satisfaction was demanded in the name of religion and justice. He was said to have brought water to Rome by aqueduct (his supposed descendant, Q. Marcius Rex, built the Aqua Marcia in 144 BC and was honoured with an equestrian statue).

Rome's last three kings, Tarquinius the First (an Etruscan immigrant), Servius Tullius and Tarquinius the Proud are in a more recognisable historical context, though this does not mean that all that writers say about them is true. Servius Tullius, in particular, appears partly as a political reformer, but also as a mythical figure. The circumstances of his infancy were legendary, and those of his death the stuff of melodrama.

As a little boy, Servius lived in the elder Tarquin's palace. One day, while he was asleep, flames were seen to play about his head, without harming him. When he awoke, they went out. Tanaquil, the queen, recognised this as a sign from heaven and told Tarquin that it meant he would be a support to their house. They accordingly reared him as a prince, and Tarquin betrothed him to his daughter. The story would be even better if he had been the child of a slave, but Livy, as always sceptical, cannot bring himself to believe that – a slave's child would never have been betrothed to a princess. His mother was obviously of high rank, a prisoner of war, who was befriended by the queen.

However, Ancus Marcius' sons, whom Tarquin had tricked out of the throne, resented his preferment and tried to assassinate Tarquin. While he lay dying, Tanaquil arranged matters so that Servius took over the reins of government, and in due course became king. Despite all the good he did for Rome, his end was unhappy.

Tarquin the First had two sons, Lucius Tarquinius, who was ambitious, and Arruns, who was not. They were married to Servius' two daughters, both called Tullia, and similarly different in character. By the good fortune of Rome, the two fierce ones were not initially married to each other. However, the bad Tullia turned the wicked Tarquin against her wimpish husband and his meek wife. Two murders later, she and Tarquin married, and then she began to egg him on against Servius. Tarquin bought support among the nobles with promises of favours, then threw Servius out of the Senate-house. As he staggered along the street, he was assassinated.

As Tullia's carriage was driving back towards her home on the Esquiline after she had been to hail her husband as king in the Forum, the driver pulled up short at the sight of Servius' mutilated body. Seizing the reins herself, she drove over her father's corpse, spattering her clothes and the carriage-wheels with blood. And that is how the street where it happened (the modern Via di S. Pietro in Vincoli) got the name Sceleratus Vicus, 'Street of Crime'.

Her husband Tarquin the Proud behaved as tyrants traditionally always behaved. He denied Servius burial and executed his supporters in the Senate. He exercised a reign of terror, inflicting death, exile or confiscation of property on those he disliked or whose property he coveted. Then a neighbouring town, Gabii, was taken over by Rome; historical writers simply plagiarised a story from the Greek Herodotus to flesh out the event. Tarquinius' son Sextus seized control of the town by trickery, and sent to ask his father what he should do next. The messenger reported that the king said nothing, but merely walked up and down in the garden, knocking off the tallest poppy-heads with his stick. Sextus understood.

The end of the monarchy

Tyrants usually violate the community's standards of sexual morality in some way. It was Tarquin's son, Sextus, who provided the last straw that made the nobles' resentment of Tarquin flare up into open rebellion and brought the monarchy to an end. He raped a noble Roman lady, Lucretia, who killed herself after telling her father and husband. Tarquin and his family were driven out of Rome and the people elected their first two consuls; the traditional date of this event was 509 BC.

That was not quite the last of the Tarquins. The deposed king obtained help from some Etruscan towns, and in particular from the king of Clusium, Lars Porsenna. Porsenna's siege of Rome produced a number of striking examples of Roman heroism and patriotism, and in the end, or so the Romans liked to believe, Porsenna was so impressed by these virtues, and by the Romans' stubborn resistance and determination to preserve their liberty, that he voluntarily withdrew.

The alternative history: Etruscans at Rome

This was a good story, but it was a cover-up. Tacitus and the elder Pliny knew that Porsenna had captured Rome and held on to it for a time. Besides, the archaeological evidence indicates that the Etruscans did not withdraw from Rome until the middle of the fifth century BC. Far from trying to restore the Tarquins, the king of Clusium apparently had had his own expansionist plans, and his eventual expulsion from Rome was achieved by the combined forces of the Latins, with help from the ruler of Cumae. However, this story was less flattering to Rome, and many preferred to ignore it in favour of a version that stressed the admirable qualities of the Roman national character.

There are traces, too, of other legends that indicate that Etruscan influence on early Rome was more thorough and long-lasting than most Romans were willing to admit. An exception was the emperor Claudius (AD 41–54), a keen antiquarian, whose first wife was of Etruscan descent, and who wrote a book on Etruscan history. In a typically long-winded and rambling speech to the Senate in AD 48, he justified the proposal to admit citizens from Gaul to office by recalling how Rome had admitted outsiders in the days of the kings. According to him, the Etruscans said that the king between the two Tarquins was not Servius, but a certain Etruscan, Caelius Vibenna, previously known as Mastarna.

A wall-painting in an Etruscan tomb at Vulci, from the fourth or third century BC, illustrating a story whose details are lost to us, shows Mastarna freeing Caelius Vibenna, while Aulus Vibenna fights someone from Falerii and another man kills Gnaeius Tarquinius Rumach ('from Rome'?). 'Mastarna' seems to be only the Etruscan word for 'magistrate'. But Aulus Vibenna at least is a real Etruscan name – it is found on a pot of the sixth century BC from Veii. Caelius Vibenna was known to Varro as an Etruscan noble (he gave his name, of course, to Rome's Caelian hill) who helped Romulus against King Tatius and the Sabines, and Varro said that the Tuscan Way in Rome was named after his followers. According to some Romans, including Cicero, the name of one of the three Roman tribes created by Romulus, the Luceres, came from another Etruscan king who helped Romulus against Tatius.

These scattered references to an 'Etruscan' history of Rome may have some basis in Etruscan cultural, if not also political, expansion into Latium at an early date. However, the Sons of the Wolf preferred to stress their Latinity, and to give credit for their success to themselves and to the gods.

The hero and the state

E very Roman schoolboy was taught the legends of early history, which exemplified the virtues that the Romans liked to think were part of the essential Roman character, and stressed in particular the principle that the welfare of Rome must come before the desires of the individual, and even before loyalty to the family group. The noblest Roman families were particularly proud to include such stories in their family histories, and, at least during the Republic, continued for a long time to model their conduct upon them. Stories of this sort were a staple component of the orations delivered at public funerals, to inspire the young men to emulation. Ennius, the author in the third century BC of Rome's first national epic, the *Annales*, wrote: '*Moribus antiquis res stat Romana virisque*' ('Upon the values and the men of old Rome stands firm').

Ennius' appeal was to traditional values, his context historical. In 340 BC the consul Titus Manlius Torquatus (said to have acquired the last name as a young man, when he fought a Battle of the Champions against a huge Gaul, slew him, and took the torque from his neck) was in command of a Roman army against the Latins. His son, stung by the taunts of a Latin cavalry commander, against orders engaged him in a duel. Torquatus, upholding military discipline, had his son executed immediately. In 140 BC his descendant found that his son, whom he had given in adoption to another Roman, had abused his position as governor in Macedonia to extort money. He publicly refused ever to see him again, and when his stricken son hanged himself the next night, he refused to attend his funeral but spent the day, as usual, in the atrium of his house seeing those who came to seek his expert advice on civil law and pontifical ritual. The story is in a collection of such moral anecdotes, 'Memorable Deeds and Sayings', published in the generation after Augustus by Valerius Maximus, who says that Manlius, like other noble Romans, kept wax images of his ancestors, including the stern Titus, as a reminder to live up to their standards.

The Torquatus of 340 BC had a legendary precedent. When Tarquin the Proud was expelled from Rome, certain young Romans, including the sons of Lucius Junius Brutus, one of Rome's first pair of consuls, formed a plot for his restoration. The plot was discovered, and they were all sentenced to death. The father did not spare his own sons; indeed, as consul, he was present, seated on the official dais, during their execution. No one paid attention to the others; all eyes, said Livy, were upon him, and upon his sons.

This model of stern subordination of personal and family interests to those of the state is not specific to one form of government. Among the Romans it is

Bronze figure of a lictor
(magistrate's attendant).
The bundle of rods and axe
he carries symbolise the
magistrates' power to inflict
punishment, including the
death penalty.

found in stories attached both to the period of the kings and to the early Republic. It is interesting that a later period also found it adaptable. One of the most famous paintings of the French Neo-classical artist Jacques-Louis David shows the consul Brutus sitting in his house, eyes downcast, while the lictors carry in the bodies of his sons. It was exhibited at the Paris Salon in 1789, several weeks after the storming of the Bastille, but it had been commissioned by the monarch.

Horatius and the Battle of the Champions

Even more famous is David's *The Oath of the Horatii*, which shows three brothers apparently resolving to fight to the death. Although later interpreted, in view of David's active participation in post-revolutionary politics, as a rallying call to the masses, it was in fact painted for the Crown some five years before the revolution as part of a project, supervised by Louis XVI's minister for the arts, for improving public morality through the use of the visual arts. The oath-scene was David's invention; it is not in the ancient story, nor in the play about the Horatii by the seventeenth-century French dramatist Pierre Corneille. The power of David's concept has made it a cult image. *Le Serment des Horaces* has been adopted as the title of a French journal launched in 1987 specialising in university research on art history.

David's picture emphasises readiness to sacrifice one's own life for the state. The ancient story includes other elements, and in particular one which would not have fitted well into the French king's didactic scheme – he would scarcely have wished to seem to sponsor sororicide.

The Romans under Tullus Hostilius, their third king, fought a war against the Albans which ended in the demolition of their city and their incorporation with the Romans. The kings of Rome and Alba agreed that, to conserve their manpower against their common enemy, the Etruscans, they should settle the issue by a Battle of the Champions. Conveniently, in each army there were triplets, the Roman Horatii and the Alban Curiatii, and they agreed to fight.

On the appointed day, for the first time known to tradition, the solemn agreement between the Romans and Albans was made by the 'fetial' procedure. The priest, bearing an uprooted plant, asked and received the king's consent to act for Rome. Then he touched with the plant Spurius Fusius, who was to utter for the Romans the formula of the oath not to depart from the terms of the treaty. 'Should they do so with evil intent and by public consent then, Jupiter, may you strike them even as I strike this pig, and the more so, in that your power and might surpass mine.' So saying, he killed the pig with a flint knife. The Albans likewise took the oath.

The champions stepped forward, watched anxiously by both the assembled armies. All three of the Albans were wounded; but then first one, then a second Horatius was killed. The last Horatius turned and ran – not, however, through cowardice, but to separate his opponents. He killed the first pursuer, then the second as he came up. The third, exhausted, could offer no

The Oath of the Horatii, *painted in 1784 by Jacques Louis David.*

resistance and was killed with a single stroke. Both sides buried their dead; their graves, said Livy, were still to be seen. Horatius received the weapons and cloaks of the Curiatii as his spoils, and marched back to Rome at the head of the Roman army.

He was met by his sister, who had been betrothed to one of the Curiatii. When she recognised the cloak she had made for him, she loosened her hair in mourning and shrieked his name. At once, Horatius stabbed her to the heart. 'Take your childish love to your betrothed. You have no thought for your brothers, living and dead, and for your country. So perish all Roman women who mourn for an enemy.'

The people were in two minds. Horatius' deed was dreadful, but at the same time, he was a national hero. He was put on trial before the king, who used the archaic procedure for *perduellio* (literally 'treason' – since Horatius had pre-empted the people's right to pass judgement), which Livy explains for his readers. If Horatius was found guilty even after appeal to the people from the magistrates' decision (*provocatio* – an ancient right of the citizen), he was to be blindfolded, hanged on a barren tree, and his corpse scourged.

The appeal went to the people. Horatius' father spoke. Had his daughter not deserved her death he would have exercised his right as a father to punish his son himself, but he begged the people that his heroism in the fight should save him. Horatius was acquitted, but his father had to perform certain rites of expiation for him, and Horatius had to pass with covered head beneath a beam slung across the road.

There was a spot in the Forum known in Livy's day as 'the Horatian Spears'; that was where, it was said, the spoils of the Curiatii had hung. Close to where the Colosseum later stood, there was a beam (*tigillum*), replaced from time to time at state expense until at least the fourth century AD, known as the *Tigillum Sororium*. This is explained as 'the Sister's Beam' from *soror*. Near it, however, were two altars, to Janus Curiatius and Juno Sororia, and the Roman religious calendar mentions a ceremony at the spot on 1 October. This suggests that false etymologies may have produced a legend to explain primitive and obsolete rituals accompanying rites of passage for the young boys of the *curiae* (ancient voting-groups of the people) and the girls reaching puberty (*sororiare* meaning the growth of breasts), as well as to account for one or two traditional topographical names. The legend also, as told in classical writers, inculcated certain values – country before life, patriotism before personal affection.

How one-eyed Horatius kept the bridge

Lars Porsenna and the Etruscan army marched upon Rome, heading for the vulnerable point, the wooden bridge across the Tiber. The Roman guards began to flee in panic but another Horatius, called Cocles ('One-Eyed'), urged a few of them to break down the end of the bridge while he did his best to hold off the enemy single-handed. Two noble Romans, Spurius Larcius and Titus Herminius (both, interestingly, names of Etruscan derivation) stayed out of shame, and helped Horatius by prolonging the resistance for a few precious minutes; he sent them back when the bridge was almost cut through, then turned to try to continue holding off the enemy until the work could be finished. His taunts actually nonplussed them for a few moments, then a shower of spears came. Horatius caught them all on his shield. As the whole army advanced, the bridge suddenly crashed down, cutting off his escape.

Calling upon father Tiber to save him, he jumped in full armour into the river and swam across. He had saved Rome, and his reward was a statue (the first, says the elder Pliny, ever set up in honour of an individual) and a plot of land. Some private individuals, Livy adds, voluntarily contributed to his maintenance during the hard times of the siege that followed.

Horatius was not always saved by his swimming. In another version, Horatius deliberately sacrificed himself for his country – and there is no mention of public honours. Indeed, there is something suspicious about the story of a public statue for a living person at so early a date. Horatius' leap into the river from the Pons Sublicius, Rome's oldest bridge, is reminiscent of a mysterious ceremony on 14 May when the Roman pontiffs, the Vestal Virgins and the praetors threw thirty straw puppets, called Argei, into the river from this bridge. Again, we may have an example of a legend growing up to explain a ritual, and perhaps also an old cult-statue, and being given also a moral dimension.

One of the most popular poems in English literature, for generations after its publication in 1842, was Lord Macaulay's 'Lay of Ancient Rome' about Horatius. Macaulay's Etruscans show a tinge of British sportsmanship; when Horatius struggled out onto the bank, 'even the ranks of Tuscany / Could scarce forbear to cheer.'

How Scaevola lost his hand

Another traditional type of tale, found also among the Greeks, is that of the secret mission behind the enemy lines. Porsenna's siege of Rome continued and food was running short. The humiliation of Rome's suffering siege, especially by an enemy who had so often been defeated in the past, determined a young aristocrat, Gaius Mucius, to undertake a great risk; but first he sought permission from the Senate (otherwise the Roman guards might take him for a deserter and kill him). Armed only with a dagger, he made his way by stealth into the Etruscan camp. The king was sitting on a platform with his secretary, and pay was being distributed to the soldiers.

Which was the king? They were dressed so much alike that Mucius could not be sure. Taking a chance, he stabbed the wrong man, and was promptly seized and hauled before Porsenna. He hurled defiant words at the king, threatening obscurely that the king need never think himself safe. When Porsenna ordered him to tell what he knew, on pain of being burned alive, Mucius cried, 'Look! See how little men think of their bodies, when their eyes are set on great glory,' and he thrust his right hand into a lighted altar-fire and held it there, as though insensible of the pain. Porsenna was so impressed that he ordered him to be set free, as a gallant enemy. Mucius, in a rather curious form of thanks, volunteered the information that three hundred young nobles had sworn to undertake this mission in succession, until one of them should succeed. The immediate result of his exploit was that Porsenna opened negotiations with the Romans, which led to peace. Mucius thereafter bore the *cognomen*, additional name, Scaevola, 'Left-handed', which in historical times belonged to a particular branch of the clan of the Mucii.

This story can be no earlier than the third century BC, and bears obvious signs of Greek influence. Romans in the sixth century BC did not generally bear a *cognomen*, despite the genealogical fancies of later generations; besides, *scaeva* (an omen from the left) was known to Romans of Varro's day as a Greek loan-word, and the adjective *scaevus* does not enter literary Latin until the second century AD. Porsenna's well-dressed secretary is another Greek touch, and the secret mission may owe something to an Athenian legend of their early king Codrus (who went to the enemy camp to be killed, in order to fulfil an oracle and save his country).

The story helps to motivate the withdrawal of Porsenna from Rome, which, as we saw, was the preferred Roman version of the history of their

Scaevola burning his hand before Lars Porsenna: Italian majolica plate, c. 1510–20.

relations with the Etruscans. It was fabricated for the family traditions of the patrician Mucii Scaevolae, a family which in the later Republic shows historical and antiquarian interests. The first one known to history was praetor in 215 BC. In the second century BC two Scaevolae, father and son, were in succession Pontifex Maximus, chief priest at Rome, and so had access to a primitive form of chronicle, the *Annales Maximi*, the chief priest's annual records of festivals and other events. A century later another member of the family helped to organise Augustus' antiquarian revival of the Saecular Games (traditionally commemorating at intervals of about 110 years the foundation of Rome.)

Naturally, the Scaevolae would want to devise an acceptable explanation for their family name, either because left-handedness was regarded as unlucky in ordinary life (though lucky from the point of view of Roman augurs), or because, as the story perhaps suggests, it laid itself open to the obvious insinuation that an ancestor had had his hand burned off as a punishment.

Ironically, the Romans came to use the story of Scaevola as part of the pageantry of punishment. By the first century AD executions by various means, and other forms of corporal punishment, were not only included as part of the entertainment in arena displays, such as wild-beast shows, but even incorporated into theatrical performances. Such performances occurred at the grand inauguration in AD 80 of the emperor Titus' new amphitheatre, the Colosseum. The poet Martial describes one charade where someone apparently was allowed the option of burning his hand off as an alternative to being burned to death inside a tunic covered in pitch:

> The other day at the morning show
> We saw Mucius put his hand in the fire.
> If you think that he was enduring and tough,
> You must be as thick as a man from Abdera.
> If they say, with the itchy shirt there, 'Burn your hand,'
> It takes a great deal more guts to say 'No'.

So a legend meant to illustrate patriotic self-sacrifice was adapted as a sensational way of demonstrating the authority of the state.

The story of the belly and the limbs

Less than twenty years after the expulsion of the king, Rome faced a double crisis, external threat from the neighbouring hill-peoples, and internal strife between the common people and the ruling class. The people revolted in protest against the cruel law which allowed creditors not only to seize the property of their debtors, but to imprison and maltreat them. Promises to change the law were not kept. There were riots, and only with the greatest difficulty was the Senate able to enrol the army to face the threat of invasion. When, however, fearing sedition at home once the army was disbanded, the Senate tried to keep them mobilised and on campaign, the whole people marched out of the city and camped three miles away on the Sacred Mount. This was known as the first Secession of the Plebs.

The Senate sent a plebeian, Menenius Agrippa, to reason with them, and he told them a parable, the story of the Belly and the Limbs.

'In the days when all the parts of a man did not, as now, agree together, but each limb had a mind of its own and could speak for itself, the other parts complained that it was unfair that they had to worry and exert themselves to provide everything for the belly, while the belly stayed quietly in the middle, doing nothing but enjoy the pleasures with which it was provided. So they conspired together that the hands should not convey food to the mouth, nor should the mouth accept what it was given, nor should the teeth chew up what they received. They intended, in their resentment, to subdue the belly in this way by starvation; but what happened was that every one of the members themselves and the body as a whole almost completely wasted away. And so it had become apparent that the belly too was not idle but performed a service, that it was no more nourished than it nourished them, returning to all the parts of the body what we depend on for life and health, when it is allocated equally among the veins, and made ready by the digestion of food – that is, the blood.'

The people recognised the parallel between the intestinal dissension in the body and their own resentment against the Senators. A compromise was agreed, and they were given magistrates of their own to protect them against arbitrary action by the consuls. And so the first tribunes of the plebs were appointed, one of them Sicinius, leader of the revolt.

Coriolanus and the siege of Rome

However, the harmony between the people and the Senate did not last long. Agriculture had been neglected during the secession, and the city was on the verge of famine. Corn had to be imported from far and wide for the next two years. The price would have to be subsidised if the people were to afford it, and there were some Senators who wanted to make the people give up their newly-won political privileges in return.

One of the most vehement spokesmen for this point of view was Gaius Marcius. He was a national hero. The previous year, as a junior officer, he led an attack on the Volscian town of Corioli and captured it, earning the name Coriolanus. Now, however, he antagonised the people against both himself and the Senate. 'I would not put up with King Tarquin,' he said, 'am I to put up with King Sicinius? Let him secede and call the plebs away to the Sacred Mount and the other hills. No one is stopping them. The prices are their own fault; let them put up with them. I dare say they will soon knuckle under and till the fields themselves, rather than secede under arms and prevent cultivation.'

The tribunes promptly summoned him for trial. The Senate were terrified. At first they tried to use their personal bully-boys to prevent the people from having meetings; eventually, they resorted to begging them to let Coriolanus off. He, however, failed to appear in court and the people sentenced him to exile (so Livy writes; Plutarch, on the other hand, has a dramatic trial scene in which Coriolanus' contemptuous behaviour further antagonises the people).

Coriolanus went to his old enemies, the Volscians, who were for the moment at peace with Rome. He conspired with one of their leaders, who by using disinformation and black propaganda panicked the Senate into ordering the immediate departure of the Volscians who were in Rome to attend a festival. Then they saw to it that this diplomatic incident blew up again into open war by the Volscians against the Romans.

Coriolanus personally led the Volscian army. First he recaptured the Volscian territories recently taken by the Romans, and then overran Latium, finally laying siege to Rome itself. Twice the Senate sent envoys to negotiate with him; the second time he refused even to give them a hearing. They sent their priests, with no more effect. Then the women of Rome appealed to Coriolanus' aged mother Veturia and his wife, Volumnia. When Coriolanus heard that they had come, with his children, he went to embrace them. His mother held him off: 'Are you my enemy or my son? Am I your mother, or a prisoner of war? When you saw Rome, did you not think of your home with its gods, and of your family? If I had had no son, Rome would not be in danger. My

Coriolanus reproached by his mother: Italian majolica dish, 1544.

misery will not last long; but think of the others who will die or become slaves.'

Then his wife and children clung to him sobbing, and the women with them broke into tears. Coriolanus was completely overwhelmed. He sent them home and withdrew the army; but whether the Volscians killed him or he spent a long life in unhappy exile, no one knew for certain.

That is the story as told, rather baldly, by Livy, under the evident influence of a source reflecting the 'popular' politics of a section of the Senate in the first century BC, but without overt criticism of either side. Livy goes no further than to suggest that Coriolanus' intransigence was not in the best interests of the Senate: with more willingness to compromise they might have got rid of the tribunate.

The best stories, however, are adaptable to suit the interests and purposes of a variety of tellers. For Plutarch, the motivating force of Coriolanus, whose father had died in his boyhood, was a desire to please his mother (called Volumnia in this version), and he showed towards her all the filial respect which he would have shown a father. His Coriolanus is paired with the Athenian Alcibiades (who also turned traitor in exile), and given some qualities to enhance the 'match'. Coriolanus, like a tragic hero, is in large part to blame for his own downfall, because of his pride and unrestrained aggression and intolerance, and he goes into exile bent on avenging himself on Rome. Plutarch's version is much more dramatic and emotional in the telling, and it is not surprising that it is the one which inspired later writers.

Shakespeare in his *Coriolanus*, both to conform to the political orthodoxy of his own day and to bolster Coriolanus' credibility as a tragic hero, gives his contemptuous arrogance some justification by developing a hint in Plutarch and presenting the people's leaders as mean-spirited, manipulative trouble-makers. On the other hand, for the Communist Bertolt Brecht, who left an unfinished play, *Coriolan*, at his death, Coriolanus is far from a hero. His mistaken pride in believing himself indispensable and irreplaceable is exposed; the common people of Rome, united, can well do without him.

Family fictions, and how history repeats itself

Every great Roman family had its own collection of family legends. Here are two from the early and middle Republic.

The Fabii were a distinguished family in the early Republic. Every year from 485 to 479 BC one of the consuls was a Fabius. During most of those years Rome had waged an indecisive war against Veii, an Etruscan city, and Rome's rival for control of vital trade routes along the Tiber valley. The Veientes frequently raided the Romans' fields, escaping before the legions could draw them into pitched battle. Other wars threatened, and the legions were needed elsewhere. Then the Fabian clan went to the Senate and said, 'Leave the Veientes to us. We will wage this war as if it were a family feud, at our own expense.'

The whole city turned out to see them march forth, 306 in number, with their leader, one of the consuls of the year (478 BC). They set up a garrison in a fort on the frontier, on the river Cremera, and there they stayed, fighting frequent skirmishes against the Veientes. But the latter devised a plan. They would sometimes leave flocks and farmhouses unguarded; their armed men, if they encountered the Fabii, would run away as if in panic. At last, the Fabii grew contemptuous of their enemy and over-confident; and so one day, as they chased some unguarded livestock, they were caught in an ambush. The date was 13 February. They were all killed – all, that is, except one, scarcely out of boyhood, in whom the Fabian line was kept alive.

That was the family story. There were some debunkers among the Greek writers, who said the Fabii were not alone, but part of a legion with four thousand others; Dionysius calls it a story 'like a fiction of legend or the theatre'. The numbers involved, and the year, are suspiciously close to those of the Spartans holding off the forces of Xerxes at the Battle of Thermopylae.

Lustre was added to the family history of the Decii by the action for which several generations were renowned. In 340 BC, before a battle against the Latins (the same battle in which the son of the consul Titus Manlius Torquatus engaged the enemy against orders, see p. 117), the sacrifice offered by the other consul, Publius Decius Mus, boded ill for his family. When the wing under his command began to be driven back by the enemy, Decius instructed a pontiff to dictate to him the formula for *devotio* (self-dedication) to the gods, so that he might save his legions.

He put on a purple-bordered toga, covered his head and, standing on a spear and touching his chin with one hand, he recited the formula. He called upon Janus, Jupiter, Mars, Quirinus, Bellona, Lares, gods new and gods native, gods of the Romans and of their enemies, and gods of the underworld, that they might prosper the might and victory of the Roman people, the Quirites, and afflict their enemies with terror and death. 'As I have uttered the words, even so on behalf of the Republic of the Roman people, the Quirites, and of the army, the legions and auxiliaries of the Roman people, the Quirites, I do devote myself – and with me the legions and auxiliaries of the enemy – to the gods of the underworld and to earth.'

He then adjusted his toga in the ritual 'Gabine manner' and rode into the midst of the enemy. The enemy were thrown into confusion and the Romans given fresh heart; and as Decius fell beneath a hail of missiles, the tide of battle turned.

Fifty-five years later, at the battle of Sentinum against a combined force of Gauls and Samnites, Decius' son, in his fourth consulship, devoted himself in exactly the same way. That was the decisive battle of the third Samnite War, and effectively settled Rome's leadership of Italy.

So far, so good; but Cicero knew of a story that the grandson followed the example of his father and grandfather at the battle of the Aufidus in 279 BC. Other sources, however, mention this Decius as still alive in 265 BC. Perhaps his *devotio* did not 'take' and he survived, in which case, according to Livy, the proper ritual was to bury a life-size effigy in the ground instead. The drawback was that the unsuccessful self-devoter could never again take part in any religious ritual.

Alternatively, the commander need not devote himself at all; he could 'volunteer' any citizen from the legions. Perhaps the third Decius simply felt that the family tradition was getting out of hand.

Legendary ladies

There were also legends about Roman women, both good and bad. We may find these more attractive than those about the self-denying heroes, but although they sometimes contain romantic or even tragic elements, a closer look will show that, for the Romans, they had the same original purpose as the stories about Rome's male heroes, that is, to encourage acceptance of Roman moral priorities, in particular self-control and self-discipline, in the interests of the Roman state and its security.

Tarpeia the traitress

Let us begin with a wicked lady, Tarpeia. A story was needed to account for the traditional name of a rock near the south-western end of the Capitoline hill in Rome.

The bare story can be told in two sentences. When king Tatius and his Sabines were laying siege to Rome in order to recover their kidnapped women-folk, Tarpeia, daughter of the Roman commander, who had gone outside the walls to fetch water, agreed to let the Sabines into the Capitoline citadel. Once inside, they threw their shields upon her and killed her.

Here the complications start. Why did Tarpeia let the Sabines in? In the straightforward Tarpeia-the-traitress version, the motive was greed. Tarpeia had agreed to betray the citadel for gold. She coveted the heavy golden armlets and rings worn by the Sabines, but when she claimed as reward 'what you wear upon your arms' (meaning the jewellery), she was instead crushed under the Sabines' heavy shields.

Propertius, a poet contemporary with Virgil and Ovid, gave the story a romantic-seeming twist (which owed a good deal to a Greek myth well-known to Roman poets) by making Tarpeia fall in love with the king as she saw him riding out in full armour. Her price for betrayal was to become Tatius' bride; the outcome, however, when she tried to claim payment, was the same, her death. To Romans, however, love was no more acceptable as a motive than lust for wealth, especially when it conflicted with patriotic duty. Propertius makes it clear that Tarpeia deserved what she got – even the Sabine enemy condemned her crime – and he heightens her guilt by following the version of the story that made her a Vestal Virgin, vowed to chastity.

There was another version of the story, in which Tarpeia was not a traitress but a heroine, acting from the highest motives. This Tarpeia planned

A coin showing Tarpeia already waist-deep in a pile of Sabine shields.

the destruction of the Sabines. When she asked for 'what they bore upon their left arms', her intention was to deprive them of the defence of their shields, and to raise the alarm for the Romans; but the Sabines saw through the ruse, and killed her. We may think her incredibly naive, but that is beside the point. Tarpeia the heroine was said to be buried at the spot bearing her name. At any rate, annual libations were made there, and this story accounted for them.

On the other hand, the Tarpeian rock had a sinister reputation. Those convicted of particularly serious offences were executed by being thrown down from it. Which offences, other than treachery, our sources do not specify, and historical instances are hard to find. In AD 33, a man from Spain was so executed on a charge of incest with his daughter, but, Tacitus says, the emperor, Tiberius, really wanted to get hold of his gold and bronze mines. In any case, this evil association required an appropriate story to account for it – hence Tarpeia the traitress, with her individualistic and unpatriotic desires.

A nice girl

Much more healthy and wholesome was the story of Cloelia (from a family which claimed several consuls in the first century of the Republic). When Lars Porsenna agreed to withdraw from Rome after Scaevola's exploit, he demanded a number of Roman hostages, who were kept in the Etruscan camp near the Tiber. Among them was an unmarried girl called Cloelia. She organised a group of fellow hostages, all girls, and led them in swimming across the river – 'among the missiles of the enemy' says Livy – and so restored them to their families.

Once again, Porsenna was torn between anger and admiration, and this time the etiquette of warfare complicated matters. Porsenna declared that her exploit outdid the likes of Horatius Cocles and Scaevola. If, as a hostage, she was not returned, he said, he would regard the treaty as broken; but, if she was returned, he undertook to send her back intact and inviolate to her people. The Romans returned her, and then Porsenna was better than his word. He presented her with half the hostages, at her choice. She chose, it is said, the boys who had not yet reached puberty, for two reasons. One was that that was more seemly in a young girl (that is, than to choose sexually mature males); the other, that boys of that age were particularly vulnerable to abuse. When peace was made again, the Romans rewarded this valour, unusual in a woman, with an equestrian statue on the Sacred Way.

The horse arrives in the story rather awkwardly, though the story is used to account for the statue, which was a Roman landmark. The original statue was replaced after being destroyed by fire in 30 BC. Horse-riding is no more probable than swimming as a normal activity for high-class and, it seems, sheltered, young Roman ladies in the early Republic. The story, as told by Livy, combines several functions. It is part of the proud tradition of a noble family; it explains a statue; and, like the story of Scaevola, it helps to explain why Porsenna left Rome. Besides all these, it carried some clear messages about the moral attitudes and sexual behaviour to be regarded as desirable – as well as some sinister hints about the treatment which both young women and young boys lacking the protection of free status or parental presence might expect to receive in Rome.

Behaviour and reputation

Great store was set upon the chastity of Roman women, and in none was it more important than in the Vestal Virgins, guardians of the sacred hearth of Vesta, whose purity was at once the symbol and the guarantee of the welfare of Rome. Death by entombment alive in an underground chamber was the punishment inflicted several times during the Republic on Virgins found (usually in times of national crisis) to have been unchaste.

Suspicion was easily provoked. In 420 BC, it was said, Postumia, whose brother had recently been fined for his part in a Roman defeat at Veii, was charged before the priests with sexual immorality. She was innocent, as it happened, but had acquired a doubtful reputation because she was rather too well-dressed and smartly got-up, and showed unsuitable independence of mind. She was judged innocent and let off with a warning. In future, the chief priest told her, she should stop making jokes, and pay more attention to holiness than to fashion in her choice of dress.

Some lucky ones had their chastity miraculously vindicated by the gods. Aemilia, a senior Virgin, had left the fire in the care of a new member, who had allowed it to go out. When the fire was found to be out, there was a great to-do in the city, and the priests decided to investigate whether Aemilia had been unchaste. She stretched out her hands toward the altar and prayed to Vesta: 'If for nearly thirty years I have devoutly and properly carried out all my sacred duties, keeping a pure mind and a chaste body, manifest yourself to help me, and do not allow me to suffer a wretched death; but if I have done any impious deed, let me cleanse the city by my punishment.' She tore off a part of her robe and threw it on the fire. From the cold ashes, a great flame sprang up.

Or there was Tuccia, who, under a similar charge, said that she would prove her innocence in deeds. She walked down to the river Tiber; the whole of Rome turned out to watch. Then, after asking Vesta's aid, she took up water in a sieve and carried it all the way to the goddess's shrine, without spilling a

Head of the Vestal Aemilia, on a coin issued by an Aemilius in 65 BC.

A marble head of a Vestal Virgin, showing the special arrangement of her hair, a style otherwise worn only by brides on their wedding-day.

drop – or, some say, to the Forum, where she poured it on the ground at the feet of the priests – whereupon her accuser mysteriously disappeared and was never seen again.

Claudia and the Great Mother

One of the highlights of the Roman year was the week-long celebration, in early April, of the Megalesia ('Great Games'), the festival of Mater Magna ('Great Mother'), or Cybele. The story of the introduction of the goddess to Rome involved members of the most prominent families, one of them a woman. In 204 BC, during the war against Hannibal in Italy, plague was rife in the army, and there were more ill omens than usual. The Sibylline books were consulted, and the usual remedy proposed – the introduction of a new cult. A prophecy was found which said that a foreign invader in Italy could be driven out if Cybele was brought from Pessinus in Phrygia to Rome. Five Roman senators went as envoys to King Attalus in Pergamum and received the sacred black stone which represented the goddess. A special boat was prepared, and the stone made the long journey across the Mediterranean until it reached the mouth of the Tiber. Ovid's version of what happened next is the most dramatic.

All the knights and the stately senators, mingled with the common people, came to the mouth of the Tuscan river to meet her. With them came in procession also mothers and daughters and brides and the Vestal Virgins. Men wearied their arms tugging at the tow-rope, but the foreign ship could scarcely make headway against the stream. There had been a long drought; the ship's keel grounded on the muddy shallows. Everyone strained to the utmost, chanting to help the effort, but the ship stuck fast, like an island in mid-sea. It was a portent; stricken, they stood shaking.

Claudia Quinta traced her descent all the way from the original Clausus, and she had beauty to match her noble ancestry. She was chaste, but that was not her reputation. Unfair rumour had injured her, making false charges. What told against her was her dress and make-up, and the elaborate hairdos with which she appeared – that, plus her readiness to answer back to severe old men. She knew she was innocent, and laughed at the lies told about her – but people in general are ready to think the worst.

She stepped forward from the line of chaste matrons and took up pure water from the river in her hands. Three times she poured it on her head, three times she raised her hands in the air – everyone watching thought she had gone out of her mind. She knelt down, her hair loosened, and gazing at the goddess's image she said:

'Fruitful mother of the gods, graciously accept a suppliant's prayer, on this condition. They say I am not chaste. If you condemn me, I will acknowledge guilt, and pay for it with my life. But if I am free of blame, demonstrate my innocence. You are chaste; follow my chaste hands.'

She gave a slight tug on the rope. This is a strange tale, but stage-plays also testify to what I say. The goddess moved; she followed her leader, and in so doing approved her.

The story had been presented in plays (probably at the festivals) and was presumably popular. There was, however, another, rather duller story. The oracle had said that the goddess was to be welcomed by the best of the Roman men and the best of the women. The senate chose as best of the men a young man who had not yet actually started on a magisterial career but who (probably not coincidentally) was cousin of the Scipio who was consul in 205 BC and went on to command the victorious final campaign against Hannibal in Africa. 'What exactly were the virtues on which they based their judgement,' says Livy rather drily, 'I would willingly pass on to posterity, if only chroniclers of that time had been specific; however, I do not intend to hazard any guesses of my own about something that was so long ago.'

Claudia (whose other name, 'Quinta', suggests that she was the youngest of five sisters) belonged to the same great Roman clan as one of the two censors of 204, the men responsible for letting the contracts for the building of the new goddess's temple. Whether the censor's influence had something to do with a relative being chosen as 'best of the women' we can only guess. Her nomination would make another honourable entry in the family's history.

The 'popular' version was perhaps originally started by someone hostile to the family, but it made a much better tale. It was also much more useful for moralising purposes, since it went into specifics. Decent women did not question the opinions of the senior men of the community; and decent women did not doll themselves up. Why should they wish to appear attractive to men other than their husbands? This was the conventional view presented by many Roman writers (though Ovid, in his intentionally 'shocking' erotic poems often takes the opposite stance). Men disciplined themselves; women had to be coerced into being good. How in the past Roman men had instilled proper ideas of behaviour was shown by several (probably apocryphal) stories – e.g. of a woman allegedly starved to death by her family for having taken the keys to the wine-cellar, or one divorced for going to the games without her husband's knowledge, or another for appearing in public unveiled.

When the story of the dashing Claudia first appeared is not known. In the first century BC Cicero ignored it, but that does not mean that it did not exist; the other version suited his purpose better. His political enemy, Publius Clodius, a descendant of the great family, had a sister, a 'merry widow', who was thought to be the real instigator of a charge of poisoning against Cicero's friend, Caelius, in 56 BC. In his defence speech, after imagining the ghost of another famous ancestor, Appius Claudius the Blind (censor 312 BC), upbraiding Clodia for her behaviour, Cicero puts his own interpretation on her life-style. 'Let us suppose,' he says, 'a woman – not *her*, of course – who gives herself to anyone and parades her lovers; who allows all sorts of self-indulgence in her private park, her Roman mansion, her beach house at Baiae; who gives money to young men' – who, in short, is a brazen hussy and spendthrift, with the habits of a whore. What had Clodia done to lay herself open to this? Appearances were against her, as against Claudia Quinta. She was rich, and entertained a lot; she had a house at a holiday resort, and went about publicly with young men. She was a widow, but she had neither taken herself out of circulation nor – the next best thing – remarried.

Divorce in Rome was frequent and easily obtained by both sexes, and remarriage by widows and divorcées generally expected. Nevertheless, the persistent moral ideal, however little honoured in practice, was the *univira*, the 'one-man woman', that is, the one who went straight from girlhood's virginity into marriage, and had relations with no other man for the rest of her life. In a society where all the women were *univirae* the men would no doubt have been able to feel more secure. Two more stories – one of them still famous today – show indirectly something of the underlying anxieties of Roman men.

Tyranny, lust and revolution: Appius and Verginia

The Claudii were one of Rome's oldest and noblest families, and they were proud of their history. In 79 BC, a Claudius who was consul had shields inscribed with his family's achievements set up on the walls of the temple of Bellona, the War-Goddess, founded almost three hundred years before by his ancestor, Appius Claudius the Blind.

However, there was at Rome an equally powerful anti-Claudian tradition that accused them of ingrained arrogance and overweening behaviour towards the people. One of the worst, so the story went, was Appius Claudius the Decemvir, consul in 451 BC. He was one of the committee of ten men (*decemviri*) set up in that year to produce Rome's first codified law. The result was the Twelve Tables; ten were produced in the first year, and two more in 450 by another committee of ten; only Appius was a member of both. This second committee, at the instigation of Appius, refused to resign after its work was done, or to hold elections, and began a reign of terror in Rome.

Appius lusted after a plebeian girl – some accounts call her, aptly, Verginia, and her father Verginius – who was already betrothed to a plebeian political activist, Icilius. When Appius failed to seduce her, he instructed one of his dependants, Marcus Claudius, to claim her as his slave. The man accordingly seized her one morning, as she entered the Forum with her attendant, calling people to witness that she was his slave. He brought her into court; Appius, of course, was trying the case.

Verginius was away with the army and unable to make a defence, and the case might have gone by default, but pressure from the bystanders forced Appius to agree to defer judgement till the following day. However, since her father was not there to take custody of her, Appius and Marcus should retain her overnight. Verginia's fiancé strongly resisted this – he knew what treatment a female slave might expect – and called on the Romans to support him. 'I am to marry her, and I intend to have a virgin as my bride. You have enslaved the people by depriving them of their political rights, but that does not mean that you can behave like owners and exercise your lust on our wives and children.'

Appius backed down for the time being and allowed Verginia to remain free overnight. Her friends hastily summoned back her father. Appius' letter ordering the army commanders to detain him arrived too late, and Verginius was there in court the following day. Appius, however, did not even allow him to make his counter-claim, but immediately pronounced in favour of Verginia's alleged owner, quelling any possibility of riot among the crowd by drawing attention to the presence of his armed escort. He granted Verginius' request to be allowed to question his daughter's attendant, in Verginia's presence.

Drawing them to the side of the Forum, Verginius grabbed a knife from a butcher's shop and stabbed his daughter to death, crying, 'Only so can I make you free!' Verginius escaped to the army and incited them to revolt, while Icilius and Verginia's uncle incited the urban populace. The result was revolution. The *decemviri* were overthrown and the people were once again able to elect their tribunes, to protect them against arbitrary coercion by magistrates.

The rape of Lucretia

Tyranny, lust and revolution are also the ingredients of one of the best-known stories from antiquity; this is Livy's account. In 509 BC King Tarquin the Proud started a war against Ardea. The cause was his own extravagance. His ambitious building schemes had drained the public funds, and he needed booty also to appease the people's resentment of the servile labour he had made them perform. During the siege of Ardea, as the king's sons sat drinking one night with their kinsman Collatinus, they argued about which had the best wife. At Collatinus' suggestion, they decided to ride back to Rome to catch their wives unprepared and find out what they were doing in their absence.

The princes' wives were found enjoying lavish dinner-parties with friends.

The suicide of Lucretia, an engraving by Marcantonio Raimondi, after a design by Raphael, c. 1511–2. The Greek inscription means: 'It is better to die than shamefully to live.'

Then the husbands rode to Collatia. There Lucretia was found busy in the activities which were typical, Romans liked to believe, of old-fashioned virtue. She was at home, seated among her slave-women, still working, late though it was, at her wool. Collatinus had won; but Lucretia's proven chastity, as well as her beauty, had quickened the lust of Sextus Tarquinius, son of the king.

A few days later, Sextus made a secret visit to Collatia and was received as a guest. That night he went with drawn sword to Lucretia's bedroom and awoke her. He declared he loved her, pleaded, threatened, but to no avail. Then he said that he would kill her and a slave, and leave the slave's naked body beside her, to make it look as if she had been caught and killed in the act of adultery. Lucretia gave in. After the rape she sent messages summoning her father and her husband to come, each with a friend; Collatinus brought Lucius Junius Brutus. When Collatinus asked, 'Is it well with you?' she answered, 'What can be well with a woman who has lost her chastity? The mark of another man is in your bed. But only my body has been violated. My mind is guiltless, as my death shall testify. Swear that you will take vengeance on the adulterer.'

All the men swore, then began to try to comfort her. She was forced, they said, so it was not her fault. It is the mind that sins, not the body, and where there was no intention, there is no guilt. Lucretia answered: 'You may decide what *he* deserves. I absolve myself of wrongdoing, but I do not free myself from punishment; and hereafter no unchaste woman shall live through my example.'

Then she stabbed herself through the heart with a knife which she had hidden in her dress. Her kinsfolk collapsed in grief, but Brutus seized the dripping knife and swore to destroy the Tarquins and abolish the monarchy. Brutus had survived under the rule of Tarquin the Proud (and so, it is said, obtained his 'brutish' *cognomen*) by pretending to be stupid and harmless; now he threw off the pretence. With Collatinus and Lucretius he took Lucretia's body to the Forum and there made a speech inflaming the people against the Tarquins. The result was revolution, and the beginning of the Roman Republic.

Lucretia: the later life of a legend

The story has exercised a fascination on artists and writers for two thousand years, from Ovid, who, though otherwise close to Livy, emphasises the erotic aspect by elaborating on Lucretia's feelings at the moment of the rape, to the present Poet Laureate, Ted Hughes. It is the subject of one of Shakespeare's two long poems (the other is *Venus and Adonis*), which Hughes sees as religious myths, acting as templates for the construction of all Shakespeare's plays from *All's Well That Ends Well* to *The Tempest*.

Many writers, such as the English dramatists Thomas Heywood and Nathaniel Lee, the Protestant reformer Heinrich Bullinger in sixteenth-century Switzerland, and Voltaire in France, wrote plays giving greater prominence to Brutus and the overthrow of the monarchy than to the fate of Lucretia. In Shakespeare, the political dimension is barely present; he concentrates on the confused internal debates of Tarquin and, especially, Lucretia, complicated by the addition of Christian ideas of sin and guilt. Ronald Duncan, the librettist for Benjamin Britten's opera *The Rape of Lucrece* (1947) introduces Christian commentators framing the action. Neither, however, tackles the problem raised, but not resolved, in Livy. Why did Lucretia have to die at all?

The apparent answer in Lucretia's final words ('hereafter no unchaste woman shall live through the example of Lucretia') is no answer at all. If Lucretia was, as her menfolk insist, innocent, why should she be regarded as setting a precedent for voluntary unchastity?

Saint Augustine stated the problem clearly. Most early Christian writers had no difficulty with the idea that loss of life was preferable even to involuntary loss of chastity. For Saint Augustine, however, the question of mental guilt or innocence was highly relevant; he refused to condemn the decision of the nuns who had chosen not to commit suicide after their rape by the Goths who sacked Rome in AD 410. He discusses Lucretia's story at length in *The City of God*, and reaches a dilemma. If Lucretia's mind consented to the rape, she was adulterous, and her death was the execution of justice; if her mind was innocent, then her death was suicide and sinful. 'If she was made an adulteress, why is she praised? If she was chaste, why was she killed?'

Rape and politics

The answer lies, from a Roman point of view, not in debate about Lucretia's guilt or innocence, but in the political aspect of the story. For the Romans, Lucretia's rape and death, like the peril and death of Verginia, are incidents within larger, political, narratives which are about the world of men.

For Livy and his contemporaries the stories had a special relevance; they saw the uncontrolled passions and desires of men who put themselves before the state as both the symptoms and the causes of the troubles of the late Republic, which ended in the collapse of what they thought of as democratic government. These had to be brought back under control; part of the programme of Augustus for mending the torn fabric of Roman society was the introduction of new and severe laws which made adultery a criminal offence, carrying severe penalties. That was the sort of lesson to be drawn from the tyrannical behaviour of Appius, and of Tarquinius and his son, and its consequences.

The women Lucretia and Verginia were the triggers for the lust of the tyrannical males Tarquin and Appius. Assault on them violated the autonomous control exercised by a husband or father within his own family, and set a bad precedent. (This was a principle recognised also in the Roman law of damages; insult or injury to a woman, or injury to a slave, was treated as damaging to the father, husband or owner.) The deaths of Lucretia, who is now 'damaged goods', and of Verginia, who seems about to be made so by force, reject any notion that such assaults may ever be regarded as tolerable, and so they preserve order and mutual respect among Roman men. The public parade of the corpses also provides the necessary provocation for the rest of the men of the community to unite against the tyrant who threatens their liberties.

Some gods old and new

As we have seen the major gods in the Roman pantheon were assimilated to or equated with the great Olympian gods of the Greeks, and their genealogies and the stories told about them by Roman writers were those told about their Olympian originals. Several foreign gods were also introduced to Rome, without being given Roman equivalents. Then there were the Romans' own lesser gods, honoured by the Romans, privately and also publicly, with shrines, offerings and rituals, but with few stories told about them, and sometimes not even any clear idea of their nature and identity.

To run through even the names of all the Roman gods would be tedious, but an example will give some idea of how little the Romans themselves could tell about them.

A forgotten god: who was Vediovis?

Vediovis (also sometimes called Veiovis or Vedius) had three festivals marked in the Roman calendar, on 1 January, 7 March and 21 May, and two temples at Rome. The first two festivals are the anniversaries, respectively, of the dedication in 194 and 192 BC of the two temples. There had been an earlier temple on the Capitol site; votive deposits from the seventh century BC have been found. Varro said that the Sabine king Titus Tatius introduced Vediovis to Rome; Ovid had the idea that the temple was in the place where Romulus set up his sanctuary. Livy thought both temples were dedicated to Jupiter.

Who was Vediovis and where did his name originate? Ovid says confidently: 'He is Jupiter when young [*iuvenis*]'. Beside his statue was an image of a she-goat; when Jupiter was an infant, the nymphs on Crete fed him with goat's milk. As for the name, 'Spelt [a kind of grain] that has not grown properly countrymen call *vegrandia*, and anything little they call *vesca*. So if that is the meaning, then may I not suspect that Vediovis is little Jove?'

In the second century AD a lawyer called Aulus Gellius published his *Noctes Atticae*, twenty volumes of little essays on a variety of topics (nowadays, he might have had a regular column on the features page of *The Times*). He tried hard to explain Vediovis. Jove and Diovis, he said, were given their names from helping (*iuvando*), and the prefix *ve-* sometimes negatived a word, so Vediovis was 'Anti-Jove', a god who did harm. Alternatively, because the statue in the shrine on the Capitol held arrows, obviously meant to do harm, many said that Vediovis was Apollo. Clearly, Gellius knew no more than anyone else.

Relief from a sarcophagus showing images of the Dioscuri and Jupiter being carried in a covered wagon, probably in a religious procession.

A few of the 'immigrant' gods have stories attached to them, usually in connection with the introduction of their worship to Rome. Here are two examples.

The Dioscuri

According to the Greeks, 'Zeus's boys' (*Dios kouroi*), Castor and Polydeuces (Pollux to the Romans), who were specially honoured at Sparta, were the brothers of Helen of Troy. Their mother was a mortal woman, Leda. Zeus, who disguised himself as a swan to seduce her, was the father of Pollux, but his twin Castor was the son of Leda's husband Tyndareus, and was mortal. However, since Pollux refused the immortality to which his parentage entitled him unless Castor could share it, Zeus allowed a compromise, by which they spent alternate days in the underworld and up above. They protected mariners at sea (and are often shown with stars on their caps), and rode on white horses.

In 499 or 496 BC the Romans fought a great battle at Lake Regillus, near Tusculum, and defeated the Latins. During the battle, two young men riding white horses appeared on the Roman side. Immediately after the fighting, they appeared again in the Roman Forum, their horses bathed in sweat, and announced the Roman victory. They watered their horses in a pool sacred to the nymph Juturna (Virgil made her Turnus' sister), then vanished. Manifestation in battle was something the Dioscuri did; the Greeks knew of one or two instances in their own history.

More than three hundred years after Lake Regillus, in 168 BC, a man called Publius Vatinius was heading for Rome late one night when two handsome young men on white horses appeared to him and announced that the Roman commander Lucius Aemilius Paullus had just defeated Perseus, king of Macedon. He reported this to the Senate, but they thought that he was playing a practical joke, and imprisoned him for contempt of their dignity. Eventually a dispatch arrived from Paullus, announcing his victory at the battle of Pydna, and Vatinius was set free and given some land as a reward. The divine visitors were said to have watered their horses at the sacred pool on that occasion too; at any rate, the adjacent temple was unaccountably open.

This temple was in fact dedicated only to Castor (it had been vowed by the Roman commander during the battle of Lake Regillus). The Romans made more of Castor, the horseman, than Pollux, the boxer; sometimes they even spoke of them as 'the Castores'. In 304 BC an annual cavalry parade was instituted in Rome on 15 July, their festival; in census years (every five years or so) it was combined with a review of membership of the state cavalry. This parade eventually lapsed, but Augustus revived it, and celebrated it with great splendour. The state cavalry paraded, sometimes to the number of five thousand, in formal robes, crowned with laurel and wearing all their military decorations, starting at Mars' temple outside the city boundary and ending at the Forum.

The Romans had in fact taken over two gods who were already established among the Latins. A bronze plaque from Lavinium, dating to the sixth or fifth century BC, has a dedication apparently transliterated from Greek, 'To the *kouroi* Castor and Pollux.' There was a spring of Juturna at Lavinium and a temple of the Dioscuri nearby at Ardea. Some identified them with the Great Gods, the Di Penates ('household protectors'), originally brought from Samothrace to Troy, and thence to Italy by Aeneas.

When Ascanius was building Alba Longa, a strange thing happened. A special temple was built in Alba for the images of the two gods, and they were brought from Lavinium to their new home. During the night, however, they disappeared, although the temple doors were shut fast, and no damage was found either to the roof or to the walls of the enclosure. In due course they were found, standing on their old pedestals in Lavinium. They were brought back to Alba, with prayers and special propitiatory sacrifices, but the same thing happened again. In the end it was decided to let them stay in Lavinium and to send some men back there from Alba to take care of them. In historical times Roman magistrates went every year to Lavinium, to sacrifice to the Penates and to Vesta; it was at Rome itself, however, in the temple of Vesta, or so they believed, that the original Penates were now kept, along with the Palladium, a sacred image of Pallas Athena, brought by Aeneas himself from Troy, which was the Luck of the Roman People.

Castor and Pollux and another immigrant, Hercules, became literally household names among the Romans, who used their names in mild oaths – but, curiously, in a gender-specific way. Women, but not usually men, said *mecastor*; both men and women said *edepol*, but women were not supposed to say *mehercle* – perhaps because they were not allowed to share in the food sacrificed to Hercules at the Ara Maxima ('greatest altar').

Hercules and Cacus

The Ara Maxima stood in the Forum Boarium (Cattle Market) at Rome and was the centre for a special cult of Hercules. It is uncertain whether he became popular with merchants because of this location, or whether, as some think, he was there because he was introduced to Rome by Phoenician traders, being identified with their god Melkart, and already worshipped by merchants because of his own journeyings, and his reputation as 'the warder-off of ills'. At any rate, the Romans had their own story to account for the cult. Their Hercules has some of the personal qualities of his Greek original. He is not only a saviour of mankind from terrible monsters, but, it is hinted, a muscleman, rather greedy and not too bright, with a quick temper.

On his return from the far West after his tenth Labour, Hercules came to the Tiber, driving the cattle which he had taken from the three-bodied monster Geryon. He paused to rest in a grassy meadow by the river. Heavy with food and drink, he dropped off to sleep, and a local shepherd, a strong, fierce man called Cacus, stole the finest of the cattle. To confuse the trail, he dragged them away backwards by their tails and hid them in a cave. Hercules was totally baffled, seeing only tracks leading away from the cave, and began to drive off the rest of the herd. Some of them began to low, and were answered by those in the cave. The trick was exposed; Hercules went after Cacus and struck him dead with his club.

That was the 'straight' story, as told by Livy. In the *Aeneid* Virgil turned the tale into a lurid supernatural fantasy, which reads almost like the screenplay for the special effects department of a film studio. Virgil's Cacus was no human being, but a hideous, fire-breathing man-monster, offspring of Vulcan, who lived in a cavern. He ate human flesh. The ground around his cave on the Aventine hill stank with freshly-shed blood, and around the entrance hung rotting human heads. He was a coward; when Hercules came after him, he turned and fled into his cave, blocking the entrance by cutting a chain and dropping a huge rock, originally installed by his father Vulcan, so that it jammed immovably between the doorposts. Hercules strained, but could not shift it, nor could he find another entrance. Finally he climbed higher up the hill and pulled up by its roots the great rock that formed the roof of the cave; thunder crashed, the earth shook and the river ran backward. Daylight poured into the foul den, showing Cacus cowering in a corner, howling. Hercules hurled down on him every missile he could lay his hands on, but Cacus spewed out great billows of thick black smoke, shot with flames, and so hid himself. Hercules leaped down into the thick of the smoke and fire, laid hold of Cacus and, literally, tied him in a knot, then strangled him until his eyes started from his head. He burst open the entrance, and hauled out the corpse.

After the death of Cacus, the local people, led by Evander, in gratitude to Hercules for ridding them of their oppressor, instituted a ritual in his honour. Every year on 12 August oxen were sacrificed and there was a feast. The cult was

A cavalry procession, led by musicians towards a shrine where sacrifice is being made: a relief from a cinerary urn (c. 100 BC).

administered by two Roman families, the Potitii and the Pinarii. The Pinarii arrived late for the first feast, and missed their share of the entrails; and so they were never ever served with that portion of the sacrifice. In 312 BC the cult was taken over by the state (Livy hints at some underhand doings). The Appius Claudius (later known as 'the Blind') who was censor in that year authorised the Potitii to instruct public slaves in the ritual, in order to hand it over to them. Within a year all the Potitii were dead, and their clan and name extinct, and a few years later Claudius went blind. (The Potitii in fact are not otherwise heard of in history, though some Pinarii survived into later times.)

The ritual had some peculiar features. No woman was allowed to share in the sacrificial meat. No other gods must be invoked. Dogs were excluded from the precinct. Plutarch had his ideas about the reasons. Other gods were not mentioned, because Hercules was merely a demigod. Hercules could not abide dogs, because of all the trouble he had been given by Cerberus, the three-headed dog guarding Hell, and because the battle in which his twin brother was killed arose because of a quarrel about a dog. Women were excluded because Carmenta (see p. 96) arrived late.

Propertius, in mock-epic style, gives a different explanation. Killing Cacus was thirsty work, and when Hercules asked to be allowed to drink at a spring in a shrine sacred to the Good Goddess (whose rites were secret and reserved to women), the priestess refused him entrance. So Hercules smashed down the door and had his drink. Then he got his own back; he told the priestess that he was setting up an altar of his own, as a thank-offering for recovering his cattle, but no women would be allowed to join in *his* rites.

Cacus and Cacu

There was another version of the story, found in Roman authors at least as early as the second century BC. The cattle belonged to a Greek shepherd called Recaranus, or Garanus, who was called 'a Hercules' because of his size and strength. His cattle were stolen by Cacus, who was Evander's slave. Evander found out, returned the cattle, and handed Cacus over for punishment.

Is this just a rationalised version of the Hercules story or, as some think, a separate, Italian story which has blended with it? To add to the confusion, 'Recaranus' and 'Garanus' both look like garbled forms of Geryon – but Hercules, not Cacus the slave, stole his cattle. Anyway, Cacus, it has been pointed out, is the Greek word for 'bad' (*kakos*), and Evander means, literally 'Goodman'. Calling the thief Cacus also helped the Romans to explain the name of a flight of steps leading up from the Forum Boarium to the Palatine.

However, that does not exhaust the stories about Cacus. Gnaeus Gellius, a Roman annalist (second century BC), said Cacus inhabited a place near the Tiber. King Marsyas had sent him as an envoy, accompanied by Megales the Phrygian, to King Tarchon the Etruscan, who imprisoned him. He escaped and went back where he had come from. Then he returned with reinforcements and seized the area around Vulturnus and Campania. When he dared to attempt to seize also those places which had been ceded to the Arcadians (i.e. Evander and his people), he was killed by Hercules, who happened to be there. Megales went to the Sabines and taught them the art of augury.

King Tarchon, who was the son or grandson of Hercules, was the founder of Etruscan Tarquinii, and knew the art of divination. One day a peasant was ploughing at Tarquinii, when out of the furrow emerged a being with grey hair and the face of a child. His name was Tages, and he proceeded to reveal to Tarchon and to the leaders of all the other Etruscan cities the art of divination from birds and from the entrails of animals. Marsyas, in Greek myth, was a satyr, and wind instrumentalist, who challenged Apollo (who played the harp) to a musical contest and lost; he was flayed for his pains. Gellius calls him a king of the Lydians, who founded a city on Lake Fucinus. There was an ancient belief that the Etruscans had come to Italy from Lydia.

This story is set in the mythological period before the foundation of Rome, but it might just contain the germ of an account of historical relations between Etruscan rulers in different parts of Italy in the sixth century BC; before then, Etruscans had spread both north and south, establishing colonies in northern Italy and as far south as Campania.

'Cacu' is well documented in Etruscan iconography. He appears, with a companion 'Artile', on a fourth-century BC bronze mirror, being ambushed by two warriors, and as their prisoner in relief carvings on no fewer than eight alabaster funerary urns, from the second century BC. This Cacus is no monster, nor even a hulking shepherd, but a handsome young man, evidently a seer and diviner. He is playing a lyre and Artile, perhaps his assistant, holds a diptych with some writing. The men ambushing him – perhaps hoping to benefit from the inside knowledge which his skills can provide – are no other than Caelius and Aulus Vibenna, whom we have already met (see p. 116). History and myth are mingling again.

How the Etruscan Cacu the seer was gradually metamorphosed into the Roman Cacus the monster – and the particular reasons why the Romans at various periods wanted to change the angle of the stories – has been the object of much modern discussion and speculation. This much appears clear: once more, we seem to have caught the Romans 'editing out' an alternative, Etruscan, history of central Italy.

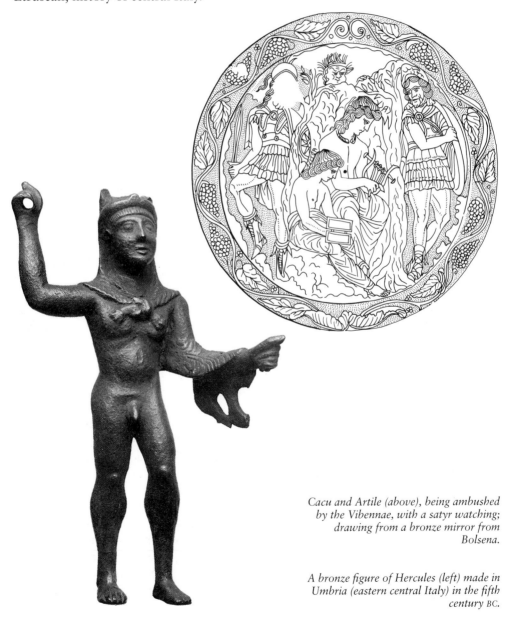

Cacu and Artile (above), being ambushed by the Vibennae, with a satyr watching; drawing from a bronze mirror from Bolsena.

A bronze figure of Hercules (left) made in Umbria (eastern central Italy) in the fifth century BC.

145

*A Lar (right), holding a
drinking-horn and a libation dish.*

*A handle of a silver patera (below):
beneath a figure of Fortune is a
country shrine, and at the foot a
woman sacrificing at an altar.*

Cults and festivals

The Romans celebrated many religious cults, both privately and publicly. In the country, farmers sacrificed to the appropriate gods before each job of work. The elder Cato, in the early second century BC, gives details in his farming manual of a number of their rituals; two hundred years later, when a romantic poet, Albius Tibullus, fantasises about living a rural idyll with his mistress playing the farmer's wife, he imagines her making little offerings of grapes or corn-ears, or libations of wine. Roman houses had a shrine at which daily offerings were made before figures of the Genius (protecting spirit) of the head of household, and of the Penates (gods of the store-cupboard), and the Lares. There were also public Lares (Lares Compitales) in the countryside and in towns, guarding crossroads where land-holdings or town districts adjoined. Their festivals were the occasion for jolly neighbourhood parties, and the emperor Augustus exploited their community function by linking their worship to that of the Genius of the emperor. Neither public Lares nor those of the household have individual names or histories.

Dozens of public religious occasions are listed in the Roman calendar, though we have details about what happened on only a few. Here are three of the most colourful.

Anna Perenna: a Roman Hogmanay

The Ides of March (15th), the day when Julius Caesar was assassinated in 44 BC, was the festival of Anna Perenna. Until about 153 BC the year began on 1 March, so the Ides fell about the time of the first full moon of the new year. On the previous day, the 14th, according to a late Roman writer, a man dressed in skins was beaten with rods and chased out of the city (exactly the same thing used to be done, on New Year's Eve, in farms on the island of Lewis).

The name Anna Perenna suggests that she was a personification of the yearly cycle; she was envisaged as an old woman. Ovid, typically, offers a number of explanations. One, perhaps his own invention, is that she was Dido's sister. After Dido's death, Carthage was invaded by local people and Anna fled by boat, arriving eventually in Latium. Aeneas met her and brought her to his palace; but his wife Lavinia was jealous and plotted her death. Warned by Dido in a dream, Anna fled and was carried off by the river Numicus. Those searching for her heard a voice from the water, saying that she was now a nymph. 'In an ever-flowing river (*amne perenne*) I hide, and Anna Perenna I am called.'

One of the Penates, with a cornucopia and a libation dish.

Wine, women and dance at a festival: a painting from a tomb in Rome.

But Ovid thinks more likely the story that, during the first Secession of the Plebs, the people who had gone to the Sacred Mount began to run out of food. There was an old woman called Anna, born outside the city at Bovillae, who was poor but industrious. With her trembling old hands she baked loaves of country bread, and every morning she brought them, piping hot, and distributed them among the people. Later they set up a statue of her, in gratitude.

Her festival was held at the first milestone along the Via Flaminia, to the north of Rome. People brought picnics and sat on the grass. Some brought tents, others built shelters of branches of reeds. They drank wine, praying for as many years as they drank cups – so, naturally, they tried to drink as many as possible. Then they would begin to sing popular songs, picked up in the theatres, and to dance. Eventually, they reeled off home, all drunk together.

Ovid adds that girls chanted ribald verses, and he explains why: they commemorated a trick played by Anna. Just after she became a goddess, Mars came to her one day for help. He had fallen in love, he said, with Minerva, and wanted to marry her (other authors say it was a goddess called Nerio who became Mars' wife). Anna kept fobbing him off, but eventually said that Minerva had agreed. Mars went home and got the bridal chamber ready, and the bride was escorted to him, with a veil on her face – but turned out to be Anna.

Nonae Caprotinae: the Feast of Slave-Women

This was held on the Nones (7th) of July, and was also a picnic day. The story about its origin is almost the Rape of the Sabines turned inside out.

Soon after 390 BC Roman territory was attacked by the Latins. They sent to Rome demanding that the Romans give them free-born virgins for marriage. The Romans were just recovering from the sack of the city by the Gauls, and wanted to avoid war so were reluctant to refuse, but they were worried that the 'brides' were really intended only as hostages. A slave girl called Tutula or, some say, Philotis, told the magistrates what to do. They picked out the prettiest and most aristocratic-looking slave women, dressed them like free-born brides, complete with gold jewellery, and sent them with Tutula (or Philotis) to the Latin camp near the city.

149

A statue of Mars from Britain, made by Gaulish or British craftsmen, probably after an Italian original.

Pretending it was a festival day for Romans, the slave women got the Latins drunk, and during the night they took away their swords, while Tutula sent the magistrates the secret signal on which they had agreed. She climbed a tall wild fig-tree and held up a lighted torch, spreading cloths behind it to conceal the light from the Latins. The magistrates urgently called out the soldiers, who tumbled out of the city and, not knowing what was going on, shouted each others' names in their confusion. They stormed the camp of the Latins while they were still asleep, and killed most of them.

All this, says Plutarch, was commemorated in the festival. Crowds of slave girls, gaily dressed (probably in their mistresses' clothes), ran out of the city gate, shouting common male personal names, like 'Gaius', 'Marcus', 'Lucius' and so on. They joked with all the men they met. Then they had playful fights with each other – a mock battle. After that, they sat and feasted under shelters made from fig-tree branches.

Varro says that the Nones were called *Caprotinae* because women in Latium sacrificed on that day to Juno Caprotina under a wild fig-tree (*caprificus*), offering her fig-juice instead of milk, and using a stick from the tree in the ritual (perhaps to hit each other in the mock fighting), and a later author adds that both slave women and free took part. The festival may have been a sort of female version of the Saturnalia in December, when masters waited on their slaves – useful as a safety valve, in maintaining social order. During the early Empire, masters left that part of the celebrations to their children; probably the mistresses stopped taking part in the Caprotine Nones as well.

The religious purpose for the festival may have been to promote fertility, in women as well as agriculture (the agricultural writer Columella recommended pollinating fig-trees in July). In the Latin town of Lanuvium at the beginning of February there was a festival of Juno Sospita ('Protectress'), who is shown wearing the skin of a goat (*caper* or *capra* according to gender) on her head. Young girls, blindfolded, entered her sacred grove with offerings of barley cakes for a sacred snake. If it ate the cakes, the girls were proved to be virgins, and the year would be fertile.

Goat or fig-tree? Plutarch has another story. There was a Roman festival called *Poplifugia* (flight of the people). No one knew what it was supposed to be commemorating; one idea was that it originated at the disappearance of Romulus, which happened near a place called Goat's Marsh. 'They go out of the city and sacrifice at the Goat's Marsh (for *capra* is their word for she-goat); and as they go out to the sacrifice they shout out native [i.e. Roman] names, like Marcus, Lucius, Gaius, imitating the way in which, on the day when Romulus vanished, they shouted to each other in alarm and confusion.' Unfortunately, Plutarch the Greek is confused, thinking that the Poplifugia (which was on 5 July) and the Nonae Caprotinae fell on the same day. The Nones in the Roman calendar were on the fifth day of the month *except* in March, May, July and October, when they were on the seventh.

Lupercalia: beating the bounds?

The festival of the Lupercalia on 15 February is easier to describe than to explain. Two colleges of priests took part, the Luperci Quintilii and Fabii; a third, the Julii, named after Julius Caesar, was instituted in 45 BC but did not continue long after his death.

Proceedings started at the Lupercal cave at the south-west corner of the Palatine hill. Animals were sacrificed, goats and, unusually, a dog, and cakes prepared by the Vestal Virgins with flour made from the first ears of the previous year's harvest. The blood on the blade of the sacrificial knife was smeared on the foreheads of two of the Luperci, and wiped off with a piece of wool soaked in milk; then the young men had to laugh. The goatskins were cut into strips. Some of them the young men girt round themselves, then, naked except for these girdles, the teams ran in different directions, originally all around the Palatine hill (later this seems to have been altered to a partial circuit, and a sprint up and down the Sacred Way in the Forum) and back to the Lupercal. On the way they struck at bystanders, especially women, with goatskin thongs.

By Augustus' time, the fun may have been getting slightly out of hand. Livy talked of the original celebrants' playful and frolicsome antics – which Valerius Maximus later took to mean that they had too much to drink. Augustus ordered that only youths old enough to have a beard were to be allowed to run. Nevertheless, the festival survived until AD 494 when Pope Gelasius I claimed it for the Church, as the Feast of Purification of the Virgin Mary.

The sacrificed dog was a puzzle. Plutarch, as usual full of ideas, had four suggestions: first, the Greeks used dogs as purificatory sacrifices, and also, in expiation, to Hecate, goddess of the underworld; second, Lupercalia was associated with wolves, and dogs were wolves' enemies; third, the Luperci were harassed by barking dogs as they ran; fourth, Pan approved of dogs, who guarded the flocks.

The antiquarian Varro interpreted the striking with thongs as a purification rite, but Ovid preferred what was probably the popular view, that it encouraged fertility; Plutarch gives both explanations. Shakespeare, in his *Julius Caesar*, picks up this detail. At the Lupercalia he has Caesar instruct his childless wife to stand in Mark Antony's way, to be struck. The most famous celebration of the festival was that of 44 BC, when Mark Antony, head of the Julian Luperci, publicly offered Julius Caesar a royal crown, which he refused three times. The occasion was probably chosen because of the crowds of spectators that gathered. This stage-managed demonstration that he had no regal ambitions did Caesar no good; one month later, he was assassinated.

Evander was supposed to have instituted a festival in honour of Pan Lycaeus, who was identified with the woodland god Faunus or with 'Inuus'. As far as aetiological explanations were wanted, the Romans believed that the Lupercalia in some way celebrated the origin of Rome (it was not the city's 'official birthday' – that came later, on 21 April). The route of the running was thought by some to be the boundary of the original Rome established by Romulus around the Palatine, starting and ending at his old nursery, the wolf's lair. The two teams were associated with Romulus and Remus. Ovid explains that once, when they were shepherd youths, while the goats sacrificed to Faunus were being cooked, a warning came that robbers were stealing the cattle. Romulus and Remus, each with a group of young men, chased off after them in different directions. Remus and his Fabii got back first with the rescued cattle, and ate up all the feast. In Christian times the race up and down the Sacred Way was ingeniously reinterpreted as representing sinful mankind running up and down hill to escape the Flood.

Such explanations, however, left a lot of details unaccounted for. Why the smearing with blood, the milk-soaked wool, and the laugh? Why the goatskin girdles and thongs? According to Plutarch, a Greek poet in the first century BC said that the blood commemorated the danger in which Amulius had placed the infants, and the milk their nourishment by the wolf. The goatskin thongs were sometimes explained as part of a purification rite (Varro, Plutarch).

A coin of 65 BC. (obverse):
Juno Sospita in a goatskin
headdress; (reverse) a woman
offering something to an
upraised serpent.

Ovid, interestingly, associates them with Juno, both as a goddess of fertility in women, and one who looks after women in childbirth, Juno Lucina, who had a temple on the Esquiline (Juno Sospita, the one with the goatskin cloak, was also worshipped at Rome, but elsewhere). Brides who want to be mothers, Ovid says, should allow themselves to be struck at the Lupercalia. Once upon a time, when Romulus was king, the birth-rate was disastrously low. 'What good did it do me,' cried Romulus, 'to have carried off the Sabine women?' There was a grove on the Esquiline, sacred to Juno. The women and their husbands went there and prayed to the goddess. Then the tops of the trees began to toss, and the voice of the goddess came from the grove: 'Let the sacred he-goat go in to [*inito* – which perhaps explains the name Inuus] Italian matrons.' The people were dumbstruck, not understanding. Then an augur, an Etruscan exile (but his name is long forgotten) killed a goat, and told the women to offer themselves to be struck with the hide, cut in strips. In the tenth month, the Romans became parents.

With the Lupercalia, one suspects, we have an example of a phenomenon dear to the hearts of students of mythology, a festival with a multiplicity of functions, which may have accumulated around one date in the calendar as a result of a long historical development. February (whose name Romans connected with purification) was the last month of the old year, a month of cleansings, purifications and preparation for new beginnings. Juno Sospita's day was the first. From the 13th to the 21st was the festival of the dead (*Parentalia*), when all temples were closed and family tombs were visited, followed on the 22nd by Loving Family day (*Caristia*). On the 27th the city bounds were walked in procession and there was a sacrifice. In March the new year began, and the new campaigning year for Rome's warriors.

The Lupercalia is integrated into the sequence of the Roman religious year. It was a festival of purification for the community, but also, it has recently been suggested, it functioned both as a fertility ritual for women and a rite of passage for young men, by symbolic re-enactment of birth and the aftermath, up to and including the time when babies, once out of the post-natal danger period, start to respond interactively – which would account for the blood, the milk, the laugh, and the association with the infant Romulus and Remus.

That may be so. For the Romans, it was an interesting day's fun, at a dreary time of year, and they had their own stories to account for it.

153

Conclusion

Roman myths and legends served a variety of purposes, and so their details were not sacrosanct; they were changed, embellished and adapted at need. Some, as we have just seen, were stories to explain the rituals of festivals or to 'domesticate' foreign gods introduced to Rome. Others celebrated the patriotic and moral values cherished, at least as ideals, as being particularly Roman, while often at the same time offering explanations for historical events, or staking a noble family's claim to a prominent place in Rome's tradition. Central, and most important, were the legends about Rome's origins and early growth. These asserted Rome's claim to have been, from the first, outstanding and undefeated among the peoples of Italy (despite the alternative versions – fairly successfully suppressed – of other peoples), whom they were destined to rule. They also claimed for the Romans a share in the cultural birthright of the Greek civilisation they had conquered. More than all this, and despite their adaptation to bolster the power of the ruler under the imperial régime, they depicted Rome itself and its people as marked out by the gods to be the destined rulers of the whole world.

John 'Warwick' Smith, View of Rome. *Watercolour, 1780. In the centre is the Colosseum, with the Arch of Constantine on the left.*

Suggestions for further reading

There was room above to give only a limited number of the legends familiar to the Romans, and those for the most part briefly. It is possible to enjoy the more elaborate, and often vivid, accounts of Greek and Roman writers through English translations. Many of the works mentioned in the text are available in Penguin Classics, whose translations, several produced within the last few years, are lively and readable. Almost all the authors cited are published in the Loeb Classical Library; the translations used in that series were often written some time ago, and appear rather old-fashioned in consequence, but they have the added advantage, for those with some knowledge of Latin or Greek, of having a parallel text in the original language.

There are a number of modern books which can enhance appreciation and understanding of Roman legends and their nature. A collection of essays on a variety of topics, including several of the legends told in the present book, is contained in *Roman Myth and Mythology* (London, 1987) by J. N. Bremmer and N. M. Horsfall, two contrasting scholars, one of whom is mainly concerned with analysing the stories to trace the development of the traditions, the other with such matters as comparative mythology, and the relation between myth and ritual. H. H. Scullard, *Festivals and Ceremonies of the Roman Republic* (London, 1981) proceeds day by day through the religious calendar of a Roman year, with descriptions of many festivals and ceremonies, and the stories told to account for them.

For the relationship between myth and history, Michael Grant, *Roman Myths* (London, original publication 1971, recently reprinted) is a readable account of the ways in which these stories were manipulated or, in some cases, invented, in successive periods of Roman history to fulfil the purposes of members of the governing élite. T. P. Wiseman, *Clio's Cosmetics* (Leicester, 1979) discusses the concept of history among Roman historical writers, particularly in the first century BC, and their view of what we would call legend. For what is now thought to be known about the actual history of early Rome, see T. J. Cornell, *The Beginnings of Rome* (London, 1995). The theory that Romulus' twin was an invention of the late fourth century BC is argued in detail in T. P. Wiseman, *Remus* (Cambridge, 1995).

The use of traditional myth in propaganda, and creation of a new personal myth by Julius Caesar, is discussed in *Divus Julius* (Oxford, 1971), by S. Weinstock. Study of similar propaganda for Rome's first emperor, Augustus, has produced much important recent work, of which readers are likely to find most interesting and accessible the discussion of the use of visual means of communication in P. Zanker, *The Power of Images in the Age of Augustus*, translated by A. Shapiro (Ann Arbor, Michigan, 1988); see also Susan Walker and Andrew Burnett, *The Image of Augustus* (London, 1981). The use of legends in visual propaganda (this time mainly under the Republic), and especially in coins, is also the subject of J. DeRose Evans: *The Art of Persuasion: political propaganda from Aeneas to Brutus* (Princeton, 1992).

Special mention should be made of I. Donaldson, *The Rapes of Lucretia: a Myth and its Transformations* (Oxford, 1982). The ideas of the Poet Laureate, Ted Hughes, on Shakespeare's version are to be found in his *Shakespeare and the Goddess of Complete Being* (London, 1992).

Norse
Myths

R. I. PAGE

To Anne-Margrethe Hustad

Picture credits

p. 163 Bergen Museum*; pp. 199, 218 (right):* Professor R. Cramp, University of Durham; *p. 229:* Bernt A. Lundberg, Statens Historiska Museum, Stockholm; *p. 165 (bottom)*: The Manx Museum and National Trust, Douglas; *pp. 228 (all), 232:* Dr Sue Margeson, Castle Museum, Norwich; *pp. 162 (right), 165 (top), 166:* Nationalmuseet, Copenhagen; *p. 167:* National Museum of Iceland, Reykjavik; *p. 218 (left):* Oldsaksamlingen, Universiteti Oslo; *p. 205 (left)*: Royal Commission on the Historical Monuments of England; *pp. 162 (left), 173 (right), 175, 183:* Statens Historiska Museum, Stockholm; *p. 173 (left)*: Uppsala University Library.

Contents

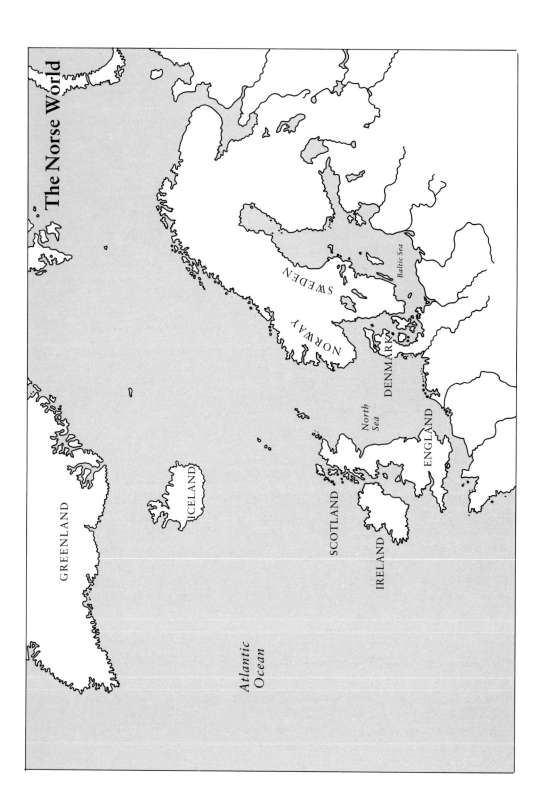

Introduction

A myth, says the *Oxford English Dictionary* profoundly, is 'a purely fictitious narrative usually involving supernatural persons, actions, or events, and embodying some popular idea concerning natural or historical phenomena'; it adds more cheerfully that the word is often used vaguely 'to include any narrative having fictitious elements'. In this book I use 'myth' neither as loosely as in the second of these definitions nor as rigorously as in the first. Certainly most of the tales retold here deal with supernatural persons and actions, and so provide a guide to pagan Norse thinking as reported by medieval writers. But not all the stories are purely fictitious. Some of those in the final chapter, treating of battle, murder and sudden death in a heroic society, have an origin in historical event, though distant. However, most chapters contain myths of the gods and goddesses of pagan Viking Scandinavia. Some of these clearly embody ideas about natural phenomena (and hence, I suppose, the reason for their creation); these are likely to appeal to readers engaged in modern cults of mysticism. Other stories may also have done this, but they are opaque, and I, not being an anthropologist or folklorist, can only guess at what the ideas were. Others again look to us now like tales told for pleasure, and that is presumably what most modern readers will take them as.

From the records that survive it is clear that the Norsemen had many gods and goddesses. Some of them are hardly known to us, as Ull, splendid archer, ski-champion and fighter, and Var, the goddess 'who takes note of oaths and specific agreements made between men and women ... and wreaks vengeance on people who break them'. Such deities are little more than names to modern readers, though in their day they, like their fellow-gods, may have had myths told of them. Inevitably, however, the body of this book records the myths of the great gods and goddesses of Scandinavia, though we should always keep in mind that what survives may be only a small, and is certainly a random, sample of what once existed.

Best known are the gods of the race of Aesir, one of the two main groups of gods in the Norse pantheon. Leading them is **Odin**, universal father, god of poetic inspiration, of mystery and magic, patron of warriors. He was married to **Frigg**, goddess who knows the fates of all men. Other gods are often referred to as Odin's children. First is **Thor**, a warrior god, defender of the Aesir against their natural enemies, the giants. He married **Sif** about whom little is known save that her hair was of gold. Other sons of Odin

A runic memorial stone from Hanning, Denmark, whose inscription ends (top left) with a hammer symbol which some have seen as a reference to Thor, although its late date, 12th century, could make it a tradesman's sign.

A one-eyed figure (left), identified as Odin on the ground that Odin is the only important one-eyed figure in Scandinavian mythology. He is said to have given an eye in return for understanding.

are **Bragi,** god of eloquence and poetry, married to the important goddess **Idunn** who kept the apples of eternal youth; and the handsome but unfortunate **Baldr,** married to **Nanna,** and who was killed by accident by the blind god **Hod.** Also defined as Odin's son is **Tyr,** the brave and wise god of war who lost his hand in helping to fetter the dread wolf Fenrir. A more mysterious figure is **Heimdall,** watchman and herald of the final battle that ends the life of the gods in this world. He is the foe of **Loki,** a baffling figure, part god and part demon, who was son of a giant Farbauti, and married to the devoted Sigyn. However, he also had issue by a giantess Angrboda, and they turned out to be sinister indeed: the wolf Fenrir, the World Serpent Iormun-gand and the supernatural creature who presided over the other world, Hel.

Side by side with the Aesir live a group of gods of the race of Vanir, deities of fertility and wealth. These are Niord, Freyr and Freyia. **Niord** is god of seafaring, fishing and riches. He married a giantess Skadi, but they could not agree. Niord's children are the twins **Freyr** and **Freyia**, who also mated together. Freyr married a giantess Gerd, and Freyia a character called Od. Freyr and Freyia control fertility and produce.

There are also a number of minor deities, Hoenir, Kvasir, Gefion, Vali, Vili, Ve, Vidar and so on, as well as a variety of other supernatural creatures below the rank of gods: dwarfs, elves, norns, witches, valkyries. But the gods' greatest enemies are the *iotnar* (singular *iotunn*), a word usually translated 'giants'; for these ancient, ugly, terrible and usually ill-intentioned creatures something like 'demons' or 'trolls' would be equally apposite.

In the translations in this book I have sought to be fluent rather than faithful to the original in every detail. This is particularly the case in the verse translations, where I have tried to make sense while keeping roughly to the lineation of the primary texts. There will always be some arbitrariness in rendering Old Norse names (and other words) in modern English prose, and I admit this in the present work. In the main, if I give a name or word in italics, it will be in the 'standard' Old Norse/Icelandic form. This will sometimes contain unusual letter forms, of which the most important are þ and ð which Norse uses for the various sounds that modern English represents by *th*. Otherwise, if the name is in Roman in continuous prose, it will be an adaptation of the standard form, without inflexional ending or accent and perhaps with some adaptation like d for ð: as Odin in the place of *Óðinn*. This will raise occasional problems when I quote Latinised forms, as Othinus instead of Odin, or Frothi for Frodi (*Fróði*). Occasionally I have completely anglicised a name or nickname: it seems absurd, for instance, to speak of Eirik blodox (*Eiríkr blóðøx*) rather than Eric Bloodaxe.

Miniature gold foils from Norway. Some have interpreted these scenes as Freyr and Gerd, for no compelling reason.

Where to find Norse myths

Mention the word 'Norsemen' and the English will think first of the Vikings, those enterprising and ruthless peoples who, in the three centuries from 800 to 1100, plundered, colonised, conquered, traded with, developed and sometimes even civilised countries east and west of Scandinavia. That these people had a pagan religion, and with it a pagan mythology of some complexity, is without doubt. How much of either can be recovered is less clear. The Vikings were illiterate save for their inscriptions, so they recorded little of their beliefs and still less of their myths. Any knowledge of these that we now have comes either from outside Scandinavia if within the Viking Age, or from within Scandinavia in the post-Viking era. Extra-Scandinavian material was written down by Christians unsympathetic to Viking ideas, beliefs and behaviour, and so is sparse. Later Scandinavian writings may derive from Viking sources, but it is difficult to know how precisely and accurately; and their expression is often affected by ways of thinking and writing that are common European and Christian.

Christianity established itself quite late in mainland Scandinavia. In Denmark there was a strong and authoritative move towards the new religion in the mid-tenth century. Norway was a little later, the end of the tenth and the first decades of the eleventh. Sweden was later still. The Icelanders, if their medieval historians were well informed, formally adopted Christianity about the year 1000. Viking colonists elsewhere may have become Christians earlier, though still late by Western European standards. The Norse settlers of East Anglia issued a coinage commemorating the Christian sainthood of King Edmund a couple of decades after they martyred him in 870. The colonisers of the Isle of Man were putting up memorial crosses in the tenth century; by then they were intermarrying with the native Christian Celts.

Of course, we need not assume that the advent of Christianity necessarily made radical changes in Norse practice or belief. It was quite possible, we are told, for an Irish Norseman to put his trust in both Christ and Thor. Rather than replace it, the Christian myth may have been added to, or may have penetrated Norse myth. The great eleventh-century cross in the churchyard of Gosforth, Cumbria, has its carved crucifixion scene, but also other sculptures interpreted as illustrations of Norse myths of the gods. At Andreas, Isle of Man, is a cross-slab fragment bearing, below one of the cross arms, the figure of a spear-carrying man savaged by a beast, apparently the god Odin attacked by the dread wolf Fenrir.

A soapstone mould for both the pagan and the Christian – Thor's hammer and Christ's cross could be produced.

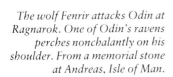

The wolf Fenrir attacks Odin at Ragnarok. One of Odin's ravens perches nonchalantly on his shoulder. From a memorial stone at Andreas, Isle of Man.

Amulet in the shape of Thor's hammer, worn as a pendant. From Rømersdal, Denmark.

For contemporary records of Viking myth, then, we go not to texts but to carvings; or to miniatures like the hammer-head amulets which occur from time to time in Viking contexts and indicate that stories of the hammer-bearing god Thor were already current; or, much less certainly, to a small group of figurines, which some have thought to be statuettes of gods with their characteristic attributes but others, more mundanely, have considered to be playing-pieces for some board game or other. If we want elaborated versions of the myths, however, we have to get them from the medieval Scandinavia of the post-Viking era, with all the problems of corruption and inaccuracy that this later provenance brings with it.

Poetic Edda

Our knowledge depends on three major sources. The first is the *Poetic Edda*, a group of loosely related texts, poems of a short or middle length. The heart of this collection fills a manuscript called the *Codex Regius*, the Royal Manuscript, so named because it was a treasure of the Royal Library at Copenhagen for centuries before it returned to its native land in 1971, following an agreement between the Danish and Icelandic governments. The *Codex Regius* is a vellum manuscript written in the second half of the thirteenth century, nearly three hundred years after Iceland's conversion to Christianity. It contains twenty-nine poems, eleven of them on mythological topics, sixteen, together with two fragments, on heroes and heroines of Germanic antiquity. There are other manuscripts preserving a few poems of a similar form and nature, while verse quotations in prose texts are evidence of yet more, now lost save for what is quoted. In effect we retain a random sample of a verse literature of unknown size, a fact that must always be in our minds when we try to draw conclusions from what survives.

Moreover, though it is comparatively easy to say where and when the *Codex Regius* was written, it is fearsomely difficult, perhaps impossible, to determine where and when the Eddic poems themselves were composed. Casually the *Codex Regius* brings together works from different dates and lands. Some of the poems may go back to the early years of the Viking Age; others may be as late as the twelfth century when Scandinavian civilisation had moved into the European Middle Ages. Some may be from Norway, others from the western settlements, perhaps from Ireland or Greenland.

The Eddic verses are more or less stanzaic, with a limited degree of metrical variation, so they present quite a homogeneous appearance. Yet the mythological poems differ a good deal in content and treatment. Some are narrative as a ballad is narrative, with a sequence of quickly changing scenes interspersed with direct speech to recount adventures of the gods. Others are question-and-answer poems, dialogues between supernatural beings serving to display mythological information. Occasionally there is a series of stanzas containing traditional wisdom or proverb attributed to one of the deities. All these reveal much of the Norse picture of their gods, but often allusively so that a listener must apply knowledge he already has to illuminate a chance reference.

An example is one of the simplest of narrative poems, *þrymskviða*, the tale of the giant-king Thrym. It opens with Thor waking in his bed and reaching for the mighty hammer that gives him power and security. It is gone, stolen. He must find it or the giants will invade the land of the gods and destroy them. His crony Loki, a deity whose qualities vary from the

A silver pendant from Iceland, with an animal-head thong hole, that may represent either Christ's cross or Thor's hammer.

cheeky and mischievous to the evil, is with him. Together they go to the home of the lovely goddess Freyia and ask for her skin of feathers so that one of them may fly over the earth in search of the hammer. Freyia gladly lends it. Loki puts on the skin and flies from Asgard (Godland) to the realm of the giants. He chances on Thrym, who boasts he has hidden the hammer and will not return it until the gods send him Freyia as his bride. Loki reports back to Thor and together they go to the home of the lovely Freyia – there is ballad-style repetition of wording here – and tell her to get a wedding dress on at once as she must go to Iotunheim (Giantland) as Thrym's bride:

> Freyia was furious, in wrath she snorted,
> The hall of the great gods shook beneath her.
> Her glittering necklace shot in pieces.
> 'Am I so mad to get a man
> That I'd drive with you to Iotunheim!'

The gods call a hasty meeting and one of them, the far-seeing Heimdall, has an inspiration. Let Thor dress up in women's clothes and drive to Iotunheim, pretending to be Freyia.

> Brawniest of gods, Thor then spoke:
> 'The gods will think that I've gone gay
> If I have to wear a wedding dress.'

The gods overcome his objections, dress him up and send him to Iotunheim with Loki disguised as his lady's maid. Thrym and the giants are, surprisingly, taken in, but Thor nearly gives the game away at the wedding feast by wolfing down and drinking up so much that Thrym is horror-struck at his bride's voracious appetite. Only Loki's quick wit saves them; he excuses 'Freyia', saying she is so infatuated with Thrym that she has not been able to touch a morsel of food for days beforehand. Thrym is eager to hurry the wedding along, and orders up the sacred hammer to bless the bride with. The moment Thor sees the hammer his heart exults. He grabs it, and flattens all the giant race. So he gets his hammer back.

The tale is wittily and broadly told. It is funny even to anyone with no previous knowledge of the Norse gods. But Freyia's wrath is funnier if you know she is the goddess of fertility and sexual love, who is notoriously 'mad to get a man'. It also helps to know something of Norse moral attitudes. Thor's horror at wearing drag is the more piquant because effeminacy in a man filled the Vikings with loathing, and Thor was aggressively tough and virile, even if not very bright. When you see the force of the jokes, you are driven to the question: what sort of poet could write such verses? We do not know their date, save that it was before the end of the thirteenth century. Could a pagan have jested like this about his gods, amused at them while relying on their support? Or is the poem the work of a mocking Christian who despised these false deities? If the latter, is this a genuine tale from Norse mythology, or is it a made-up thing, composed to throw scorn on the old faith? The debate continues.

Again, there is the case of the poem called *Hávamál*, the Chant of the High One. This is a complex work, made up of a number of individual stanza sequences which were collected together under the single heading at some early date. When is a matter of controversy. Some would have it this is a chance selection of ancient verses linked by the personality of the great god Odin, the High One himself. Others interpret it as a learned compilation and edition from perhaps the twelfth century. In either case most scholars accept that *Hávamál* incorporates matter of great antiquity, probably from the Viking Age: it tells something of the Viking world-picture.

Much of the poem is in proverbial mode, useful if rather down-to-earth advice on how to lead your life. There is talk of friendship, its obligations and benefits, of the duties of hospitality, of the importance of caution, keeping your wits about you, of poverty and its troubles, of whom you can trust and whom you can't, of the need to be well thought of, and so on – all subjects appropriate to a god of worldly wisdom. There is magical material, chants and spells, suited to a god of magic. And there is the occasional narrative sequence. Immediately after a group of wisdom stanzas addressed to an unknown Loddfafnir, immediately before a catalogue of magical practices that someone, presumably Odin, has mastered, are a couple of baffling verses:

> I mind I hung on the windswept tree
> Nine whole nights,
> Stabbed by the spear, given to Odin,
> Myself to myself.
> Of that tree no man knows
> What roots it springs from.
>
> No bread they gave me, no drink from the horn,
> Down I peered.
> I took up runes, howling I took them up,
> And back again I fell.

This is weird stuff indeed. The hearers must have understood the circumstances (though of course if this is a chance-preserved gobbet of a longer poem, the original may have given more detail), but what were they? Nowhere else in Norse literature, I think, survives any version of this myth, so we must guess at its meaning and context. It seems to represent something like a shamanistic test Odin took upon himself in order to learn esoteric magic, that of the runic letters. There are things in Norse record that match some of its details. We know that at the great temple of Uppsala, Sweden, beasts and men hung from the trees of the sacred grove, sacrifices to the gods. We know Odin was nicknamed 'God of the Hanged'. We know the spear was his special weapon. We know he had skills in runes and that this strange script was believed to give access to supernatural powers. But we have no surviving story about Odin that confirms this short and cryptic passage of *Hávamál*. Moreover, as it is related here, the tale shows disturbing similarities to the Christian myth: Christ hanging on the cross-beam, pierced by a spear, tormented by thirst, achieving the fullness of his Godhead by his willing self-sacrifice. Were there two myths here, perhaps ultimately related? Or did one invade the world of the other?

A third example is from the poem *Lokasenna*, Loki Quarrelling. Here Loki is the evil one, excluded from the company of the other gods and goddesses. They give a party and Loki is not invited. So he pushes his way in and engages in unseemly banter with each of those present. Each indelicate allusion – by Loki or his opponent – takes up one stanza. For example, when the god Tyr interposes to defend one of his fellows:

Loki said:
'Shut up, Tyr. You were never fit
To reconcile two foes.
Let me mention that right hand of yours
That Fenrir tore away.'

Tyr said:
'So I've lost a hand. You've lost Hrodrsvitnir.
Each suffers sorrowful loss.
The wolf too is wretched; he must wait
Enchained till the world's end.'

Here I have quoted practically all that *Lokasenna* relates of this myth, yet the audience must have known more of it or the verses would make no sense to them. We are lucky to know the whole tale, for Snorri Sturluson (1179–1241) wrote a detailed summary in his *Prose Edda*. In two separate passages Snorri told of Tyr's encounter with the ferocious wolf Fenrir, who seems in *Lokasenna* to have also the name or nickname of Hrodrsvitnir. Tyr, said Snorri, was the boldest of the gods, the patron of brave warriors. The wolf Fenrir was one of the monstrous brood of Loki, born to a giant woman. The gods heard a prophecy that the wolf and his kin would one day destroy the world, so they seized the beast to be brought up under their control. Only Tyr had the courage to tend him. Things were quiet while the wolf was a cub, but when the gods saw how huge he was growing they got anxious and decided to chain him up. How to put the chain on? They tried to trick the wolf (and it is worth noting that treachery and cunning were part of the gods' moral code). They persuaded him to let himself be fettered, pretending it was a test of his strength to get out; the tougher the chain, the greater the prestige in breaking it. Unfortunately, however strong the fetter, the wolf shattered it.

The only answer was to get those skilled craftsmen, the dwarfs, to make a custom-built chain, from six elements: the sound of a cat prowling, a woman's beard, a mountain's root, a bear's sinews, a fish's breath and a bird's spittle, all things with little or no physical entity. The dwarfs accepted the commission. Not surprisingly, from these materials they produced a very slender chain indeed, but one immensely strong for all that. Then the gods tried to trick the wolf into putting it on, arguing that anyone who could destroy iron bands would easily break out of this. But their own casuistry defeated them, for the wolf retorted there was no prestige in snapping such a slim chain unless it had been made with guile, and in that case he wanted nothing to do with it. Eventually, however, fearing that his courage would be questioned, Fenrir agreed but only on condition that, as a pledge of good faith, one of the gods should put his hand into the wolf's jaws while he was chained up. The gods looked at one another in perplexity. None wanted this office. At last the brave Tyr accepted it. They fettered the wolf with the deceitful chain. He struggled to escape, could not, and bit off Tyr's hand. 'Then they all laughed – except Tyr.'

The gods took Fenrir and tied him to a rock with a sword wedged between his jaws to stop him biting. They left him there, and *þar liggr hann til ragnarøkrs*, 'there he lies until the end of the world'.

Prose Edda

This tale introduces us to the second of the great collections of mythological material, the *Prose Edda*. Snorri Sturluson was a very rich Icelandic farmer, local leader, territorial magnate, ambassador, and something of a quisling in the service of the imperialistic Norwegian king, Hakon Hakonarson. Withal he was an educated man, having an unmatched knowledge of his country's antiquities and literature. He was himself a poet, and compiled his *Prose Edda* in the 1220s as a handbook of mythology for budding poets.

The book falls into four sections: a prologue; *Gylfaginning*, Fooling Gylfi; *Skáldskaparmál*, the Diction of Poetry; and *Háttatal*, the List of Verse Forms. The last is the least relevant to our subject: a series of definitions, with technical descriptions and examples, of the various and complex forms of line and stanza used by early Norse court poets. The first three sections belong more coherently together. Their purpose is explained in a passage from *Skáldskaparmál*, addressing young poets 'who want to learn poetic diction and to get themselves a wide vocabulary of traditional terms, or who want to be able to follow what is expressed elliptically in verse'. Snorri's book is an explication of the mythological allusions common in traditional verse, to help newcomers to the art to get them right. These poets of the thirteenth century would have been Christians, yet their verses were expected to abound in references to a pagan mythology that had been dead, more or less, for over two hundred years. Without instruction they might make mistakes.

To take an example. If your poem had to mention gold, you could refer to it as 'Frodi's meal'. It would then be helpful to know of the mythical king Frodi of Denmark, who had a quern that would grind out whatever its owner asked for. Frodi wanted gold, and kept his mill-slaves Fenia and Menia toiling day and night grinding out wealth for him. Or you could call gold 'Kraki's seed' in a reference to the legendary Danish king Hrolf Kraki. Chased by an avenging enemy, he scattered his golden plunder behind him as a sower broadcasts seed. If you had not these stories in mind, you might mistakenly call gold 'the seed of Frodi' or 'the meal of Kraki'. To give a modern parallel. Recently I heard a radio chat-show in which the hostess interviewed a famous guest who had radically changed his career in mid-life. She asked: 'Did you come to do this after careful thought? Or did you see, as it were, a blinding light on the road to Emmaus?' Had she had access to a modern Christian equivalent of Snorri's *Edda*, or even had she read the *Acts of the Apostles*, she might not have confused the road to Emmaus with the road to Damascus.

But Snorri too was a Christian, and could hardly tell such tales as though they were the truth, particularly tales that related adventures of the pagan gods. So he distanced himself from his subject in a number of ways. He composed a prologue full of early anthropological observation: how in primitive times men realised there was order in the universe, and deduced it must have a ruler; how the most splendid of early communities was Troy in Turkey, with twelve kingdoms each with a prince of superhuman qualities, and one high king above all. Snorri traced one of these royal dynasties to a son called Tror: 'we call him Thor'. Thor went out adventuring, met up with a beautiful witch called Sibil, 'whom we call Sif', and by her spawned a race full of the names of great heroes and one in particular, Odin. Odin had supernatural powers (as did his wife Frigg), for which he knew his name would 'be honoured beyond all kings'. He left Asia and travelled north, setting his sons in charge of kingdoms there, organising communities on the Trojan pattern. From these incomers from Asia (who were hence called *Aesir*, which is the common Old Norse word for 'gods') descended the great kings of Scandinavia. Here Snorri has taken an orthodox Christian position, identifying the pagan gods as ancient heroes deified by their ignorant followers.

The first part proper of Snorri's *Edda*, *Gylfaginning*, sets its material in a narrative frame. Gylfi was a Swedish king, something of a philosopher. He was perplexed by the Aesir, since all things seemed to work according to their will. Were they gods, or did they get their power from gods whom they worshipped? He set off to find out, disguised as a tramp, Gangleri. But the Aesir spotted him coming and prepared an illusion for him; hence this section's title, 'Fooling Gylfi'. When he came to the land of the Aesir, he saw an enormous hall which turned out to be full of people disporting themselves. At one end were three thrones, each occupied by a king: the first king was called High, the second Just-as-High, the third simply Third. These august rulers were prepared to answer Gylfi's questions. He asked about the gods and received in reply encyclopaedic lore, folk-tale, legend. By this device Snorri was able to tell his myths through intermediaries, not committing himself to their truth. He could also tell them in a detached, witty, drily ironical style which is a joy to read.

Some of his material Snorri certainly had from poems like those of the *Poetic Edda*, though they may not have been identical with the ones that have come down to us. As evidence for what he writes, he sometimes quotes passages from verses represented in the *Codex Regius*, as here in a passage telling of the great warriors whom Odin picks from the battlefield and takes

Gangleri questions the three kings: High, Just-as-High and Third.

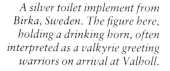

A silver toilet implement from Birka, Sweden. The figure here, holding a drinking horn, often interpreted as a valkyrie greeting warriors on arrival at Valholl.

173

to live with him in his great hall of Valholl. Snorri makes High say:

Every day when they have got up, they put on their war-gear and go out into the arena and fight, each pouncing on the other. This is their idea of sport. And when dinner-time approaches, they ride home to Valholl and sit down at their drink; as it says in this verse:

> All the great champions
> In Odin's circle
> Battle together each day.
> They choose who shall die,
> Ride from the fight,
> And sit together in peace again.

The verse occurs in just this form in the question-and-answer poem *Vafþrúð-nismál* in the *Codex Regius*.

But Snorri also makes it clear that he knew poems that have not survived independently: witness his story of Niord, god of sea travel and mercantile adventure, who made a *mésalliance* with the giantess Skadi and had to compromise on living conditions.

Skadi wanted to live where her father had lived, in the hills called Thrymheim. On the other hand Niord wanted to live near the sea. So they came to an agreement that they should stay in turns, nine days at Thrymheim and the next nine at Noatun [Niord's seaside residence]. And when Niord came back to Noatun from the hills he proclaimed this verse:

> I'm bored with the hills, I didn't stay long
> Nine nights only.
> Wolves' howling I hated
> Compared with swans' singing.

And Skadi said:

> I couldn't sleep by the ocean's beds
> For the sea-bird's screaming.
> Every dawn it wakens me,
> The gull flying in from the sea.

So Skadi went to the hills and lived in Thrymheim. She usually wears skis and carries a bow for shooting animals. And she is known as the ski-ing goddess.

The verses are known only from Snorri's *Edda* but must derive from a full-length poem now lost.

In other cases again we have no clear idea where Snorri got his story from, though the amount of detail he gives shows he had full sources which may have been folk-tale or tradition. To this group perhaps belongs the tale of how the gods planned a defensive wall round their territory to guard it from giant attack. They found a builder who, though they did not realise it at the time, was of giant kin. He agreed to construct the wall for a fee: the sun, the moon and the goddess Freyia. He was allowed no help save from his cart-horse Svadilfoeri, and he had to finish the job in three seasons or he would lose everything. Thor was not at home when this was arranged, but Loki was, and he advised the gods to accept the contract, thinking the task was impossible. The gods agreed, and bound themselves by oaths to keep the bargain.

The builder worked all day, and by night brought out his horse to fetch stones. When the gods saw the horse at work they were horrified to find how much it could pull at a load – it worked twice as hard even as the builder! Time was nearly up, the wall practically complete. The gods were terrified they would lose, and assailed Loki, blaming him for his bad advice. Loki in turn was frightened, and devised a plot to stop the builder from winning. He turned himself into a mare. On the last night the builder drove his horse to get the final load of materials; out popped the mare and whinnied at the horse, which went frantic and broke its traces, trying to get at its mate. The two galloped away to the woods and were absent all night, so the builder could not get his task finished. At that he fell into a giant rage, and this made the gods realise at last that he was of enemy kin. At the critical moment Thor came home and saw the danger. He swung his mighty hammer, smashing the giant's skull in splinters. But the last laugh was on Loki. He gave birth to a monstrous foal with eight legs. This grew into the famous horse Sleipnir, which was Odin's favourite mount.

As evidence for this tale, Snorri quotes two verses from the great Eddic poem *Voluspá*, The Wise Woman's Prophecy. They are quite inadequate to explain the detail that Snorri's version contains. So, either he made up the

This design, incised on a stone in Gotland, Sweden, shows an eight-legged horse, usually assumed to represent Odin's favourite mount Sleipnir.

whole tale himself – and this is unlikely – or he had some source that we cannot trace.

The second part proper of Snorri's *Edda*, *Skáldskaparmál*, also has a narrative frame. Again there is a visitor to the Aesir, who again are not identified as gods though they have the same names as gods. This visitor is Aegir, a king skilled in magic. Again the Aesir spot him in advance and prepare both reception and deception. They give him a great welcome and prepare a feast in his honour, sitting him next to Bragi whose name is that of the god of poetry. Bragi tells of the exploits of the Aesir. So the traditional myths are expounded, ending with a very important one for Snorri's purpose. This tells of two dwarfs, Fialar and Galar, who killed a creature Kvasir and mixed his blood with honey, so making the mead that turns anyone who drinks it into a poet. The dwarfs kept their mead in three cauldrons. A giant, Suttung, took it from them, and Odin in his turn plotted to steal it. He seduced the giant's daughter who was so infatuated that she let him take three drinks of the mead, which completely emptied the cauldrons. Then Odin turned himself into an eagle and flew off over the mountains. When Suttung discovered his loss, he put on his own eagle skin and rose in pursuit, nearly catching Odin up. The Aesir saw Odin's peril as he hovered over their dwellings, so they quickly put out into the courtyard all their pails and jars. Odin spewed up the mead into them, and there it remains, waiting to be distributed to anyone who aspires to be a poet. Thus, says Snorri (or perhaps Bragi), poetry can be called 'Odin's plunder' or 'Odin's discovery' or 'Odin's drink'.

Here Snorri has got to the main purpose of writing his *Edda*: a discussion of the language and imagery of poetry, how its metaphors can be understood in terms of Norse mythology. Now the narrative frame of *Skáldskaparmál* recedes into the background, and Snorri is content to ask questions. Why is gold referred to as 'the hair of Sif', or as 'the otter's blood-money', or as 'Aegir's fire'? And he gives the stories that explain the images. Or he tells of the appropriate metaphors to be used of the various gods: 'How do you refer to Tyr? By calling him "the one-handed god", "the wolf's feeder".' We know why: Snorri told us the story in *Gylfaginning*. 'How do you refer to Hod? By calling him "the blind god", "Baldr's killer", "shooter of the mistletoe",' referring to the Baldr tragedy, a most important myth which I discuss later. This type of metaphor, *kenning* as it is named in Old Norse, may be a myth in shorthand. It is an essential feature of Norse court poetry.

Skaldic verse

This introduces naturally the third of our major sources for Norse myth, the compositions of the court poets, the skalds as they are usually called. The *Poetic Edda* is anonymous; in contrast, many skaldic verses are attributed to named poets. Their biographies may be preserved or their political allegiances known. Moreover, their verses often refer to contemporary events which can be dated on independent evidence. Thus with skaldic verse it is possible to build up a chronology of writings, to date many of the poems at any rate to within a decade or so. The practice of composing skaldic verse began perhaps in the ninth century and continued through the Viking Age into the Middle Ages; but of course, save for occasional stanzas cut in runes, little of it was written down until the advent of Christianity and Roman literacy. So we have the familiar problem. We have to trust to Christian records of a pre- or proto-Christian era. We have to assume accurate oral transmission of verse until the period of writing down. And we have to accept that the later attribution of verses to named poets is sound. Using skaldic verse as evidence is clearly perilous.

Skaldic poetry was usually highly mannered and technically elaborate, as befits a form of verse designed for songs in praise of Scandinavian kings and nobles. It could also be the vehicle for occasional verse, to celebrate great occasions or simply for impromptu comment on happenings the poet observed or took part in. As well as a complex verse form, most skaldic poems had a complex language pattern with sentences intermingled and employing unusual words in place of common ones, and making frequent use of kennings. It is in these kennings that myths may be concealed.

For instance, the poet Einar Skalaglamm composed a poem, *Vellekla*, in honour of the great earl Hakon of Lade, near Trondheim in Norway, towards the end of the tenth century. He opened it with a formal request to his patron for a hearing:

> Great-hearted land's protector,
> I beg you to listen to the yeasty surf
> Of the dwellers of the fiord's bone.
> Hear, earl, Kvasir's blood.

On its first performance, the listeners must have scratched their heads a bit at this until they managed to work out the various periphrases. 'Kvasir's blood' is easy enough when you know it was made into mead, a special sort of mead that gives poetic inspiration; hence the kenning can be used for a specific example of poetic inspiration, an individual poem. 'The yeasty surf of the dwellers of the fiord's bone' is trickier, more involved. 'The fiord's bone' is the rocky shore or cliff of a fiord. 'The dwellers of the fiord's bone' are, or at least may be, dwarfs, since every schoolboy knows that dwarfs live in crags or great boulders. Here the dwarfs are Fialar and Galar. Their 'yeasty surf' would be their mead; hence again we have a kenning for poetry, a poem. All the poet has said in these lines is 'Please be quiet and listen while I'm reciting', but it sounds more impressive this way. However, it does depend on audience participation: if they cannot remember the myth and unravel the riddle, they will be baffled by the verse.

Luckily, not all skaldic verse is as hard to follow as this. Some skalds wrote comparatively straightforward verse, while still exploiting mythological thought patterns. When the great tenth-century Icelandic poet Egil Skalla-grimsson lost two of his sons, he composed a bitter lament scolding his patron, the poet's god Odin, for betraying him. It was hard to compose in such circumstances, he said. 'It is not a propitious time for the theft of Vidrir.' Vidrir is another name for Odin; his theft was the mead of poetry. But though Odin had injured him, he had also, by his gift of poetry, strengthened Egil. 'If I look upon things properly, Mimir's friend has brought me recompense for my grief.' Mimir was Odin's friend because his wise head, cut off and pickled, told Odin many secrets about the future.

Again, a skald might praise his lord in an almost Eddic form, writing a simple narrative verse in a scene set amongst the gods. When Eric Bloodaxe, exiled king of both Norway and York, came to grief in battle in the mid-tenth century, his fiercely pagan wife commissioned an appropriate funeral ode. Only a few verses of it survive. They begin in Odin's hall:

> Odin said:
> 'What dream was that? I rose at dawn
> To clear Valholl for a slaughtered army.
> I roused my great champions; bade the Valkyries wake,
> Strew the benches, wash out the beer-mugs,
> Bring out the wine for a prince who was coming.
> From earth I am looking for
> Such noble fighting-men
> As will make my heart exult.'

He asks his companion Bragi what the thunderous noise outside is. Bragi thinks it is the god Baldr returning home. Odin tells him not to be daft; it's obviously Eric and the army of the dead who have been killed with him. He sends out his two greatest heroes to welcome the king. One of them, Sigmund, heroic but not unduly intelligent, asks why Odin expects Eric rather than someone else. Odin explains patiently that Eric is a great warrior: 'because he has reddened his sword, carried a bloody blade, in many lands'. Sigmund asks reasonably: 'If he seemed so valiant, why rob him of victory?' Odin makes the veiled reply:

> 'What's to come cannot be known.
> The grey wolf glares at the homes of the gods.'

Eric was a fairly mediocre king, unsuccessful in most of his ventures. By treating him like this the poet has shown him as one of the greatest fighters, fit to mix with the heroes of antiquity, fit to form part of Odin's defending army when the grey wolf Fenrir escapes his bonds and takes ferocious vengeance on the gods.

In some cases mythological tales may be more directly the subject of a skald's verses. An example is the poem *Haustlǫng*, Autumn-long, so called because it took its writer Thiodolf a whole autumn to finish. The poem describes a shield the skald had been given, decorated with a group of scenes portraying a couple of stories of the gods. One told the tale of Idunn, a useful goddess since she kept in a chest the apples that gave renewed youth. Snorri, who knew *Haustlǫng*, tells her story plainly.

Three of the Aesir, Odin, Loki and Hoenir, were on an expedition, and one day seized and killed an ox for supper. They tried to cook it, but whenever they checked the meat was not ready. Above them was an oak, and in its branches an eagle. The eagle revealed it was responsible for the cooking failure; the beef would never be done unless the eagle got its share. The gods accepted this and invited the bird to help itself. So it did, too freely for Loki's taste. Loki was furious, picked up a staff and beat at the eagle. The staff stuck to the eagle which flew off, with Loki, who was also stuck to the staff, hanging on behind. Loki, shaken and battered, was terrified and pleaded to be let loose. The eagle agreed on condition that Loki promised to entice Idunn out of her stronghold among the gods, bringing her apples with her. So Loki and the others got home safely.

Loki faithfully kept his bargain, luring Idunn out into the woods. The eagle, now revealed as a giant Thiazi, swooped upon her and carried her off to his home in Thrymheim. The gods, apple-less, began to grow old and feeble. They were puzzled at what had happened to Idunn until someone remembered she had last been seen with Loki. So they arrested Loki and threatened him with death unless he found Idunn and brought her back. Loki transformed himself into a hawk and flew off to Thrymheim. Luckily the giant was out fishing and Idunn at home alone. Loki turned her into a nut, picked her up in his talons and flew off. Thiazi, finding Idunn gone, put on his eagle shape and went off in pursuit, flapping so violently that his wings caused tempests. The Aesir saw the hawk struggling, chased by an eagle, and realised the situation. They heaped up a pile of woodchips just inside their walls, and when the hawk had flown safely in, they lit the wood. The eagle was flying so violently it could not stop. Into the fire it went and its wings were destroyed. The Aesir killed Thiazi.

Snorri has a sequel to this tale. Thiazi had a butch daughter called Skadi. When she heard her father had been killed, she grabbed her weapons and armour and rushed off to seek revenge. The Aesir thought it best to placate her, and offered her one of themselves in marriage. But she had to choose by the feet, seeing no more. So the gods held an ankle contest. Skadi saw a very elegant pair of feet, and, guessing it was the beautiful god Baldr, she picked that one. It turned out to be the elderly Niord. As we have seen, their marriage did not take.

Haustlǫng has twelve stanzas on the Thiazi story. Each describes an episode or situation: the first shows Thiazi, in bird's form, watching the Aesir trying to cook their ox, the second reports Thiazi's claim that he prevented the meat being done, the third the gods' offer of some of their meat to Thiazi while Loki worked hard keeping the fire going, the fourth Thiazi's greed in taking such a huge helping, the fifth Loki striking at Thiazi with the staff, and so on. While this is easy enough to follow if you already know the story, it would be tricky – especially considering the contorted language of the verses – to understand the plot if you don't. Again the poem demands audience participation.

Such are the main sources of Norse mythology. There are many others, some minor in the amount of information preserved though they may be major in its importance. To take two examples: as well as the *Prose Edda*, Snorri compiled a Norwegian history called *Heimskringla*, Circle of the World. This comprises biographies of Norwegian kings from the first 'historical' monarch, Harald, nicknamed the Fine-haired, at the end of the ninth century. Before Harald's story there is a book called *Ynglingasaga*, the History of the Kings of the Yngling Dynasty, and here are tales of legendary kings and some of the gods. When Saxo Grammaticus wrote in Latin his history of Denmark, *Gesta Danorum*, early in the thirteenth century, he built upon a lot of mythological and legendary lore, some of it inconsistent with the material we find in, say, Snorri.

From this mixture of sources from different places and times, and responding to different literary demands, it is not likely that we shall gain a coherent account of Norse mythology. There is a confusion of tales: some belong in clear sequences, others are apparently scattered aimlessly about. How much is genuine Norse legend, how much literary invention, is hard to tell. What the myths have to do with Norse belief is also a matter of controversy. A myth, we are told, should employ 'some popular idea concerning natural or historical phenomena'. How far the myths retold here do that is for the reader to decide.

Aesir, Vanir and a few kings

I n the Norse myths there are two groups of gods, the *Aesir* (the singular
of this noun is *Áss*) and the *Vanir* (singular *Vanr*). Despite Snorri, the
word *Áss* is not derived from *Asia*: that is a typical bit of medieval 'learned'
etymology. *Áss* derives from a common Germanic word for 'god'. It has a
parallel in Old English *ōs* (a word that survives today only as the first element
of masculine personal names like *Oswald*, *Osbert*), and there is a Gothic
plural form in a Latin text, *ansis* which is translated *semideos*, 'demi-gods'.
Vanr is a more problematic word. As the dictionaries admit, 'there is no
shortage of etymologies for it', but a tempting one links it with Old Norse
vinr, 'friend', and Latin *Venus*, 'goddess of physical love'.

The renowned French student of comparative religion, Georges Dumézil,
argued that the distinction between the Aesir and the Vanir is an ancient
one, to be found in the religions of other Indo-European peoples. The Vanir,
he thinks, were originally gods of inferior status, accepted into the superior
group only after a period of some conflict. This is certainly reflected in the
relationship between the two god types as reported in *Heimskringla*, though
there it has become a struggle between neighbouring peoples:

Odin took an army to attack the Vanir. They made a valiant defence of their country,
and each side in turn had victory. Each plundered the others' land, doing much damage.
And when the two peoples had had enough of this, they set up a peace conference, made
a truce, and hostages were exchanged. The Vanir gave their most distinguished men, the
rich Niord and his son Freyr. In return the Aesir gave the man called Hoenir, saying
he was very proper to have authority. He was a big man, very good-looking. With him
the Aesir sent one Mimir, a very shrewd man, and in return the Vanir gave the most
intelligent one in their group. He was called Kvasir.

When Hoenir came to Vanaland, he was given authority at once. Mimir taught
him everything he should say. And when Hoenir was in attendance at legal moots and
gatherings without Mimir at hand, and any difficult case came before him, he always
gave the same answer. 'Let someone else decide', he would say. Then the Vanir suspected
that the Aesir had tricked them over the hostage agreement. They seized hold of Mimir,
cut off his head and sent it to the Aesir. Odin picked it up, smeared it with herbs so
that it would not rot, and chanted spells over it. This gave it such power that it spoke
to him, telling him many occult secrets.

Odin set up Niord and Freyr as sacrifical priests, and they were cult-leaders among
the Aesir. Niord's daughter was Freyia. She was a sacrifical priestess. She was the first
to teach the Aesir the practice called *seiðr* [magic] which was common among the Vanir.
When Niord lived among the Vanir he had mated with his own sister, for that was legal
with them. Their children were Freyr and Freyia. But among the Aesir it was forbidden
to mate within this degree of kindred.

Much of this legend is confirmed by allusions in Eddic verses. In the poem *Vafþrúðnismál* the question is asked: 'Where did Niord come from to live among the sons of the Aesir? He controls hundreds of shrines and temples, yet he wasn't born among the Aesir.' The answer is given: 'The wise powers created him in the land of the Vanir, and gave him to the gods as hostage. At the end of the world he will return again to live among the wise Vanir.'

For all the best scandal about the gods, turn to *Lokasenna*, where the insults traded between Loki and his opponents usually reveal some disgraceful act or practice of one or the other. Niord has boasted of his son, loved by all and a prince among gods. Loki retorts:

'Stop it, Niord. Control yourself.
I won't hide this any longer.
That son of yours you begat on your sister,
And that's no less than expected.'

When Freyia intervenes, Loki lashes out at her:

'Shut up, Freyia. I know you in full.
You're not exactly free from fault.
All the Aesir and elves who are in this hall,
All have been lovers of yours.'

And in his next riposte, he accuses her of being caught in the act with her own brother.

In these verses the distinctive character of the Vanir is affirmed – distinctive but rather sinister, or at least unorthodox. The practice of *seiðr*, for instance, was useful but could be dangerous. It was a form of magic that gave its practitioners power, either to harm others or to achieve esoteric knowledge. Snorri says that Odin knew it, presumably taught by Freyia:

Odin had that skill – indeed he practised it himself – which brought with it great power. It was called *seiðr*. By using it he could learn the fates of men and events still in the future. He could bring death, ill-fortune or sickness to men, or take intellect or strength from one and transfer it to another. But this sorcery, when it was performed, carried with it such effeminacy that it was thought shameful for men to have anything to do with it. So its practice was taught to the priestesses.

In the main, however, the Vanir brought benefits to mankind. Dumézil sees them as 'givers of health, youth, fecundity and happiness'. He speaks of twin deities, and we can think of Freyr and Freyia as twins (as well as mates). Niord too should have a twin sister (and mate), and she can perhaps be traced, though not precisely in Norse myth. Tacitus, the first-century Roman historian, reported a goddess worshipped by Germanic tribes of the North Sea neighbourhood. She was called Nerthus (an exact cognate of the name Niord), which Tacitus glossed as 'mother earth'. She brought peace and fertility to her devotees. Within the Norse sources, Niord is a god of wealth, rich lands, mercantile enterprise and fisheries. Freyr is god of favourable weather and so of produce, of peace and prosperity, and his appropriately virile statue

A phallic figurine from Rällinge, Sweden, perhaps representing the fertility god Freyr.

in the great temple of Uppsala was invoked for fruitful marriages. Freyia 'is very fond of love songs. It is a good thing to pray to her in affairs of the heart.'

Because of the central importance of such themes to daily life in the Middle Ages, there must have been many myths of these Vanir gods, but surprisingly few of them survive. Of some we have hints. For instance, Freyia was married to a little-known god Od, who went off on his travels leaving Freyia weeping. Thereafter she went in search of him, taking upon herself a variety of strange names. There were presumably stories of her adventures, but there survive only a few allusions in Snorri and the poets. When Freyia wept for Od, her tears turned to gold, so a group of kennings for gold includes 'Freyia's weeping', 'the thawing of the eyelid of Freyia', and so on.

Most detailed of our records of the myths of the Vanir is that of Freyr's passion for a giant-girl, Gerd, a love-tale appropriate to a god of fertility and physical desire. It is told in the Eddic poem *Fǫr Skírnis*, Skirnir's Journey, and paraphrased in Snorri's *Edda*. Odin has a great throne, Hlidskialf, from which he can survey all worlds. One day Freyr climbed into it and was punished for his presumption. He looked northwards (and every schoolboy knows that in the north live giants). There he saw the most beautiful girl with shining arms. He fell for her at once and languished, sick for love. Niord, worried at his son's condition, sent for Freyr's squire Skirnir and told him to enquire the reason. Skirnir asked Freyr why he sat moping, appealing to him for the sake of their childhood friendship to reveal his secret. Freyr confessed his love, and begged Skirnir to go a-wooing for him. The journey was likely to be a dangerous one. In recognition of this, Freyr had to give Skirnir his splendid horse and one of his greatest treasures, a sword that would fight of its own accord. Skirnir rode to the giant's dwelling, which was surrounded by howling guard dogs. The shepherd sitting outside advised him against trying to get in. Skirnir persisted. Gerd, following the dictates of northern hospitality, invited him in for a drink of mead, and asked his errand. Skirnir declared Freyr's love, and offered her gifts if she would respond: eleven golden apples and a ring that reproduced itself every ninth night, clear indications of the immense wealth the Vanr had at his disposal. She rejected them; she had enough gold already. So Skirnir resorted to threats, which got more and more outrageous (and to some degree more and more cryptic) until at last she gave in. She arranged a tryst for nine days' time, promising to give herself to Freyr then. Skirnir rode back. Freyr was so eager for news that he was waiting outside. Skirnir gave his message. Freyr's response will smite the heart of all true lovers:

> 'A night is long. Two are long.
> How shall I last out for three?
> Often a month has gone quicker for me
> Than such a half wedding night.'

For all its obscurities, *Fọr Skírnis* relates one of the more transparent of Norse myths. The name Gerd has been linked to the common Old Norse noun *garðr*, 'enclosed plot, field' (as in the modern dialectal and specific English word 'garth'), and the coupling of Freyr and Gerd is seen to be an expression of the sacred marriage of the god of fertility to the cultivated land. Ultimately *Fọr Skírnis* has a happy ending. But it is left to the sardonic Loki to point out the implications in a typical stanza in *Lokasenna*:

> 'You had Gymir's daughter [Gerd] bought with gold;
> That's what you gave your sword for.
> But when Muspell's sons ride across Mirkwood,
> You wretch, you won't know what to fight with.'

Muspell's sons will be part of the destroying host to attack the gods at the world's end. Freyr will fight to protect the gods, but how can he without the wondrous sword that he gave up in a moment of passion?

Next, a significant tale about Freyr, whose implications are, however, questionable. It comes from Snorri's *Heimskringla*, and so treats Freyr as though he were an early king, not a god; another aspect of that writer's euhemeristic approach to the pagan Norse deities. This affects the story's content. Niord and Freyr are defined as successive kings of the Swedes. Freyr was very popular; in his days harvests were good and there was a long-standing peace, which the Swedes attributed to their king. He established the great temple at Uppsala, applying to it all the money paid in taxes and tribute.

Freyr fell sick, and as the illness gained on him, his men considered what policy to follow. They let few people come near him, and they built a great mound, put a door in it and three windows. When Freyr was dead, they carried his body secretly into the mound, and told the Swedes he was still alive. There they kept him for three years. All the tax money they emptied into the mound, gold in at one window, silver at the second, and the bronze coinage at the third. The period of peace and fertility continued ... When all the Swedes realised that Freyr was dead, yet peace and good harvests still went on, they concluded that so it would be as long as Freyr remained in Sweden, so they refused to cremate him. They called him *veraldargoð*, 'the god of worldly things', and ever afterwards sacrificed to him for peace and good harvests.

Certainly there are some elements in this story – the riches, the fertility – that are characteristic of the god Freyr's adventures, but in fact it is a celebration of kingship as well as godhead. After all, the name *Freyr* was originally a common noun meaning 'lord', related to the Old English word *frea*, used of both earthly and heavenly kings. It seems from the later medieval tales that early Scandinavian kings were revered in proportion to their ability to bring their peoples the blessings of peace and prosperity, to secure productive seasons for crops and cattle. According to some legendary accounts kings who failed in this were killed off. One such wretch, recorded in Snorri's *Heimskringla*, was the fugitive Swedish king Olaf, nicknamed the Tree-trimmer because he fled to the west of the country and vigorously cleared

A reconstruction of the temple at Uppsala, from Olaus Magnus' History of the Northern Peoples published in 1555.

the forests and tilled the land. Other exiles, seeing how fertile the soil was, joined him:

And such a flood of people poured into his territories that the land could not support them all. So there arose great famine and starvation. The Swedes put this at their king's door, because Swedes make a practice of attributing to their king both good seasons and bad. King Olaf was not one for celebrating sacrifices. The Swedes took a poor view of this, thinking it was the cause of the famine. So they gathered together in a band and suddenly fell upon Olaf. They caught him in his house and burnt him in it. Thus they gave him to Odin, sacrificing him to get themselves a good harvest. That was by Lake Vänern.

In his tale of Freyr, Snorri told a royal story which is also a religious one. It resembles an anecdote Saxo Grammaticus tells of the Danish king Frothi, also famed for the long period of peace he brought his people. When Frothi died his retainers wanted to keep it secret so that the land's tranquil condition would remain. They embalmed the body and had it carried round the countryside in a litter, as though the king were too infirm to travel in any other way. Only when the body began to putrefy did they give it proper burial.

This too looks like a transformed religious myth. The name *Frothi* may be related to the adjective *fróðr*, 'fruitful, fertile'. His posthumous progress through the countryside (perhaps to bring an abundant harvest) can be likened to that of Nerthus, *terra mater*, mother earth, in Tacitus's account:

In an island of the ocean is a sacred grove, and in it a consecrated cart covered with a drape. One priest only is allowed to touch it. He becomes aware that the goddess has entered her sacred chariot, and he attends her with great reverence as she is drawn along by her heifers. Then the days are full of rejoicing; the places she thinks worthy of her visit are in festive guise. No-one goes to war. No-one bears arms. All steel is locked away. Only then are peace and tranquillity recognised, only then loved, until the same priest returns the goddess to her temple, having had her fill of human society. Straightaway the cart, the drape, and, if you are prepared to believe it, the goddess herself are washed in a remote lake. Slaves perform this duty, and the same lake immediately engulfs them. From this comes an awesome terror and a feeling of pious ignorance as to what that may be which only those on the verge of death may see.

In turn, the story of a dead king being carried round his realm to ensure that prosperity continued has some little similarity with the tale of the accidental death of the semi-legendary Norwegian king Halfdan the Black, father of Harald the Fine-haired. Snorri tells it in an early section of *Heimskringla*. Halfdan was driving from a feast in Hadeland, and his route took him over the frozen Randsfiord. It was spring and the ice was treacherous. It broke as they were crossing, and Halfdan and all his suite drowned. The bodies were recovered. Halfdan had been a king particularly successful in bringing fertile seasons to his people. The men of Ringerike brought his body home for burial there. To this the people of his other dominions, Rømerike, Vestfold and Heidmark, objected, for they thought that the productive seasons would continue in whatever region the body was entombed. So everybody wanted it. They came to a statesmanlike compromise, chopping the body into four bits and burying a piece in each of the provinces. Hence, claims Snorri, there are four distinct places in Norway called Halfdan's Mound.

The link of the name *Frothi* with the adjective *fróðr*, 'fertile, burgeoning', suggests that it could be a by-name of Freyr. A chapter in the *Ynglingasaga* of Snorri's *Heimskringla* makes it clear that the two names are intimately linked. Snorri takes Freyr to be a Swedish king, successor to Niord in this office. He describes his rule thus:

He was blessed in friends and fertile seasons as his father had been. Freyr built a great temple at Uppsala, set up his main residence there, and applied to it all his tax-income, his lands and free capital. Then was established the royal treasury of Uppsala, which has continued ever since. In Freyr's days there began 'the peace of Frothi', when there were also fertile seasons in all lands. The Swedes attributed this to Freyr.

Peace and fertility are closely linked in Norse phrase, for it is common to read of sacrifices made *til árs ok friðar*, 'for fruitfulness and peace'. The primitive cult of Nerthus, as we have seen, was also one of peace. Place-names and early references in the sagas confirm this connection between the Vanir and fertile peacefulness. Freyr's name is quite common in Norwegian and Swedish place-names with second elements with meanings like 'meadow', 'field', referring, I suppose, to pieces of land producing rich crops. Niord and Freyr were both wealthy. Indeed, Snorri (or rather High in *Gylfaginning*) says that Niord 'is so rich and blessed with property that he can give wealth of land or of cash to anyone who appeals to him for it'. Freyr owns important treasures like the boar Gullinbursti which lightened darkness with the glitter of its golden bristles. He has a ship with enviable qualities: it can accommodate the whole Aesir band with weapons and armour, it can draw a favourable wind the moment the sail is hoisted, and it can be taken from the sea when not in use and folded up like a cloth and put into a pouch. Freyr's father too had a link with ships and the sea.

For all their differences, the tales of Freyr, Frothi, Halfdan (and in a different mode Nerthus) have common elements, themes that can be supported in different degrees by other early Scandinavian and indeed Germanic stories, that of Olaf Tree-trimmer being only one. The themes are: a deity/king who provides peace and plenty for a people; rich harvests which are connected in popular thought with the continuity of possession of his body, to ensure which abundance the deity/king travels about his realm in a carriage.

Behind legends like these lies some common Scandinavian or probably Germanic myth, and perhaps even some religious ritual derived from it. The Vanir were clearly important deities in the practical concerns of Norse religious activity. They supplied and controlled the wealth on which Norse society, agricultural and mercantile, depended. Not surprisingly, therefore, they are often named as gods to whom sacrifices were dedicated. Paradoxically, it may be this very practical importance that accounts for the comparatively few myths that survive about a major group of gods like this. The twelfth-

The three great gods in the temple at Uppsala. Thor sits in the middle with Odin to his left. Freyr should stand to his right, but the goddess Frigg has been placed there in error. Again from Olaus Magnus' History of the Northern Peoples.

century historian Adam of Bremen compiled a description of the great heathen temple at Uppsala, and the rites conducted there. Within the temple were three major images of gods; one of them, called by Adam *Fricco*, was certainly Freyr, 'doling out peace and delight to mortals'. Adam gives a short account of the great spring sacrifices, but adds disappointingly: 'The chants that are usually sung in the observance of such celebrations are various and unsavoury, so it is best to say nothing about them'.

Inevitably, pagan observances shocked Christian writers and they preferred not to speak of them. If the rites were those of deities who influenced the daily round of life, the economics of agriculture or cattle-raising, the success of trading voyages or fishing, they would be the more dangerous in a proto-Christian society; people would want to carry on with them since the continuity of their communities depended on their success as farmers or seamen. That made it more important for professional Christians to ensure that these gods of the countryside and of the sea were suppressed and their myths forgotten or replaced by Christian equivalents.

Odin and Thor

The two most famous and powerful of the Aesir, Odin and Thor, stand in sharp contrast to one another: Odin, god of poets and kings, of warriors, of magic; and Thor who appealed to the everyday Viking, the Icelandic or Norwegian man-in-the-fiord. Dumézil viewed the two as types and classified them accordingly. In his division of gods into functions and constituencies, he sees Odin as sovereign god, as king, priest, magician. Thor, he thinks, exhibits the features of the warrior god, one essentially tough and aggressive. There is something in this distinction, though it is simplistic as applied to Viking Age myth or belief. Certainly Thor fights to save the gods from their mortal enemies, the giants; but Odin too has close links with battle, protecting his chosen champions and ultimately gathering them to himself.

Odin

Of the two, Odin was far the more complex in character. This complexity arose, some scholars think, from the circumstance that over the centuries Odin took to himself characteristics and areas of activity that had earlier belonged to other gods. The variety of Odin's nature is mirrored by the large number of names applied to him, names that are not quite nicknames but have something of that quality; what the Norse called *heiti*, a noun related to the verb *heita*, 'to be called'.

Snorri, this time as Third in *Gylfaginning*, says that Odin is the oldest and the most eminent of the gods, in control of all things. The other gods obey him as children do their father – this, of course, was many years ago. Third also calls him *Alfǫðr*, All-father, but he also names him Father of the Slain (*Valfǫðr*), God of the Hanged (*Hangaguð*), God of Captives (*Haptaguð*), God of Cargoes (*Farmaguð*), and, he adds, Odin gave himself even more names on his visit to King Geirrod. Third then quotes a verse list from the poem *Grímnismál*:

'I call myself Grim   Thunn, Unn,
And Ganglari,   Helblindi, Har,
Herian, Hialmberi,   Sann, Svipall,
Thekkr, Thridi,   Sanngetal ...'

And so on for another sixteen lines. No wonder Gangleri bursts out in reply:

'A hell of a lot of names you've given him. My god, what a lot of learning a man must have to be able to tell in detail how each name came into being'.

What in fact a man needs is a grounding in Norse etymology, at any rate for some of the names. *Grímr* is usually interpreted as 'the masked one, the hooded one'. *Herian* is related to the noun *herr*, 'army', and *Hiálmberi* contains the word *hiálmr*, 'helmet'. *Hár* most obviously means 'the high one', but an alternative etymology – suggested but by no means proven – makes it mean 'the blind one'. *Svipall* is linked to the adjective *svipull*, 'changeable, capricious'. In the rest of this verse there are names meaning 'inflamer' (*Hnikarr*), 'weak-eyed' (*Bileygr*), 'fiery-eyed' (*Báleygr*), 'evil-doer' (*Bǫlverkr*), 'long-hood' (*Síðhǫttr*), 'father of victory' (*Sigfǫðr*), 'the blind one' (*Blindi*), 'the one with the magic staff' (*Gǫndlir*), 'gelding' (*Iálkr*), 'feeder' (*Kialarr*), 'destroyer' (*Viðurr*), 'terror' (*Yggr*), 'wind' (*Váfuðr*) and 'god of men' (*Veratýr*). The names show different sides of Odin's character, or something of his variety of action: the god of war and giver of victory, the god of magic, the sinister god, the terrifying and awesome god, the god who could control the winds, the god whose word could not be trusted. Some names enshrine myths. The fact that Odin practised *seiðr*, which could call his masculinity into question, might lead to the name *Iálkr*. The many stories where Odin travels in disguise would account for names like *Grímr* and *Síðhǫttr*. Names like *Bileygr*, *Blindi* and perhaps *Hár* recall that Odin was one-eyed, for he pledged one eye in return for a drink from the well Mimisbrunn, which is the source of wisdom and mother-wit.

Names that evoke warfare and armour suggest the god of battle, the supporter of great fighters, the god who picks for his army the greatest of warriors, men like Eric Bloodaxe. But by virtue of this activity Odin also shows himself faithless, changeable, capricious; after helping a great champion for some time, he will betray him, letting him be killed so that he can come to join Odin in Valholl. Indeed, faithlessness is part of Odin's general nature, as it is part of the way of life of the Vikings, many of whom must have taken Odin as their personal god.

Breach of faith is one of the themes of the Eddic poem *Hávamál*. Therein Odin speaks from his experience of the world, pondering cynically on the treachery men and women show towards one another:

> Loving a woman whose heart is false
> Is like driving an unshod horse over slippery ice,
> A mettled two-year-old, not fully broken;
> Or like handling a rudderless ship in a fierce gale,
> Or like a cripple catching reindeer on the thawing fells.

But in equity he adds:

> Yet now I'll speak plainly. I know both sides.
> Men's minds are treacherous to women.
> When our intent is most false, we speak most fairly;
> That deceives the wisest hearts.

Thereafter he hints at two adventures illustrating these different treacheries. The myths are not told in full, and of the first we have no more information than *Hávamál* supplies. The second can be filled out from other sources.

The first tells of one of Odin's love intrigues that failed. He fell for a girl, apparently a giantess, referred to only as 'Billing's daughter'. He approached her bed, but she begged him to return at nightfall since it would be unseemly for anyone else to know of their mutual passions. Back came Odin at the appointed time, and found all the household guards wide awake, keeping watch with burning torches. He fled, and stole back early next morning. The guards were now asleep, and Odin hoped to slake his desires. But the girl had tied a guard dog to her bed to keep him off.

The second is a story we know already, of Odin's theft of the poetic mead from the giant Suttung. The *Hávamál* poet concentrates on one aspect, Odin's seduction of the giant's daughter Gunnlod in his quest for the drink. By his allusive method the writer requires his audience to fill out the gaps in his tale from their own knowledge:

> The ancient giant I sought out. Now I'm back again.
> Little would I have got by silence there.
> Many words I spoke to my own glory
> In the halls of Suttung.

(Elsewhere *Hávamál* says much about the importance of eloquence to the man who would command success.)

> In a golden chair Gunnlod gave me
> A drink of that precious mead.
> A poor return I made her
> For her true heart,
> For her troubled mind.

There follows an obscure verse, perhaps out of order, that indicates the way Odin penetrated Suttung's rock-girt hall by boring through the crags – or does it tell how he got out again?

> With Rati's mouth I made myself space
> And gnawed through the rock.
> Above and below stood the paths of the giants.
> Thus I risked my neck.

There follows a difficult stanza about the poetic mead, and then:

> I have my doubts if I would ever have escaped
> From the halls of the giants,
> Had I not used that good woman Gunnlod
> Whom I clasped in my arms.

And finally:

> Odin, I think, swore his ring-oath.
> How can his word be trusted?
> He left Suttung swindled of his mead
> And Gunnlod in tears.

We know from elsewhere, including a source from Anglo-Saxon history, that the Vikings held a ring-oath – an oath sworn on a holy ring – in particular reverence. Yet Odin violated his.

There is more than this to the story of Odin stealing the mead, though we cannot always recover it. For instance, part of *Hávamál* is a temperance-tract warning against over-drinking:

> Not so good as people claim
> Is ale for the sons of men.
> The more drink he takes, the less a man
> Knows the thoughts of his mind.

Upon which follow the verses:

> The heron of oblivion it is called
> That hovers over drinking parties.
> It takes a man's mind away.
> With this bird's feathers I was fettered
> In Gunnlod's court.

> Drunk I got,
> Very drunk indeed,
> At the wise Fialar's hall.
> In one thing only is drinking good
> That a man at last recovers his wits.

An intoxicated Odin seducing Gunnlod is a new image. Moreover, if these two verses are linked, Gunnlod's court and Fialar's hall are the same place; Odin stole the mead not from the giant Suttung but from Fialar, one of the dwarfs who made the drink from Kvasir's blood.

Snorri adds a prologue to the story. The dwarfs Fialar and Galar had originally brewed the mead, he says, but Suttung took it over in compensation for the death of his father and mother, a giant Gilling and his wife. The dwarfs had invited Gilling for a row in their boat. It had capsized and Gilling was drowned. Gilling's wife wept copiously, so copiously that Fialar could stand the howling no longer. He encouraged her to seek consolation by going to the doorway and looking out over the place where the tragedy had happened. She agreed. As she stood in the doorway Galar dropped a millstone on her head and killed her. Suttung took exception to all this, and plotted revenge. He grabbed the dwarfs and rowed them out to a skerry that was submerged at high tide. There he threatened to maroon them unless they paid blood-money, and they agreed to give him the mead. He took it home and entrusted it to his daughter Gunnlod.

Odin determined to get hold of the mead. As he walked towards Suttung's stronghold he came to a meadow where nine thralls were mowing. They were the farmhands of Baugi, Suttung's brother. Being thralls they were not very bright, and were using blunt scythes. Odin offered to whet the scythes, and the slaves were agreeably surprised at how much better they then cut. They asked if they could buy Odin's whetstone. He threw it up among them, and they all grabbed for it. What with the confusion and what with the sharp scythes, they managed to cut one another's throats and expired. Odin went on to the farm. Baugi was perturbed that he had lost his entire workforce, but Odin offered to do all their jobs in exchange for one drink of Suttung's mead. He introduced himself as Bolverk, which ought to have put even a giant on his guard, since it means Evil-doer. However, all Baugi did was point out he had no control over Suttung's mead, but he agreed to see what he could do to help Odin with his wish. Bolverk slaved through the summer, and when winter came he asked Baugi for his pay. Baugi went with him to Suttung, but that giant refused to give him a single drop of mead. Baugi and Bolverk plotted to get some nevertheless, and together they drilled a hole through the rock wall to get to the drink. Bolverk turned himself into a snake and wriggled through the hole, and the rest of the story we know.

The tale illustrates several of Odin's unattractive attributes: his low cunning and self-seeking, his ability to change his shape, his propensity for disguises and false names, his recourse to treachery. For a marginally more positive view of the god we should look at his pretensions to being a god of knowledge. Already we have seen ways he achieved wisdom: by sacrificing himself on the tree; by pawning one eye in return for a drink from the well of knowledge. There are others: he could make the dead talk; he could question the wise; he could use the full powers of *seiðr*; he had two ravens, Hugin and Munin, who flew across the word gathering news for him.

Odin's study of cosmology and of past and future events is important to us, for it is enshrined in the small group of wisdom poems which provide much of our knowledge of Norse belief and myth. One of them is *Vafþrúðnismál*, the record of a contest of skill and science between Odin and a giant, Vafthrudnir, renowned for his deep knowledge. The poem opens with a conversation between Odin and his wife Frigg, Odin asking for advice he has no intention of taking. Shall he visit Vafthrudnir to find out how much he knows? Frigg, a dutiful wife, sends him off hoping he will return safely. He reaches Vafthrudnir's hall, addresses him less than tactfully, is nevertheless invited in and interrogated. Typically, Odin gives a false name, Gagnrad. The giant questions Gagnrad briefly, and finding him knowledgeable, suggests a contest: they shall test each other's skills, the loser to forfeit his head. So Gagnrad begins asking Vafthrudnir about the origins of the world, the nature of the gods, the end of all things. The giant replies competently until Gagnrad cheats with his final question: what did Odin whisper into the ear of his son Baldr as the dead god was being put on the funeral pyre? Only Odin knows the answer to this, so the giant realises he has been outwitted:

> No man knows what, in those far-off times,
> You spoke in the ear of your son.
> Doomed I have spoken my old tales
> And told the fate of the gods.
> Now I know it was with Odin I fought,
> Always the wisest of all.

Another wisdom poem with Odin as its protagonist is *Grímnismál*. This is set in a more elaborate narrative frame, given in a prose introduction in the *Codex Regius* text. It tells of two young princes, Agnar aged ten and Geirrod, eight. They went out fishing, and the wind blew them out to sea. They were wrecked on a shore near a small farmer's shack. They stayed with the farmer and his wife that winter, and the farmer took particular notice of Geirrod. When spring came, a ship was found for them. As they were embarking, the farmer gave Geirrod some private instructions. When the ship came to their native land, Geirrod, who was standing in the bows, jumped ashore and pushed the boat back out to sea, leaving his elder brother stranded on it. Geirrod went home, found his father had died in the meantime, was hailed as his successor and grew to be a glorious prince. The rightful heir, Agnar, drifted away in the boat, landed in some desolate place and was taken up by giants living there.

This conflict between two brothers caused strife in higher places, for Odin was Geirrod's patron while Frigg was Agnar's. One day the couple were sitting in their high seat seeing what was happening throughout the world, when Odin observed tactlessly, 'Look at your foster-son Agnar. He's begetting children on a giantess in a cave. Whereas my foster-son Geirrod is a king ruling his country'. Frigg retorted acidly, 'Geirrod is a miser, so stingy with his entertainment that he tortures guests if he thinks too many have come'. This was a slander and they quarrelled over it. Odin bet his wife he could show it to be false.

Odin disguised himself and went to Geirrod's hall to test Frigg's accusation. But Frigg was more cunning than her man. She sent a messenger to Geirrod warning him of this doubtful stranger who had entered his land. Geirrod was taken in, and he made Odin captive. Odin was swathed in a blue-black cloak and gave his name as Grimnir, both of which should have warned Geirrod, had he been bright enough. Geirrod wanted more information. Grimnir stood on his right to remain silent, so Geirrod had him tortured. He built two great fires, set Grimnir between them and left him there for eight days, so scorched that his cloak burned on him. Geirrod had a ten-year-old son whom, with doubtful tact, he had named Agnar after his brother. The young Agnar pitied Grimnir, and brought him a horn full of drink. Grimnir's thanks, and prophecy that Agnar should be rewarded with the throne, opens the verse.

Grimnir then shows the range of his knowledge, naming the courts of the various gods, the supernatural beasts that inhabit their world, telling of the creation of the firmament and the gods' treasures, all things that should waken his audience to his real identity. He ends by foretelling Geirrod's death by the sword, and announcing his name:

'Now you can see Odin.
Approach me if you can.'

The sequel is in prose:

King Geirrod was sitting with his sword half-drawn on his lap. When he heard that his visitor was Odin, he jumped up, wanting to take Odin away from the fire. His sword slipped from his grasp, hilt-down. The king's foot tripped and he fell headlong on to the sword. It skewered him through and he was killed. Then Odin vanished. And Agnar was king there for many years after.

Thor

To turn from the deceitful, sinister and complex Odin to the simple-minded and straightforward Thor is something of a relief. Thor is a battler, his enemies the gods' enemies: giants, monsters and primeval forces. Snorri sums him up:

Thor is the foremost of the gods. He is called Thor-of-the-Aesir or Charioteer-Thor. He is the strongest of all the gods and men ... He has three valuable properties. The first is the hammer Miollnir which the frost-monsters and the cliff-giants recognise the moment it is raised on high (which is not surprising – it has bashed in the skulls of many of their fathers and family). A second splendid thing he owns, his belt of strength; when he buckles it round him his godlike power doubles. A third thing he has which is of the greatest value: his iron gloves. He mustn't be without them when he swings his hammer.

Many myths about Thor survive. Some of them are adduced in early skaldic poems, which shows their great age and perhaps implies a practical worship of the god in Viking times. It may be significant here that Thor is the only god invoked in Viking memorial inscriptions, where such phrases as 'Thor hallow these runes' and 'Thor hallow these monuments' display him as a protecting deity. Yet the myths are not always easy to get at, nor easy to explain in terms other than simple narrative – is there any 'popular idea concerning natural . . . phenomena' behind them?

Take the example of Thor's encounter with the giant Geirrod (no relation to the king Geirrod with whom Odin drew conclusions). Towards the end of the heathen age of Scandinavia, the Icelandic poet Eilif Godrunarson wrote a poem which we now know as *Þórsdrápa*, the verses about Thor. This survives because it is quoted in Snorri's *Skáldskaparmál*, but it is generally thought of as one of the most dark and difficult of skaldic poems. Snorri gave an interpretation in telling his tale, but who is to say he was right? Snorri's version runs thus.

The trouble began as usual with Loki. One day he was trying out Frigg's falcon-suit in which he could fly around looking like a bird. He came to Geirrod's hall, touched down on the window-sill and looked in. Geirrod did not like this bird watching him, and ordered a servant to catch it. The servant clambered up the wall, and Loki, seeing how severe the climb was, waited till the last minute before flying away, just to annoy the man. Alas, he then found his feet were stuck and he could not escape. Geirrod could see by the falcon's eyes that it was really a man in disguise, and required to know who. When Loki stayed silent, he was shut in a box for three months without food. This friendly persuasion worked, for when Geirrod took him out, Loki was ready to confess. Geirrod offered him his life if he could lure Thor to Geirrod's hall without his mighty hammer and his belt of strength.

What inducement Loki offered Thor for this is not told, but the great god set off unarmed and Loki went along with him. On the way they put up at a giantess's house, and she told Thor the truth about Geirrod's blood-thirsty nature, and lent him a belt of strength, a staff and some iron gloves – you never knew when they might come in handy. When Thor came to the huge river Vimur, he buckled on his belt, took the staff in his hand and waded across, with Loki holding on to the belt. When Thor got midway, the river suddenly rose till it reached his shoulders. He looked about, and there standing in a cleft of the hills and astride the river was Geirrod's daughter Gialp. She it was who had made the water rise. Snorri is too well bred to say how, but presumably she was pissing into the river (which sounds proper for a folk-tale, though some anthropologists and folklorists would prefer her to be menstruating). Thor remarked philosophically, 'Dam a river at its source', and hurled a great rock at her. Then he waded to the bank and heaved himself out by tugging at a rowan. That is why, says Snorri, we call the rowan 'Thor's deliverance'.

This part of the tale is supported by an Eddic stanza that Snorri quotes, perhaps indicating he had a longer poetic version available to him, from which he constructs his prose:

> Rise not, Vimur, since I fain would wade
> Through you to the giants' courts.
> Know if you rise, so will my godlike strength
> Rise up to the high heavens.

Thor continued his way to Geirrod's where he and Loki were shown to a goat-house, hardly fit lodging for deities of their distinction. Inside was a single piece of furniture, a chair. Thor sat on it, and it began to lift under him, pressing him towards the roof. He pushed against the rafters with the giantess's staff to keep himself down, and there was a crack and a scream. Under the seat were Geirrod's daughters trying to crush Thor against the roof. He had broken their backs. Here too there is a verse quotation in Snorri's *Edda*, though it is preserved in only one manuscript:

> One time only I used all my strength
> In the courts of the giants;
> When Gialp and Greip, Geirrod's daughters,
> Tried to lift me to the heavens.

Next Geirrod summoned Thor to his hall which was lit and heated by two great fires. As Thor entered, Geirrod took up a pair of tongs, picked from the fire a red-hot ingot of iron and flung it at the god. Luckily Thor had the iron gloves on. He caught the missile and aimed it back at Geirrod. The giant rushed for protection behind an iron pillar. The ingot crashed through pillar, Geirrod, the wall behind, and into the ground outside. So ends Snorri's story. The final section finds support in a curious passage in

Saxo Grammaticus's *Gesta Danorum*. Recounting an adventurous expedition that the Danes mounted to the north of Scandinavia, Saxo describes some of the terrifying sights they met. They came to a town, an early example of urban decay; within it was a stone hall in sore need of sweeping and garnishing. Therein the Danes saw 'a shattered piece of rock, and not far off on a raised platform an old man, his body pierced, sitting opposite the pile of broken stone'. The Danish leader Thorkell explained to his followers that 'once the god Thor, infuriated by the insolence of the giants, had driven a red-hot steel through the belly of the hostile Geruthus; flying further it had destroyed and thrust through the mountain's sides'. Nearby were the bodies of women, their backs broken.

An odd tale, and one that is as meat and drink to the hungry mythologist. Imaginative interpretations abound. To select a few: is this a myth embodying an initiation test of the manhood of a young warrior; the unarmed Thor facing attack from natural and animal enemies? Does it show divine strength in conflict with the forces of nature; does Thor, here a young and virile god, face the threats posed by 'the dual forces of excessive attachment to the female objects of his primary bonding and the destructive rivalry with the father'? I conclude that of making many interpretations of books there is no end, and much study of them is a weariness of the flesh.

Other stories survive which recount Thor's strife with giants: that of his contest with Hrungnir, for instance. *Lokasenna* treats it as a well-known tale. Towards the end of that poem Loki becomes so outrageous that Thor arrives to quieten him. Loki gives him a sardonic welcome, 'Why are you rampaging about like that?' Thor replies with threats:

> Shut up, you feeble wretch. My mighty hammer,
> Miollnir, will stop your mouth.
> With my right hand I'll smash you with Hrungnir's killer
> So that every bone in your body shatters.

His next verse repeats the offer:

> Hrungnir's killer will send you to Hel,
> Down to the gates of death.

Skaldic poems have other allusions to Thor's destruction of Hrungnir, but again it is Snorri who gives the extended version.

Hrungnir was an ugly giant, with a stone head and a stone heart. His immensely thick shield was of stone, and his weapon was a whetstone, huge enough to be carried on his shoulder. He and Odin quarrelled over the merits of their horses. Odin rode off and Hrungnir followed in fury, galloping so fast that when he came to Asgard he couldn't stop, but crashed through the gates into the court.

The gods courteously invited him in for a drink. Very drunk he got, and began to boast of how he would destroy the gods and kidnap the goddesses. The Aesir sent for Thor who arrived in a great rage, demanding to know who had asked this enemy in and given him liquor. Hrungnir claimed Odin's protection, but agreed to fight Thor on neutral ground, at the border of their territories.

Back went Hrungnir to collect his shield and whetstone. The other giants speculated uneasily on the outcome of the duel, worried that Hrungnir might lose. So they prepared an enormous clay figure of a warrior, with a heart taken from a mare (for only this was big enough, and even this quaked when Thor appeared). Hrungnir stood prepared to receive Thor, with the clay giant, pissing himself with terror, as his second. Thor's second was his servant Thialfi, who was a champion runner and arrived first. He told Hrungnir a disgraceful fib, claiming that the giant should not stand with his shield in front of him since Thor was travelling underground and would get at him from below. So Hrungnir stood on his shield and held his whetstone ready.

Thor arrived in his usual godlike rage and slung his hammer at Hrungnir. Hrungnir retaliated with his whetstone. The two missiles clashed in the middle, the whetstone flew in pieces, part falling to the ground (whence derive all the whetstone rocks of the world). The rest embedded itself in Thor's head and down he fell. Miollnir the hammer followed through and shattered Hrungnir's skull so that he too fell, with his leg upon Thor. Meanwhile Thialfi was butchering the clay giant.

There lay Thor, pinned to the ground by the giant's leg. Nobody could move it until Thor's three-year-old son Magni came and lifted it easily. Thor said politely that he reckoned his son would grow up to be strong.

Thor came home, but the whetstone was wedged in his head. The gods appealed to a witch called Groa, wife of a mysterious Aurvandil. She chanted charms over Thor and the stone fragment loosened. Thor wanted to reward her, so he told her how once he had waded across the chill stream Elivagar, carrying Aurvandil in a basket. One of Aurvandil's toes stuck out of the basket and was frozen. Thor broke it off, threw it into the sky and it became a star. This so delighted Groa that she forgot her charms and the whetstone remained in Thor's head. That is why it is just not done to throw whetstones about in the house; if you do, the fragment quivers in Thor's head. From this myth derive such kennings as 'leaf of Hrungnir's sole' for 'shield', and 'splitter of Hrungnir's skull' for 'Thor'.

Thor is also called 'foe of the World Serpent' in allusion to his struggles with the great monster Iormungand who lurks in the ocean's depths. The tale is illustrated in Viking Age carvings. It is known in some detail from an Eddic poem, *Hymiskviða*. There, however, it forms only one of a series of contests of strength between the terrible giant Hymir and the god Thor, who was visiting him in an effort to seize his great cauldron for the gods to brew beer in. Snorri, who had other source material, relates the story in more telling and elegant terms. He gives no reason for Thor's stay with the giant, merely saying he was on a journey and put up there for the night.

Next morning Hymir was ready to go fishing. Thor wanted to join him but Hymir rejected the offer, saying Thor was too feeble and might get chilled

The Gosforth fishing stone depicting Thor fishing for the World Serpent Iormungand which was so strong that his foot went through the bottom of the boat when he hooked it. The second figure in the boat may be the giant Hymir.

on the open sea. Thor got angry and insisted, so Hymir made him find his own bait. He went to Hymir's herd of oxen, chose the biggest and tore its head off. This he took to the rowing boat that Hymir had launched. The two took up the oars and soon reached the fishing grounds for flat-fish. Thor wanted to go further out and continued rowing. Soon Hymir warned they had better stop, otherwise there was danger of meeting the World Serpent. To Hymir's consternation Thor carried on. At last he took out a great line and a huge hook, put the ox-head on it and threw it overboard. The World Serpent took the bait and the hook lodged in its jaws. The monster jerked back and Thor's hands rapped against the gunwale. At that he lost his temper and heaved so hard on the line that his feet went through the boat's bottom and struck the sea-ground. He hauled the serpent in as far as the gunwale, and there the two glared at one another, the serpent spitting venom. Thor was just going to kill it with his hammer when Hymir, in terror, hacked through Thor's line and the monster escaped. Thor threw his hammer after it, and, says Snorri, or rather High, some say he killed the World Serpent, 'but I disagree; I think it is true to tell you that the World Serpent is still alive, lurking in the encircling ocean'. Thor was so furious with Hymir that he knocked him overboard and himself waded ashore.

The Thor myths I have recounted, though differing widely in detail, have a common theme, Thor's struggle against monstrous beings who can be thought of as enemies of the gods, and presumably also of humans. Extant are other myths of this sort, as well as hints in skaldic kennings of myths that have not survived to us. There are also the stories of how Thor, absent from Asgard, returned just in time to save the gods from trouble, as in the matter of the giant builder who fortified Asgard.

Thor was a specially honoured god in Viking times. In the temple at Uppsala, says Adam of Bremen, there were statues of three gods who can be identified with Thor, Odin and Freyr. Thor, 'the most powerful of them', was placed in the middle: 'he commands the air, he governs thunder and lightning, winds and rainstorms, fair weather and crops'. If disease or famine threaten, Thor is the god sacrificed to. This is not how the Norwegian or Icelandic myths show Thor, but it would account for his popularity in communities built upon agriculture or fisheries. Thor is the only god whose name formed numerous compound personal names in Viking times, both masculine (as *Thorsteinn, Thorfinnr*) and feminine (as *Thorgerðr, Thorgunnr*). The later Icelandic sagas tell of people who venerated Thor as their individual god, as Thorolf from the island of Mostr in western Norway. He 'kept the temple of Thor on the island, was a great friend of Thor, and that is why he was called Thorolf'. In a moment of political crisis he 'held a great sacrificial feast, and consulted his beloved friend Thor as to whether he should come to terms with the king or leave the country and find another way of life for himself; and the consultation directed Thorolf to Iceland'. Nearing that country he threw overboard the wooden posts that had supported the formal seat of honour in his Norwegian ancestral hall. 'Thor was cut on one. Thorolf decided he would settle in Iceland at the place where Thor came to land.' The settlers followed the floating posts and found them driven ashore on a headland in the west of Iceland. 'That,' says the saga, 'has been called Thorsnes ever since.' It still is.

Baldr and Loki

A famous Norse myth involves two gods quite different in character from those introduced hitherto: Baldr and Loki. Baldr is often named but little known in Norse legend. Snorri says he is Odin's son, the best of gods, fair of complexion and nature, wise, eloquent and full of grace. Yet he is ineffectual. He may be something of a god of law, for his son Forseti controls the great judgment-hall Glitnir where he resolves all disputes. But of the father Snorri admits that no ruling he makes will hold. Baldr must have been something of a fighter too for his name is invoked in kennings for warriors.

Loki has already appeared in this book, and it must be clear that he is a complex figure, part god, part demon. In *Þrymskviða* he was shown to be enterprising, witty, the supporter of Thor while making that great god something of a figure of fun. In the tale of the giant-architect who fortified Asgard, he is shown to be artful, not always wise in his judgment. He brings the gods into trouble through lack of forethought. In the myth of Idunn's apples he betrayed the gods, and only recovered his position with them after threats to his life. At the world's end he is to be one of the leaders of the anarchical army that will destroy the gods; and specifically he is the enemy of the god Heimdall. Snorri sums up the contradictions of his character:

Counted among the Aesir is one whom some call the slanderer of the gods, the father of deceit, the disgrace of all gods and men. He is called Loki or Loptr, son of the giant Farbauti . . . Loki is good-looking, pleasing in appearance, but evil by nature and capricious in his habits. Beyond all others he has the sort of mentality that we call cunning, and he devises plots about everything. He has often brought the Aesir into the greatest difficulties, and got them out again by his crafty schemes.

Snorri then lists Loki's illegitimate children by a giantess Angrboda. Her name is a sinister one; it means 'harbinger of grief'. The list of her brood explains this: Fenrir the wolf, Iormungand the World Serpent, and Hel the goddess of the dead. 'And when the gods realised these three siblings were being brought up in Iotunheim, they pursued oracles, and learned that they would bring them immense harm and disaster. All could understand they must expect great evil, first because of the mother's nature, but more so because of the father's.' Odin went to capture the three. He threw Iormungand into the depths of the ocean, and there he remained encircling the inhabited world. Hel he cast into the underworld, to receive all who died of sickness and old age. What happened to Fenrir we have already seen.

The complex figure of Loki has attracted the interest of many scholars, some of whom have even written perceptively about him. Perhaps the most important of recent contributions is that of Georges Dumézil, who sees in the god/demon a reflection of a demonic figure, Syrdon, who appears in a number of Caucasian legends, and argues a common origin for them. If this is true, the concept of Loki as fundamentally at odds with the great gods is an ancient one.

Baldr

It is convenient to begin the myth of Baldr with the relatively late *Baldrs draumar*, Baldr's Dreams, a poem which is not in the *Codex Regius* but in a shorter collection of Eddic material, MS AM 748 4°. This is a question-and-answer poem, beginning as most such do, with a bit of narrative:

> The Aesir came swiftly all to a council,
> The Asyniur [goddesses] too, all in conclave,
> And the mighty powers mulled it over,
> Why Baldr was troubled with dreams of ill omen.

Odin takes action, saddles his horse, rides to the realm of the dead, summons up a dead seeress and asks her to explain. She is reluctant, ending all her pronouncements with the bitter remark, 'Against my will I have spoken. Now I shall keep silent'. Each time Odin is too powerful for her, beginning his questions with:

> Be not silent, witch! I will still question.
> I must know further till I know all.

The re-animated sybil continues helping Odin with his enquiries. Why are there such preparations in the realm of the dead? Answer: they are expecting Baldr to appear; they are brewing mead for him. How will Baldr die? Hod will be his killer, will take the life of Odin's son. Who will avenge this deed?

> In western dwellings Vali will be born of Rind.
> One night old, he will avenge Odin's son.
> He will not wash hands, he will not comb hair,
> Until Baldr's killer is burned on the pyre.

A stanza from *Lokasenna* reveals Loki's responsibility for the crime. Retorting to a threat from Odin's wife, Frigg, he boasts:

> I made sure that never again
> Will you see Baldr riding back home.

Loki has been the *ráðbani*, 'planner of the killing'; the innocent Hod was the *handbani*, 'hit-man'.

From hints like this Snorri builds up the tale of deceit and evil. It begins with Loki's motiveless malignity, his envy of Baldr. The shining god had had ominous dreams, foreboding death. On behalf of the gods Frigg acted to prevent mishap. She took oaths from all creatures not to harm Baldr: from 'fire and water, iron and all sorts of metal, rocks, earth, trees, diseases, beasts, birds, poison, snakes'. All swore. Baldr became the centre of a game. Since he couldn't be harmed, the gods stood round and used him for target practice, attacking with arrows or spears, swords or axes, stones. Nothing could hurt him. Loki planned disaster. Disguising himself, he went to Frigg and asked why Baldr could not take harm. She told him about the oaths. He asked whether there was anything that had not sworn. Frigg gave the fatal secret away. 'West of Valholl grows a slip of tree called mistletoe. It seemed too young to be asked for an oath.' Loki tore up the tree shoot from the ground, and took it to where the gods were playing. The blind god Hod was standing about doing nothing. 'Why aren't you shooting at Baldr?' 'In the first place I can't see him; in the second, I've nothing to shoot with.' Loki tempted Hod, pointing out what a splendid thing it was to demonstrate Baldr's invulnerability. 'I'll show you where he's standing. Shoot this shaft at him.' Hod shot at Loki's directions, and Baldr fell dead.

Consternation and grief filled the gods. The game had been played at their moot-place, a sacred spot. There they could not take vengeance on Baldr's killer though they knew perfectly well who it was. And they could hardly speak for tears. Frigg showed a woman's practical sense. She sought out someone with the courage to ride to Hel to seek out Baldr and find if he could be allowed to return to Asgard. The great hero Hermod agreed to take this perilous journey, riding Odin's magnificent horse Sleipnir. Meanwhile the gods prepared Baldr's body for the pyre.

This they planned to build in Baldr's ship Hringhorni. It had been drawn ashore, and they could not shift it to the sea. They sent for a witch Hyrokkin, who with a single shove sent it afloat so fast that the runners burst into flames and the whole earth quaked. They carried Baldr's body aboard, and his widow Nanna collapsed with grief and was also put on the pyre. An odd dwarf happened to be passing by, and Thor kicked him on for luck. Treasures were also piled on, including the magical gold ring Draupnir.

Meanwhile Hermod rode the long, dark path to the river Gioll that divides this world from the next. Over its bridge he rode, making it echo as though five legions of the dead were crossing. He came to the gates of Hel, spurred his horse and jumped over. There in the great hall he found Baldr. Hermod asked for his release. Baldr was so much loved, he said. But Hel was sceptical. 'If everything in the world, living and non-living, weeps for him, then he can go back to the Aesir; but he shall be kept in Hel if anything objects or refuses to weep.'

Hermod took back this message. The gods sent ambassadors throughout the world to ask for Baldr to be wept out of Hel, and everything and everyone complied: men, creatures, earth, rocks, trees, all metals. As the messengers were making their way back, they came upon a cave in which sat a giantess named – she said – Thokk. They bade her weep Baldr out of Hel. She retorted with this verse:

> Dry tears are all that Thokk will shed
> At Baldr's funeral pyre.
> Quick or dead, man's son has never served me,
> Let Hel keep her property.

Snorri adds: 'men guess this must have been Loki Laufeyiarson, who has done the greatest wickedness among the Aesir'.

The myth is easily recognised. Though this version has its distinctive Norse features, its type is represented among many mythologies. The myth of the 'dying god', who may also be a resurrected god, is of course central to Christian experience – or at least was before some bishops of the Church of England reformulated its belief. It is also found in, for instance, the Osiris legend of ancient Egypt, that of Adonis from the Near East, and, in heroic rather than mythological form, the Finnish tale of Lemminkainen. Whether there is an archetypal pattern in this or influence of one civilisation's myth upon another is in dispute.

Snorri's story does not end here. Though the gods could not destroy Baldr's killer, they could punish him. Indeed, they became so enraged that Loki fled, taking refuge in a safe house with a door in each wall so that he could keep watch in all directions. By day he became a salmon, living in concealment in a nearby waterfall. When ashore he took the precaution of working out how the Aesir might try to trap him. He thought up the principle of the fishing net, and made up a prototype out of linen thread to see how it would work. Nets have been made that way ever since.

Odin settled into his great throne Hlidskialf. From that eminence he spotted Loki, and directed the gods as to how to find him. When Loki saw them advancing, he threw his net into the fire and fled to the waterfall. The net flared up, but left its pattern clearly to be seen in the ashes. The wise god Kvasir saw it and realised its purpose; so the gods made a similar net and went to the rapids to try to catch Loki. They dragged the river, but twice Loki evaded them, by hugging the shingled bottom or leaping the net. The third time Thor was in wait, and as Loki leapt the net, Thor grabbed him. The gods set to securing him.

They tied him to three great rocks, one beneath his shoulders, one beneath his loins, the third under his knees. In case he was too comfortable, they suspended a venomous snake over him so that its poison dripped on to him. His faithful wife tried to help him by interposing a bowl. However, each time the bowl fills up she has to go off to empty it, and the poison drips on his face. At this he shudders vehemently, and so earthquakes are made. But Loki still lies securely enchained until he is fated to escape and precipitate the final day of this world.

Such is Baldr's story as it is told, hinted at or alluded to in Norwegian/Icelandic writings. Further east, in Denmark, there was a different tradition, one much less picturesque. Saxo Grammaticus recorded it in his *Gesta Danorum*. He thought himself as writing history, not mythology; hence his story is of kings (or at the most of demi-gods and other supernatural creatures),

Figures on the Gosforth Cross (left and above). The lower ones perhaps represent Loki and his wife. Loki is bound and his wife saves him from the poison that drips onto him. This is the gods' vengeance for the death of Baldr.

not of gods. The tale is set in pre-Hamletian Denmark, where Hotherus and Balderus are rivals to the throne, as well as to the favours of the lovely princess Nanna, daughter of Hotherus's foster-father Gevarus. Hotherus was a mere mortal, albeit a talented one, a skilled athlete and musician. Balderus was of more doubtful parentage, being the son of a certain Othinus of Uppsala who, says Saxo scathingly, 'was at that time credited by the whole of Europe with the false title of divinity'. Hence Balderus was a *semideus*, 'half-god'. Hotherus was Nanna's chosen lover, but Balderus fell for her on seeing her bathing, as many a good man before or since.

The stage is set for struggle between Hotherus and Balderus, fighting for the possession of Nanna and control of kingdoms in Sweden and Denmark. Balderus is god-descended, but against this Hotherus has help on several occasions from a group, or possibly groups, of supernatural women (*silvestres virgines, nymphae*, 'wood-nymphs') who control victory and give useful tactical advice. From them he gets a coat of proof which will be helpful in war.

Balderus could not be wounded by steel, so Hotherus needed a special sword to penetrate his thick hide. This he took by force from a supernatural creature, a *satyrus* called Mimingus, who lived in a cave amidst frozen wildernesses. He also seized an arm-ring that had the power of increasing its owner's wealth. Armed with these, Hotherus went adventuring. Meanwhile Balderus accosted Nanna, asked for her in marriage, and got her reply that, being a mortal, it was not seemly for her to mate with a god. This threw Balderus into a love-lorn state.

Hotherus, indignant at Balderus's importunity, gathered a sea-borne army, attacked Balderus and defeated him, even though Balderus had the support of Othinus, Thor and other so-called gods. Balderus fled. Hotherus wedded Nanna. However, this did not finish off his rival. Balderus returned and beat Hotherus in a series of battles. A depressed Hotherus wandered through the forests and again came upon the wood-nymphs. He complained they had not been very successful in giving him victory. They advised him to be philosophical, but suggested more practically that he should steal the supernatural food that gave Balderus his special strength. Curiously encouraged by this, Hotherus again attacked Balderus. After a day of inconclusive fighting with huge loss of life, Hotherus prospected the enemy camp, traced the three nymphs who looked after Balderus's food, tracked them down in disguise and gained (apparently, for there seems to be a loss in the text here) a taste of it. He also got hold of a belt that ensured victory.

Coming back he chanced upon Balderus whom he wounded severely with his magic sword. Bravely Balderus continued the battle the next day from his litter, but his wound was too serious, and he declined and died within three days. Many years later Balderus was avenged when Othinus begat a son, Bous, on Rinda, daughter of the king of Ruthenia. Bous met Hotherus in battle and killed him.

Different as these two versions of the Baldr myth are, they have common details which must come from a common original. Found in both Snorri and Saxo are: the names Baldr/Balderus; Hod (*Hǫðr*)/Hotherus; Nanna; Baldr's immunity from harm save that inflicted by a special weapon; Hod's killing of Baldr; the magical ring Draupnir. From West Norse sources outside Snorri, and also in Saxo, come the name Rind/Rinda as the mother of Baldr's avenger; Baldr as a respected fighter. Yet the variations between the two traditions are immense. Saxo has Nanna married to Hotherus, not Balderus. Balderus is the aggressor, not the kindly and innocent victim. The avenger is called Bous, not Vali (though to confuse the issue, I have to admit that the verse from *Baldrs draumar* that gives this information requires an emendation of the text). But the main difference between the two versions is that in Saxo there is no room for Loki's wicked intervention.

Loki

In the Norse version Loki's part is genuinely devilish. He plays the role of the gods' enemy, motivated only by the desire to destroy. He takes the same part in the battle that ends this world's rule. Naturally there are similarities with the Devil figure in Christian myth, and that may have influenced the late Norse viewpoint. In the tale of the abduction of Idunn, Loki also plays a spoiling game, though there he is forced to it by the straits he finds himself in. At other times his acts are impish rather than devilish. He does trivial works of mischief, which may however have serious consequences.

'Why is gold called "Sif's hair"?', asks Snorri in *Skáldskaparmál*; then he answers his own question. One day Loki cut off all Sif's hair. He did it *til lævísi*, which I would translate 'in sheer vandalism'. Sif's husband Thor lost his temper and was about to beat Loki up, but he hastily promised to go to the elves, very skilled artificers, who would forge a new head of hair for Sif out of gold. This would grow to her scalp like a second crop. So some dwarfs made Loki the hair, and also a ship (Skidbladnir) and a spear (Gungnir). Loki was so impressed that he rashly made a bet – the wager was his own head – with a dwarf called Brokk, who had a craftsman brother, Eitri. The bet was that Eitri couldn't make three things as fine. Eitri set to work, put a pig's skin into the furnace and told Brokk to blow on the bellows and not to stop till Eitri said the word. Brokk started work. As soon as Eitri went off, a fly settled on Brokk's arm and began biting. Brokk ignored it, and when Eitri came back he opened the furnace and took out a boar with bristles of gold which glittered so brightly that they lightened the darkest night. Next Eitri put an ingot of gold into the furnace, and again set Brokk to work with the bellows. Along came the fly again and nibbled at Brokk's neck. Brokk took no notice, and in due course the goldsmith came back and took from the furnace a gold ring called Draupnir. Every ninth night, eight more rings, equal to it in weight, would drip from it. The third time Eitri put iron into the furnace. This time the fly bit at Brokk's eyelids so that blood dripped into his eyes, and for a brief moment Brokk let go the bellows to brush it away. When Eitri came back he said his work was nearly

spoiled, but he took from the furnace a hammer. Because of the fly's inter-
ference the shaft was just too short. It would never miss its target and would
return to the thrower's hand; yet it was so small it would fit inside a man's
shirt. Snorri never tells us, but we can be pretty sure the fly was Loki in
one of his disguises.

How to decide who had won? Odin, Thor and Freyr were the judges.
Loki gave the spear to Odin, the golden hair to Thor, and the ship to Freyr.
Then it was Brokk's turn. He gave Odin the ring, Freyr the boar, and Thor
the hammer. The gods wanted a weapon to defend them against the giants,
so they judged the hammer the best of these treasures. Loki had lost and
must forfeit his head. He tried to buy himself out. 'No chance,' said Brokk.

Loki fled, but Thor caught up with him and handed him over. Brokk
prepared to cut off Loki's head, but that legalistic god had a flash of inspiration:
he could lose his head, but his neck was still his own. So instead Brokk
sewed up his mouth, presumably to stop his impish speech in future.

The story has a clear structural purpose within the sequence of Norse
myth as Snorri recounts it: to explain how the great treasures of the gods
came into being. How far that is an original plan, a real part of Viking Age
myth, is unknown. In the tale Loki has no godlike attributes. The most one
can say is that he has the supernatural quality of being a shape-shifter, able
to take on the attributes of other creatures – but in Norse narrative humans
can do this too.

Another of Snorri's tales, that of Thor's expedition to the court of the
giant king Utgard-Loki, shows this muted version of the Loki figure. Thor
set off on this visit for no defined reason. His companions were Loki and,
later, Thialfi. After a surprising adventure with a giant, Skrymir, they reached
Utgard-Loki's monstrous palace, where the giant's trickery humbled them.
Utgard-Loki challenged them to compete with his own retainers in divers
skills. Thialfi chose athletics since he could run faster than anyone. But when
matched against the local champion, Hugi, he lost easily. That is because
Hugi means 'thought', and thought is swifter than anything. Thor competed
last, in three contests. He tried to drink off the contents of a horn and failed
wretchedly. Afterwards he learned that the other end of the horn was in
the sea. His swigging made the tide go out but that was all. The second
contest was a silly one: could he pick up Utgard-Loki's rather big cat? He
couldn't, but that was because the cat was impersonated by the World Serpent,
so long that nobody, even Thor, could raise it. For the third contest Thor
suggested a wrestling match, and the giant contemptuously pitted him against
an old woman, Elli, who brought Thor down on one knee. That is because
Elli means 'old age', something that eventually defeats the strongest.

Loki's test, an eating contest, opened the games. Loki bet he could wolf
down food faster than anyone else. Utgard-Loki set against him a certain
Logi. The two sat at opposite ends of a table, with a wooden trencher full
of meat between them. They set off eating as ravenously as they could and
met exactly in the middle. Whereas Loki had eaten all the meat off his bones,

Logi had consumed meat, bones, trencher and all. 'And the general opinion was that Loki had lost.' Only later did the gods realise that *Logi* means 'fire', most voracious of all elements.

This side of Loki – a simple figure of fun with no pretence to divinity – must be taken into account, but I suspect his darker, powerful side is more important. Unfortunately, we know too little about the myths that must have circulated about this god, and what we know is varied and sketchy. There survive tantalising references to tales, as that of a struggle between Loki and the strange god Heimdall, a feud to be reawakened at the world's end. On this myth the Icelandic poet Ulf Uggason has an important verse in his poem *Húsdrápa*, composed *c.* 1000. Snorri claims that Ulf wrote a good deal about the story in his poem, but all that remains is the cryptic:

> The gods' famed road-warden, eminent in wisdom,
> Took off for Singastein with Farbauti's crafty son.
> Son of eight mothers and one, powerful in mind,
> He first took possession of the brilliant *hafnýra*.

Again the audience has to spot the references. Heimdall was the guardian of the paths of the gods: he it is who, on the final day, will blow his horn to signal the approach of hostile forces. He was also that obstetric curiosity, born to nine mothers. Farbauti's son was Loki. So somehow Loki and Heimdall went to Singastein where Heimdall got hold of a *hafnýra*, a curious word that occurs only in this verse. Literally it means 'sea-kidney', and anyone may have a guess at what that might be. Snorri came up with an answer in his *Skáldskaparmál*. 'Heimdall is the visitor to ... Singastein. That was when he fought with Loki for the *Brísingamen* ... They were in the guise of seals.' Apparently Singastein was a rock in the ocean, hence the gods' peculiar disguises. The *Brísingamen* is well known (though what it has to do with 'sea-kidneys' I haven't the least idea). It was a famous and glorious gold necklace, some time the property of Freyia. According to a late text, it was made by four dwarfs, and the goddess so coveted it that she slept with each dwarf in turn and got the necklace as payment. Which sounds typical of her. More than this we do not know, save that at the world's end Loki was to seek out Heimdall and fight him to the death.

Beginnings, middles and ends

Most – perhaps all – peoples ponder on the distant past and the distant future: how did this world begin and what was there before; what are the limits of the world and how are they set; how was man created (seldom why); how will the world come to its end, and then what will happen? Such ponderings are a potent source of myth, specifically here of Norse myth. The answers the Norsemen gave these questions are unlikely to be coherent and are certainly not comprehensive. Nor need we assume there was a single, orthodox belief to be expressed.

A good place to begin is with the early part of the great Eddic poem *Vǫluspá*, The Wise Woman's Prophecy. This probably dates from *c*.1000, when Christ was beginning to exercise a strong influence on Norse affairs. So the poem as we have it may show Norse myth infiltrated by Judaeo-Christian. Moreover, the *Codex Regius* text of this poem shows it already in mutilated state; there are obvious gaps in it and there are likely to be interpolations that are harder to trace. Even our primary source is thus defective. The poem is presented as the pronouncement of an unspecified *vǫlva*, 'prophet-ess, sybil', at the insistence of Valfodr, one of Odin's many names. He had asked her to relate 'the ancient tales of men', the first things she could remember. From her memories of primeval times, she went on to speak of later, though still ancient, events, and finally to the future which she foretold, presumably to Odin's apprehension. Of the earliest state of the universe she says:

> It was in distant times
> When nothing was;
> Neither sand nor sea
> Nor chill waves;
> No earth at all
> Nor the high heavens;
> The great void only
> And growth nowhere.

So far so clear. But then the story becomes so allusive as to be cryptic. Bur's sons, she says, raised up lands and shaped Midgard, the central enclosed territory of inhabited earth. Greenery spread over it, but the heavens were not yet planned. The sun, moon and stars did not know their functions and places. So the gods – the word here is *regin* which means something like 'organising powers' – sat in conclave, discussed the situation, and determined the hours of day and night and the division of time into years. They met together on a plain called Idavoll, perhaps meaning Evergreen Field. There they built houses and temples, set up forges, made tools and worked precious metals. So they lived in bliss, wealthy beyond need, and playing some sort of board game with golden pieces by which, think some, they determined the world's course. Then disaster struck. The problem is we do not know what it was. It was connected somehow with the arrival of three monstrous giant women, but at this stanza any continuity the poem had is broken. Snorri Sturluson himself did not know the answer.

Even an amateur cosmographer can pick plenty of black holes in the *Vǫluspá* story. There are too many things unexplained. Who were Bur's sons (Odin and his two brothers?) and where did they spring from? Who made the heavenly bodies? What was the origin of the gods, and how did they achieve their 'organising power'? And so on. This lack of information in *Vǫluspá* may, of course, be the effect of that poem's defective transmission and record. Snorri obviously found difficulties, but he made a rather better effort at explaining the creation, largely by interpreting the additional material found in the question-and-answer poem *Vafþrúðnismál*. When Gangleri/Gylfi questioned the three mysterious kings, one of his first enquiries was, 'What was the beginning? How did everything begin? What was there before?' High replied by reciting the *Vǫluspá* verse I have quoted (and indeed, reciting a better form of it than appears in *Codex Regius*). But the kings obviously thought this was inadequate, for they went on to add to the account, though it is not always easy to see what they meant. They define a universe, part freezing (called Niflheim, Land of Fog), part hot and blazing (called Muspell). These two regions stand on either side of the Great Void (Ginnungagap). A river flowed into Ginnungagap, and froze over, layer upon layer, forming a fundament. Where hot and cold met, the rime began to melt, and its drops, quickened by the warmth, formed a frost-giant, Ymir. From him, by a remarkable feat of parthenogenesis, the race of frost-giants descended: 'beneath his left arm grew a man and a woman, and one of his feet begot a son on the other.'

Gangleri tried to understand the logistics of the situation: what did Ymir live on? 'The next thing that happened, as the rime continued dripping, was that it formed a cow called Audhumla. Four rivers of milk flowed from its teats, and it fed Ymir.' But what did the cow live on? 'It licked the rime-stones since they were salty. The first day it had been licking the stones, in the evening there appeared from the stones a man's hair, the second day a man's head, and the third the whole man. He was called Buri.' Buri mated (but Gangleri forgot to ask with whom) and begot a son called Bor who married a giantess by whom he had three sons, Odin, Vili and Ve.

There were giants in the earth in those days, and the same thing happened to them as happened to those of Noah's time. Odin, Vili and Ve slew Ymir, and so much blood poured from his wounds as to drown nearly all his progeny. One called Bergelmir escaped with his family by jumping into his *lúðr*, a word that seems to mean 'chest, coffin', but which Snorri apparently equated with 'ark'. Ymir's corpse was not wasted. Odin and his brothers carried it to Ginnungagap, and set it in the midst. His flesh was made into the earth, his bones into crags; his teeth and bits of his shattered bones became shingle and small rocks. His blood was standing water and sea, encompassing the earth on all sides. More elegantly, the brothers created the sky out of Ymir's skull, and under each cardinal point of the compass they put a dwarf (where did they come from, I wonder?), presumably to hold it up. Odd sparks and molten particles that shot up out of Muspell they caught and set in the heavens, some fixed to the sky and others moving freely beneath it. The brothers had still not finished recycling Ymir. They took his brows and made them into a protecting wall to keep men safe from the giants; within this wall was Midgard, the central enclosure where humans dwelt. Ymir's brains they threw into the sky to form clouds. High justifies this story by citing stanzas from another question-and-answer poem, *Grímnismál*:

> From Ymir's flesh was the world fashioned,
> And from his blood the sea.
> Crags from his bones, trees from his hair,
> And the vault of heaven from his skull.

> And from his brows the genial gods
> Made Midgard for mankind.
> And from his brains were all those
> Harsh storm-clouds created.

Within this world were to dwell a variety of beings, men, gods, monsters, giants and elves. The geographical relationship of their different dwelling-places to each other is unclear, and probably always was. Snorri made a stab at defining it. The giants, he said, live by the deep ocean, at the outer edge of the circular world. Men reside nearer the centre, in their protected land called Midgard. Elves are of two sorts: swarthy ones who lurk within the earth, and brilliant ones who live in Alfheim. The gods and goddesses make their home in Asgard, each within his or her own sanctuary. At the most sacred place of all, at the earth's centre, the gods hold their daily courts, under the great ash-tree Yggdrasil, whose boughs spread over the whole world. Beneath one of its roots is Mimir's well, wherein is hidden all wisdom and good sense. When Odin wanted to gain wisdom by taking a single drink from this well, he was required to leave behind one of his eyes as a pledge. Hence Odin is always portrayed as one-eyed. There is a second spring beneath the tree's roots, called the Well of Fate. By this is a great hall in which live three demi-goddesses called Urd, Verdandi and Skuld (meaning something like Fated, Happening, What Must Be). These are the Norns who shape the course of men's lives. At this point Snorri suggests there is a confusion in Norse myth, for he also mentions individual norns, attached to a man at his birth and controlling his destiny, not always for the happiest. As Gangleri comments: 'If norns control men's destinies, they arrange things jolly unfairly; some people have a good and splendid life, some have not much success or glory; some have long life, some a short one'. And to this eternal problem

High has no very convincing solution.

There is nothing eternal about the state of this world. Even the great world-ash is subject to attack. Snorri quotes a verse from *Grímnismál* about the tree's enemies:

> The ash Yggdrasil endures hardship
> More than men can know.
> The hart bites its crown, its sides decay,
> The serpent Nidhogg tears its roots.

The Norns try to preserve it by pouring over its branches water and mud from the Well of Fate. This magical liquid helps to stop the rot. In the end the tree is to fall, as are the gods themselves. They are as mortal as man.

Another myth tells the beginnings of mankind. The primary source is a couple of stanzas in *Vǫluspá*. The text of the poem is in disarray here, nor can we be sure if these verses are original or late interpolations. Certainly the details of the story are confused, and its beginning (its end too) is abrupt:

> Until from that band there came three
> Mighty, great-hearted Aesir to that dwelling.
> By the shore they found two of little strength,
> Ask and Embla, beings without destiny.
>
> No breath they had, no living soul,
> No flow of blood, no voice, no colour.
> Odin gave breath, Hoenir gave soul,
> Lodur gave both blood and colour.

Snorri had to make sense of these stanzas for his *Prose Edda*. He succeeded, but by adding and altering. He makes Gylfi ask where the people who inhabit the world come from. High answers:

Bor's sons [Odin, Vili and Ve, an alteration from the *Vǫluspá* version here] were walking by the sea-shore, and came upon two logs. They picked them up and shaped them into human beings. The first gave them breath and life, the second understanding and motion, the third form, speech, hearing and sight. They gave them clothes and names. The man was called Ask [ash tree], the woman Embla [perhaps 'elm' or 'vine']. From them descend the races of men who have been given a dwelling-place below Midgard.

For the beginnings of social class in this world, we turn to another, rather unusual, poem called *Rígsþula* or sometimes *Rígsmál*, the Tale of Rig. Though it is an Eddic poem it does not appear in the *Codex Regius*. Its primary text is in a manuscript of Snorri's *Prose Edda*. The story tells of Heimdall, a rather shadowy god, indeed so shadowy it is not always clear if he is *Áss* or *Vanr*. He went on his travels, taking the name of Rig which has been linked to an Old Irish word *ríg*, 'king', since the poem tells of the origin of royal and other ranks. Thus there is a suspicion of Celtic influence on the myth. The poem's prose introduction runs:

In ancient histories men say that one of the Aesir, the one called Heimdall, was off on his travels. He walked out to the sea-shore, came upon a farmstead, and gave his name as Rig. This poem follows that history.

The god is defined as *kunnigr, rammr* and *roskr*, knowing, tough and vigorous, suitable qualities for the work he will do in the poem. In the farm kitchen sat two aged people, Ai and Edda (Great-grandpa and Great-grandma). They welcomed Rig and dined him as best they could on coarse bread and broth. Then they all went to bed, Rig lying between the couple. In nine months Edda gave birth to a boy-child. They called him Thrall. He grew up to be strong, but rough and ugly, capable of hard, menial toil. He married a suitable mate and they raised a family, all with vulgar names. These would do the heavy work on the farm: muck-spreading, tending the beasts, peat-digging. So arose the race of slaves.

Rig walked on and came to a more prosperous-looking house. Inside sat a well-dressed couple. The man was a skilled workman and farmer, the woman was spinning. They were called Afi and Amma, Grandpa and Grandma. They welcomed Rig and presumably (there seems to be a lacuna in the poem here) gave him a rather better supper than his former hosts. They went to bed, Rig again between the pair. Nine months later Amma bore a boy-child, ruddy-faced and with peering eyes. They called him Karl. He grew up to be a craftsman, skilful worker and farmer. His bride was keeper of the household, looking after the linen, holding the keys to the locked chests. Their family formed the race of yeoman farmers.

On walked Rig and came to a splendid mansion, occupied by another couple, Fadir and Modir, Father and Mother. Fadir was checking his armoury, making sure his bow and arrows were in good order. Modir seems to have been occupied with her appearance; certainly she was very fashionably dressed. She took her best linen cloth and set out a sumptuous supper on a silver service, fine bread, pork and roast fowl, with wine to drink. They sat and chatted; then to bed as before. Nine months later Modir bore a boy-child, fair-haired, clear of complexion and with eyes as keen as serpents. He was called Earl. He grew up to be the aristocratic sportsman and fighter, learning to shoot, wield a spear, fence, ride and swim. This son Rig acknowledged, taking an interest in his education, teaching him about runes, granting him estates. The lad grew into a great and wealthy warrior, a generous prince. He married and had aristocratic children. The youngest was called Konr, and here the poet indulges in a pun: *Konr ungr*, 'the young Konr' becomes *konungr*, 'king'. And at that the poem breaks off.

The myth is transparent. All human beings derive ultimately from the gods, but they are not equal. Indeed, the poem *Voluspá* opens with a call for silence from all Heimdall's kin, great and small. The greatness or smallness of a man's social position depended on family. This applied in particular to kingship, for the meaning of the word 'king', *konungr* in Old Norse, *cyning* in Old English, is 'man of kin'. A man or woman's skills, appearance, rights and duties derived from the social position (s)he was born to. Norse life was aristocratic, fixed in social dimension, its ranks set firmly.

For mankind death is a necessary end, we are told, which will come when it will come. Yet many peoples have been reluctant to see death as an end, preferring to think it a transition to another life; and they have evolved myths to expound this. Norsemen were no more willing than most to meet their end, and they have many tales that tell of life after death: a shadowy life in a grave-mound; a life that allows the dead to walk again; a life of revelry within a holy mountain; and so on. These, though delightfully improbable, are hardly mythology. Their variety suggests there was no very clear-cut or coherent view of the dead that applied to the whole of pagan Scandinavia. Mythological stories and references confirm this variety of attitudes, giving inconsistent accounts, some of them very slight indeed. For instance, Snorri's *Prose Edda* lists, among the goddesses, a little-known one called Gefion: 'she is a virgin, and those girls who die as virgins are her servants'.

A stanza from the Eddic poem *Hárbarðslióð* also tells of a division of responsibility for or claim on the dead:

> Odin owns the fighting-men who die in battle,
> And Thor takes the race of slaves.

An alternative disposition is recorded in *Grímnismál*:

> That place is called Folkvang where Freyia disposes
> Of seating-places in her hall.
> Each day she picks out half the slain,
> The other half has Odin.

To the outgoing warriors of Viking times, the myth with the greatest appeal was that of Odin taking to himself those who died in war. Freyia's share is usually not mentioned, though Odin is certainly seen to be exercising discrimination, picking out the ones who show themselves most valiant. His assistants are demi-goddesses, valkyries; indeed the word *valkyria* (*valr*, 'those slain in fight'; -*kyria*, connected with the verb *kiósa*, 'choose') means 'one who picks from among the war-dead'. When King Hakon the Good of Norway died of wounds received in battle *c.* 960, his court poet, Eyvind (nicknamed 'despoiler of poets' because he stole other skalds' ideas), composed a funeral ode for him. Though Hakon had been a Christian – hence his sobriquet – Eyvind modelled his dirge on *Eiríksmál*, the pagan poem written for Eric Bloodaxe. It begins with two valkyries, Gondul and Skogul, being briefed for a mission:

> Gautatyr [Odin] sent Gondul and Skogul
> To choose among the kings;
> Which one of Yngvi's race should go to Odin
> And dwell in Valholl.

> They came upon Biorn's brother [Hakon], clad in mail-coat,
> A glorious king beneath his battle-banner.
> Lances levelled, pennant fluttered,
> As the clash of war began.

Hakon is a star performer:

> So the sword in the prince's hand
> Bit Odin's gear [armour] as though plunged into water.

> Spear-points clattered, shields smashed,
> Swords hammered into men's skulls.

The valkyries, recognising the talent, choose Hakon to join Odin's forces. Hakon is not impressed; he sees no future in dying in battle:

> 'Why did you thus dispose the fight, Gondul?
> Did we deserve no success from the gods?'

The retort is:

> 'It was we who allowed you to hold the field,
> And made your enemies flee.'

Hakon is still not satisfied, particularly since he distrusts Odin who is notoriously *illúðigr*, 'black-hearted'. Though the valkyries promise him safe conduct to Odin's hall, and plenty to drink when he gets there, he insists on holding on to his arms and armour:

> 'Always guard helmet and mail-coat well.
> It's good to have them at hand.'

The gods welcome Hakon to their land, but the poem concludes with an ominous verse looking to Odin's need for such men in his army.

> Unchained, wolf Fenrir will invade men's homes
> Before so good a king returns to these desolate tracks.

Life in Odin's hall, Valholl, is good if you like that sort of thing. *Grímnismál* tells quite a lot about it, and Snorri takes up this information into his *Edda*, expanding and rationalising it, and commenting quizzically. Since the battle-dead of centuries have been collected into Valholl – and Snorri implies all of them, not part only – it has to be an enormous building:

> Five hundred doors and forty more
> In Valholl I think there are.
> Eight hundred warriors at a time
> Will pass each door to fight the wolf.

Even then, says Snorri balefully, and even with all those to be added from future wars, they will not seem too many when Fenrir attacks. The commissariat for this mighty army is the cook Andhrimnir, who has a great cauldron Eldhrimnir. Into this every day the cook puts the meat of the great boar-pig Saehrimnir, to make pork stew for the fighters. Each night the pig is whole again. The drink is mead, also produced by an unconventional process. A goat Heidrun lives on the roof of Valholl, feeding on the foliage of a tree called Lerad; from the goat's teats flows so much mead that she fills a great barrel every day. 'That', says Gangleri wonderingly – or perhaps ironically – 'is a jolly convenient goat to have. And it must be an extraordinary tree it feeds on.'

Odin himself is more abstemious. As he presides over the feasting he takes only wine, which serves as food and drink for him. Meat put before him he feeds to his pet wolves Geri and Freki.

There is a further shadowy place mentioned in the literature as the abode of the dead. It is called Hel, governed by a goddess of the same name: a wretched place divided from the world of men by the river Gioll, over which arches the bridge called Giallarbru. It was this way that Hermod rode when he visited the realm of the dead to seek out Baldr. Snorri describes precisely how to get to Hel: *niðr ok norðr liggr Helvegr*, 'the road to Hel runs downwards and northwards'.

From time to time but insistently in this book, and throughout the Eddic and skaldic literatures too, there has been mention of the end of the world, the great calamity that Odin tries to evade by assembling his army of chosen and veteran warriors. This is *Ragnarǫk*. The word is a compound. Its first element, *ragna-*, is the possessive plural of the word *reginn* which we have seen used of the gods as organising powers. The second part, *-rǫk*, means literally 'marvels, fate, doom'. Thus the compound literally means 'fate/ wonders of the gods', but quite early the second element became confused with the word *røkkr*, 'twilight'; hence Wagner's *Götterdämmerung*, 'twilight of the gods'.

The gods know that Ragnarok is inevitable. It has been prophesied that they will be destroyed in this final battle, yet they prepare for it. Their greatness is shown in their defiance in face of a fate that they cannot avoid. Again, *Vǫluspá* is our primary source for the detail of this struggle, though numbers of other poems allude to it. Snorri took over the *Vǫluspá* account, quoting freely from it as well as interpreting it liberally. The final age of this world is to open with terrifying omens. There will be a fierce winter, *fimbulvetr*, 'the monstrous winter'; 'those winters go three in a row with no summer in between'. Strife will fill the world, even strife within families which cuts at the heart of Norse social thinking. Ethical bonds will dissolve. There will succeed:

> An age of axes, an age of swords, shattered shields,
> An age of tempests, an age of wolves, before the age of men crashes down.

Here there is an echo of the terrors that presage the coming of Antichrist in Judaeo-Christian mythology, and we should keep in mind that *Vǫluspá* probably dates from a time when Norse paganism was giving way before Christianity.

There are natural portents. High had explained to Gangleri that the sun and moon race across the heavens pursued by wolves trying to eat them. At Ragnarok, we now learn, the wolves will catch up.

One wolf will gulp down the sun, and men will think that a great disaster. The other wolf will catch the moon, and he will not produce much improvement either. The stars will fall from the sky. And this too will happen; all the earth and the mountains will quake so that the woods are loosened up from the ground, and the crags totter, and all fetters and bonds will shatter and tear apart. And then the wolf Fenrir will get free.

The attack on the gods is confusedly told in the poetic sources and in Snorri's prose version. It needs a good deal of rationalisation to get a coherent

A monster swallowing a male figure (above) which may of course be interpreted as Odin meeting his fate at Ragnarok. From the church of Torpo, Hallingdal, Norway.

A man fighting a monster on the Gosforth Cross – Odin at Ragnarok again?

story, and what follows here is only one such. There are three main invading forces. From the sea slithers the great World Serpent Iormungand, in fighting mood. It creates tidal waves which loosen the ship Naglfar (a name which Snorri interprets as 'nail-ship', made from the uncut nails of the dead, an excellent reason why anyone should keep his nails well-manicured). In this ship is the giant Hrym, and apparently the sons of Muspell too, whoever they may be. Loki, also freed from his bonds, is the helmsman. From the south advances the fire-demon Surt with his army (which some think includes Muspell's sons). Most fearsome of all, the ravening Fenrir races forward, his jaws agape so that, says Snorri, the upper one touches the heavens, the lower the earth. 'He would open them wider if only there were space.'

Heimdall blows his horn to summon the gods to war council. Odin consults Mimir's head but it is too late. The gods arm. Freyr fights Surt, but he is inadequately armed – he has given his splendid sword to Skirnir – and so he is cut down. Thor manages to destroy Iormungand, but is overcome by its venom and falls dead. Fenrir gulps Odin down. Odin's son, Vidar, avenges his father either, according to *Vǫluspá*, by stabbing Fenrir to the heart, or, according to Snorri and *Vafþrúðnismál*, by stepping with a heavily-shod foot on its lower jaw, pulling upwards on its upper jaw, and tearing it in two. (Where did he find space for that, I wonder.) Snorri adds two more duels, neither, I think, otherwise supported. Garm, a monstrous hound, and Tyr kill each other, as do the traditional enemies Loki and Heimdall. Thereupon Surt scatters fire over the whole earth, and it burns away.

The tale is nicely schematised, but it is hardly satisfactory. It tells so little. There is no general scheme of battle between the forces of the gods and those of darkness. What about the other gods whose names we know? What happens to the goddesses? Where are Odin's chosen warriors, who have trained so hard for this fixture?

Nevertheless, Ragnarok means the end of the old gods' regime. Yet though I have elsewhere translated the phrase 'the end of the world', it is in fact not the close of everything. *Vǫluspá*, and Snorri following it, tell of a new beginning, perhaps intended as heralding a new world purged of the treachery of the old one, or at least punishing such wickedness. Obviously there is likelihood of Christian influence upon Norse myth here. Gangleri asks the significant question:

What happens after heaven, earth and the whole world is burnt up, and the gods are all dead, and all the great warriors, and all humankind? Didn't you tell me that every human being must live throughout all time in some world or another?

Third gives the grim answer, 'There will be many good forms of life and many bad', and then provides examples of each. If you have been virtuous you may live on in delightful surroundings, which could mean enjoying drinking in the hall called Brimir, or having, I suppose, a life of ease in the golden hall Sindri. In contrast – and here Snorri quotes from *Vǫluspá* – there is another hall in a place with the unpromising name *Nástrǫnd*, 'corpse-beaches'.

Its doors face northwards, not a good sign. It is built of interwoven serpents, whose poison floods the building. Those who lodge here are the oath-breakers and brutal murderers.

But there is another renewal. The visionary of *Vǫluspá* puts it thus:

> A second earth she sees arise
> From out of the sea, green once more,
> The cataracts tumble, the eagle flies over them,
> Hunting fish in the mountain streams.

> The Aesir meet again on Idavoll
> And speak of the mighty World Serpent,
> And call to mind the mighty judgments
> And the ancient mysteries of the Great God himself.

There is even a reference to that strange board game that was a feature of the early (and innocent?) life of the old gods:

> Then again will be found in the grass
> Those wondrous golden playing-pieces,
> Those they had owned in ancient times.

Whether in consequence, or simply afterwards, a golden age will come. Fields will flourish unsown – one of man's perpetual dreams – and all ills will be cured. Baldr will return, and the children of the old gods will take over their heritage. According to Snorri (not in *Vǫluspá* but in *Vafþrúðnismál*), two humans will survive the holocaust, nourished by the morning dews. From them the new race of men will be born.

So the whole sad business starts again. Gangleri would doubtless have wanted to know more, but High shuts him up firmly. 'If you want to know anything after this, I've no idea where you are going to learn it from. I've heard nobody tell the future of the world beyond this point. So make the most of what you have learnt.' Which is probably as far as any philosopher has got.

Gods and Heroes

S o far the myths of gods and goddesses have shown them in some isolation
from mankind. They have told of actions that affect deities only (as
in the Baldr myth), or of often stormy relationships between gods and
other supernatural creatures – giants, demons, dwarfs and so on (as in the
story of Idunn's kidnapping). Odin had an interest in the warrior class, helping
professional fighters before betraying them. Inevitably the gods are linked
to humanity in the cosmic creation and destruction tales. But otherwise, in
the myths included here, there has been little connection so far between god
and man.

However, there is one powerful myth – powerful in its enduring effect
on European culture – that illustrates the way an action of the Aesir could
affect the fates of individual humans, a myth that connects an adventure
of the gods with a cycle of legends of heroic kings and fighting men. This
turns on a question asked in my first chapter and not yet answered: why
is gold referred to as 'the otter's blood-money'? The story is told in one of
the Eddic poems, *Reginsmál*, the Tale of Regin, together with its prose introduction in the *Codex Regius*. Snorri has a version in the *Prose Edda*, and
it also occurs, essentially linked to heroic actions, in a late medieval Icelandic
saga called *Volsunga saga*, the History of the Volsungs, about which more
later.

The tale begins with a rich farmer called Hreidmar. He had magical
skills, and not surprisingly all his three sons had peculiar characteristics. Two
of them were shape-changers, Fafnir and Otr. The third was a dwarf, Regin.
Like all dwarfs he was a fine craftsman, in particular a smith. He was also,
says the *Codex Regius* ominously, 'knowledgeable, savage and skilled in
magic'. Otr had the curious practice of turning into an otter (which is what
his name means) and living in a torrential river, eating the fish he caught.
This was his undoing.

One day a trio of gods, Odin, Hoenir and Loki, were out on one of
their expeditions, and as usual Loki got them into trouble. This time by an
incautious though excusable act. They came to a waterfall, and on the river-
bank nearby spotted an otter devouring a salmon. Like all otters, says *Volsunga
saga* (and it would be interesting to know if this is a fact of natural history),
this otter was eating with its eyes shut. The saga's explanation is that the
otter couldn't bear to see his meal getting less the more he ate of it. In any
case, the otter did not see the gods approaching. Loki threw a stone at it,

killed it, and so in one blow gained both an otter skin and a salmon. The gods thought this a lucky strike until they came to Hreidmar's house and asked for a night's lodging. They boasted of their catch and showed Hreidmar the otter skin. The farmer and his sons recognised it, grabbed hold of the three gods and demanded compensation. The Aesir agreed to fill the skin with gold and then pile gold all over it until it was completely covered. Loki was sent off to find the wherewithal.

Luckily he knew of a dwarf called Andvari; dwarfs, being skilled craftsmen, usually had plenty of gold about them. This dwarf again was an odd character. He assumed the form of a pike, and lived in a waterfall catching fish. Loki borrowed a net from the sea-goddess Ran and caught the pike. *Reginsmál* records the conversation between them. Loki asked:

> 'What sort of fish is this, swimming in the flood,
> Yet it cannot save itself from disaster?
> Ransom your life from the realm of death
> And get me gleaming gold.'

> 'Andvari's my name, Oin my father's,
> Through many a torrent I've swum.
> In ancient times a cheerless fate
> Decreed I should wade in water.'

As ransom Loki demanded all Andvari's gold. The dwarf paid up, but tried to hold back a single ring (presumably an arm- not a finger-ring) since this had magical properties that would help him recoup his fortunes. Loki exacted the ring from Andvari. Leaving for the security of his home in a rock, the dwarf cursed whoever held his treasure:

> 'That gold [the word could also mean 'ring'] that Gust once owned
> Shall be the death of two brothers,
> Shall be the downfall of eight princes.
> In my wealth shall no man delight.'

Loki brought back his plunder, and Odin, coveting the ring, kept it for himself. The rest of the treasure the Aesir used in stuffing the otter skin and covering it with gold. Hreidmar inspected their effort, and spotted a single otter hair uncovered. Reluctantly Odin pulled off the ring and covered the hair. As the gods departed from Hreidmar's hall Loki revealed the dwarf's curse:

> 'To you now gold, great ransom
> Is rendered for my life.
> For your son no fortune will follow.
> This will bring death to both.'

So it did. Fafnir and Regin asked for their share of the blood-money, but Hreidmar would not pay up. Fafnir killed his father, took the treasure away to the wilderness and there hoarded it. And there he stayed, taking on the form of a dragon, until Regin contrived his death.

Shaw's 'perfect Wagnerite' will recognise some of this, at any rate in outline: a golden treasure, a ring that is accursed, got by treachery from a dwarf; a body to be covered with gold, and a ring that must be piled on to complete the process. The prologue to *Der Ring des Nibelungen, Das Rheingold*, has reflections also of myths told earlier in this book: a stronghold for the gods built by giants under a contract that is to be renounced; a goddess who keeps the apples of youth and who is seized by giants with the result that the gods become aged and wan. Clearly Wagner derived a good deal of his matter from Norse myth, adapting it to his own intellectual purposes. Yet much of Wagner's music drama is taken up with the adventures of two heroes, father and son, Siegmund and Siegfried, whose ambiguous relationship to the gods and particularly to Odin (Wagner's *Wotan*) leads to disaster.

Norse tradition too shows this connection between the myth of the cursed ring and a family of hero-kings. I say 'Norse tradition' but in fact the material is essentially central European rather than Norse, though it is the literature of medieval Scandinavia that preserves it most completely. Behind the legendary names that the Norse writers record, certain historical characters can be discerned. The king called *Gunnarr* was probably the *Gundaharius* of the fifth-century Burgundian dynasty, while the villainous *Atli* is a reflection of the ferocious Hunnish leader *Attila* who died in 451. The king *Iǫrmunrekr* represents *Ermanaric*, the fourth-century king of the Ostro-Goths, while *Hiálprekr* may be the sixth-century Merovingian *Chilperic*. The order in which these characters appear in the Scandinavian cycle defies chronology.

The Norse legends are related in a group of heroic poems of the *Poetic Edda*. Though I call them a group, they diverge widely in date and form. Some are probably from quite early in the Viking Age, others as late as the twelfth century. Some are straightforward narrative verse, broken by stanzas of dialogue. Others have verse narrative and speech interspersed with sections of narrative prose, and the relationship between verse and prose passages has led to discussion and indeed controversy. Others again tell a story from the standpoint of one of its characters, looking back upon past events. For all their variety, there is a good deal of similarity of content and theme: their events are fierce feuds, carried on by kings of cruel temperament, often assisted by women of equal ferocity. Kings are arrogant, often avaricious, eager for glory or afraid of seeming cowardly. The general atmosphere is pagan, as all Christians will readily confirm.

Part of the whole tale Snorri recorded in his *Prose Edda*. More important for the complete narrative is the version in *Vǫlsunga saga*, a prose re-telling from the thirteenth century, extant in one early manuscript from *c.*1400. In essence *Vǫlsunga saga* reproduces the Eddic poems, linking them into one continuous story, and also preserving material from sources that no longer exist. The effect is sometimes inconsistent, for the poems do not always tell identical stories. In addition there are minor Norse sources (including Saxo Grammaticus), a very considerable amount of information in medieval German works – though some of this diverges from the Norse – and even brief references from Anglo-Saxon England showing that at any rate parts of the legend were known there.

The Scandinavian version begins with a king called Volsung, the founder of a great dynasty in Hunland, thought to be descended from Odin. He begot ten sons and a daughter, though only one son, Sigmund, and his twin sister, Signy, are named. Volsung was a tough king and a fine warrior, and kept great state in a splendid hall which had a tree growing in its midst. A powerful king, Siggeir of Gautland (Götaland, Sweden), wooed Signy, and a marriage was arranged. Naturally there was a great wedding feast. As all were seated round the central fires, in came an unknown figure, an old man, one-eyed, wearing a cape and with his face covered with a hood. Who could it be but Odin, though nobody recognised him? He was carrying a sword. He plunged it into the tree's trunk and announced that the man who could pull it out again could keep it. Then off he went. All the guests tried to pull the sword out, but only Sigmund succeeded. When they examined the weapon, everyone agreed it was the finest sword ever seen. Siggeir wanted to buy it, but Sigmund refused, and so ill-will grew between the families. (The sword in the tree motif recurs, of course, in Wagner's *Die Walküre*.)

Siggeir cut the wedding feast short and returned home, taking Signy with him much against her will. However, Siggeir had given Volsung and his sons a return invitation to visit Gautland in three months' time. When Volsung arrived there, he found Siggeir with an army mustered against him. His pride would not let him retreat, though he was now advanced in years. So they joined battle. Despite a valiant resistance, Volsung and all his men were killed, only the ten sons surviving as captives.

At Signy's suggestion they were chained to a log in the middle of the woods and left there. Each night a she-wolf came from her lair and ate one of the sons until Sigmund alone was left. At this rather late point Signy had a brainwave. She sent her servant with a jar of honey, which he smeared all over Sigmund's face and into his mouth. When the wolf arrived as usual, she sniffed the honey and began to lick Sigmund's face; at last she put her tongue into his mouth to get the honey. Sigmund bit into the wolf's tongue, and she jumped back, straining with her feet at the log so that it cracked in pieces. Sigmund bit on her tongue so that it tore from its roots. The wolf it was that died.

So Sigmund became free, and hid in the woods with Signy's connivance. There the pair plotted revenge. Signy sent her two sons to see if they could help her brother, but they proved feeble so Sigmund killed them off. Strangely enough Siggeir seems not to have noticed their disappearance. Signy decided she must have a son by her brother if he were to be tough enough to help in the act of vengeance. So she changed shapes with a comely witch, visited her brother and slept with him. From this union a son, Sinfiotli, was born; and a very harsh character he turned out to be. (The incestuous coupling that results in the birth of a hero is also reflected in *Die Walküre*.)

Father and son had a spell of battle training, and then made their way to Siggeir's hall, hiding in the entrance lobby. There Signy's latest two children spotted them, so Sinfiotli sliced them up with his sword and threw the remains into the hall. Even the lethargic Siggeir reacted at this, ordering the intruders to be seized. After the usual gallant resistance Sigmund and Sinfiotli were taken, and buried alive in a turf mound so that they would die in protracted agony. But Signy threw a piece of meat into the mound before it was closed up. When they examined it they found there was a sword stuck into the joint. Between them they sawed their way out of the mound, set fire to Siggeir's hall and burnt him alive. Signy refused to leave her husband, realising that her behaviour could not allow escape. So she died with him.

This ferocious tale has no extant source, though its origin is implied in a bit of verse quoted to illustrate the two kinsmen's escape from the mound. As the verse says:

> With strength they cut the massive slab,
> Sigmund with his sword and Sinfiotli.

Apparently here as elsewhere the author of *Vǫlsunga saga* has turned a poem he knew (but which hasn't come down to us) into rather pedestrian prose.

Sigmund and his son/nephew shipped themselves back to his ancestral lands, and Sigmund took power there, marrying a woman Borghild and having by her two sons, one of whom, Helgi, was to become famous. So ends the first episode in the Volsung story.

Vǫlsunga saga's second section reports the adventures of Helgi and his uncle Sinfiotli. It derives in part from an Eddic poem, *The first lay of Helgi Hunding's Killer*, which we can supplement from the more complex material of a second lay on that hero. As a young man Helgi went on a freebooting expedition with Sinfiotli, and attacked and killed a king called Hunding. Hunding's sons took exception, and when Helgi refused to pay them blood-money, they called up an army and fought him. They were beaten, and several lost their lives. Returning from the battle Helgi met a party of women, one of whom was a king's daughter Sigrun. By profession she was a valkyrie. She complained she was being given in marriage to a weakling, King Hoddbrodd, and Helgi volunteered to save her from this dread fate. He brought his force to Hoddbrodd's land where the home guard were awaiting them. After a disgraceful scene of mutual insult between the leaders of the two armies, Helgi attacked and destroyed his enemy with the assistance of Sigrun's valkyries. Helgi settled down with Sigrun and is heard of no more in the *Vǫlsunga saga*, though the second lay relates his death at the hands of an avenger.

Sinfiotli continued his piracy and met up with an attractive woman who was also being courted by Borghild's brother. Sinfiotli struck his rival down. Returning, he was surprised to find he was unwelcome to Borghild. Sigmund insisted that Sinfiotli should remain with them. Borghild prepared her brother's wake, with a splendid feast. As was the custom, she served the drink and took a full horn to Sinfiotli. He thought the liquor cloudy and wouldn't drink: so Sigmund finished it off. But then, Sigmund could drink poison without taking harm; Sinfiotli couldn't. Borghild brought a second round. 'The drink has been tampered with', said Sinfiotli. Again Sigmund drank it off. Borghild tried a third time. 'There's poison in this drink', said Sinfiotli. By now Sigmund was drunk and incapable of judgment. 'Strain it through your moustache then', he advised. Sinfiotli did and fell down dead. Sigmund, broken with grief, took the body to the shore of the fiord where he came upon a man (could this be Odin again?) with a boat so small it would take only one passenger. Sigmund loaded the body on to the boat and prepared to walk round the fiord side; but as he did, the boat vanished. Sigmund returned home and banished his vengeful queen who died soon after.

Sigmund married again, a king's daughter Hiordis. His unsuccessful rival in love was one of Hunding's sons, Lyngvi. Lyngvi felt this was the last straw and resolved to destroy Sigmund. He invaded Hunland and offered battle. There was a tough fight, with Sigmund, now an old man, defending himself courageously. In the midst of the strife appeared a man, one-eyed, with a black cloak and floppy hat, and carrying a spear (Odin!). The man stood in Sigmund's path with his spear aloft. Sigmund's sword shattered against the spear, and at that the battle turned against the defenders and Sigmund was mortally wounded. (A similar occurrence is in *Die Walküre*.)

The pregnant Hiordis had been put in a place of safety in the woods, with all the royal treasure. She went out to seek among the wounded, finding Sigmund in his death agonies. Sigmund prophesied the greatness of the son who would be born to them, and instructed Hiordis to preserve the fragments of his sword for the child's benefit. Thereupon he died, and Hiordis was taken into the protection of a group of passing Vikings led by the king of Denmark's son.

Vǫlsunga saga's third section relates the exploits of Hiordis's son by Sigmund. This was to be the greatest of Germanic heroes, Sigurd (Wagner's *Siegfried*). It is here that the heroic legend of the Volsungs links to the god myth of the great gold treasure with its fatal ring. Sigurd was fostered with honour in the king of Denmark's court. His tutor there was the smith Regin, disaffected brother of Fafnir, now a dragon guarding his stolen wealth. Regin taught Sigurd accomplishments suited to a prince, but also tried to make him discontented with his position as a dependent at court. 'Who was looking after Sigurd's rightful royal inheritance?' 'The Danish king and his son.' But did Sigurd trust them? Did they treat him generously enough? Why didn't he have his own horse?

Sigurd replied he could have a horse — or anything else he wanted — for the asking. The king gave him freedom to choose from his stud. When Sigurd went to pick out the best horse, he met an old bearded man otherwise unknown to him. We are not told the man was one-eyed, but we may suspect it. Obviously Odin. The stranger advised Sigurd how to select a horse and between them they chose one that Sleipnir had sired (and so must have admirable qualities). They named it Grani.

Next Regin put into Sigurd's mind the desire for money, saying he knew where there was treasure for the taking. A dragon called Fafnir guarded it, and had its lair on a heath not far off. But Sigurd would need a sword to kill the monster with. Regin forged the lad a sword, but when the hero chopped at an anvil with it, the blade shattered. Regin made a second, better one. It smashed just like the first. Sigurd went to his mother and asked for the bits of his father's sword that she had kept by her all these years. With this metal, obviously skilfully balanced, Regin made a new blade, so tough it would slice through an anvil, yet so sharp it would cut a strand of wool drifting down the river. Before attacking the dragon, Sigurd mounted an expedition against his father's killers and destroyed them. Now he was ready for Fafnir.

With Regin he went up on to the heath and traced the tracks Fafnir made when he went to his watering hole. They were enormous and made Sigurd apprehensive. Regin advised him to dig a pit along the track so that when the dragon crawled to the water, he could lurk in it and stab the beast in the soft underbelly. Sigurd prepared his trap, but was interrupted by an old man (who could it be?) who advised him to dig a row of pits so that the dragon's blood would flow into them and do Sigurd no harm. Sigurd took this advice, and struck Fafnir his death-blow. The Eddic poem *Fáfnismál*, the Tale of Fafnir, records the exchanges between the dying Fafnir and his victor. These include warnings to the lad of the fate the treasure would bring him:

> 'The ringing gold, the glow-red treasure,
> The rings will bring you to your death.'

Sigurd was unmoved:

> 'For every man in fullness of time
> Must descend to his death.'

When the monster was safely despatched, Regin came up, cut out its heart and drank some of its blood. Then he asked Sigurd to roast the heart for him. Sigurd spitted it on a stake which he held over a fire. When it looked ready and juice was frothing out of it, Sigurd felt it with his finger to test if it was properly done. The meat was hot, and Sigurd popped his finger into his mouth to cool it. The moment Fafnir's blood came on to his tongue, he found he could understand the language of birds. Above him in a tree perched a flock of nuthatches, twittering together. One said:

> 'There sits Sigurd spattered with blood.
> He's brazing Fafnir's heart on the fire.
> That ring-scatterer [prince] would seem wiser to me
> If he ate the glittering serpent's heart.'

Other birds joined in, revealing Regin's intended treachery to the lad, and suggesting Sigurd should lop off the smith's head, take all the riches to himself and go off and learn wisdom from the valkyrie Brynhild who lay in a charmed sleep on Hind Fell. Sigurd approved this advice, drew his sword and beheaded Regin. He ate some of the dragon's heart, and kept the rest for future use, leaped on his horse Grani and traced Fafnir's tracks to his lair. There he

*All the Sigurd carvings illustrated opposite
are on the doorway from Hylestad church,
Oldsaksamling, Oslo, Norway.*
TOP LEFT *Sigurd, the right-hand figure, tests
his sword to destruction. Regin looks on
crossly.* MIDDLE LEFT *Regin and his helper
forge another new sword from the fragments
of Sigmund's blade.* BOTTOM LEFT *Sigurd
stabs the dragon in the belly.*
TOP RIGHT *Regin sleeps while Sigurd
roasts Fafnir's heart and tests it to see if it's
ready. As he tastes the blood, he understands
the speech of the birds in the trees above him.*
MIDDLE RIGHT *Sigurd follows the
birds' advice and kills off Regin.* BOTTOM
RIGHT *Sigurd's horse Grani, loaded with
treasure acquired from Fafnir the dragon.*

*A runic memorial inscription (right) set
within a snake-like form. The carver took the
snake to be Fafnir, and carved Sigurd
beneath, stabbing the dragon in the belly.*

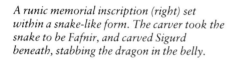

found more treasures than two or three ordinary horses could carry; yet he loaded them all on Grani, sprang into the saddle and rode away.

This is the point where Sigurd's affairs, hitherto fairly straightforward, become tangled, for he found himself involved with two strong-minded women, Brynhild and Gudrun, his future bride. There is also a confusion of traditions: it is not easy to derive a simple story from the various sources. *Vǫlsunga saga* tells how Sigurd rode up on to Hind Fell, and saw in the distance a blazing fire. When he came closer, he found it surrounded a fortress. Within lay an armoured figure fast asleep. Sigurd slit open the armour – his sword cut metal as if it were cloth – and found it was a woman, the valkyrie Brynhild whom Odin had put to sleep for disobedience. Sigurd woke her and was entranced by her beauty and intelligence. He fell for her and she for him, and they swore mutual faith.

Then follows a confusion in the tale. Sigurd rode away (why?) and came to the home of Heimir, Brynhild's foster-father, where his splendid appearance caused a sensation. Brynhild was now staying at Heimir's (how did she get there?), and again Sigurd made his profession of love to her. This time she was apprehensive, for she was a valkyrie, happy when leading a battle-force. He was fated to marry Gudrun, Giuki's daughter. Sigurd denied this would happen, and again he and Brynhild swore vows of devotion. Sigurd gave her a gold ring: indeed, the gold ring.

And so to the hall of Giuki, south of the Rhine. Giuki had a wife, the witch Grimhild, three sons, Gunnar, Hogni and Guttorm, and a daughter Gudrun. Brynhild was Gudrun's friend, and the two consulted about the future. Brynhild interpreted Gudrun's dreams, foretelling her unhappy fate: she would marry Sigurd and lose him.

Sigurd reached Giuki's hall with all his treasure. Giuki welcomed him in, and Grimhild soon recognised that Sigurd would be a great asset to the family. If only he were not in love with Brynhild. Grimhild solved the problem by giving Sigurd an enchanted drink that made him forget his old love. To retain Sigurd's support, Giuki offered him the hand of his daughter Gudrun, and Sigurd, blissfully oblivious of Brynhild, accepted. They had a splendid wedding, and to bind the alliance, Gunnar, Hogni and Sigurd swore blood-brotherhood. After that the men of the family went off a-pirating, and returned home rich with plunder. Sigurd gave Gudrun some of Fafnir's heart to eat, 'and after that she was much crueller than before, as well as wiser'.

Meanwhile Gunnar was getting restless for a bit of married life. He decided to court Brynhild, and Sigurd agreed to help. She would marry only the man who rode through the encircling fire to her hall, and Gunnar tried to do it. His horse shied away and wouldn't enter the flame. Gunnar asked to borrow Grani, but even Grani wouldn't go on with Gunnar up. So Sigurd and Gunnar exchanged appearances (how, I wonder), and Sigurd mounted Grani and charged through the flames. Within her hall sat Brynhild, majestic in armour and helmet. Sigurd/Gunnar announced that he had ridden the fire and was entitled to her hand. She accepted, welcoming him to her home and her bed. Sigurd/Gunnar laid his drawn sword between them as they slept. Then he took back the great gold ring, exchanging it for another. There-after he rode back through the flames and the two friends changed into their own guises. A great wedding feast was held for Brynhild and Gunnar, and now, when it was too late, Sigurd remembered his meeting with Brynhild. But he made no sign.

Shortly afterwards Gudrun and Brynhild had a quarrel over precedence. Brynhild claimed her husband was the greater, as he had ridden through the ring of fire to her. Gudrun revealed what had really happened, that it was Sigurd in Gunnar's guise who had ridden the flame wall, and she had the great ring to prove it. Brynhild went white with anger and plotted ven-geance on Sigurd and Gudrun, the man and woman who had shamed her, and on Gunnar, the husband who had taken her by deceit. Sigurd's soft answers could not turn away her wrath.

Brynhild spoke to her husband, warning him of the danger of having so eminent a fighter as Sigurd in his household:

'Back shall I go where I used to be,
Living together with my father's kin.
There will I sit and sleep my life away
Unless you make sure of Sigurd's death,
Unless you become a prince greater than all others.'

Gunnar was now in a tricky position. He could not harm Sigurd for they were bloodbrothers, yet he would like the treasure to be his. Hogni could not attack Sigurd either; indeed he felt more engaged by his oath than Gunnar was. Then Gunnar had a bright idea. Why not get their young brother Guttorm to do the killing – he was not involved in the compact? The two brothers urged Guttorm to the murder, offering him money and power. They gave him enchanted food (which sounds distinctly unpalatable) to charm him. Grimhild added her persuasions, and Guttorm fell.

Sigurd was lying abed, unsuspecting. Guttorm went twice to his room, but Sigurd was awake and his looks so terrifying that Guttorm ran off in panic. But on the third occasion Sigurd slept, and Guttorm thrust him through with his sword. Sigurd awoke at the blow, grabbed for his sword and threw it at Guttorm as he escaped through the doorway. It sliced him through at the waist, and half fell back into the room, half out. Gudrun, who had been asleep in Sigurd's arms, awoke drenched with blood, and her grief was uncontrolled. Sigurd died, accusing Brynhild of responsibility for the deed, but recognising it had long been fated to happen. When Brynhild heard Gudrun's bitter moan of misery, she laughed aloud. Then she made Gunnar understand the implications of the killing: now the brothers would not have Sigurd's support when they rode into battle. As they prepared Sigurd's burial, Brynhild stabbed herself, and begged to be put on the funeral pyre with him, with the drawn sword lying between them as it had done so long ago. So ended the great hero, after a life of peril, glory and treachery. (Wagnerites will recognise much of the plots of *Siegfried* and *Götterdämmerung* here.)

The last sections of *Volsunga saga* relate the terrible fate of Gudrun after her husband's death. For a time she hid in the wilderness, and then lived in exile in Denmark. There her brothers found her, and brought compensation for her ills. Grimhild produced another of her enchanted drinks that made Gudrun forget her wrongs. Then, with doubtful tact, they betrothed her to Atli, Brynhild's brother, much against her will. Atli coveted the treasure that Sigurd had left, and which was now in the brothers' power. He invited Gunnar and Hogni to visit him, intending treachery. Gudrun tried to warn them, but failed; the brothers were seduced by the possibility of inheriting Atli's kingdom. So they went. When they disembarked in Atli's territory, the treachery was revealed, but Gunnar and Hogni rode boldly to Atli's hall. There they fought a pitched battle against Atli's men, and when their sister saw them hard pressed she took sword and armour and joined in on their side. There was terrible slaughter, but in the end Gunnar and Hogni were captured and put in chains.

Gunnar was made an offer. He could save his life if he revealed where the hoard was hidden. 'Let me see my brother Hogni's heart cut out of his body first.' But Atli's men cut out the heart of a cowardly slave and showed it to Gunnar as Hogni's. Gunnar didn't believe it. The heart was quivering in terror as Hogni's never did. So they cut out Hogni's heart, and he laughed scornfully the while. They took the heart to Gunnar and he recognised it. 'Only I know where the gold is now Hogni cannot tell you. I was in doubt while we both lived, but now I alone have the decision. The Rhine shall hold that gold before Huns wear it on their arms.'

Atli put Gunnar in a pit with poisonous snakes. His hands were bound,

Gunnar lies bound in the snake-pit, trying to charm the snakes. It avails him little. Also on the doorway from Hylestad church, Oldsaksamling, Oslo, Norway.

but Gudrun threw a harp into the pit, and he charmed the serpents by playing to them with his toes. However, in the end a venomous adder dug its fangs into him and he died.

Both Atli and Gudrun had friends to mourn, so they arranged a joint wake in reconciliation, or so Atli thought. For the feast Gudrun served up the hearts of her sons by Atli, mixed their blood with the festive wine and fashioned their skulls into drinking cups. Thereafter she and one of Hogni's sons stabbed Atli and set fire to his hall. There is no doubt that eating dragon's heart will bring out the worst in a woman.

Yet Gudrun's griefs were still not complete. Her lovely daughter Svanhild was betrothed to the elderly King Iormunrek. He suspected her of infidelity and had her trampled beneath his horses' hooves. Avenging her, Gudrun's surviving sons took Iormunrek in his hall and chopped off his arms and legs. Before they could kill him he shouted to his men to stone his assailants to death, and so they perished. But by that time, according to Snorri, Fafnir's inheritance, the cursed gold, had been hidden in the River Rhine. 'And it has never been found since.'

Suggestions for further reading

The study of Norse myths is a complex business, and this book can only simplify it. Even the sources I describe are more complicated than I make them out to be – there are variant readings of texts, and variant translations and interpretations. All I have tried to do here is draw a general picture. Those who want to know more have access to a full and authoritative translation of Snorri's *Edda* in A. Faulkes, *Snorri Sturluson: Edda* (London, 1987). This is excellent in its accuracy and closeness to the original but in consequence loses in fluency and readability: nevertheless it is much to be commended. There is no equivalent translation of the *Poetic Edda* though there have been many attempts. Most recently W. H. Auden and P. B. Taylor compiled *Norse Poems* (London, 1981). This has most of the Eddic verse in it, though the treatment is often idiosyncratic as in their reorganisation of *Hávamál*. For a text of that most important poem it is perhaps best to go to the rather antique version and translation, D. E. Martin Clarke, *The Hávamál* (Cambridge, 1923). U. Dronke's *The Poetic Edda*, vol. 2, *Mythological Poems* (Oxford, 1997) has convenient translations of and notes on several of the poems quoted here.

The verses of the skalds are hard to come by in translation, partly because of the fearsome problems of rendering their language and construction into readable English. Some of the poems I mention, together with a competent introduction, are in E. O. G. Turville-Petre, *Scaldic Poetry* (Oxford, 1976). The text of *Ynglingasaga* can be found in L. M. Hollander's translation of *Heimskringla: history of the kings of Norway* (Austin, Texas, 1964), and there is also a convenient Everyman's Library edition. A very useful translation of Saxo Grammaticus's *Gesta Danorum* has appeared, the relevant early part being *Saxo Grammaticus: the history of the Danes*, vol. 1, translated by Peter Fisher (Cambridge, 1979). A good text, with translation and introduction, of *Volsunga saga* is R. G. Finch, *The saga of the Volsungs* (Nelson's Icelandic Texts, Edinburgh and London, 1965), while U. Dronke's *The Poetic Edda*, vol. 1, *Heroic Poems* (Oxford, 1969), gives the four poems whose material provides the later episodes of that saga, with a translation that sometimes makes them sound more poetic than they really are. My own *Chronicles of the Vikings* (London, 1995) includes several translated texts relevant to this book.

A good introduction to the modern study of Norse mythology is in the first chapter, 'Mythology and mythography', in C. J. Clover and J. Lindow, *Old Norse-Icelandic literature: a critical guide* (Cornell, Ithaca, 1985). Other chapters are helpful in giving the literary background to much of what I say here. For an up-to-date summary of the relevant medieval literature there is J. Kristjánsson, *Eddas and Sagas*, translated by P. Foote (Reykjavík, 1988). In English perhaps the best available general work on Norse mythology is still E. O. G. Turville-Petre, *Myth and Religion of the North: the religion of ancient Scandinavia* (London, 1964), useful despite being marred by numerous literal misprints and inconsistencies. Georges Dumézil's views can be found, though not criticised, in an English translation, *Gods of the Ancient Northmen*, edited by E. Haugen (Berkeley and Los Angeles, 1973). Convenient reference works for the further study of Norse myths are R. Simek, *Dictionary of Northern Mythology* (Cambridge/Woodbridge, 1993) and A. Orchard, *Dictionary of Norse Myth and Legend* (London, 1997).

Egyptian Myths

GEORGE HART

To my mother and father

Picture credits
pp. 240, 255, 263, 275 (right): New York, The Metropolitan Museum of Art: Rogers Fund and Henry Walters Gift, 1916 (16.1.3); Gift of Edward S. Harkness, 1926 (26.7.1412); Rogers Fund, 1945 (45.2.11); Fletcher Fund, 1950 (50.85); *p. 244*: Turin, Museo Egizio; *p. 246*: Paris, Musée du Louvre; *pp. 249, 283 (bottom), 286*: Franco Maria Ricci editore, Milan, from *Nella Sede della Verità* by A. Fornari and M. Tosi (photo Franco Lovera, Turin). Other photos British Museum.

Quotations used in the text are reprinted by permission of the following:
pp. 239, 293: Faber and Faber Ltd, from 'Little Gidding' from *Four Quartets* by T.S. Eliot and from *Collected Poems 1909-1962* by T.S. Eliot; *p. 251*: Routledge and Kegan Paul; *p. 260*: Oxford University Press; *p. 285*: Princeton University Press.

Contents

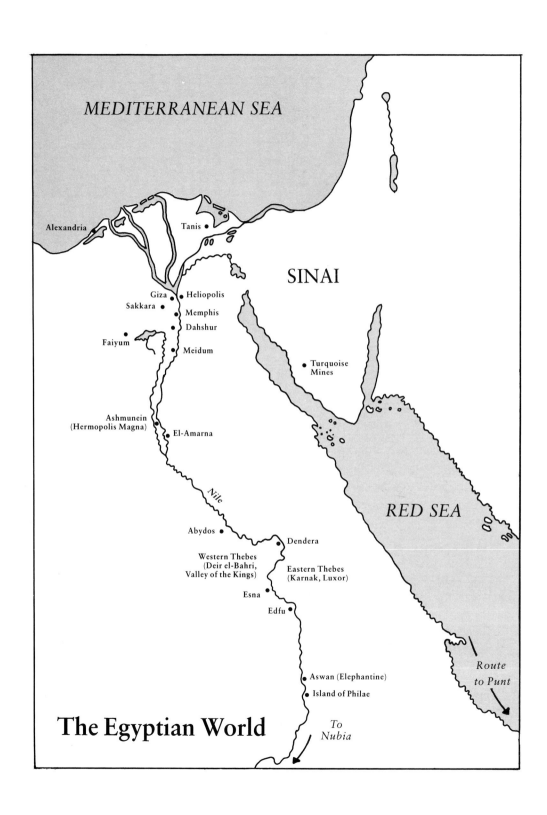

MEDITERRANEAN SEA

Alexandria

Tanis

SINAI

Giza • Heliopolis
Sakkara •
• Memphis
• Dahshur
Faiyum •
• Meidum

Turquoise
Mines

Ashmunein
(Hermopolis Magna)
• El-Amarna

Nile

RED SEA

Abydos •
• Dendera
Western Thebes
(Deir el-Bahri,
Valley of the Kings)
Eastern Thebes
(Karnak, Luxor)
Esna •
• Edfu

Aswan (Elephantine)
• Island of Philae

Route
to Punt

The Egyptian World

To
Nubia

Introduction

Egyptian mythology is a rich and perplexing panorama of visual and written images. In an attempt to clarify some aspects, I have divided the subject into two broad categories. The most manageable material is quite straightforward and includes the tales and legends involving escapism to exotic lands, amusement at the exploits of magicians and the apotheosis of historical heroes.

The other category is what I venture to call 'myths of the higher consciousness'. My personal view is that these formed an active, integral element in ancient Egyptian government and society; they are far from being a series of fossilised *mémoires* on gods and goddesses. Those concerning the origins of the cosmos, the concept of lawful succession to the throne and the vision of a regenerative journey made by the sun at night, stand out as the projections of the ancient Egyptians' thoughts, hopes and fears about the human condition and the troubles experienced in the course of one lifetime.

Investigation of natural phenomena and confrontation with the 'mysterious' mattered deeply to the ancient Egyptians, even if there was not always an explanation and if the result was occasionally incomprehensible and contradictory. Consequently, metaphysical myths of creation and magical formulae directed against the forces of chaos – manifest in the threat of the underworld snake Apophis – signify the ancient Egyptian quest for ultimate knowledge. This is echoed in what has been called the modern dilemma:

'We shall not cease from exploration
And the end of all our exploring
Will be to arrive where we started
And know the place for the first time . . . '
(from T. S. Eliot, *Little Gidding*)

But it is not only on modern times that Egyptian myths have left their mark. Throughout the last two and a half thousand years, foreign visitors to the Nile Valley have recorded their reactions to the vast pantheon of deities inscribed on tombs, temples and papyri. Herodotus, the fifth-century Greek historian and ethnographer, gives some accounts of Egyptian religion but is respectfully reticent about divulging sacred rites:

I have held converse with the priests of Hephaistos [Ptah] at Memphis. I went to Thebes and to Heliopolis intent on discovering if the information I gathered in Memphis would be verified, since the Heliopolitans are regarded as the wisest of Egyptians. As to their explanations of the 'sacred', I am not keen on fully disclosing that knowledge except perhaps in giving the names of certain rituals which I consider to be already 'common currency' among men.
(*Histories* II, chapter 3)

In a similar vein are the comments by the entertaining novelist Apuleius, who has his hero Lucius undergo degrading adventures while in the form of an ass, and who Isis transforms as an initiate into her mysteries. In contrast, however, the xenophobic Roman satirist Juvenal openly mocks Egyptian beliefs and scorns the cult of Isis. Even ordinary tourists in late antiquity have left their impressions (unforgivably as graffiti) about Egypt's complex mythology: 'I, Dioskorammon, looked upon this nonsense and found it bewildering!' (scratched on the wall of the tomb of Ramesses VI in the Valley of the Kings).

But Egyptian myths, though seemingly outlandish to some, have survived because the society out of which they originated considered them crucial to the creation of a view of the world. Scribes, priests and story-tellers transmitted myths to explain aetiological phenomena, to provide data for the continuity of existence in the afterlife and to exhibit the versatility of their imaginations. So whether as part of a religious quest or anthropological investigation or whether for an adventure into the surreal, the myths and legends of ancient Egypt leave us richer for their speculation and imagery.

Pectoral of princess Sit-Hathor-Yunet depicting in gold and semi-precious stones two falcons flanking the cartouche of Senwosret II (1897–1878 BC). The princess' royal name, Kha-Kheperre, involves the image of the scarab beetle and the sun's rays breaking out on the eastern horizon at dawn.

Creation legends

The creation of the world, by whom and how, were subjects of constant interest to the Egyptians. Three cosmogonies were formulated based upon the traditions of three ancient cities – Heliopolis, Hermopolis and Memphis.

Major sources

At the outset of this book we must plunge deep into documents crucial to our understanding of the ancient Egyptian view of the cosmos. Columns of hieroglyphs were carved 4,300 years ago in the vestibule and sarcophagus hall of the pyramid of King Wenis (*c.* 2350 BC) at Sakkara, necropolis of the royal capital of Memphis, with the intention of securing a hereafter for the monarch in the vicinity of the sun god. Subsequent rulers of the Old Kingdom (*c.* 2649–2152 BC) continued this tradition. Known as *Pyramid Texts*, this corpus of spells and speculations gives us the opportunity to evaluate the complex imagery centred upon the Egyptian pantheon. It also forms the earliest religious compilation in the world.

In the next major era of Egyptian civilisation, called the Middle Kingdom (2040–1783 BC), we find that the prerogatives of royalty in defining status in the afterlife through magical inscriptions were usurped by provincial governors and court dignitaries. Their coffins became supernatural caskets painted with funerary formulae addressed to Anubis and Osiris, amuletic 'Eyes of Horus', luxury goods, basic rations, hundreds of tightly written spells (published by Egyptologists under the title *Coffin Texts*) and maps of the netherworld – all designed to neutralise the forces of chaos and to fortify the owner's spirit with hopes of joining the sun god's entourage. Scattered throughout these *Pyramid* and *Coffin Texts* can be found vital comments about the myth of the creator god of Heliopolis, provided of course you control your frustration at the ancient Egyptian editor's scorn for sustained logical analysis. Much later in date, at the beginning of the third century BC, a British Museum papyrus (also known as Papyrus Bremner-Rhind), traces by means of graphic phraseology the development of life from the creator god. (Although Ptolemaic in date this papyrus is likely to have evolved from an original written down at least a thousand years earlier.)

For the survival of the metaphysical account of creation by Ptah, god of Memphis, we are indebted to King Shabaka (712–698 BC), who belonged

The Shabaka stone bearing an inscription carved around 700 BC which is our main source for the metaphysical creation myth devised by the priests of Ptah at Memphis. It was supposedly saved by order of King Shabaka but subsequently used as a mill-stone.

to the expansionist Nubian dynasty whose capital was near Gebel Barkal in the Sudan. He followed up the invasion of Memphis of his predecessor Piye (formerly read Piankhi) with a more permanent occupying force. On a tour of inspection of the Temple of Ptah, Shabaka was horrified to discover that its most sacred papyrus scroll, containing a drama version of the accession of the god Horus to the throne of Egypt and the Memphite myth of the creator god, was being devoured by worms. He immediately ordered that the remaining undamaged text of the scroll be incised on a slab of black granite. His pious intentions, however, were partially thwarted: prior to its acquisition by the British Museum, the 'Shabaka Stone' was used as a mill-stone, as the deep gouge in its centre and the radials emanating from it testify.

Early scholars studying the original date of the 'Memphite theology' copied onto the stone believed that the language of the text pointed towards an Old Kingdom prototype. More careful scrutiny of the epithets of Ptah and the thought structure has led to the rejection of a date in the third millennium BC in favour of a Ramesside (*c.* 13th century BC) or later origin of this remarkable myth.

Our evidence for Amun as the creator god of Hermopolis rests primarily on Papyrus Leiden I 350, a vast encomium of the god emphasising his exclusive, procreative role. In addition, the New Kingdom temples of Deir el-Bahri and Luxor reveal Amun deserting his mysterious confines in the sky for sexual union with the reigning queen of Egypt, thereby fathering the future monarch. Finally, in the Graeco-Roman era, the last centuries of temple decoration in Egypt, such as at Esna and Edfu, when priestly scribes often gave obscure and enigmatic theological compositions to the sculptors to carve, the hieroglyphs preserve accounts of creation which are imaginative and rich in subtle allusions but seem to have lost direction in terms of cosmic revelation.

The sun god of Heliopolis

Under the suburbs of north-east Cairo lie the ruins of Yunu, once counted among the foremost and most ancient sanctuaries in Egypt. It was known as Heliopolis, or City of the Sun, to Herodotus, the Greek historian who visited the region in the fifth century BC, well over two thousand years after the first dedications had been made at its shrines. Here the intellectuals at the time of the unification of Upper and Lower Egypt (*c.* 3000 BC) began to formulate a cosmogony to explain the vital elements of their universe, culminating in their significant input into the *Pyramid Texts* of Dynasties V and VI.

Before the development of a structured cosmos there existed in darkness a limitless ocean of inert water. It was envisaged as the primeval being called Nu or Nun. No temples were ever built to honour it, but the nature of Nu is present in many cult sanctuaries in the form of the sacred lake which symbolises the 'non-existence' before creation. In fact, this vast expanse of lifeless water never ceased to be and after creation was imagined to surround the celestial firmament guarding the sun, moon, stars and earth as well as the boundaries of the underworld. There was always a fear in the Egyptian mind that Nu would crash through the sky and drown the earth. Such a destruction is hinted at in Spell 1130 of the *Coffin Texts* in Faulkner's 1973 edition where we read: 'mounds will be cities and cities become mounds and mansion will destroy mansion'. When this *Götterdämmerung* ('twilight of the gods') occurs the only survivors will be the gods Atum and Osiris in the form of snakes, 'unknown to mankind and unseen by other gods'.

Atum, 'lord of Heliopolis' and 'lord to the limits of the sky', constitutes the demiurge, the creator of the world, who rose out of Nu at the beginning of time to create the elements of the universe. As the sun god, he self-developed into a being and stood on a raised mound, an image suggestive of the banks and islands that re-emerge after the season of the Nile inundation. (It was natural that the régime of the River, source of Egypt's life and prosperity, should influence the concepts of creation just as the early scribes' environment dictated the signs of the hieroglyphic script.) This primeval mound became formalised as the *Benben*, a firm pyramidal elevation to support the sun god; the actual stone relic, perhaps regarded as the petrified semen of Atum, was alleged to survive in the *Hewet-Benben* (Mansion of the Benben) in Heliopolis.

The underlying notion of the name Atum is one of totality, thus as the sun god he is the *Monad*, the supreme being and quintessence of all the

The sun god Re-Horakhti before the Benben (primeval mound) of Heliopolis. Pyramidion of Ramose from Deir el-Medina, c. 1300 BC.

forces and elements of nature. Therefore, he contains within himself the life-force of every other deity yet to come into being. In Egyptian thought totality had a positive power, as in the idea of completing an eternity of existence, and a destructive aspect, as in consigning an enemy to the flames. This dualism inherent in the Monad allows for the future birth of a constructive goddess such as Isis as well as a god of chaos and confusion such as Seth.

But how was a male principle in solitary splendour going to give birth to his progeny? Here the ingenuity of the Heliopolitan theologians was bound-less. Two accounts evolved of how the life-giving essence in Atum passed from his body to produce a god and goddess. Utterance 527 of the *Pyramid Texts* makes the unequivocal statement that Atum masturbated in Heliopolis: 'Taking his phallus in his grip and ejaculating through it to give birth to the twins Shu and Tefnut'. This direct imagery only makes sense if we remem-ber that Atum possessed inside himself the prototype of every cosmic power and divine being. Otherwise, the word-picture of an orgasm by an ithyphallic sun god becomes a scurrilous caricature instead of an evocation of a sublime and mysterious act of creation.

In Utterance 600, however, the priests offer another explanation for the birth of Atum's children, relying on the assonance of words with similar consonantal skeletons. Punning was a useful tool of instruction in ancient Egypt, as shown by one example from a British Museum papyrus concerned with the interpretation of dreams: seeing a 'large cat' in a dream meant a 'bumper harvest' because the two phrases contained phonemes, or syllables, that were quite similar. So while not denying that the Egyptian sense of humour was pervasive and is all too often overlooked, we ought to regard the puns in the creation myths as attempts to convey intellectual concepts and not to elicit laughter at verbal dexterity – or, of course, groans at excruciating facetiousness. Atum is addressed as the god who 'spluttered out Shu and spat up Tefnut'. Shu is the mucus of Atum in as much as his name – from a root meaning 'void' or 'empty', an apt notion for the air god – is not too dissimilar to the word whose consonantal value is *yshsh* (no vowels are written in hieroglyphs) and which means 'sneeze' or 'splutter'. In the case of Tefnut, whose name eludes precise interpretation and is sometimes guessed to mean 'dew' or 'moisture in the air', the first two consonants of her name form the word *tf*, translated as 'spit'. Extracts from the Papyrus Bremner-Rhind bring together the salient points surrounding the procreative act of the Monad:

All manifestations came into being after I developed ... no sky existed no earth existed ... I created on my own every being ... my fist became my spouse ... I copulated with my hand ... I sneezed out Shu ... I spat out Tefnut ... Next Shu and Tefnut produced Geb and Nut ... Geb and Nut then gave birth to Osiris ... Seth, Isis and Nephthys ... ultimately they produced the population of this land.

The deities named here form the *Pesdjet* of Heliopolis, a group of nine gods and goddesses for which the Greek term *Ennead* is frequently used. Obviously the nine deities can be restricted to the genealogy devised at Heliopolis, but the notion of a coterie of gods and goddesses was transferable; the Temple of Abydos had an Ennead of seven deities while there were fifteen members of the Ennead in the Karnak temple. Probably because signs grouped in threes in Egyptian hieroglyphs conveyed the idea of an indeterminate plural, the concept of nine gods and goddesses indicates a plural of plurals, sufficient to cover a pantheon of any number of deities in any temple.

The first deities Atum created, Shu and Tefnut, could be represented as lions, as, for example, on the ivory headrest of Tutankhamun. In vignettes from the *Book of the Dead* Shu, wearing the ostrich plume which is in fact the hieroglyph for his name, raises his arms to support the body of the sky goddess Nut arched over her consort, the earth god Geb. Shu's role in the Heliopolitan cosmogony seems suppressed, no doubt because he had a strong solar streak in his nature that could not be allowed to approximate to the sun god *par excellence*. He encompassed the concept of air permeated by the rays of the sun – a notion used by the pharaoh Akhenaten in the earlier didactic name of the Aten, paramount sun god for less than two decades in the fourteenth century BC: 'Live Re-Horakhty rejoicing on the horizon – in his name as Shu who is in the Aten [i.e. sun disc]'.

Lioness-headed Tefnut escapes definitive categorisation. Her association with moisture or dew is attested in the *Pyramid Texts*, where there is also a passage suggesting that she is the atmosphere of the underworld. Perhaps the emphasis should be placed on her automatic access to the sun god, since as his daughter she becomes equated with his all-powerful solar eye.

The Heliopolitan view of the cosmos: the sky goddess Nut arches her body over her supine consort the earth god Geb from whom she is separated by the air god Shu, c. 1300 BC.

By natural processes Shu and Tefnut gave birth to Geb and Nut. Egyptians viewed the earth as a male principle and the sky female, in contrast to Indo-European mythology. Geb, the earth god, personified the land of Egypt and through him the link was established with the throne of the reigning pharaoh. The sky goddess Nut became one of the most represented deities from the elder Ennead. Her body is stretched across Geb but, after giving birth to four children, she is separated from him by Shu in accordance with the directive of Atum. Beyond her is Nu and non-existence. The ornate paintings of her in the sarcophagus hall of the tomb of Ramesses VI (1156–1148 BC) in the Valley of the Kings stress her importance – here the sun god journeys across the firmament along the underside of Nut's arched body; on reaching the western horizon at the end of the allotted twelve hours of day, the sun god is swallowed by the sky goddess; he traverses the inside length of her body during the hours of night, and at dawn Nut gives birth to the sun god on the eastern horizon amidst a display of redness that is the blood of parturition.

At this point in the genealogy, the priests of Heliopolis evolved a clever transition that incorporated the Osiris cycle of myths into the solar corpus. It lies in the fact that Nut bore Geb four children – Osiris, Isis, Seth and Nephthys. This created a connection between the elder cosmic deities of the Ennead and the political world. It also subordinated the upstart god Osiris, not attestable epigraphically or archaeologically before Dynasty V (2465–2323 BC), to the position of great-grandson of the sun god, thereby emphasising the impressive antiquity of the Monad. The legend of Osiris will be considered later but it is worth noting here that in completing the Ennead of Heliopolis the four offspring of Nut and Geb represent the perpetual cycle of life and death in the universe following Atum's act of creation. The Osiris cycle conforms to the dualism of the cosmic order established by the sun god and a balance is struck between the opposing principles of totality: Osiris *completes* a legitimate reign in Egypt; Seth *destroys* the lawful possessor of the throne of Geb. But more later.

The theogony of Heliopolis

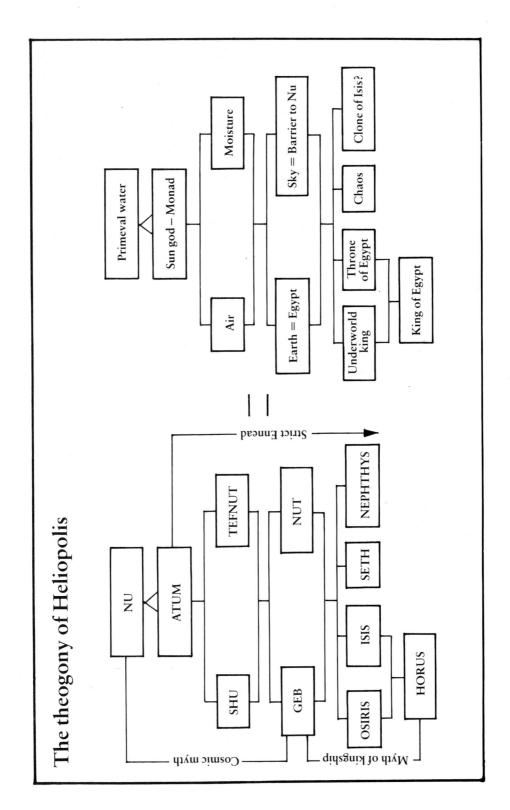

The imagery of the lotus flower seems to have been employed by the priests of Heliopolis to help explain the birth of the sun god Atum. Out of Nu emerged a lotus, together with the primeval mound, from which the sun god, still self-developed, rose as a child. The lotus itself was later identified with the god Nefertum (worshipped at Memphis); as a result there are spells in the *Book of the Dead* to transform the deceased into Nefertum because he is 'the lotus at the nose of the sun god'. In Cairo Museum the most beautiful portrayal of this concept can be found in the painted wooden lotus flower with the head of the child sun god emerging. It was found in the Valley of the Kings and is an iconographical identification of Tutankhamun with the newly-born sun god.

Before concluding the creation myth of Heliopolis we ought to mention the role of the Phoenix, the symbolism of the lotus and the coalescence of Atum with other manifestations of the sun god. The Phoenix, which the Greek writer Herodotus heard about in Egypt in the fifth century BC but did not see except in pictures on mythological papyri or wall carvings, originally took the form of a yellow wagtail but changed to a heron with long head plumes. In hieroglyphs it was called the *Benu*, the etymology of which means to 'rise in brilliance'. Self-evolved, the Benu became the symbol of the birth of the sun god. This is stated in Utterance 600 of the *Pyramid Texts* in an invocation to Atum: '... you rose up, as the Benben, in the Mansion of the Benu in Heliopolis'.

Herodotus was far from convinced about the existence of the Phoenix but related the story the priests had told him. The Herodotean Phoenix is a bird like an eagle, sporting gold and red plumage. On the death of its parent every five hundred years it flies from the Arabian peninsula to Egypt. It carries the body of its dead parent embalmed in an egg of myrrh and buries it in the Temple of the Sun God. The differences between the Phoenix of Herodotus and other classical authors, and the Benu of the ancient Egyptian sources are serious enough to make us question if the two birds are in any way related. However, Herodotus may have been confused by the evidence given to him. The bird he saw in pictures was certainly not the Benu, either in the shape he describes or in its gorgeous colouring; it was probably the Egyptian vulture or the Horus falcon. The mention of incense adds an authentic flavour, since it was highly valued in Egyptian temple ritual. The embalming myrrh of Herodotus' description could feasibly have been used in Heliopolis at this period in Egyptian civilisation, having come from the kingdoms of southern Arabia via the Red Sea trade routes.

For the rest, we ought not to forget that no-one knows the position of Herodotus' informants in the priestly hierarchy – upper echelons experienced in Heliopolitan theology or novices still learning. Indeed, some explanations of the Benu might have defeated the translators, especially since there are no records of Herodotus' time to inform us of any of the complexities of this bird that might have arisen during the two millennia following its first attestation in the *Pyramid Texts*. For example, we know that the Benu

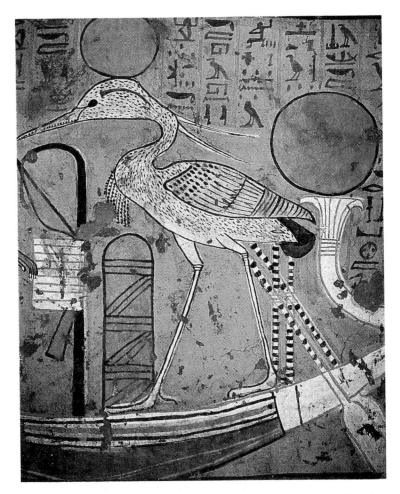

The Benu bird, or phoenix, manifestation of the sun god creator of Heliopolis.
Tomb of Arinefer at Deir el-Medina, Western Thebes, c. 1300 BC.

was incorporated in funerary rituals and had here come to play a role in ensuring the resurrection of the deceased in the underworld. The strongest point of contact between the Benu and the Phoenix is the connection that both have with the Temple of the Sun at Heliopolis.

Finally, the inner complexity of the Monad could project other manifestations. The coalescence of Atum with three aspects of the sun already existed by the time the *Pyramid Texts* were being inscribed. 'Re' is a basic word for sun indicating its physical presence in the sky and also the name of the sun god 'shining in his disk'; Khepri is the image of the sun propelled by a scarab beetle, an analogy taken from nature; Harakhti is the hawk soaring on the horizon, far off and distant as the sun itself. The names combine: for example, Re-Atum or Re-Harakhti. However, the essence of the myth of Heliopolis is not confused by this multiplicity of forms, each of which is an attempt to capture in a name an aspect of the sun god creator.

Ptah of Memphis

Ptah, 'south of his wall', was the god of Memphis, the ancient political capital of Egypt. In fact, in the New Kingdom (1550–1070 BC) his temple there, *Hewet-ka-Ptah* (Mansion of the spirit of Ptah), gave the name for the whole region and is ultimately the origin, via Greek, of the word Egypt itself. The ruins of Memphis today – for tourists mainly a calcite sphinx of Amenhotep II and a colossal statue of Ramesses II – offer little indication of the flourishing cosmopolitan city it once was. But leaving aside whatever splendid now-vanished monuments adorned the capital, Memphis demands our attention as the guardian of an intellectual tradition of cosmogony devised to assert the role of Ptah as most ancient and pre-eminent of gods. For it was here that the priests of Ptah formulated the metaphysical synthesis of creation preserved on the previously mentioned Shabaka Stone originally set up in their temple.

Before describing the contents of the Shabaka Stone, a word or two about Ptah as a creator god might be helpful. In the *Coffin Texts* and documents of the Ramesside era there are references to Ptah as being responsible for fashioning gods and the sun and for the ripening of vegetation. But even earlier in the Old Kingdom, Ptah's nature as a supreme artisan was fully developed and his High Priest at Memphis was called 'Greatest of the controllers of craftsmen'. From the reign of Ramesses II (1290–1224 BC) we find that the god Ptah coalesces with the deity Ta-tenen. The name Ta-tenen means 'the land which has become distinguishable', in other words, distinguishable from the primeval waters. Thus Ta-tenen risen from Nu can be equated with the primeval mound imagery already described. Now we can look at the Memphite account of creation beginning in column 53 of the Shabaka Stone.

Ptah gave life to the other gods (including Atum of Heliopolis) by means of his heart and his tongue. The conception of thought in the heart and the speech of the tongue determine the action of every limb. Ptah's presence is universal in the heart and mouths of 'all gods, all people, all cattle, all creeping things that live'. Ptah is superior to Atum, who brought his Ennead into being 'by his semen and his fingers'. The Ennead of Ptah is the teeth and lips in his mouth, so that by pronouncing the identity of everything the authority of his utterance was such that all creation came into being. Whatever the eyes see, the ears hear and the nose breathes goes straight to the heart, and the conclusion reached by the heart is then spoken by the tongue. This is how Ptah commanded all the gods into existence and how he became Ta-tenen, 'from whom all life emerged'. Having managed the birth of the gods, Ptah created for them cities, sanctuaries, shrines and perpetual offerings.

From this myth Ptah is seen to be an intellectual principle of creation amalgamated with the physical image of Ta-tenen as the primeval mound. It is a complete synthesis of mind and the material world. Known as the 'logos doctrine', there is a resounding echo of this impressive philosophical approach to the cosmos formulated by the priests of Memphis in the following passage from the New Testament:

In the beginning was the Word and the Word was with God
and the Word was God.
The same was in the beginning with God.
All things were made by Him; and without Him was not
anything made that was made.
In Him was life; and the life was the light of men.
(St John's Gospel, Chapter 1, Verses 1–4)

This similarity of thought has received much attention. What has never been emphasised, however, is the small but mind-destroying step from his recognition of a possible creator-intelligence (eloquently propounded both by the priests of Memphis and St John) to the dogma of predestiny. The perfidious 'bridge' is the argument that since the supreme deity is both artisan of the human race and commander of order in the universe, his words have consequently planned all future events. Such a subservient acceptance of the idea of a pre-ordained course for the human race can be found in the verses of a poet quoted by Scheherazade:

Go on your way and be comforted,
Child of the Faithful;
He who has moulded the world in His hands
Holds it and us in His hands forever.
What He has written you cannot alter,
What He has not written never shall be ...
Walk on light-hearted, caring and carrying nothing
Leaving all to Him;
Fear not what man may do, grieve not at sorrow,
Especially plan not, for He has planned all things ...
(*The Arabian Nights*, translated by Powys Mathers)

The priests of Memphis had argued and speculated in order to evolve the advanced principles of the logos doctrine. At times there must have been heated questioning of the nature of Ptah. But from this positive process emerged the Memphite cosmogony inscribed on the Shabaka Stone. Had a stultifying climate of unnegotiable religious tenets existed in pharaonic Egypt, it would have suppressed the initiatives of the priests of Ptah to grapple with what Omar Khayyam in Fitzgerald's *Rubaiyat* called the 'quarrel of the universe'.

The Ogdoad of Hermopolis

El-Ashmunein is a site in Middle Egypt that was once a prosperous city boasting an impressive temple built in honour of the god Djeheuty, better known by his Greek name of Thoth. The ruins are vast but overgrown and to unravel them demands full concentration, even for specialists. Although several archaeological expeditions, including the intensive British Museum excavations of the 1980s, have extended our knowledge about different developments on this site, most visitors to el-Ashmunein today will only be able to explore the huge Christian basilica constructed from re-used Roman columns and masonry. Because the region was the major cult centre of Thoth, god of wisdom and transmitter of the knowledge of hieroglyphs to the ancient Egyptians, the Greeks (who equated Thoth with their Hermes) referred to it as Hermopolis. In the Egyptian language, Hermopolis is called Khemnu, from which the modern Arabic name of el-Ashmunein ultimately derives, via Coptic. Khemnu means 'Eight Town' and was home to the eight primordial deities commonly known as the *Ogdoad* (a group of eight).

The myth of creation involving the Ogdoad is almost scientific in its concern with the physical composition of primeval matter. The original cosmic substance is seen as more complex than Nu, although Nu is counted among the mythical beings that it comprises. Admittedly the cosmology of Hermopolis lacks the imagery that surrounds the myth of the sun god of Heliopolis and the precision of the Memphite theology, but its scant statements probably result from the almost utter destruction or 'unexcavation' of inscribed pharaonic material at the site of el-Ashmunein. In fact, most evidence about the Ogdoad is drawn from Theban monuments pieced together in 1929 by the German Egyptologist Kurt Sethe in a masterly survey called 'Amun und die acht urgotter von Hermopolis'.

The number of either gods or goddesses in the Hermopolitan myth is far from fortuitous. We can see that four was regarded as the concept of a balanced totality: the Egyptians recognised four cardinal points, the Heliopolis myth gives the goddess Nut four children and the viscera extracted during embalming are protected by the four 'sons of Horus' with four goddesses guarding them in turn. Consequently the concept of eight is totality intensified – according to Spell 76 of the *Coffin Texts*, the god Shu created eight 'infinite beings' to help support the body of the sky goddess.

The eight of Hermopolis (structured as four couples) were personified entities within the primeval matter, with the gods envisaged as frogs and the goddesses as snakes. In the succinct phraseology of Henri Frankfort in his thought-provoking *Kingship and the Gods*, '. . . chaos had been conceptualised in eight weird creatures fit to inhabit the primeval slime'. The names of these eight deities survive, but it is difficult in some cases to conjure the exact mental image which ancient Egyptians would have seen. The following table gives the basic notion of each couple but ignores any divergence of concept which may have existed between the male and female principle:

Gods (frogs)	Goddesses (snakes)	Concept
Nu	Naunet	primeval waters
Heh	Hauhet	flood force
Kek	Kauket	darkness
Amun	Amaunet	concealed dynamism

In the case of Heh, philological evidence convincingly shows that the conventional translation of 'infinity' confuses two distinct words with similar consonantal stems.

At some point these entities who comprised the primordial substance interacted explosively and snapped whatever balanced tensions had contained their elemental powers. The formulators of the Hermopolitan cosmogony were convinced that the Ogdoad predated the Ennead of Heliopolis and were responsible for the origin of the sun. Accordingly, from the burst of energy released within the churned-up primal matter, the primeval mound was thrust clear. Its location later became Hermopolis, but its original emergence was described as the Isle of Flame because the sun god was born on it and the cosmos witnessed the fiery glow of the first sunrise. It was the primacy of the Ogdoad in this cataclysmic event that seems to have been paramount in the Hermopolis myth. In Egyptian terms, the Ogdoad are 'the fathers and the mothers who came into being at the start, who gave birth to the sun and who created Atum'. Events then develop in the newly created universe, but three pairs of the Ogdoad take no further interest and stay immune and immutable in the vortex. Amun and Amaunet, however, throw in their lot with the new order, and so desert Hermopolis for Thebes.

Finally, a tomb at Tuna el-Gebel, the desert necropolis for el-Ashmunein, adds an intriguing complication to the creation myth. Constructed in the style of a miniature temple shortly after the conquest of Egypt by Alexander the Great in 332 BC, it belonged to Petosiris, High Priest of Thoth at Hermopolis. He was also priest of the Ogdoad, but their withdrawal from the Hermopolitan scene after the Isle of Flame episode of the cosmogony

The ibis-headed god Thoth, head of the Ogdoad of creator deities of Hermopolis, in his role of divine scribe at the judgement of the dead. Before him is the Devourer of Evil Hearts and Osiris god of the underworld. Tomb of Petosiris at El-Mazauwaka, Dakhla Oasis. Hellenistic period.

meant that Thoth had taken the role of 'Lord of Khemnu'. Petosiris in his autobiographical inscriptions draws attention to the restorations he made to the temple complex at Hermopolis, severely damaged during the turmoil of the second Persian domination of Egypt in 343 BC. He revitalised the temple rituals, drew up a new rota for the priests and improved their promotion prospects. He conducted the foundation ceremony for a limestone temple to the sun god Re, who is referred to as the 'child in the Isle of Flame'. That conforms to the Hermopolitan myth, but now a new symbol of creation comes to the forefront. Petosiris describes how he built an enclosure around an area of the temple which had been vandalised by hooligans. He calls it the 'birthplace of every god' and states that there was outrage throughout Egypt at the damage. The reason for this outrage was that the relics of the cosmic egg from which the sun god broke out were buried there. Therefore, a new image of the sun god emerging from an egg had been introduced at Hermopolis. Possibly this scenario is an intrusion into the original myth, evolving around Thoth, who flew carrying the cosmic egg to the primeval mound at Khemnu for the birth of the sun god.

Amun the transcendent creator

During the New Kingdom Theban priests reached the heights of eloquence in hymns to the god Amun that extolled his uniqueness as creator. Like the analysis of the nature of the sun god Aten inscribed in the tomb of Ay at el-Amarna, these paeons, particularly the stanzas of Papyrus Leiden I 350, aimed to demonstrate that all elements of the physical universe were manifestations of a lone demiurge. There is a conflation of all notions of creation into the personality of Amun, a synthesis which emphasises how Amun transcends all other deities in his being 'beyond the sky and deeper than the underworld'. Time and again the Egyptian poet-priests tried to interpret Amun's inexplicability. His mystery is contained in his name – since his essence is imperceptible, he cannot be called by any term that hints at his inner nature, and so the name Amun has the underlying notion of 'hidden-ness' and probably best translates as 'the one who conceals himself'. His identity is so secret that no other god knows his true name. Amun – to venture a touch of lese-majesty – is the ultimate godfather, whose associates never know the extent of his involvements so that their safest policy is *omerta* (the Sicilian mafia code of silence). In the words of the Leiden hymn, Amun is 'too great to inquire into and too powerful to know'; the penalty for trying to get illicit information on his identity is expressly stated as instantaneous death.

Amun is synonymous with the growth of Thebes as a major religious capital. His prominence in that region is already attested in the Middle Kingdom, particularly as a god with procreative powers similar to the ancient ithyphallic deity Min, the primeval god of Coptos. His epithet to describe this possession of unfailing fertility is 'Bull of his mother', and the finest iconography of Amun in this character can be found on the peripteral chapel

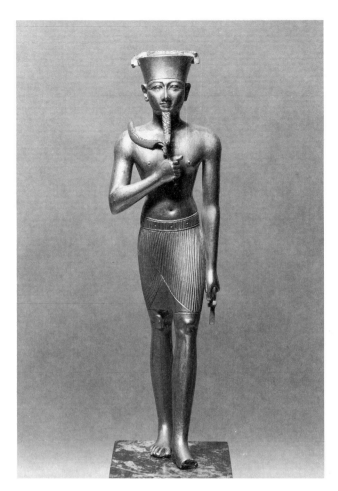

Gold statuette of the god Amun, transcendent creator and solar deity, holding the 'ankh' sign of life in one hand and the scimitar, symbol of power and foreign conquest, in the other.

of Senwosret I (1971–1926 BC) reconstructed in the open air museum at Karnak temple. It was, however, in the five centuries of the New Kingdom that Amun became undisputed head of the Egyptian pantheon (except for an eclipse of two decades when the 'sun disk' of the pharaoh Akhenaten was promoted to paramount god). Amun as universal ruler in his title of 'Lord of the thrones of the Two Lands' and 'King of the Gods' had such impressive temples built for him at Thebes that rumours of Thebes' splendour spread beyond the frontiers of Egypt into the world of composers of Greek epic poetry, as in Achilles' comments on Agamemnon:

I hate his gifts.
Not if he gave me ten times as much, and twenty times over as he possessed now, not if more should come to him from elsewhere ... all that is brought in to Thebes of Egypt, where the greatest possessions live up in the houses, Thebes of the hundred gates, where through each of the gates two hundred fighting men came forth to war with horses and chariots ... not even so would Agamemnon have his way with my spirit until he had made good to me all this heartrending insolence.
(from Homer's *Iliad*, Book IX, translated by Richmond Lattimore)

There were shrines to him, of course, elsewhere in Egypt and in the period following the New Kingdom the monarchs of Dynasties XXI–XXII (c. 1070–715 BC) redeployed colossal monuments from the reign of Ramesses II to build a huge temple to Amun, the northern equivalent of Karnak, at Tanis in the Delta. But it is to the columned halls, obelisks, colossal statues, wall-reliefs and hieroglyphic inscriptions of the Theban temples that we look to gain the true impression of Amun's superiority. Thebes was naturally thought of as the location of the emergence of the primeval mound at the beginning of time. It was the supreme 'city' and all other towns in Egypt could only try to imitate it and would only achieve pale reflections.

In the Hermopolitan creation myth, Amun is one of the elemental forces of the Ogdoad. But as the unique deity of the Theban theology he is transcendental, above creation and pre-existing the joint efforts of the Ogdoad to bring about the primeval mound. The Theban intellectuals must have struggled long and hard to resolve this problem. Amun as 'he who fashioned himself' generated himself into existence before all other matter existed. Without specific details of this mysterious event, the atmosphere of the occasion is evoked by the image of his 'fluid' becoming welded together with his body to form a cosmic egg. Once emerged, Amun forms the primeval matter – the elements of the Ogdoad of which he himself is a part. In this respect he becomes the 'First one who gave birth to the First ones'. But the universe was dark, silent and motionless. It seems that Amun was the creative burst of energy that stirred the Ogdoad into action. Kurt Sethe in his monograph interpreted Amun's role as similar to the 'Spirit of God' in Genesis that 'moved upon the face of the waters' – in other words, Amun was a stimulating breeze across primeval matter, stirring it into a vortex out of which the primordial mound would emerge. This is a tempting suggestion and the notion of wind is in keeping with Amun's invisibility. The Leiden hymn gives another rather amusing image of Amun initiating the activity of creation. The setting is the deadly quiet cosmos across which suddenly booms the voice of the 'Great Honker', not surprisingly 'opening every eye' and causing commotion in the cosmos. Amun in the form of this primeval goose set the whole process of creation in motion with his piercing screech.

The Theban theologians extensively develop the idea that all seemingly important deities are merely projections of Amun. Hence he does not stay in oblivion with the post-creation Ogdoad but becomes Ta-tenen, the primordial mound. He develops as the sun god, distant in the sky, continually rejuvenating in the cycle of sunset/sunrise. Therefore, his name on monuments as Amun-Re is legion. The Ennead of Heliopolis is a manifestation of Amun. In fact, every god is a projected image of Amun, and three gods in particular form a unity that is 'Amun': Re is his face, Ptah his body, and Amun his hidden identity.

As a postscript we can mention an aspect of Amun as a primeval deity that was probably restricted to the Theban region. If the creator god and assimilator of other deities described in the Leiden hymn proved to be too philosophical and intangible for some minds, then the Theban priests could provide a very concrete image of Amun as a primordial being. On the west bank of Thebes there is a site called Medinet Habu, much visited for its massive mortuary temple of the pharaoh Ramesses III (1194–1163 BC). Within its boundary walls is another temple lying to the north of the western fortified gate. Its construction in its present form dates from Dynasty XVIII with the joint reigns of Hatshepsut and Tuthmosis III (beginning about 1479 BC) through to the Graeco-Roman occupation into the reign of Antoninus Pius (AD 138–161). The statue of Amun of Karnak would regularly be brought to this sanctuary with the sole purpose of greeting his ancestor, a primeval form of himself imagined as a snake. The snake was described as 'Kem-atef' or 'The one who has completed his moment'. This could be a reference to the darting swiftness of a snake and with it an inherent analogy of the burst of energy from Amun at the creation. It could also be suggestive of the snake shedding its skin and hence symbolic of the procreative power of Amun and the continual cycle of renewal of life. The Greek writer Plutarch (c. AD 40–120) described the snake as 'Kneph', mentioning that the inhabitants of Thebes worshipped it to the exclusion of all other gods. In that statement Plutarch was decidedly wrong, but his epithets for the snake are drawn from traditions that accurately reflected this ancestral form of Amun as 'unbegotten and immortal'.

Khnum and the Theban theogony

The god Khnum, a ram-headed god of the cataract region of the Nile, introduces a new emphasis in creation myths in that his main concern is with the making of humans. He is thought to have moulded the human form on a potter's wheel. Elsewhere, in the Heliopolitan and Hermopolitan myths

The creator god Khnum in his manifestation as a ram. At his temple at Esna the myth explained how Khnum created mankind on the potter's wheel. Late Period.

for example, the human race is all but ignored in favour of cosmic issues. But in the myth of Khnum there is a progressive link between the gods and the people of the world. The ram, Khnum's sacred creature, is a symbol of procreativity in the natural world. At Aswan in the Nile cataract, Khnum controlled the caverns of Hapy, the god of the inundation. Before the modern irrigation projects at Aswan, culminating in the High Dam (which destroyed the natural regime of the Nile), the River would flood annually. The water covered the fields and on receding left a mantle of the rich silt it had carried with it from the Sudan. On the fertile mud Egyptian farmers grew barley and emmer-wheat and harvests normally resulted in a surplus of grain. So the inundation meant prosperity, and Khnum its controller was seen as a benefactor to the people of Egypt. A ruined sanctuary of Khnum as 'lord of the cataract' sprawls over the southern end of the island of Elephantine at Aswan.

In the temple of Esna in Upper Egypt Khnum was celebrated as the creator of all people. The town of Esna today, apart from occasional Islamic architecture of merit, is a squalid urban cluster. The main street leading to the temple from the River is just north of the ancient ceremonial approach, now buried deep below the modern town. All that survives of Khnum's temple is the hypostyle hall predominantly Roman in date. The inscriptions on the columns and walls are in the deliberately complex form of the hieroglyphic script favoured by the priest-scribes of the Graeco-Roman era. Nevertheless, it is from the calender liturgies and hymns carved at Esna that we derive the clearest understanding of Khnum as creator and god of the potter's wheel.

Khnum's actions in moulding the human body on the wheel are explicitly stated and survive as a detailed anatomical record. He orientated the blood-stream to flow over the bones and attached the skin to the body's frame. He installed a respiratory system in the body, vertebrae to support it and an apparatus for digestion. In keeping with his procreative responsibilities he designed the sexual organs to allow maximum comfort without loss of efficiency during intercourse. He supervised conception in the womb and initiated the stages of labour. Chanted at the Festival of the Potter's Wheel, the above hymn must have sounded like a metrical medical manual. Other descriptions emphasise that Khnum's moulding on the wheel is a continual process and not just restricted to Egyptians but to those who speak foreign languages as well. He is thus a universal creator who formed gods and people, animals, birds, fish and reptiles.

It has been suggested that the idea of Khnum moulding a human being on the potter's wheel, which goes far back in Egypt in reliefs and inscriptions of the Temple of Esna, could have influenced the traditions that the Greek poet Hesiod (c. 700 BC) drew upon for the making of Pandora which he describes both in his *Theogony* and *Works and Days*. There Zeus instructed Hephaistos to mould a woman, Pandora, out of clay, who would bring mankind limitless miseries. But it is quite probable that the Hesiodic concept of Pandora is an independent tradition – certainly the malicious intentions of Zeus are far from the spirit of the philanthropic Khnum. There are also later Middle Eastern surmises upon the idea of the creation of people on the potter's wheel. For instance, Omar Khayyam, in Fitzgerald's *Rubaiyat*, contains a scene in a potter's shop in Iran, probably Naishapur, around AD 1200. The 'clay population' converse with one another, each with a human angst: 'Then said another – "Surely not in vain my substance from the common earth was ta'en that He who subtly wrought me into shape should stamp me back to common earth again"'.

We can now move from the general encomium at Esna about Khnum's importance in human life to an interesting commission that the god Amun entrusted to him at Thebes. The episode is known as the Theban theogony. This describes the 'marriage' (actually a brief sexual encounter) between the god Amun and the great royal wife. There are in fact two examples of the theogony in Theban temples: one relating to the birth of Queen Hatshepsut at Deir el-Bahri and the other, which we will follow through here, concerning the pharaoh Amenhotep III (1391–1353 BC).

The procreative form of Amun, with his self-renewing energy conjured up by the epithet 'Ka-mutef' or 'Bull of his mother', predominates in the Temple of Luxor on the east bank at Thebes. Near to the sanctuary, which in its present form bears the cartouches of Alexander the Great, Amenhotep III gave orders for the construction of an apartment where the results of Amun's unfailing sexual powers could be unfurled in a series of reliefs that enhanced the monarch's own divinity. The pharaoh was called from the Pyramid era onwards (in particular from c. 2500 BC) the 'Son of the sun god' – this was in addition to being the early manifestation of the god Horus. The sandstone reliefs at Luxor, now horrendously pitted, define this kinship to the creator god, the status now held by Amun, in a 'royal wedding' documentary.

From the hieroglyphs it is clear that Amun, 'the one who conceals himself', has taken on the guise of the pharaoh Tuthmosis IV (1401–1391 BC) in order to make the earthly projection of himself a reassuring figure for the queen involved. However, the depictions show Amun in his traditional iconography as state god: anthropomorphic, beard of divinity with the curled tip and a crown of two high plumes. The first scene chronologically shows Queen Mut-em-wiya, great royal wife of Tuthmosis IV, seated opposite Amun on a long couch which can also be read as the hieroglyph for sky. So we can assume that the scenario is symbolically Amun's place in the heavens far removed from the palace bedroom. The sexual union is discreetly represented – both Mut-em-wiya and Amun are clothed in their linen garments but their legs are in a formalised entanglement; Amun's right hand extends the 'ankh', sign of life, to the nose of Mut-em-wiya for her to breathe in its vitality. This is the moment of orgasm and of transmission of the god's semen into the queen. Supporting the sky-couch with their heads and holding the feet of the god and queen are the protective scorpion goddess Serket and the demiurge-goddess Neith.

The next scene brings Khnum onto the stage. Amun, holding his sceptre of dominion and the sign of life, approaches the ram-headed Khnum who carries similar regalia. Instructions are passed on to Khnum. Now Khnum comes into his own. He sits on a throne, his hands resting on the heads of the two child-beings he has just moulded, who stand on the stylised potter's wheel. One figure is the future King Amenhotep III, and the other represents the 'ka' or eternal life-force of the pharaoh. The goddess Hathor, in one aspect guardian of royalty, is seated by the wheel and holds up the 'ankh' sign to the two figures. Mystery then surrounds the method of implantation of these moulded beings into the womb of the queen by Khnum. We are then shown the birth of Amenhotep III. Queen Mut-em-wiya is seated on a cube-shaped chair in the centre of a gigantic couch guarded by lion-head terminals. Both her posture and her chair are stylisations of the real-life situation where women knelt over the 'brick of pregnancy' (representing the goddess Meskhenet) to give birth. Two midwives hold on to the arms of Mut-em-wiya, but unfortunately there is a large gash in the sandstone damaging details around the queen's abdomen. These surrounding reliefs, however, indicate that there has been a successful delivery of Amenhotep III and his 'ka'.

The Theban theogony is incapable of any interpretation suggesting that Amun is abusing his prerogative as supreme god in order to enjoy a one-night stand with the Queen of Egypt. Their union is a far cry from the indiscriminate lusts of certain Greek deities whom Lord Byron clearly had in mind when he wrote:

> What men call gallantry, and gods adultery,
> Is much more common when the climate's sultry.
> (Don Juan, *Canto* I:LXIII)

In Egypt for the god-pharaoh to be proclaimed as the offspring of the king of the gods constituted a propaganda myth aimed at 'hierarchising' the monarchs into second-in-command in the cosmos. The reputation of his predecessor was in no way tarnished. The queen was elevated – albeit momentarily – to consort of the supreme god in an intimacy beyond the reach of the pharaoh himself. The god Amun became manifest early on in a calculated liaison with Mut-em-wiya with the purpose of engendering a future regent to control Egypt in his name. To borrow phrases from W. B. Yeats' *Leda and the Swan* – the queen of Egypt in her lovemaking with the king of the gods could well have 'put on his knowledge and his power'. Furthermore, Amun's motivation in ensuring that the heir to the throne of Egypt would be totally unassailable, through an extraterrestrial input of DNA, creates a mood light-years away from the turbulent passion of the Greek god Zeus that led to the disasters of:

> The broken wall, the burning roof and tower
> and Agamemnon dead.

The myth of kingship

The legitimate succession of a pharaoh to the throne of Egypt was on the one hand a very practical affair, possibly involving a stabilising period of co-regency with the previous monarch, and on the other an event hallowed by mythological precedent. The basic dogma of the ruler-cult proclaimed that the pharaoh was the earthly manifestation of the sky god Horus. So the myth of the transmission of kingship from Osiris via the machinations of Isis to her son Horus is vital to understanding the status and power of the sovereign in ancient Egypt and shall be explained here.

The records from which it is possible to piece together the myth of kingship are varied in nature and date. In the case of Osiris as monarch of Egypt before his departure to become king of the underworld I have concentrated on the *Pyramid Texts*, spells on the coffins of courtiers in the Middle Kingdom and the stela of Amenmose in the Louvre Museum. Ancient Egyptian sources are noticeably reticent about the murder of Osiris and the usurpation of the throne by Seth, but there are intriguing references such as in the stela of Ikhernofret in Berlin Museum (no. 1204), and in a Ptolemaic papyrus (no. 3008 in Berlin Museum) concerned with the grief of Isis. I have used Papyrus Chester Beatty I, an extremely lively papyrus in the Dublin Museum as documentation for the violent, salacious and hilarious episodes of the struggle between Seth and Horus for the throne. The eventual vindication of Horus as the rightful ruler of Egypt draws upon the Shabaka Stone, the Middle Kingdom Ramesseum Dramatic Papyrus and the play concerning the annihilation of Seth inscribed on the wall of the ambulatory passage in Edfu Temple, dating to the Ptolemaic period. Finally, at the end of the myth as it is found in pharaonic sources, I have appended a brief synopsis of the account called 'Concerning Isis and Osiris' by the Greek author Plutarch (*c.* AD 40–120), where original Egyptian elements have been interwoven with Hellenistic concepts.

The murder of Osiris

From the creation myth devised by the priests of Heliopolis we can observe a clever link between the cosmic deities and the gods and goddesses who figure in the story of the transmission of kingship. Geb the earth god and Nut the sky goddess produced four children – Osiris, Isis, Seth and Nephthys. By this genealogy there is a descent from the sun god creator to the possessor of the throne of Egypt. Osiris was the firstborn of the offspring of Geb and Nut. His birthplace was near Memphis at Rosetau in the western desert necropolis. This spot was particularly apt for the birth of Osiris since his pre-eminent role is that of the god of the underworld and Rosetau, or 'Mouth of the passage-ways', is the symbolic entrance into Osiris' nether realm. An epithet, originally for a funerary deity at Abydos, which Osiris often carries is 'Khenta-mentiu', or 'Foremost of the Westerners', a title which similarly emphasises Osiris' status as ruler of those buried in the desert cemeteries whence their spirits hoped for access into the underworld.

As the eldest son of Geb and Nut, Osiris inherited the right to govern the land of Egypt. In the traditions of kingship preserved in the New Kingdom papyrus known as the Turin Royal Canon, Egypt in predynastic times was under the rule of a succession of gods – Ptah, Re, Shu, Geb, Osiris, Seth and Horus. (We have to ignore here its continuation with Thoth, Maet and the Followers of Horus.) Osiris' consort was his sister Isis, thus providing a divine prototype for marriage between full or half-brothers and sisters in the royal family. The prosperity of Egypt during his reign is conjured up in eloquent phraseology on the stela of Amenmose (c. 1400 BC during Dynasty XVIII) in the Louvre Museum. There, Osiris is described as commanding all resources and elements in a way that brings good fortune and abundance to the land. Through his power the waters of Nu are kept under control, favourable breezes blow from the north, plants flourish and all animal life follows a perfect pattern of procreation. Also Osiris receives immense respect from other gods and governs the system of stars in the sky. Of his cult centres throughout Egypt the mid-Delta sanctuary of Djedu (Busiris) and his Upper Egyptian temple at Abydos are paramount. His regalia consists of the crook and flail sceptres and tall plumed 'atef' crown described as 'sky-piercing'. So like many stories throughout history we begin with a benevolent and successful king and queen, Osiris and Isis, ruling in a golden age.

This idyllic scene is now shattered by the usurpation of the throne by Seth, Osiris' antagonist-brother. Tradition maintained that Seth ripped himself from the womb of Nut in Upper Egypt at Naqada where his major temple in the south was later erected. Violence and chaos became attributes of Seth but despite his 'bad press' in the myth of kingship we ought not to overlook the fact that occasions stand out when support for this god was strong. Certainly on present archaeological evidence Seth is a god of greater antiquity than Osiris, since we find the composite creature which represents him on the late predynastic macehead of King Scorpion, a ruler of Upper Egypt, in the Ashmolean Museum, Oxford. (At present no archaeological proof exists for Osiris before Dynasty V, c. 2465 BC.) The Seth animal has a slightly crescent-shaped proboscis and two upright projections from the top of its head and – if represented in complete quadrupedic form rather than just the head on an anthropomorphic body – it has an erect forked tail.

In the *Pyramid Texts* there are tantalising references to Osiris suffering a fatal attack from this creature. He is described as 'falling on his side' on

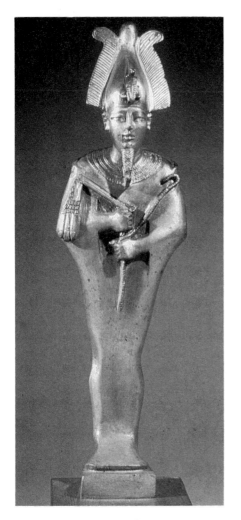

ABOVE LEFT The god Osiris, who in the myth of kingship inherits the throne from Geb, is murdered by Seth and becomes ruler of the underworld. His distinctive 'atef' crown comprises ram-horns and ostrich feathers. Late-Period bronze.

ABOVE RIGHT Seth, god of chaotic forces and opponent of Osiris and Horus in the myth of kingship. Outside this myth, Seth was regarded as an ancient and prestigious deity. Here, above the head of his heraldic creature, he wears the Double Crown of a pharaoh. Late-Period bronze.

the river bank at Nedyet in the district of Abydos. His murder is confirmed by the grief displayed in the weeping of Isis. The spells painted on the coffins of courtiers in the Middle Kingdom identify the murderer of Osiris unequivocally as Seth, and declare that he attacked Osiris in Gahesty and killed him by the river at Nedyet. These sparse details reflect the horror held by the Egyptians of the assassination of the monarch and violent transfer of power – it was a theme not to be developed or dwelt upon. It is interesting to note that historically there are relatively few instances of bloody *coups d'état* during the first two thousand years of dynastic Egypt. In fact there are several inscriptions that try to suppress the idea that Osiris was murdered – although subsequent events do not make sense without his death. An example is the hymn on the stela of Amenmose where Osiris is portrayed as invincible, a slayer of foes and crusher of conspirators, although a little later in the text Isis is searching for his body. Similarly the valuable inscription on the stela of Ikhernofret in Berlin Museum re-interprets the event into a victory-procession for the adherent of Osiris. This stela gives an insight into the rituals in honour of Osiris held at his major cult centre at Abydos: Ikhernofret was an official of King Senwosret III (1878–1841 BC) commissioned by the pharaoh to organise the annual festival of Osiris at Abydos and adorn the sacred image of the god with gold. During the ceremonies the statue of Osiris in the regalia of kingship, decked out with lapis lazuli, turquoise and gold, was carried on the 'Neshmet' boat. The ancient canine deity Wepwawet acted as the champion of Osiris during this procession. There follows the suppression of the assassination of Osiris: the 'Neshmet' boat is symbolically attacked but during the combat it is the foes of Osiris who are killed by the river at Nedyet. Illogically, the next stage of the ceremony is to conduct the funerary boat of Osiris to his tomb in the desert of Abydos at Peqer. Incidentally, this tomb was located towards the desert cliffs in the region called by the Arabs 'Umm el-Ga'ab' or 'Mother of Pots' from the vast quantity of pottery offered on the early dynastic royal monument that had become re-interpreted as the god's sepulchre.

With Osiris dead, Seth becomes ruler of Egypt, with his sister Nephthys as his consort. However, the sympathies of Nephthys are with her sister Isis who is distraught at the death of Osiris. Isis determines to use her immense magical powers to recover the body of Osiris and to resurrect it sufficiently to conceive a son to avenge the monstrous usurpation and murder. Tirelessly she and Nephthys roam Egypt lamenting Osiris until eventually his body is located at Abydos. Other cult centres claimed to be the resting place of Osiris' body – or parts of it – such as the Abaton on Biga Island just south of the First Cataract of the Nile at Aswan or Herakleopolis where the burial was held to be under the 'Naret-tree', but it is at Abydos that we find the fullest documentation of the next episode in the myth.

Therefore, let us go into the shrine of the god Sokar in the Temple of King Sety I (1306–1290 BC), at Abydos. This temple is renowned for the most exquisite reliefs to have survived in Egyptian art, primarily in the seven sanctuaries and in the suite of inner apartments dedicated to Osiris, Isis and Horus. The Sokar sanctuary has suffered severe damage but two representations give explicit visual indications of the impregnation of Isis with the seed of Osiris. In the inscription of Amenmose the goddess Isis discovers the body of Osiris, shades it with her wings (she can take the form of a kite) and creates the breath of life with her wings so that Osiris revives from death and impregnates her. Similarly on the walls of the Abydos temple this act of procreation involves the magic of Isis and her transformation into a sparrow hawk to receive the seed of Osiris. One representation shows Isis and (by anticipation) Horus at either end of the lion-headed bed of mummification. Osiris, whose putrefaction has been halted by the skills of Isis, raises one arm to his head which Isis is holding and grasps his phallus in the other hand to stimulate it into orgasm. The other depiction follows on from this act with Isis as the sparrow hawk pressing herself down upon the phallus of Osiris. Osiris' role in the myth of kingship in Egypt is now completed. He descends into Duat, the underworld, and reigns there as Lord of Eternity. In Egyptian religious thought it was not the earthly rule of Osiris that was significant but the miracle of his resurrection from death, offering the hope of a continuity of existence for everyone in the underworld where one of Osiris' titles proclaims him as 'ruler of the living'. As can be seen, the main protagonist has become the goddess Isis, the hieroglyphs of whose name contain the symbol of the throne.

The vengeance of Horus

The resulting child of Isis and Osiris is the hawk god Horus. His name means the 'Far-Above-One', derived from the imagery of the soaring of the hawk. Horus is a complex deity into whom have been amalgamated concepts not directly involved in the myth of kingship – the idea of the god as a vulnerable child or as the sky-falcon whose eyes are the sun and moon. However, all diverse elements were skilfully woven into a tapestry, the sum total of whose different emphases was the god Horus with whom the sovereign of Egypt identified.

The hawk Horus,
god of kingship.
Ptolemaic period bronze.

Horus was born in the North East Delta at Khemmis. For his own security against Seth, Isis hid Horus in the papyrus marshes. During his early years he is called Har-pa-khered or 'Horus the child', referred to by the Greeks as Harpokrates. He is vulnerable and dependent on the magic of the goddess Isis for protection (see the chapter *Isis 'Great in Magic'*). When he reaches his maturity as Har-wer or 'Horus the Elder' (Haroeris in Greek) he is ready to struggle for his rightful patrimony, the throne of Egypt, but as we shall see the goddess Isis is crucial still in helping him achieve this end.

Horus takes his claim to the kingship of Egypt to a tribunal of major gods presided over by the sun god Re of Heliopolis. He has chosen a propitious moment to submit his case – when Thoth, god of wisdom, is presenting the sun god with the 'Sacred Eye', symbolic of cosmic order, justice and kingship. The air god Shu urges the immediate approval of Horus' claim and Thoth adds that such a decision would be a 'million times right'. Isis in her excitement prepares the north wind to carry the good news to Osiris in the underworld. However, the gods have begun to act prematurely since Re intervenes to point out that their decision does not yet have his ratification. He deplores their insistence that Horus already possesses the royal name-ring (i.e. the cartouche in which the hieroglyphs spelling two of the five names of a monarch were written) and the White Crown of Upper Egypt. Seth suggests that he and Horus should go outside the courtroom and settle the matter by hand-to-hand combat. Thoth tries to restore some notion of the procedures of a law court and emphasises that Horus has a good case since he is the son of Osiris. The sun god, however, is not impressed and clearly prefers Seth 'great of strength'.

An impasse is reached and lasts eighty years. To try and break it, the gods eventually agree on sending a letter to the great creator goddess Neith. The letter is dispatched in the name of Re and is couched in deferential terms to the goddess, seeking her advice. In contrast an impatient and curt reply comes from Neith, stressing the clear-cut evidence in favour of Horus who should inherit the office of Osiris – otherwise 'the sky will crash down' at this offence against justice. Neith is also an astute judge since she realises that Seth must be given a consolation prize and urges Re to give him his two daughters Anat and Astarte as wives. These Middle Eastern goddesses had become incorporated in the Egyptian pantheon in the New Kingdom, as had the important Syrian gods Baal and Reshep. Since Seth has an affinity with foreign warrior gods the gift of these two goddesses is quite apt. The gods of the tribunal approve Neith's advice, except for Re. He finds the decision totally unacceptable and turns on Horus to abuse him. He accuses Horus of being a weakling, a youngster with halitosis and certainly not strong enough to wield authority. The tribunal of gods now becomes exasperated and a minor god called Baba has the audacity to tell Re 'Your shrine is empty' which is tantamount to saying that no one takes him seriously any more. Re now exhibits a remarkable sensitivity to this remark, abandoning the tribunal to go off to his pavilion and sulk. The situation is saved, however, by

Hathor, 'mistress of the southern sycamore', who is another daughter of Re and a goddess of love and joy. Hathor goes to Re's pavilion, stands in front of him and pulls up her dress to reveal her nakedness. For some reason this display provokes Re to laughter. He returns to the courtroom and tells Horus and Seth to submit their cases.

Seth, who is portrayed in this papyrus as a swaggerer and boaster, claims he deserves the throne of Egypt by virtue of his unassailable strength. Only he is competent to repel Apophis, the arch enemy of the sun god, on the journey through the underworld. This claim meets with approval since Apophis was a very real threat to the existence of the cosmos. But Thoth and Anhur (a warrior god originating near Abydos) question whether it is lawful to give an inheritance to the brother while the son is capable of taking it. A counter-claim argues that Seth as the elder of the two disputants deserves the office. (It is here that the papyrus refers to Horus and Seth as brothers, an independent tradition conflated into the 'uncle-nephew' account.) At this point Isis loses patience and intervenes on behalf of Horus, gaining the tribunal's sympathy. This infuriates Seth who threatens to kill one god a day with his 4500lb sceptre. He takes an oath in the name of Re to protest that he will not recognise any court in which Isis participates. Re removes the proceedings to an island, giving orders to the ferryman Nemty not to row across any women resembling Isis.

But this move underestimates the guile and magic of Isis. Disguised as an old crone carrying a bowl of flour and wearing a gold signet ring, Isis approaches Nemty. Her request is for the ferryman to row her across to the island so that she can give the flour for food to a hungry young herdsman who has been tending cattle for five days. Nemty informs her that he has received orders to ferry no women across to the island but has to admit that the old woman does not seem to be the goddess Isis. In a touch of realism which you might encounter in Egypt today, bargaining now begins over the price of the journey. Nemty is contemptuous of a cake which Isis offers and only agrees to ferry her across in exchange for the gold signet ring which he duly receives.

Once on the island Isis sees the gods having a break and eating bread. Uttering a spell to change herself into a beautiful young woman, she catches the eye of Seth who is immediately excited with desire. He comes over alone to Isis and introduces himself. Isis cleverly traps Seth into an admission of guilt – she pretends to be a herdsman's widow whose son is being threatened by a stranger with the confiscation of his father's cattle and eviction from his home. She implores Seth to act as her son's defender. Seth feels great indignation at the injustice she and her son are suffering. This is, of course, precisely what Isis had hoped for since by analogy it is the contest for the inheritance of Osiris. For her own safety she changes into a kite and flies onto an acacia, informing Seth that his verdict has condemned him. Amazingly, Seth bursts into tears and goes off to complain to Re about the trickery of Isis. Re has no option but to tell Seth that he has not been too bright in condemning himself. Seth now shows a vindictive streak and asks for Nemty the ferryman to be brought to the tribunal. Nemty is found guilty of disobedience and has his toes cut off as punishment. The court now moves to a mountain in the western desert. The tribunal awards the throne of Egypt to Horus but the execution of this decision is thwarted by the successful appeal of Seth to challenge Horus to a contest.

Thus begins a series of episodes aimed at discrediting Seth. The first is almost ridiculous in its concept. Seth challenges Horus that they should both change into hippopotami and submerge themselves under the water for three months. If either of them surfaces before this time then he will lose his claim to the throne. Horus agrees and they both plunge, as hippopotami, into the water. Isis suddenly becomes concerned that Seth intends to kill her son underwater and decides to eliminate him. She makes a copper harpoon and hurls it at the spot where they submerged. Her first throw misses the mark and strikes Horus. She conjures it out of him when he naturally complains. On her second attempt she makes a direct hit on Seth but when he pleads with her that there is a brother-sister blood bond between them she relents and conjures the harpoon out of his body.

The next sequence is quite bizarre. Horus emerges from the water in a rage at Isis for sparing the life of Seth. He cuts off her head and carries it with him into the desert mountains. Isis' body becomes a flint statue and remains headless. Re inquires of Thoth who the strange decapitated statue represents. Thoth tells Re the story of what has happened and Re promptly becomes angry and avows that Horus will be punished and gives orders for the desert to be searched. (At some point, not mentioned in the papyrus, Isis' head is restored.) Seth discovers Horus lying under a tree in an oasis of the western desert. He pounces on him and gouges out his eyes, burying them in the desert where they turn into lotus flowers. Naturally he assumes that this is the end of his adversary and on his return to Re denies ever having found Horus. However, Hathor comes across the distressed Horus and rubs his eyes with gazelle milk. Magically, they are perfectly healed. When Re is informed of events he finally loses his patience and summons Horus and Seth. He orders them to stop quarrelling as they are getting on everyone's nerves.

Seth, the supreme trickster, apparently accepts a reconciliation and invites Horus to a feast at his home. Later that night Seth makes a homosexual approach to Horus who, unbeknown to Seth, deflects the attack and with his hands between his thighs catches the semen of Seth. Horus informs Isis who is horrified when he holds out his hand with the semen in it. Obviously regarding her son's hand as polluted, she cuts it off and throws it into the marshes; her magic manufactures Horus a new hand. She then devises a ploy to make Seth's trickery rebound on himself. With scented unguent Isis arouses Horus' phallus and stores his semen in a jar. She goes into the garden and spreads the semen on the lettuces, Seth's favourite plants. Soon Seth comes and eats the very same lettuces. He then plans to make Horus a laughing-stock before the gods and proclaims in the court that he has homosexually dominated Horus which leads to the other gods expressing their contempt for Horus by spitting in front of him. In return Horus laughs and accuses Seth of telling lies, suggesting that their respective semen be summoned to discover its location. Thoth, with his arm on Horus, summons the semen of Seth to come forth, which it does, only not from Horus but from the marshwater. Holding Seth's arm, Thoth then summons Horus' semen which emerges as a gold sun disk from the head of Seth. By this scurrilous episode Seth is humiliated and Horus vindicated.

Still Seth refuses to admit defeat and suggests a ludicrous contest which cannot but seem a monument to misspent energy: the rivals must make ships of stone to race against each other. Horus craftily builds a ship of pinewood, coated with a limestone plaster to give it the appearance of stone. Seth sees it launched and then cuts off a mountain peak to shape a boat 138 cubits (70 m) long. Before the assembled gods Seth's boat sinks. In anger Seth turns into a hippopotamus and shatters Horus' boat. Horus seizes a weapon but is prevented by the gods from killing Seth. In sheer frustration Horus sails to the cult sanctuary of the goddess Neith at Sais and explains his incomprehension at how, with so many judgements in his favour, he still does not have his rightful inheritance.

Meanwhile, Thoth persuades Re to write a letter to Osiris in the underworld. In it Osiris is given a full royal title which eulogises his powers. Osiris' response to the question of the decision between Horus and Seth is to accentuate his own role in making the gods strong with emmer-wheat and barley and thereby not to defraud his son Horus. In pique Re replies that the gods would have had barley and emmer-wheat whether Osiris existed or not. Threats now come from the underworld: Osiris points out that he has at his command bloodthirsty agents who are in awe of no god or goddess and would willingly search out and bring back to him the heart of any wrongdoer. In addition the stars in the sky, the gods and mankind all descend into the Western Horizon and so into the realm of Osiris. On the sober reflection of these facts the tribunal of gods are now unanimous in vindicating Horus and establishing him upon the throne of his father. Seth suffers a final humiliation when, as Isis' prisoner, he is led before the gods to relinquish his claim to the throne of Egypt. Re, however, still feels a special regard for Seth and announces that Seth will accompany him in the sky and that his voice will be the thunder in the heavens.

The Edfu drama

As stressed in the account given in the papyrus Chester Beatty I, the claim of Horus to the throne is vindicated but Seth is protected by Re, the sun god. If, however, we go to the major temple of Horus at Edfu in Upper Egypt, we are confronted with the same outcome for Horus but the treatment of Seth is totally destructive. At Edfu the tradition of the annihilation of

Seth was portrayed vividly in the form of a drama acted annually at the Festival of Victory. Both hieroglyphs and vignettes were used to encapsulate the essential features of the play. The temple in its present form dates to the Ptolemaic era but was built across more ancient structures on that site. Similarly, although the drama in its surviving form is dated to the reign of Ptolemy IX (*c.*110 BC), its origin is much earlier, probably with a prototype of New Kingdom date.

In the drama Seth is in the form of a hippopotamus and is shown in different scenes pierced by harpoons. The victors are the king and Horus urged on by Isis. Harpooning the hippopotamus is an ancient royal ritual which we find on cylinder seal impressions from the First Dynasty (*c.* 3000–2770 BC). At Edfu, the scenes involve ten harpoons, each piercing a different part of the hippopotamus' anatomy. Certainly a model hippopotamus would have been manufactured for the Festival and have been the 'villain' of the show. In the vignettes the hippopotamus is shown diminutive in stature so that it could be contained and trapped if there was any magical animation from the wall. The viciousness and total destruction brought about by the spearing at the hands of Horus is conveyed both by vignette and hieroglyphs:

Harpoon	Part of Seth injured
First	Snout – nostrils severed
Second	Forehead
Third	Neck
Fourth	Back of head
Fifth	Ribs
Sixth	Vertebrae
Seventh	Testicles
Eighth	Haunches
Ninth	Legs
Tenth	Hocks

The symbol of the triumph of the god Horus is the depiction of him riding the back of the Seth-hippopotamus and spearing its head. Horus wears the Double Crown of Upper and Lower Egypt. Most noticeable is the aggression of Isis in the Edfu drama, since it is such a contrast to the Isis who exhibits compassion for her brother Seth in the papyrus of the struggle for the throne. At the dismemberment of the hippopotamus Isis urges the distribution of the limbs to various deities, with the bones going to cats and the fat to worms. In a final ritual a hippopotamus cake is solemnly sliced up and eaten – the ultimate annihilation of Seth.

The ritual drama of kingship

To complete our survey of pharaonic sources on the myth of kingship we ought to mention two documents that appear to be ritual dramas enacted during state or temple ceremonies. They differ from the Edfu drama in being universal in conception and less concerned with graphic descriptions of the

Relief from the drama depicting the triumph of the god Horus over the god Seth in the form of a hippopotamus. Outer ambulatory of the Temple of Edfu, Ptolemaic period.

humbling of Seth. The first is inscribed on the Shabaka Stone, our source of information about the Memphite creation legend.

On the stone a section deals with the judgement of Horus and Seth in a form involving dialogue between the gods and a scribe's explanatory notes. The earth god Geb is the presiding judge at the tribunal of gods. His first decision attempts to reconcile the claims of the two plaintiffs: Seth will rule over Upper Egypt, to include his birthplace of Su, while Horus will have Lower Egypt, to include a site where, according to another tradition, Osiris drowned in the Nile. 'Geb said to Horus and Seth "I have separated you".' But Geb then decides that Horus (editorial gloss here: 'he is the son of his son, his firstborn') should have a greater portion than Seth. Consequently he awards Horus the inheritance of all Egypt. Horus then is acclaimed as the 'Uniter of his land' at Memphis and equated with the Memphite deity 'Ta-tenen, south of the wall, lord of eternity'. Finally, the concept of Horus, now wearing the crowns of Upper and Lower Egypt, as uniter of the two lands is emphasised.

We now pass onto the Ramesseum Dramatic Papyrus, now in the British Museum, discovered at Thebes in 1895 and dating to the Middle Kingdom. It is an elaborate document consisting of 138 columns of text complemented by a series of over thirty vignettes along the lower edge. The event that had occasioned its compilation was the Jubilee Festival of King Senwosret I (1971–1926 BC), although the surviving papyrus dates from the time of Amenemhat III four reigns later (1844–1797 BC). The forty-six separate scenes of this drama follow a definite pattern: first, a statement of the action; second, the mythological explanation of its meaning; then the conversation between the gods with the pharaoh himself acting the role of Horus; and finally, stage directions. If we isolate the elements relating to the transmission of kingship we begin with the possession of the Sacred Eye (the most powerful amuletic symbol in ancient Egypt) by Horus – the episode of his loss of sight after Seth's attack is glossed over. Then a scene concerns the punishment of cattle for trampling on Osiris in his role as god of grain: oxen are treading barley in order to thresh it and Horus orders them to desist – 'Do not beat this, my father'. The oxen have to continue so that bread can be made but they are beaten as supporters of Seth. The drama also includes mock combat between Horus and Seth with Geb urging the cessation of hostilities.

In reviewing the king's regalia we come across a few significant points not brought out in the myth so far. The monarch has two sceptres which become interpreted as an absorption into the royal person of the strength of his enemy Seth. This refers to the legend of Seth being wounded in his testicles, a counterbalance to the injury to Horus' eyes: Thoth exhorts Horus to assume his enemy's power by taking up the two sceptres which represent Seth's testicles. Also in the drama the king wears a ritual corselet called the *Qeni*. This embodies all the immortal vitality of Osiris, and by strapping the *Qeni* to his chest and back the monarch symbolically enacts a union between the murdered Osiris and his avenging son Horus.

Plutarch's version

The Greek writer Plutarch (AD *c*. 40–*c*. 120) compiled a volume called *Peri Isidos Kai Osiridos*, Concerning Isis and Osiris, probably a few years before his death. He dedicated it to Klea, a priestess at Delphi who seems likely to have been a devotee of Isis. Plutarch's work is a rich amalgam of Egyptian traditions surviving in earlier writers like Manetho, a priestly historian who lived during the reigns of the first two Ptolemies, or Hekataios of Abdera (*fl.* 300 BC), combined with Greek speculations as found in Pythagoras (*fl. c*. 530 BC), Plato (429–347 BC), the Stoics (*fl. c*. 300 BC) and Gnostics (*fl. c*. AD 200). Plutarch covers topics such as the purification rituals of the priests, the cult of the synthetic Graeco-Egyptian deity Sarapis and animal cults. The following account of the myth of kingship, using the Greek names of the gods, is preserved by Plutarch.

The god Kronos (Geb) and the goddess Rhea (Nut) had illicit intercourse. Helios (the sun god) tried to prevent Rhea from giving birth at any time in the year. However, Hermes (Thoth) managed to add five days to the year by beating the moon in a game of draughts. These became the birthdays of five deities – Osiris, Apollo (Horus the Elder), Typhon (Seth), Isis and Nephthys. Later, the kingship of Osiris dragged the Egyptians out of savagery and into civilisation: he taught people how to cultivate the fields and establish laws; he journeyed through the world, turning people towards civilised communities not by force of arms but through eloquence and song. On his return Typhon devised a plot with seventy-two fellow-conspirators to overthrow Osiris. They had an exquisitely decorated chest made, exactly to the measurements of Osiris. At a banquet Typhon offered the chest to whomever fitted inside it and suspicion was allayed by lots of people trying it. Of course when Osiris got inside the lid was slammed down and bolted. The chest was thrown into the Tanitic branch of the Nile and carried out into the Mediterranean sea. Isis wandered around in a state of distress and eventually learned of the fate of the chest. During her peregrinations, incidentally, she adopted the jackal god Anubis as her guardian – apparently unperturbed that he was the offspring of an illicit liaison between her sister Nephthys and Osiris. She pursued the chest to Byblos in the Lebanon where it had been enveloped in a magnificent heath-tree which the king had cut down to form a pillar in his palace. Isis sat by a fountain and befriended the handmaids of the queen of Byblos. She breathed on their skin a fragrance which drew the attention of the queen who sent for Isis and made her the nurse of her young son. At night, in order to give the child immortality, Isis set fire to him and in the shape of a swallow flew around the pillar in which the chest containing Osiris was hidden. Her laments brought the queen to the room, and she had hysterics when she saw her son on fire. This understandable reaction broke the magic of the spell. Isis then demanded the pillar and cut out the chest, donating the outer wood, which was coated with fragrant unguent and wrapped in linen, to her temple at Byblos. She brought the chest back to Egypt but neglected it on one occasion when she went to visit her son Apollo (already born in this version) who was being brought up in Buto. By chance that night Typhon was out hunting and came across the chest. He cut the body of Osiris into fourteen pieces and scattered them throughout the land. Isis went in a papyrus skiff in search of each part and held a burial ceremony wherever she found one. This accounts for the numerous tombs of Osiris claimed at different sanctuaries in Egypt. Isis failed to recover his phallus which Typhon had thrown in the Nile and which had provided a meal for the lepidotus, phragus and oxyrhynchus fish.

Osiris himself had trained Apollo for battle, and when he came up from the underworld, he was satisfied that Apollo was determined to avenge him. The battle between Typhon and Apollo lasted for many days, but Apollo proved the victor at last. Apollo was angered at Isis who led Typhon in bonds but then freed him. He ripped the crown off Isis' head but Hermes replaced it with the cow-horn head-dress – an insignia shared by Isis and Hathor. Typhon tried to get a charge of illegitimacy against Apollo but the gods did not approve, and Typhon was vanquished in two more battles. And thus ends Plutarch's account of the myth of kingship.

Isis 'Great in Magic'

The goddess Isis had a well-earned reputation for exceptional guile, tenacity and cleverness. Several myths reflecting these characteristics survive in magical cults written on papyrus scrolls or in a most elaborate form carved on stelae. The stories of Isis comprise the spells of healing so pertinent to the daily life of ordinary Egyptians, the common ailments, fears and threats which preoccupied them: such as childbirth, fevers, headaches, gastric disorders; crocodiles, snakes, scorpions and malicious worms.

Some spells clearly form an integral element in physicians' manuals and were meant to be recited over a patient. One device aimed at alleviating pain was to identify the sick person with a figure in mythology eventually cured by the intervention of a powerful deity. For example, in a spell designed to relieve the pain of stomach cramps the sick person is called Horus in his form of a young child. The mother represents Isis and concludes that the agony stems from alien worms which have to be driven out. Consequently nineteen magical signs are drawn on the tender regions of the abdomen in order to force the parasites out of the body. Similarly, in a British Museum Medical papyrus (no. 10059), the ingenuity of Isis cures a fever or a burn in the following way. The patient becomes the young Horus scorched in the desert. Isis arrives and asks if water is available; she is given a negative reply. 'Never mind', she asserts, 'water is within my mouth and a Nile flood between my thighs'. This spell is recited over a concoction of human milk, gum and cat hairs, which is then applied to the sufferer. Thus the patient's fever or burns are cooled.

Isis and the seven scorpions

From an elaborate compilation of spells and amuletic vignettes carved on the Metternich Stela (Metropolitan Museum, New York) we can unravel the myth of Isis and the seven scorpions. The purpose of including this story on the stela was to protect the owner against the ever-present danger of a scorpion bite. The scene at the beginning finds Isis weaving the mummy shroud for her husband Osiris, murdered by Seth who wanted his throne. Thoth, god of wisdom, advises Isis to go into hiding with her young son Horus. She must protect Horus against Seth's machinations and raise him to adulthood to avenge Osiris' murder.

The myth of kingship on the stela now gives way to the relating of

ABOVE LEFT *The goddess Isis suckling her child Horus, a symbol of her protective magical powers. Late-Period bronze.*

ABOVE RIGHT *Upper part of the Metternich stela depicting Horus as a child. It is inscribed with magical texts that were recited to cure ailments and to protect against animal bites. One such text recounts Horus' cure of poisonous bites by the god Thoth.*

Isis' magical powers to cure venomous stings. Isis leaves her house in the evening with an escort of seven scorpions. (Incidentally, seven is a number of tremendous potency in Egyptian magic – for example, seven knots are required in procedures to cure headaches or postnatal breast problems.) Three of the scorpions, Petet, Tjetet and Matet, precede Isis and ensure that her path is safe. Under her palanquin are two more scorpions, Mesetet and Mesetetef, while the remaining two, Tefen and Befen, protect the rear. Isis impresses upon the scorpions the need for extreme caution so that they do not alert Seth to their whereabouts. She even instructs them not to get into conversation with anyone they meet on the way. It is hard at this point to suppress amusement at the bizarre image of a loquacious scorpion exchanging pleasantries with a perplexed Egyptian villager. Eventually Isis reaches her destination of the Town of the Two Sisters in the Nile Delta. A wealthy noblewoman sees the strange party arrive and quickly shuts the door of her house. The seven scorpions all find this extremely galling and plot their revenge on the inhospitable woman. In preparation, six scorpions load their individual poisons on the sting of the seventh, Tefen.

The temple of Isis on the island of Philae as seen by the 19th-century artist David Roberts. Now transported to the neighbouring island of Agilkia, this temple was the last to hold out against the advent of Christianity. Ptolemaic and Roman period.

Meanwhile, a humble peasant girl offers Isis the haven of her simple house. This girl is of course the counterpart to the unfriendly wealthy woman, allowing for an unobtrusive touch of social comment in the structure of the story. Next we find that Tefen has crawled under the door of the wealthy woman's house and has stung her son. Distraught, the woman roams around the town seeking help for her child who is on the verge of death. Her inhospitability to Isis is now repaid because no-one answers her calls for assistance. However, Isis, in Egyptian eyes the supreme example of a devoted mother, cannot tolerate the death of an innocent child and undertakes to revive the woman's son. Holding the boy she utters words of great magical power. Naming each of the scorpions, thereby dominating them, Isis causes their combined poison to become ineffectual in the child. By extension the words of her spell will be applicable to any child suffering a scorpion sting, if recited together with the administering of a 'medical prescription' of barley-bread, garlic and salt. Once over her distress and seeing her son healthy, the woman who had refused Isis shelter becomes contrite: she brings out her worldly wealth and makes a present of it to Isis and to the peasant girl who had shown true Egyptian hospitality to a stranger.

Isis and the secret nature of the sun god

The underlying feature of this myth is to emphasise both the potency of Isis' magic and the power that derives from the knowledge of the quintessential personality of a name. It is preserved through its use as a spell to 'ward off poison'. Its source is Papyrus 1993 in the Turin Museum and it dates to Dynasty XIX (*c.* 1200 BC), although a more fragmentary version survives in Papyrus Chester Beatty XI in the British Museum (no. 10691).

The character of Isis is succinctly portrayed at the start of the myth: 'Isis was a clever woman ... more intelligent than countless gods ... she was ignorant of nothing in heaven or on earth'. Her scheme was to discover the secret name of the sun god, the supreme deity, and it would, if successful, rank her and her son Horus next to him at the head of the pantheon.

Her plan was to wound the sun god with his own strength. Every day he journeyed across the firmament from the Eastern to the Western Horizon in his 'Boat of Millions' (i.e. Millions of Years). In this myth the sun god, progressing in years, is unflatteringly depicted as letting his mouth drop open on one occasion (possibly through nodding-off to sleep) and dribbling saliva to the ground. This was the chance that Isis was waiting for. She mixed his saliva with earth and used her magic to fashion out of it a live venomous snake. Knowing the habits of the sun god, Isis left the snake at the crossroads by which he would pass when he came out for a stroll from his palace which he used when visiting Egypt. As planned, the snake bit the sun god who immediately felt a furnace raging inside him. He yelled out to the sky and his Ennead came rushing to discover the problem. The sun god, bitten by his own venom, was trembling all over as the poison took hold of him: 'You gods who originated from me ... something painful has attacked me but I do not know its nature. I did not see it with my eyes. I did not create it with my hand ... There is no agony to match this'. The other gods, despite the hopes of the supreme deity that their magic and wisdom might cure him, can only mourn his lost vigour, the source of all life. The dramatic entrance of Isis oozing sympathy gives the sun god hope and he relates his misfortune to her. He is in a bad way – freezing and burning at the same time, sweating, shivering and sporadically losing his vision.

Isis now proposes her deal – her magic in exchange for his secret name. For him to divulge his exclusive name would mean a loss of prestige and the insecurity of someone else knowing his hidden nature and quintessential identity. So he prevaricates and reels off many of his other names:

> Creator of the heavens and the earth
> Moulder of the Mountains
> Creator of the water for the 'Great Flood' [primeval cow goddess]
> Maker of the bull for the cow in order to bring sexual pleasure into being
> Controller of the Inundation
> Khepri in the morning
> Re at noon
> Atum in the evening.

Isis indicates that his secret name was not included and seems to intensify the raging poison. Finally, the sun god can take the torment no longer and acquiesces. He agrees to tell her his secret name on the understanding that she in turn binds her son Horus with an oath not to divulge it to any other being. It is worth noting that since the pharaoh of Egypt was the manifestation of the god Horus then he too would share in this powerful knowledge. Infuriatingly, the papyrus scroll does not reveal the name that the sun god told Isis but proceeds to give the words of the spell the goddess recited to cure him – a formula which, if accompanied by a draught of 'scorpion's herb' mixed with beer or wine, will heal anyone suffering from a poisonous sting.

The myth of cataclysm

The myth of cataclysm is a major example of the temporary disturbance of the rapport between gods and mankind. The underlying factors were the deep suspicions of the sun god towards men and the over-reaching confidence of the human race – the result was rebellion and a catastrophic death toll.

The relationship between the human race and the gods depended on a myriad of diverse microcosms scattered throughout the Nile Valley. These were the temples, each governed by a hierarchy of priests. The priests' responsibilities, entrusted to them by the pharaoh, included daily rituals of reciting religious formulae and providing victuals in the sanctuary. If this service was performed correctly and no offerings were deficient then the gods and goddesses in each temple would feel satisfied and act benignly towards Egypt.

The detailed liturgy which a High Priest delivered was a response to the order of the universe established by the creator god at the beginning of time. This cosmic structure was personified as Maat, the goddess of truth, right and orderly conduct. Pharaohs are frequently shown holding her effigy, the form of a kneeling woman with an ostrich-feather on her head, to indicate their allegiance to the laws of the creator god. All the stages of making an offering or attending to the divine statue were rigorously documented on temple papyri. On the walls of the temples themselves it is the pharaoh who can be seen symbolically carrying out the requisite rituals in the inner sanctum, in a way visually indicating personal responsibility for the actions of his appointed representatives in the higher echelons of the priesthood.

This system created a mood of optimism in the people, who believed that the deities of the Egyptian pantheon were on the side of the human race. Individuals could of course transgress and be punished by a god or goddess as a result of their misdemeanour. Fine examples of this lapse of respect towards the gods, dating to Dynasty XIX (c. 1307–1196 BC), are found in the stelae from the village of workers on the royal tombs, known today as Deir el-Medina. Originally dedicated in local temples, these stelae reflect penitence for human errors and humbly request the offended deity for release from punishment. The draughtsman Neferabu managed to upset a god and a goddess on separate occasions and left votive stelae to them emphasising his contrition. On one stela, in the Turin Museum, Neferabu has clearly offended Meretseger, 'she who loves silence', a snake goddess residing on the peak overlooking the royal necropolis for which she was responsible.

For his offence, not specified, Meretseger caused Neferabu to be in agony
– his pain is likened to the last stages of pregnancy. Eventually the goddess
relented and brought 'sweet breezes' to cure him. On the other stela, in the
British Museum, Neferabu admits that he took an oath in the name of the
god Ptah Lord of Maat but swore falsely. Consequently, the god caused Neferabu to see 'darkness by day' – he struck him blind. Neferabu professes the
justice of Ptah's action and begs for mercy from the god.

It was also possible for a monarch to govern in a way that upset the
gods. The reign of the pharaoh Akhenaten (1353–1335 BC) saw the supremacy
of the sun disc, called the Aten, the closure of temples and the eclipse of
the traditional pantheon, including Amun-Re. When his son Tutankhamun
succeeded to the throne of Egypt there was a reversal of Akhenaten's policies
and the established temples were back in business. On a stela set up in the
Karnak temple (now in the Cairo Museum) the pharaoh describes the mood
of the traditional gods at the excesses of Akhenaten:

... the temples of the gods and goddesses ... were in ruins. Their shrines were deserted
and overgrown. Their sanctuaries were as non-existent and their courts were used as roads
... the gods turned their backs upon this land ... If anyone made a prayer to a god
for advice he would never respond – and the same applied to a goddess. Their hearts
ached inside them and they inflicted damage left right and centre.

The restorations made by Tutankhamun, particularly for Amun-Re and Ptah,
rectified the distress throughout the land and the gods and goddesses once
again became favourable towards Egypt.

The cataclysm myth survives as an element in a corpus of magical spells
called the *Book of the Divine Cow* aimed at protecting the body of the
sovereign. The earliest copy of sections of this book is found on the interior
of the outermost of the four gilded shrines that fitted over the sarcophagus
of Tutankhamun (r. 1333–1323 BC), originally in his tomb in the Valley of
the Kings and now in the Cairo Museum. There is a longer version of this
text in a side room off the sarcophagus-chamber of the tomb of Sety I in
the royal valley. Other royal tombs from the Nineteenth and Twentieth
Dynasties carry portions of this work so that we can put together a reasonably
full account of the myth. The role of the Divine Cow will become clear as
the sequel to the myth of cataclysm.

The scene is set in the era when Egypt was under the direct rule of
the sun god Re. This period is of course unquantifiable in terms of history
and belongs to a remote mythological past – although it is interesting to
note that an important historical papyrus (the Turin Royal Canon) and
Manetho's survey of dynasties begin with Egypt under the kingship of a series
of gods, before the unification of the country under the first pharaoh around
3000 BC. In an infuriatingly unspecific manner, the *Book of the Divine Cow*
describes the human race as 'plotting evil plans' against Re – possibly there
was the feeling that he had grown too old to govern. Certainly, later in
historical times, pharaohs took elaborate precautions to avoid the impression
that age was against them being effective rulers: the essence of the Jubilee

The lioness goddess Sakhmet, the instrument of vengeance used by the sun god against mankind. Black granite statue from the precinct of the temple of the goddess Mut at Karnak, c. 1350 BC.

Festivals lay in ceremonies designed to rejuvenate the prowess of the monarch, and the presence of the sun god was conjured up in the imagery of a temple cult-statue whose bones were of silver, flesh of gold and hair of lapis lazuli. Learning of mankind's plot against him Re summons a secret council of the gods in his Great Palace, and is apparently unwilling to warn the human race.

Re first addresses Nu, the primeval material out of which he arose at the time of creation. In his statement he mentions how mankind emerged from the tears of his eyes – a pun on the similar sound between 'men' and 'tear' in the Egyptian language (i.e. a phoneme) – and now they are conspiring against him. He wants to know Nu's opinion before he kills the entire human race. Nu's reply is that the Eye of Re, the solar eye, will be the instrument to terrorise and slay mankind. Re now becomes aware that men know he is angry over their plot and discovers that they have fled into the deserts of Egypt. The gods in unison urge Re to take vengeance on the conspirators.

The symbol of the Eye of Re is complex but an underlying feature of it is that it can form an entity independent of the sun god himself – even to the extent of going off on journeys to remote regions and having to be enticed back. Here the Eye of Re becomes his daughter, the goddess Hathor. Most often we find Hathor in the role of a divine mother-figure to the pharaoh, suckling him with her milk, as a guardian of the Theban necropolis or as the goddess of love and joy whom the Greeks equated with Aphrodite. In the myth of cataclysm, however, Hathor becomes a deity of invincible destructive powers, pursuing men in the desert and slaughtering them. When she returns to Re she exults in the lust for blood, glorying in the massacre. To complicate the nature of the Eye of Re the myth now explains how Hathor became transformed into the goddess Sakhmet – a ferocious leonine deity whose name means the 'Powerful One'. Thus the myth provides us with the vivid imagery of a raging lioness wading in blood who savaged mankind in an ecstasy of slaughter.

The Eye of Re now rests, recuperating her strength for further killing the next day. But the sun god himself has changed his mood from vengeance to sympathy for mankind. We are given no clues as to the reason for this transformation. Possibly it is the realisation that the temples of Egypt would be without their priestly occupants and consequently their altars would be empty of offerings for the gods. The cosmic pattern that the creator god had established would thus become deficient. Possibly the *volte-face* had to do with the reluctance of Re to consign beings created out of matter from himself (i.e. his tears) to oblivion. This last possibility would be in keeping with the Egyptian belief that no element of the body ought to be alientated into another's possession or destroyed – hence the four funerary jars to contain the organs eviscerated as part of the process of mummification.

Whatever the reason, Re organises the rescue of mankind from the fierce and merciless goddess whose blood-lust is totally beyond control. The gods only have the night to save the human race before the goddess wakes up. Re therefore sends his personal messengers to run at top speed – the Egyptian says 'to run like the body's shadow' – to Aswan and bring back a large quantity of red ochre. He then tells no less a personage than the 'One of the sidelock of Heliopolis', an epithet for the High Priest of the sun god, to squeeze the red ochre into a substance that slave girls can mix with barley beer. Soon seven thousand jars of this popular drink have been filled with beer that looks like human blood. Towards the end of the night Re and his entourage carry the jars to the place where the goddess will come to continue her slaughter and there they flood the region with the blood-beer to a height of 'three palms', about 22.5 cm. In the morning the goddess sees the 'blood' and, rejoicing in the unexpected bonus, drinks deeply and becomes intoxicated. As a result she fails to find the remainder of mankind left over from the previous massacre.

The rest of this compilation, following the punishment and near extermination of the human race, is concerned primarily with the rebirth and ascension of the sun god, and therefore of the monarch, into heaven on the back of the 'Divine Cow'. Both the shrine of Tutankhamun and the tomb of Sety I have depictions of the Cow 'Mehet wer' or 'Great Flood' who forms the celestial firmament, identifying with the sky goddess Nut. Thus Re, now a cynical sun god and weary of mankind, eventually leaves Egypt. But it is not a total abdication of responsibility because Re appoints Thoth, god of wisdom, as his regent or deputy to keep control of the human race. From Thoth, on the orders of Re, people are given knowledge of the 'sacred words' (i.e. hieroglyphs) in which all scientific wisdom, medicine and mathematics are embodied.

The underworld journey
of the sun god

From 1492 to 1070 BC almost all pharaohs were buried in the royal necropolis on the West Bank of Thebes, fittingly described today as the Valley of the Kings. The rock-cut sepulchres originally contained valuable funerary equipment and the sarcophagi held royal mummies decorated with exquisite jewellery. Despite the venomous sting of Meretseger, the snake goddess dwelling on the peak dominating the valley, and the (erratic) vigilance of the necropolis guards, tomb robbers were able to plunder the treasures of the pharaohs – including a few items from the burial of Tutankhamun which, after being resealed, miraculously escaped being looted until Howard Carter's excavation in 1922. Thankfully there existed no ancient illegal art market demanding fragments of the complicated and confusing designs painted on the walls of the royal tombs. However, these paintings were left to suffer the ravages of the salt inherent in the Theban limestone, occasional torrents of rain and the scrawls in some instances of Greek and Coptic tourists nearly two thousand years ago. It is on these walls that there survives a rich panorama, in spite of the natural damage or multilations, of the Egyptian underworld.

The fertile imagination of the ancient Egyptian religious speculators evolved numerous images and symbols, the sum total of which would emphasise the security of the sun god on his underworld journey and his transformation from the god who descended into the dark regions of the netherworld each night into a regenerated deity emerging each dawn, full of energy and life. Manu was the western mountain where Re began his journey after setting; Duat was the underworld through which he travelled; Bakhu was the eastern mountain above which he rose in the morning.

Three major compositions survive which depict the dangers successfully negotiated by Re in the underworld and dispel doubts about his safe emergence into the sky. These complex compilations evolved over centuries and acquired additions which often obscure rather than elucidate enigmatic scenes or texts. Sometimes the ancient scribal draughtsmen were unable to make sense of their working documents which accumulated over generations, with the consequence that some inscriptions read as exotic gibberish. On other occasions sheets of the papyri scrolls may have suffered extensive wear and tear and become too illegible to copy onto the wall. In these cases the draughtsmen

LEFT *Underworld scene showing the sky goddess Nut and birth symbolism. Tomb of Ramesses VI, Valley of the Kings, c. 1150 BC.*

BELOW *'Flesh of Re'. Ram-headed form of the sun god, protected by a gigantic snake, journeying in his boat through the underworld. Valley of the Kings, c. 1300 BC.*

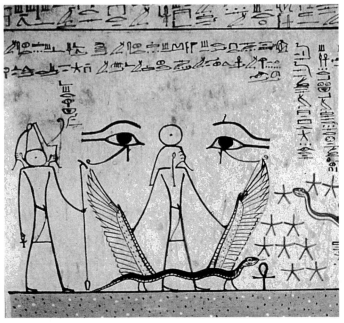

'Sacred Eyes' and a winged snake with legs beside a two-headed figure wearing the red and white crowns of united Egypt. An image from the Book of Am-Duat in the tomb of Tuthmosis III (1479–1425 BC), Valley of the Kings.

wrote into the composition the hieroglyphs *Gem Wesh* meaning 'original source found defective'. The earliest of these compilations is the *Book of Am-Duat*, the 'Book of What is in the Underworld'. Visitors to the tombs of Tuthmosis III (1425 BC) and Amenhotep II (1401 BC) can see complete versions of this book in the schematic designs on the walls of the burial chambers. The tombs of Sety I (1290 BC) and Ramesses VI (1143 BC) have eleven out of twelve scenarios, these scenarios symbolising the twelve hours of the night. The second composition, the *Book of Gates*, can be found in part in its earliest appearance in the tomb of Horemheb (1307 BC) but the fullest versions are in the tomb of Ramesses VI and on the immaculately carved sarcophagus of Sety I which, having been turned down by the then niggardly Trustees of the British Museum, was purchased by Sir John Soane and can be inspected in his museum in Lincoln's Inn Fields in London. In the tomb of Ramesses VI there is a complete copy of the latest and rarest of these three compositions known as the *Book of Caverns*.

The Book of Am-Duat

The sun god makes his underworld journey through Twelve Scenarios, to become reborn as Khepri the scarab-beetle. At the outset of his journey the sun god is at the Western Horizon approaching the River of Wernes along which he will travel. In a prologue the essence of this composition emphasising its magical power is formulated: 'Knowledge of the power of those in the underworld. Knowledge of their actions – knowing the sacred rituals for Re, knowing the hidden dynamism, knowing the hours and gods, knowing the gates and paths where the great god passes, knowing the powerful and the destroyed'.

Re starts his journey through the First Scenario (or Hour) of Duat and is depicted as a ram-headed god in a shrine and is called 'Flesh'. This description highlights the netherworld form of Re which will eventually transmute into Khepri. He travels in his solar boat and his crew consists of two gods at the prow named 'Path-opener' and 'Mind', as well as a goddess called the 'Lady of the Boat' who wears cow horns and a sun-disc, hawk-headed 'Horus the Adorer' and, by the steering oars, four deities named 'Bull of Truth', 'Vigilant', 'Will' and 'Guide of the Boat'. On either side of Re are groups of deities shown in individual squares – for example, there are two sets of nine baboons who open the doors for Re and sing to him as he enters the underworld, and twelve serpent goddesses who light up the darkness.

Re sails into the Second Hour of Night where he establishes landrights for the grain gods of the region of Wernes. The Third Hour is when Re revives Osiris by giving him 'Will' and 'Mind' – energy to decide and act. In the Fourth Scenario a distinctive motif appears in the form of a slanted passageway with two open doors. There are guardian snakes, some from the realm of mythical beings possessing a human head and four short legs, or three snake heads and two wings. That these snakes will not harm Re or his entourage is confirmed by magical epithets indicating their self-sufficiency in food: 'living on the breath of his mouth' or 'living on the voice of the gods guarding the road'. The passage is the way to the underworld from the traditional entrance of 'Ro-setau, or 'Gate of the passageways'. Through this route is access to the body of Sokar, a necropolis-god of Memphis, and to the tomb of Osiris.

In the Fifth Hour Re has reached a crucial stage on his journey and one which is full of imagery of resurrection. The solar boat is towed towards a mound out of which a head emerges called 'Flesh of Isis who is above the sand of the land of Sokar'. Below is the interior of this mound across which Re is being towed. Its gate is guarded by four heads spurting flames. A pellet of sand rests on the back of the two-headed leonine earth god Aker. Emerging out of this is Sokar, hawk-headed, standing on the back of a serpent with a human head at one end and three snake heads at the other. Sokar here is the manifestation of the underworld body of Re in a primeval form, animated by the passing of the sun god above. The tow-rope is actually held over the mound of Sokar by a scarab beetle emerging from a desert mound in the upper register of the painting. Isis and Nephthys in the shape of kites flank this mound which represents the desert tomb of Osiris. Again the sun god is overcoming death by emerging from the mound called 'Night' as Khepri the scarab-beetle – a visual representation of the belief of the Egyptian theologians that life and death are a continual cycle without one suppressing the other. In this image of the mound the sun god is contained in Osiris but not restricted in 'permanent' death.

During the Sixth Hour Re in his boat comes to a halt before a seated representation of the god Thoth as a baboon holding a sacred ibis. Thoth's purpose is to found a city for the gods in the fields and for the kings of Upper and Lower Egypt. Here also is depicted the body of Khepri encoiled within a five-headed serpent – the sun god visits his manifestation as an underworld corpse. This possibly appears bizarre to our rationality so here are a few sentences from a synthesis made by a Dutch scholar called Kristensen which might clarify the thought processes of the Egyptians on life and death:

... all that lives and all that grows is the result of an inexplicable and completely mysterious cooperation of heterogeneous factors ... Life and Death appear to be irreconcilable opposites: yet together they form everlasting life. Neither predominates; they alternate or, most aptly, they produce one another. Universal life is the totality of death and life; in it hostile forces are reconciled and have abandoned their individual independence ... the sun, when it goes down, does not die but reaches the hidden fountain of its life. Becoming or arriving is the nature of Khepri ... But every arising occurs in and from death, which thus appears to be potential life. Darkness is the cradle of light; in it the sun finds the power to arise ... Absolute life has its home in the realm of death.
(Quoted by N. Rambova in A. Piankoff, 'Mythological Papyrus: texts', in *Bollingen Series* XL.3 [Pantheon Books 1957] pp. 29–30)

Some violent scenes follow in the Seventh Hour as Re sails through. Protected by the coils of a snake is a god called 'Flesh of Osiris', in front of whom

The cat of the sun god symbolically decapitates Apophis, the underworld snake of chaos. Tomb of Nakht-Amun (c. 1290 BC), Deir el-Medina, Western Thebes.

a knife-brandishing deity with feline ears has decapitated enemies, while another – the 'Punisher' – holds rebels caught in a rope. The opponents of Osiris have been captured and annihilated. Before Re in the solar boat is the scene of his arch-enemy Apophis being overthrown. Apophis is a gigantic snake symbolising the force of non-existence and a perpetual threat to the sun god whom he attempts to swallow. Despite the indestructibility of Apophis, the representations on the royal tomb walls attempt to vanquish him by magic so that he appears in a state of being destroyed or subdued whenever the sun god is in his vicinity. There the snake lies extended for about 240 m. The scorpion-goddess Serket and the god called 'Director of the Knives' hold the head and tail of Apophis whose head and body are pierced with knife blades.

In the Eighth Hour Re is towed, with nine symbols of his power before him in the form of human-headed staves to which is attached a package from which emerges a knife. These emblems destroy his enemies. Around are gated compartments where various deities are shown accompanied by the sign for linen clothing. Some of these figures are mummiform; some are seated with human heads; others with the head of a bull, goat, rat, ichneumon, crocodile or hippopotamus; and others take the form of cobras. They respond to the call of Re as he passes by their 'caverns' with a variety of cries likened, for example, to tom-cats, a river bank falling into the Nile flood, or a nest of birds. In the Ninth Hour Re meets twelve fire-spitting cobras who guard Osiris and who 'live on the blood of those whom they slaughter'. He also sails past gods holding palm-branch sceptres who are responsible for carving trees or plants.

In the Tenth Hour symbols appear of the imminent resurrection of Re at dawn. The scarab beetle holds the egg from which he will emerge in the

Eastern Horizon and two sun disks are shown ready to be propelled into the sky. In front of the solar boat an armed escort of twelve gods checks the security of the approach to the Eastern Horizon. Re addresses them: 'Be swift with your arrows, target your spears and draw your bows. Punish my enemies lurking in the darkness near the gate'. The Eleventh Hour graphically depicts the destruction of these underworld enemies who are thrown into the fire pits, each with a goddess spitting fire into it. These enemies are shown as bound captives, as destroyed souls, as shadows and as lopped-off heads. In a sixth, larger pit four rebels are shown upside-down. Horus makes a speech over this wholesale massacre: '... you are fallen into fiery pits and cannot escape ... the knife of she who directs the knife blades slashes into you, she cuts you to bits and butchers you. You will never see the ones who live on earth'.

Now the sun god has reached the Twelfth Hour and the climax of his journey through the underworld. The solar boat is towed into the tail of a gigantic serpent in whose body Re sheds his underworld manifestation and is born out of the snake's mouth as Khepri the scarab beetle. In this shape Re rests above the head of the air god Shu whose arms seal the underworld. Re then sails up from the East in the day boat to 'shine between the thighs of Nut'.

Tabulation of the sun god's progress in the Am-Duat

Scenario	Name of underworld city/region	Name of the Hour goddess
1	Great City	Splitter of the heads of Re's enemies
2	Field of Wernes	The Wise, Guardian of her lord
3	Field of the Grain gods and Water of Osiris	Slicer of Souls
4	Cavern of the Life of Forms	Great of Power
5	Cavern of Sokar	She on her boat
6	Deep Water	Proficient leader
7	Cavern of Osiris, City of the Mysterious Cave	Repeller of the Snake
8	City of the God's Sarcophagi	Mistress of the Night
9	City of the Living Manifestations	Adorer
10	City of Deep Water and Steep Banks	Beheader of Rebels
11	City of Corpse-Counting	The Star, repulser of rebels
12	Cavern at the end of darkness, City of the Appearance of Birth	Beholder of the beauty of Re

The Book of Caverns

This latest compilation glorifies the sun god as bringer of life and brightness into the dark realm of the underworld, envisaged as a sequence of caverns. The paintings depict Re progressing through Duat, illuminating the caverns of the gods; they also show the penalty for enemies and rebels in gruesome detail. This interplay of good fortune against just punishments makes the *Books of Caverns* a psychological tableau. It stands apart from the other underworld compositions in its intensity of concentration on reward and punishment. Overall, the effect is one of remembering the vivid execution of the enemies when perhaps the benefits of the journey of Re should be paramount.

The beginning shows Re on foot descending into the underworld. He is confronted with a series of ovals containing figures of gods and goddesses. Each oval is a sarcophagus enveloping a body which the power of Re can

Underworld scene of Ramesses VI before the ram-headed sun god, amid gods in shrines and defeated enemies hanging upside down. Valley of the Kings, c. 1150 BC.

vivify on his journey. In the First Cavern Re demonstrates his knowledge of secret names to ward off danger and attack by identifying the guardian deities. For example, here are some of the terms he uses to address three huge serpents:

'Stinger in your cavern, frightener – submit and give way! I enter the West to provide for Osiris and place his opponents in the executioner's.

Fearful Visage in your cavern to whom those in the underworld hand over the souls of the place of destruction . . .

Encircler of Rosetau for the ruler of Duat . . .'

The naming of the snake and assertion of his own power enables Re to progress through the cavern, greeting the deities in their sarcophagi. Immediately we follow his path our eyes fall to the lower register of the painting where bound prisoners and decapitated enemies march along.

The punishment continues in the Second Cavern where some upside-down enemies have had their hearts torn out and placed at their feet. Here the sun god meets some gods in their coffins whose heads are those of shrew mice and catfish. These are primeval symbols associated with Horus of Leto-polis and Osiris. Progressing into the Third Cavern Re treads a path across Aker, the two-headed leonine earth god. Below is Osiris depicted as ithyphallic to indicate his revival through the light of Re. A eulogy on his beauty and benefactions greets the sun god in the Fourth Cavern.

In the Fifth Cavern Re witnesses the total annihilation of his opponents. A number of cauldrons are filled with upside-down beheaded corpses, heads, hearts, souls and shadows. Re addresses two goddesses beside one of the cauldrons to ensure that potential as well as past enemies will be similarly executed: 'Goddesses of the powerful flame stirring cauldrons with bones burning the souls, corpses, flesh and shadow of my opponents – Look I pass close to you, I destroy my enemies. You will stay in your caves, your fire will heat my cauldrons, your souls will not abandon here nor join my entour-age'. The Fifth Cavern is, however, visually dominated by two large, standing figures stretching across the height of three registers of paintings. So the sun god will meet 'The Secret One', a representation of Nut, the sky goddess, surrounded by solar disks and images of resurrection. He will also encounter the ithyphallic Osiris.

But now Re has arrived at the Sixth Cavern where his foes are being decapitated. It is time for him to leave the slaughtering behind and the image of the scarab beetle pushing the sun disk prevails in the upper registers of the final scene. Towed towards the Eastern Horizon the boat holds Re repre-sented as the scarab beetle and ram-headed god. The transformation occurs so that the scarab beetle form of the sun god then moves towards the east – but its head has amalgamated with the underworld image of Re so that we see a hybrid solar creature consisting of the body of a scarab beetle and the head of a ram. It is a time of rebirth and therefore the symbol of the sun as a child sucking its finger can be seen resting its foot on the solar disk about to emerge from the Eastern Mountain.

The Book of Gates

This composition is one of the most dramatically presented in royal tombs, notably for its recurring motif of a gigantic serpent spitting fire as it guards a gateway through Duat. A prologue locates the start of the sun god's journey in the Western Desert mountains from where Re passes through a gate protected by a snake into the underworld. Re is represented as anthropomorphic up to his shoulders, which are surmounted by a ram's head and sun disk. He holds the sceptre of dominion. His title is given as the 'Flesh of Re' which is his underworld corporeal manifestation. He stands in his solar boat in a shrine which is surrounded by a serpent with a vast number of coils called 'Mehen' or the 'Encircler'. Also in the boat are two personified qualities of the sun god depicted as standing human male figures – at the prow is Sia or 'Mind'/'Perception' while by the steering oars stands Heka or 'Magic'. The papyriform boat is towed by four dwellers of the underworld. This is the theme of continuity that runs through the whole *Book of Gates* inasmuch as it shows in the central register the sun god's safe journey along the River of Duat. The registers above and below give us glimpses of action on the two banks of the river. In this First Scenario 'Flesh of Re' is towed past his form of Atum, creator god of Heliopolis, who is supervising the destruction of enemies lying prone on the ground or marching in a line of bound captives. Their sins are specified as blasphemy against Re, perjury and murder. Atum speaks to these criminals:

'... I am the son born of his father, I am the father born from his son [i.e. Atum and Re are together in a continual cycle of renewal]. You are bound with strong ropes ... Your bodies will be hacked up, your soul will become non-existent. You will not see Re in his manifestations as he journeys in the secret region'.

The gateways themselves, such as the one Re now passes to enter the Second Scenario, are highly stylised but clearly indicate that they are sturdy double bastions and crenellated with ornaments known as the 'Khekheru' which make their appearance historically in the Step Pyramid complex of King Djoser at Sakkara (*c.* 2600 BC). Nine mummiform gods line the outer walls of the gateway with a special guardian at the entrance and exit of the passageway between the bastions. A fire-spitting cobra rears up above each tower of the gate while a serpent balanced on its tail reaches from the ground to the height of the wall, guarding the actual door. Each of these protective divinities is named so that the sun god merely has to pronounce their identity from his secret knowledge in order to pass safely into the region beyond the gate. In the Second Scenario 'Flesh of Re' greets twelve gods of barley emerging from a lake of fire which acts as a deterrent against birds but by magic does not harm the grain. The boat of the sun god is imagined as passing through a pole with bull-head terminals, representing the Boat of Earth, indicating the power of Re to counter all obstacles by his power to transform himself. On the bank Atum leans on his staff before a hopelessly entangled Apophis, the underworld snake enemy of Re who has here been overthrown.

The sun god is towed past the Third Gate into a region where he sees jackal and cobra gods guarding lakes. The jackal gods protect the Lake of Life from the inhabitants of the underworld because it is sacred and exclusive to the sun god. The Lake of the Cobras guards the flame with which the enemies of Re are annihilated. Also in this region 'Flesh of Re' passes an immensely intricately coiled snake called Hereret. The snake lies in a depression on either side of which are goddesses described as the 'Hours of the Underworld'. Their task is to swallow whatever Hereret might exude or give birth to so that it is rendered harmless.

In the Fourth Scenario a series of twelve gods can be seen on the bank carrying a long rope with extensive lengths of it yet unrolled. Their task is to measure the crops and divide allotted fields among the inhabitants of the underworld. There is general acclaim in the inscriptions that this has been done satisfactorily. On the other bank the god Horus leaning on his staff is preceded by sixteen male figures whom the inscriptions divide into the four traditional races of mankind as perceived through Egyptian eyes: Four Men – these are the 'cattle of Re' in Duat in Egypt and in the deserts, that is, the exclusive element of the human race who can be called Egyptian; Four Middle Easterners – these are the inhabitants of Palestine and Syria whom the lioness goddess Sakhmet is said to have created; Four Nubians – these represent the settled inhabitants and nomadic tribes of regions south of Egypt's natural frontier of the First Cataract of the Nile at Aswan; and Four Libyans – the goddess Sakhmet also created the tribes of the Western Desert and Mediterranean seaboard along the Libyan coast.

The 'Flesh of Re' is now towed past the Fifth Gate and immediately enters the Hall of Osiris. The god Osiris, ruler of Duat, is enthroned on a dais and holds the crook sceptre and ankh, sign of life. Before him on the shoulders of a mummiform deity is a pair of scales for weighing the hearts of those seeking to dwell in Duat in order to judge if their earthly lives have been blameless enough for this privilege. In a papyriform boat a pig is being beaten by an ape, symbolising the humiliation of Seth, the enemy of Osiris. Beyond this hall of the Fifth Scenario the sun god watches the repelling of Apophis who is carried by twelve gods. Human heads emerge from the body of Apophis representing his previous victims and whom Re vivifies. Apophis is described as 'eyeless, noseless, earless, breathing by his roars, living upon his own shouting' in order to symbolise his incapacity for destruction. Further on, twelve gods pull a twisted rope from the mouth of a deity called Aken, each twist representing an hour of the underworld.

'Flesh of Re' is now in the Sixth Scenario, being towed toward poles surmounted by jackal heads to which enemies have been tied ready for beheading. On one bank are gods tending ears of grain and reapers with sickles to provide suitable food and beer offerings for the sun god and Osiris. Beyond the Seventh Gate are gods carrying a rope, from the coils of which emerge emblems like whips, hawk and human heads and stars. These create mysteries in honour of Re but the inscriptions leave us ignorant of the details.

In contrast to the rather staid Seventh Scenario the region beyond the Eighth Gate provides 'Flesh of Re' with the most activity. On the bank he sees the twelve gods who form a council to provide nine souls, shown with bird bodies but human heads and arms, with food on their Island of Flame. He approaches his form of Atum, who leans on his staff contemplating a pool in which men are represented in prone positions. These are water gods connected with the Primeval Flood. Re gives them powers of mobility, breathing and swimming, so that they do not remain static in the element over which they are supposed to exercise benign influence. On the other bank Horus is herding the enemies of Osiris towards a fire-belching snake with mummiform gods emanating from its coils. These enemies have polluted the ceremonies of the god's temple so Horus exhorts the serpent to 'open its jaws, belch out the flame ... burn their corpses, destroy their souls with the conflagration'.

In the Ninth Scenario 'Flesh of Re' follows deities with nets swinging and spearers ready to annihilate Apophis who is lying in wait in the sun god's path. On the bank the sun god sees the crowns of Upper and Lower Egypt and, on the back of a leonine heraldic creature, a god called 'His two faces' consisting of the heads of Horus and Seth placed together on his neck, symbolising the peaceful union of North and South Egypt and hinting at any absence of conflict between the two traditional enemies.

Beyond the Tenth Gate 'Flesh of Re' joins a procession in which another boat travels bearing a front-facing male head. This is the 'Face of the Disk', an element of the sun god himself on its journey to rebirth. On the bank is a dramatic chaining of the snake Apophis. His head is bound by the scorpion goddess Serket who stretches herself full length along the chain. Sixteen gods stand on the snake's back holding the chain and are supported in this task by a massive fist emerging from the ground – no chances are to be taken with this ferocious creature. At the tail end of Apophis stands Osiris, before whom the snaked body rises to show four chained serpent-offspring. Extra protection is provided by five figures on this end coil who represent the earth god Geb and the Sons of Horus.

In the Eleventh Scenario – in addition to the symbolic overthrow and binding of Apophis – four baboons announce the approach of Re in the Eastern Horizon. The final Twelfth Scenario encapsulates the everlasting cycle of the birth of the sun god. From his primeval water the god Nu raises a boat in which travels the sun god as Khepri the scarab beetle and as a disk. Above Nu the sky goddess leans down, her feet resting on the head of Osiris representing Duat. To emphasise the successful completion of his journey a sun disk pushes through the desert sand at the point where Re will rise at dawn.

The three intricate religious compositions just reviewed are often initially puzzling to modern eyes. They can be seen as a medley of garbled inscriptions and an endless roll-call of names. But of course the unhindered journey of the sun god through Duat was a cornerstone of Egyptian belief. Beyond the executions of enemies, the destruction of Apophis, the mummiform deities and the gods in their sarcophagi lies the realm of life. Duat is not a region of despair, and the ancient Egyptian would *not* echo the poem's lines:

> This is the dead land
> This is cactus land
> Here the stone images
> Are raised, here they receive
> The supplication of a dead man's hand
> Under the twinkle of a fading star.
> (from T. S. Eliot, *The Hollow Man*)

These dark sentiments would be rejected because in Duat there is the amalgam of two great gods – Re becomes Osiris and Osiris becomes Re. The underworld god is the past form of the sun god out of whom the sun is born again. In Spell 17 in the *Book of the Dead* we find the following statement and an explanatory gloss:

> 'I am Yesterday, I am Tomorrow
> What does this mean?
> Osiris is Yesterday and Re is Tomorrow'.

The passage of the 'Flesh of Re' through Duat is a process of energising the sun god into Khepri for a new birth. Life and death are a continuum, each eternally engendering the other.

Tabulation of the sun god's journey in the *Book of Gates*

Scenario	Guardian serpent	Name of gate
1	Guardian of the Desert	He of the hidden name (Osiris)
2	Enveloper	Intense of Flame
3	Stinger	Lady of Nourishment
4	Flame-face	One of Action
5	Eye of Flame	Lady of Continuity
6	Darting of Eye	Throne of her Lord
7	Hidden of Eye	Gleaming One
8	Flame-face	Red-hot
9	Earth-tusk	Exalted in Veneration
10	Binder	Sacred
11	Effluent One	Hidden of Access
12	He of the Dawn & Enveloper	Sacred of Power

From history into legend

The characters in this chapter were each, posthumously, translated from history into legend by becoming the subject of either a cult or a tale. Each can be proved archaeologically to have existed in reality.

Imhotep

Imhotep was the architect of the step pyramid complex of King Djoser (2630–2611 BC) at Sakkara, which in grandeur of concept is unrivalled and which was the first colossal stone edifice to be built. The pyramid suggests a gigantic stairway for the monarch's ascent to the sky, while the surrounding buildings originally provided the temple for the royal cult and pavilions and shrines for the eternal celebration of Djoser's jubilee festivals. A limestone bust from a lost statue of King Djoser (called Netjeri-khet on his monuments) preserves the name and titles of Imhotep:

Seal-bearer of the King of Lower Egypt, one who is near the head of the King [i.e. vizier], Director of the Great Mansion, Royal representative, High Priest of Heliopolis, Imhotep, the carpenter and the sculptor. . . .

From stone vessels discovered in the galleries about 30 m below the pyramid we can add the title 'Chief Lector priest'. Thus, the highest religious and secular offices in the Egyptian administration belonged to Imhotep.

In addition to the pyramid complex Imhotep was the architect of a sanctuary to the sun god at Heliopolis, dedicated by Djoser and surviving today only in fragments of high quality reliefs. His name has also been found in a graffito on the enclosure wall of the unfinished pyramid of King Sekhemkhet (2611–2603 BC), successor to Djoser. This is the latest historical attestation we have for Imhotep so we can assume that he died about 4600 years ago.

His reputation as an experienced architect led to his adoption by the scribes of Egypt as the most eminent practitioner of their craft. He became regarded as a source of intellectual inspiration and a number of moral maxims were alleged to have been committed to papyrus in his name. One reference is in a partly pessimistic, partly hedonistic composition known as the *Harper's song*, the finest copy of which is in Papyrus Harris 500 in the British Museum:

I have heard the words of Imhotep and Hor-dedef [a son of King Khufu] whose maxims are frequently quoted – and what is the state of their monuments now? Their walls are smashed and their places have disappeared – just as if they had never existed.

ABOVE *The step pyramid at Sakkara, constructed by the 'historical' Imhotep for the pharaoh Djoser, c. 2600 BC.*

LEFT *Seated statuette of Imhotep as the embodiment of scribal wisdom. Late-Period bronze.*

If the song was originally written in the reign of a king called Intef, as the introduction boasts, then Imhotep's funerary monument had already become dilapidated or lost by 2000 BC. However, his name lived on in his writings as another document, also in the British Museum, can testify. Its purpose is to extol the professional scribe and it does so by choosing judicious references to illustrate the immortality of literature:

A book is of more value than the house of a master-builder or a tomb in the western desert. . . . Is there anyone around today like Hor-dedef? Is there anyone else like Imhotep? . . . Those wise men who foretold the future. . . . They might be gone and their names fade from memory – except that their writings keep them remembered.

At some point, through a shift in the Egyptian psychological view of the status of Imhotep, his role as a sage became enhanced by attributing his birth to the direct intervention of one of the major gods. Imhotep became 'son of Ptah' creator god of Memphis, whose nature as a god of craftsman particularly suited the fathering of an offspring renowned for sculptural skill. From the Saite period (Dynasty XXVI) there is ample evidence of a vigorous cult centred around Imhotep son of Ptah at Memphis and Sakkara. Hundreds of bronzes depict him in an iconography which subtly emphasise his wisdom and divine parent. He is represented seated with a papyrus scroll across his knees, wearing a skullcap and a long linen kilt. We can interpret the papyrus as suggesting the sources of knowledge kept by scribes in the 'House of Life'. The headgear identifies Imhotep with Ptah, and his priestly linen garment symbolises his religious purity.

His main temple was in North Sakkara with a subsidiary sanctuary in Memphis, south-west of the main Ptah temple. However, by the Ptolemaic period his cult had spread south to Thebes where provision was made for his worship in the Temple of Ptah at Karnak. In the reign of the Roman Emperor Tiberius an elaborate eulogy to Imhotep was carved on the fourth gate before his temple. He shared honours at Thebes with Amenhotep son of Hapu, a deified 'Director of all royal works' who had lived in the reign of the pharaoh Amenhotep III (1403–1365 BC). At the temple of Deir el-Medina in Western Thebes, Imhotep is depicted with his mythical mother Khereduankh, in the guise of the goddess Hathor. To complete the sacred triad of which the Egyptians were so fond, he is given a wife who is called 'God's sister', Renpet-nefret.

As his cult spread, more and more emphasis was placed on his role as a supreme physician readily identifiable with the Greek Asklepios. This aspect was particularly prominent in his Ptolemaic sanctuary in Western Thebes, on the upper terrace of Queen Hatshepsut's temple at Deir el-Bahri, as well as in the Temple of Hathor at Dendera, where an important eulogy to Imhotep connects him by inference to the sanatorium there. Elsewhere we find attempts to enhance his deification such as at one town in the Delta where, in a development reminiscent of the elevation of the statues of the Virgin Mary under early theologians, Khereduankh the mother of Imhotep becomes regarded as the offspring of a god, in this case Banebdjedet, the sacred ram-deity of Mendes.

The cult of Imhotep became a focal point for married couples desiring a son. A good example of his procreative powers is carved on perhaps the most poignant stela in the British Museum's collection. It is the autobiography of a woman called Taimhotep who was born in 73 BC during the reign of Ptolemy XII Neos Dionysos. When she was fourteen, she married Psherenptah, High Priest of Ptah of Memphis. Three pregnancies produced daughters. Together, Taimhotep and Psherenptah prayed to Imohtep son of Ptah for a son. Imhotep appeared to Psherenptah in a dream or revelation with a proposal: a major embellishment to his sanctuary in Ankh-tawi (the Memphite necropolis where Imhotep was buried) in exchange for a male child. Psherenptah consequently commissioned a gold statue and dedicated it to Imhotep's sanctuary, whereupon Taimhotep conceived a son. On the Feast of Imhotep in 46 BC Taimhotep gave birth to Pedibast. The rewards of motherhood were short-lived, however, because Taimhotep died in 42 BC when she was thirty. The rest of the stela comprises a moving lament on the inevitability of death. Despite this, Imhotep's positive intervention had changed the couple's life. It was this immediacy of Imhotep son of Ptah as resolver of human problems, often medical, that ensured the popularity of his cult into the Roman period.

Commander Djeheuty

The military campaigns of the pharaoh Tuthmosis III (1490–1439 BC) established Egyptian authority either by occupation-forces or by favourable trading tactics over an area stretching from the Sudan to Syria. In particular his battle against a Middle-Eastern confederacy in front of the Canaanite city of Megiddo and the subsequent seven-month siege brought about the capitulation of 330 enemy princes. But the pharaoh was still compelled to make regular parades of military might in the Levant and continual punitive strikes against Syrian armies. Occasionally we learn about his military personnel, such as Amenemhab who killed the elephant that threatened the king's life in a hunt near the Euphrates.

Likewise, we can assume that Garrison Commander Djeheuty was an acclaimed warrior on the pharaoh's general staff. Inscriptions from his Theban tomb give an idea of his historical status:

King's follower in every foreign land ... overseer of northern countries ... supplier of storehouses with lapis lazuli, silver and gold.

Accordingly his career as a governor in the Middle East was at a time of maximum Egyptian sovereignty and control of foreign wealth – lapis lazuli came via trade-routes from Afghanistan and silver from mines in Anatolia. His posthumous fame led to him becoming the hero of an escapade set in the time of Tuthmosis III's conquests but one which is probably quite fictional.

The source for the tale is a Ramesside papyrus in the British Museum written at least 150 years after Djeheuty's death.

The setting is an Egyptian siege of the port of Joppa on the coast of Palestine. Djeheuty is in conference with the Prince of Joppa in an attempt to persuade him that he, Djeheuty, intends to turn traitor and, together with his wife and children, come over to the enemy camp. As proof of Djeheuty's sincerity the Prince of Joppa demands to see the sceptre of authority of Tuthmosis III kept in the Egyptian High Command's tent. Djeheuty brings the sceptre but only to deliver the Prince of Joppa a stunning blow on the head. He then binds him in metal fetters. The ruse now adopted by Djeheuty has great similarity to the tale of *Ali Baba and the Forty Thieves*. Djeheuty organises 200 soldiers with fetters and bonds to be carried in 200 sealed baskets by 500 troops. Their orders are to enter Joppa and fetter its inhabitants. Djeheuty arranges for false information to be passed on to the herald of the Prince of Joppa to the effect that the Prince's forces have captured Djeheuty and his family, and that the 200 baskets are part of the tribute now destined for the city. This message is taken to the Princess of Joppa who gives orders for the city gates to be opened to admit the 200 baskets. The Egyptian troops then overrun Joppa and take its inhabitants as prisoners, bound in fetters. The papyrus closes with Djeheuty writing a letter to Tuthmosis III informing him of the victory which he suggests should be used to fill the Temple of Amun-Re with slaves.

Ramesses II and the Princess of Hatti

From the Nile Delta down to Nubia, temples, statues and stelae will not let you forget that Egypt was once ruled by Ramesses II (1290–1224 BC). His Delta residence was in fact so opulent that it inspired eulogies:

... The sun rises and sets within its limits. Its west is the Temple of Amun, its south the Temple of Seth, the goddess Astarte shines in its east and the goddess Wadjet appears in its north.

On the walls and pylons of most of his temples you can read in scenes and in hieroglyph the official version of the pharaoh's battle against the Hittities at Kadesh on the River Orontes in 1285 BC. But despite the propaganda-machine extolling his prowess it is clear that his intention to dislodge the Hittites from Syria and north Lebanon had failed. After a cold war both Hittites and Egyptians agreed on a non-aggression pact, officially sealed in the names of the deities of each state in 1269 BC. Thirteen years later stelae at Karnak, Elephantine and Abu Simbel proclaim an international wedding between Ramesses II and the daughter of the Great Prince of Hatti (the Hittite king). However, the two arch enemies are now fully reconciled by a legal treaty and a diplomatic marriage. The Egyptian account pretends that the Great Prince of Hatti, attributing drought in his land to the influence of Ramasses II with the Hittite storm god, decides to send his daughter and

Granite head and shoulders of the pharaoh Ramesses II (1290–1224 BC) whose alliance with the Hittites was strengthened by a diplomatic marriage.

limitless tribute to Egypt. The pharaoh intercedes with the god Seth to keep storms out of the skies during the princess's journey. On her arrival in Egypt Ramesses II was struck by her beauty. He announced that her status was to be 'King's wife, Maat-nefru-Re'. She appears to have been joined by a second Hittite princess, who became another wife of Ramesses II, and she ended her days in the Royal Harem in the Faiyum province.

A thousand years after the historical marriage we can follow Ramesses II and Queen Maat-nefru-Re into legend via a Ptolemaic stela in the Louvre Museum. It was discovered in a now-vanished sanctuary near the Temple of Khonsu at Karnak and was a forgery by the priests who knew the historical facts of the Hittite princess, even remembering an element of her Egyptian name. The purpose of the stela seems to have been twofold: to emphasise the hierarchical order of the two forms of the god Khonsu and, in the face of the recent Persian and Greek conquests of Egypt, to indulge in subtle nationalism by setting the tale in the era of Ramesses II when a native-born Egyptian pharaoh ruled the country.

The stela begins with a conflation of the royal titulary of Ramesses II and Tuthmosis IV. Ramesses II is then said to be in Naharin, a region in the Upper Euphrates. Historically, Ramesses II had never emulated the achievements of Tuthmosis I and Tuthmosis III who set up stelae on the banks of the Euphrates, since the Hittites thwarted his ambitions in North Syria at the battle of Kudesh. However, in the stela, Ramesses II receives tribute of precious metal, lapis lazuli, turquoise and valuable timber. The Prince of Bakhtan set his daughter at the head of his tribute. The location of Bakhtan might be purely imaginary but a good case has been made for its identification with Bactria. Ramesses II is captivated by her beauty and bestows on her the title 'Great Royal Wife, Nefru-Re'.

Later, Ramesses II was celebrating the 'Beautiful Festival of the Valley' in honour of Amun-Re at Thebes when a messenger from Bakhtan arrives with presents for Queen Nefru-Re. He also brings bad news about the Queen's younger sister who was dangerously ill. Her name is given as Bentresh, which may be part Egyptian and part Canaanite and means 'Daughter of Joy'. This would be analogous to the actual name of Ramesses II's daughter-wife Bint-Anat. Ramesses II summons the research-fellows in the House of Life and his palace staff, all in all an assembly of his top academics, physicians and magicians. The Royal Scribe Djeheuty-em-hab is selected to go to Bakhtan to ascertain Princess Bentresh's malady. (Egyptian doctors had a wide reputation in the ancient Near East – in the fact in the Persian dominion of Egypt shortly before this stela was composed the chief physician Wadjahorresne spent time at the court of King Darius I in Iran.) Djeheuty-em-hab diagnoses that Bentresh is possessed by hostile spirits and that only a god could contend with them. Bakhtan is so remote that it is nearly three years after the news of the sickness of Princess Bentresh first reached Ramesses II that the request for divine assistance comes to him.

At this point the god Khonsu, son of Amun-Re and Mut, is consulted by Ramesses who makes a plea for Bentresh. The first and most senior form of Khonsu is 'Khonsu in Thebes Nefer-hotep'. However, the priests manipulate matters such that the response comes from a specialised manifestation of the god, called 'Khonsu-fulfiller-of-schemes', whose skill lay in expelling 'disease-demons'. From ritual inclinations (noddings) of the god's statue, the decision is taken to send 'Khonsu-fulfiller-of-schemes', protected by magical amulets from the senior Khonsu, in a great flotilla together with horses and chariots to Bakhtan. When the god reaches Bentresh seventeen months later his power to cure is immediate and the princess recovers fully. The major spirit which had caused her illness now acknowledges the supremacy of Khonsu and, surprisingly, persuades the god to make the Prince of Bakhtan initiate a feast day in his (i.e. the spirit's) honour.

The Prince of Bakhtan then becomes reluctant to let the god's statue leave and he keeps it in his country for three years and nine months. But he then has a dream in which the god, in the form of a golden falcon, appears to come at him from his shrine and soar up into the sky in the direction of Egypt. The Prince realises his mistake and sends the statue back to Thebes with great tribute. On arrival, 'Khonsu-fulfiller-of-schemes' presents these gifts from Bakhtan to the senior 'Khonsu in Thebes Nefer-hotep' – minus a few items which his priesthood kept as commission for the arduous journey.

Tales of fantasy

The stories in this section have been chosen as examples of how wonders of magic, exotic location and extraordinary adventures provided an excellent vehicle for scribes to structure an escape from routine life. Although the contents of these papyri are a valued legacy of Ancient Egyptian literature, their origins lie in the repertoire of storytellers. The oral traditions from which they grew were the-entertainment/media of Egyptian villagers. The tales might become most elaborate under scribal editing but the humble sources from which they sprang were never scorned. The vizier Ptahhotep, the author of a wisdom text, *Instruction of Ptahhotep*, in about 2400 BC, comments: 'the art of good speech is certainly a rarity but that does not rule out your discovery of it in the mouths of the women who turn grindstones'.

A cycle of tales of magic set in the Pyramid Era in early Dynasty IV (*c.* 2550 BC) are preserved in Berlin Papyrus 3033, popularly known as the Westcar Papyrus after the English traveller who acquired them on his visit to Egypt in 1823–4. The language of the document is classical Middle Kingdom Egyptian (*c.* 2040–*c.* 1783 BC), although the papyrus itself is a slightly later copy which dates to the early sixteenth century BC. The strong historical context of this cycle of legends is embroidered by the scribe with the entertainment centred around great magicians whose fame had lasted nearly a thousand years by the time the papyrus was written. There were originally five tales but the first one is all but lost and the second is woefully fragmentary. So we begin with the third tale where Baufre, son of King Khufu (*r. c.* 2550 BC), builder of the Great Pyramid at Giza, is about to relate a wonder performed by a magician in the reign of King Sneferu, Khufu's father.

Djadja-em-ankh and his power over water

On one occasion King Sneferu – a pharaoh well documented in historical inscriptions and a prolific constructor of pyramids at Meidum and Dahshur – wanders around his palace frustrated with boredom. He sends for Djadja-em-ankh, his chief lector-priest. In ancient Egypt this title literally read: 'The one who carries the ritual book'; in other words, an official designated to hold ceremonial papyri, normally in a religious or funerary context. This may have been when pronouncing liturgy in a temple, or when reciting the spell for 'opening the mouth', at the tombside where the mummified corpse has living faculties magically restored to it.

In this particular instance, however, Djadja-em-ankh has the role of court magician whose secret spells are contained in the papyrus which he holds. Sneferu asks his magician for some ideas on alleviating his ennui. Djadja-em-ankh suggests that the king needs a breath of fresh air in the delightful environment of the palace lake where wildfowl and scenery would combine to cheer him up, especially if some beautiful girls from the royal harem rowed across the lake in front of him. The king thinks this a brilliant idea and organises a boat to be filled with twenty girls who have not born children, whose hair is finely braided and whose figures are curvaceous. Even more exciting to the king's mind is his own instruction that instead of their normal linen dresses the girls would wear only nets of faience beads. They are given oars that have been overlaid with gold leaf and start to row up and down in front of the pharaoh.

All goes well until the lead stroke, playing with her braided hair, loses her hair-clasp pendant of high-quality turquoise in the lake. (Some of these fish-shaped hair pendants survive in museum collections.) Upset, she stops rowing and so causes the boat to come to a halt. When Sneferu finds out what has happened, he offers to replace the lost pendant so that the rowing can continue. We know that he sent expeditions to the turquoise mining region of Maghara in the Sinai peninsula and so had a fair supply. Using a colloquial expression, the girl replies: 'I prefer my pot to one like it', meaning that she considers the lost turquoise to have been of exceptional quality, not to be matched. Rather petulantly King Sneferu turns to his magician and more or less tells him that since the outing was his idea he can solve the dilemma. Obediently Djadja-em-ankh does so by reciting a magic spell (which, infuriatingly, the papyrus does not divulge). The lake is over 6 m deep and upon the magic words half of it rises up to form a wall of water over 12 m high, revealing the lake bottom and the pendant. Djadja-em-ankh retrieves it and restores it to the girl. With another magical utterance he restores the lake to its previous condition. All this excitement becomes an excuse for a celebratory feast and Djadja-em-ankh is well rewarded for his magical powers.

Djedi and his power to restore life

In the next tale Prince Hordedef, another son of Khufu, and one who posthumously had a reputation as the wise author of a book of instructions on life, tells his father of the amazing magical skill of one of his own subjects. Khufu is intrigued, especially when he learns that this magician, called Djedi, knows about the secret apartments in the sanctuary of Thoth, god of wisdom, because Khufu himself had been trying to find out about them in order to make an architectural replica in one of his own temples. Consequently Prince Hordedef sails south from Memphis to the town of Djed-Sneferu where Djedi lives. Djedi is in good health and has a tremendous appetite – 500 loaves a day plus half an ox and 100 jugs of beer – not bad for someone who had reached the age of 110 (a model age among ancient Egyptians). When the prince arrives, in a splendid sedan chair, Djedi is stretched out on a mat in front of his house having an oil-massage. After an elaborate exchange of courtesies, he gathers together his valuable scrolls and sets off with Hordedef for the royal residence.

Djedi enters the main court of the palace and is received by King Khufu, who is eager to see him perform some of the spectacular magic involving the reunion of dismembered bodies that he has been told about. Djedi agrees to perform and Khufu quite callously gives orders for a prisoner to be brought as the assistant. Here Djedi quickly displays his humanity by refusing to perform on a human being, protesting that mankind are 'illustrious cattle', a reference to the concept that the human race is the herd of the creator god. As a result a goose is chosen. It is decapitated and its head placed at the eastern side of the court, its body at the west. Djedi utters his magic spell, which again we are not able to read. The goose's body waddles across to its head, which is also animated, and they join together and start to honk. Similar successes are achieved in the case of a wading water-fowl (perhaps a flamingo) and an ox. Unfortunately an earlier reference to Djedi being able to tame a wild lion to walk behind him is not developed by the scribe of this papyrus.

Khufu now broaches the subject of the number of secret apartments in the sanctuary of Thoth. Djedi denies knowing the answer himself, but says it can be found in a chest in a storeroom in the sanctuary of the sun god at Heliopolis. Furthermore, Djedi is not destined to be the one to bring the chest to the palace.

The tale now incorporates a prophecy concerning a future change of royal family, which in history we recognise as the emergence of Dynasty V in about 2465 BC. Djedi tells King Khufu that the chest will be retrieved by Ruddedet, the wife of a priest of the sun god who will bear three children sired by Re himself. The throne of Egypt will pass to them. Khufu becomes depressed at these words but Djedi encourages him by revealing that Khufu's son and grandson will inherit the throne before the prophecy comes to pass. (Historically the succession of the throne in Dynasty IV was more complex than Djedi's prophecy – the papyrus ignores the problem of Radjedef, Khufu's immediate successor, who built his pyramid at Abu Rawesh north of Giza, and seemingly regards the last ruler, Shepseskaf, as too insignificant to count.) Ruddedet will give birth, states Djedi, in early winter when the Nile flood has receded. Khufu, who wants to visit a major sanctuary of Re at Sakhbu to commemorate the birth, to which he seems reconciled, tells Djedi that the journey will be hampered since the 'Two-Fish Nile branch' in the Delta which he has to negotiate will be empty. Djedi informs Khufu that his magic will cause about 2 m of water to appear in the dried-up canal, so that the visit will not be impeded. The reward for Djedi's skill in magic and prophecy is to be given a place in the royal household with Prince Hordedef and with vastly increased food rations.

The enchanted island

This tale is normally called by egyptologists *The Shipwrecked Sailor* but the ancient scribe definitely put its emphasis more on the exotic location of the mysterious island and on the supernatural creature living there. The source of this adventure is a papyrus in the Moscow Museum which dates to the Middle Kingdom, the classical era of Egyptian literature. (It probably dates in particular to some time in the nineteenth century BC). It is relevant that this period of Egyptian civilisation witnessed the expansion of pharaonic power in Nubia, south of the granite frontier at Aswan. There was an intensification of control over the goldmines, with massive fortresses being constructed around the Second Cataract of the Nile. In addition there was a spirit of exploration involving royal agents being sent into the Sudan to investigate lucrative trade routes.

At the beginning of *The Enchanted Island* an unnamed envoy is returning from an exploratory trade mission in Nubia. From historical inscriptions, like the autobiography of Governor Harkhuf (about 2240 BC) carved on the front of his tomb at Qubbet el-Hawa at Aswan, we know the luxury goods which would be looked for by the pharaoh – incense, ebony, elephant tusks and panther skins. The envoy is in an acute state of depression because he has clearly been unsuccessful on the expedition and he is worried how to explain his boat empty of valuables to the king. One man in his entourage – the actual 'shipwrecked sailor' of the story – exhorts him to look on the bright side. The expedition has suffered no loss of life *en route* and is now safely out of Nubia on the Egyptian side of the First Cataract. The sailor insists on telling the envoy a yarn about an adventure he once had.

He was on an expedition bound for the royal mines, using a route that involved navigating on the Red Sea. The boat was impressive, being 60 m long and 40 m wide. His companions (there were 120 sailors altogether) were fearless, unintimidated by the natural elements and able to foretell when a storm was brewing. But a too sudden squall brought a 4 m-high wave so that – as the papyrus says – 'the boat died'. All the crew were lost at sea with the exception of himself who was cash ashore on an island.

For three days he hid under the protection of trees until his thirst drove him to explore the island. He found he had been shipwrecked in a veritable Garden of Eden – he was surrounded by ripe figs, grapes, vegetables and cucumbers and an abundance of fish and wildfowl. Having eaten to excess, he then lit a fire and made a burnt-offering to the gods to show his gratitude for having survived. Obviously the smoke gave away his whereabouts because the trees promptly started to crash to the ground and the island seemed to shudder. To his consternation he saw a gigantic snake about 16 m long approaching. It was a creature of legend: covered in gold scales, it had eyebrows made of lapis lazuli and, like a god, it wore a beard which hung down a metre.

The snake, which had the power of human speech, reared up and demanded an explanation from the sailor as to how he had come to the island. The accompanying threat that if the answer was not given quickly the snake would spit flames and reduce the sailor to ashes left the latter incoherent with terror. So the snake became more benign and carried the sailor in its jaws without injury to its dwelling. Reassured, the sailor related the story of the shipwreck (in an account which is almost verbatim the original description – a feature common to the oral tradition of poetry or story-telling). The snake told the sailor that a divine force had drawn him to the 'island of the Ka'. This phrase is difficult to translate – the 'Ka' is the life-force of a person born at the same time as the physical body but surviving physical death as a spiritual entity. One egyptologist has suggested that 'phantom island' might be a possible rendering. However, since the 'Ka' is a magical power, capable of bringing to reality inanimate representations of, for example, bread, beer jugs, incense, linen clothing and animals, then 'the Enchanted Island' is probably the snake's meaning. The sailor was then told that his sojourn on the island would last four months, until his friends would sail past and rescue him. The snake emphasised that the sailor would reach home and die in his own town. Burial in Egypt was of paramount importance since only then would the correct funerary rituals be performed. Also the snake pointed out that the experience of a calamity could be compensated by the feelings of relief when the situation had improved.

The next development is that the snake gives his own story within the framework of the sailor's tale, which in turn is a diversion for the low spirits of the envoy. This storyteller's ruse of tales within tales, occurring here in a simple form nearly 4,000 years ago, is the basis for some of the most elaborate concoctions of Princess Scheherazade in *The Arabian Nights' Entertainments*. On the Enchanted Island there were originally seventy-five snakes. One day all the others were killed by a falling star (this was probably a reference to a meteorite) which burned them up in flames. The one surviving snake was desolated but eventually overcame his grief. However, to the sailor he reflects on the contentment of family life. Moved by his tale, the sailor avows that on his return to Egypt he will proclaim the magnanimity of the snake to strangers like himself and send a cargo of exotic goods such as fragrant oil and myrrh to the island. The snake in laughter replies that the island has more valuable produce than the sailor could ever hope to see. He calls himself the 'Prince of Punt' – the land from where Egypt obtained incense, goods and produce of Equatorial Africa, situated in the region of the River Atbara – and moreover, once the sailor has gone away the island will disappear below the waves of the Red Sea. (Of course by this clever device the storyteller ensured that no-one could be so prosaic as to check out the facts of the sailor's yarn.)

Four months later a boat with a crew of his friends approached close by the island and was hailed by the sailor who had climbed a high tree. The benevolent snake sped him on his way with a gift of a rich cargo consisting of myrrh, oil, perfumed unguent, eye paint, giraffe tails, elephant tusks,

Tribute from Nubia of the sort referred to by the sailor and the gigantic serpent in the tale of the enchanted island. Note in particular the giraffe with the monkey climbing up its neck. Tomb of Rekhmire, Western Thebes, c. 1450 BC.

greyhounds, monkeys and baboons. On the West Bank at Thebes, if you look at the walls of Queen Hatshepsut's temple at Deir el-Bahari and of the rock tomb of the vizier Rekhmire, you can see exactly this kind of produce coming from southern countries into Egypt. Two months later – with the switch from the Red Sea to the River Nile glossed over – the sailor reached the royal residence and handed over his goods. He was rewarded by the pharaoh with an endowment of serfs and was made a palace official. The irony of the successful outcome of the sailor's adventure, in contrast to the dismal failure of the envoy to whom the tale has been told, makes for a sardonic ending. The envoy uses an analogy between the futility of giving water at dawn to a goose that is going to be slaughtered later in the morning and in his own case the hopelessness of being cheered up briefly before facing the pharaoh.

To indicate that the conclusion of the tale has been reached the papyrus finishes with the words: 'It has come from its beginning to its end just as found in the writing – the work of the scribe excellent of fingers, Imeny's son Imen-aa, may he live may he prosper may he be healthy'.

The metamorphoses of Bata

In the British Museum there is a papyrus (no. 10183) commonly referred to as the *Tale of the Two Brothers*, immaculately written in the Hieratic script by the scribe Inena who lived around the last quarter of the thirteenth century BC. It is an intricate concoction of mythology, folklore and humour. Although some of the events might seem far-fetched, we are never remote from human emotions and foibles.

Two brothers, Anubis (the elder) and Bata live in the same house. (The fact that they bear the names of Egyptian deities vaguely connects them with the world of myth through the legend of the Jackal Nome of Upper Egypt as it survives in a later and complex document known as Papyrus Jumilhac.) Anubis has a wife who is regrettably never named. Bata lives with them but sleeps in the cattle stable and acts as a general handyman in making clothes for Anubis and in bearing the brunt of agricultural work. His unfailing strength has gained him a good reputation. He has the gift of understanding the speech of the cattle which he tends so that when they tell him 'The grass of such-and-such a place is delicious' he takes them there to graze. This gives good results in terms of increased calving.

One day in the ploughing season when the brothers are sowing barley and emmer-seed in the fields, the supply runs out. Bata is sent to fetch some more. He finds his brother's wife braiding her hair and rather peremptorily asks her to get up and give him a supply of seed as quickly as possible. Not surprisingly, she tells him not to interrupt her coiffure session and to go to the storage bin to collect the seed himself. Bata takes a large jar to carry the maximum amount of seed. His brother's wife inquires how much he is carrying, to which he answers 'Three sacks of barley and two of emmer-wheat'. This would be an impressive load equivalent to eleven bushels. His brother's wife becomes sexually stimulated at seeing his energy. She grabs hold of Bata, suggesting that there is now an opportunity to sleep together for an hour. It will be good for him, she asserts, and she will undertake to make him fine linen clothes. Bata's moral behaviour finds this proposition horrific and he becomes as fierce as a leopard in his rage. It is unacceptable to entertain such an iniquitous idea since he lives like a son with her and his older brother. However, he promises that the matter will be divulged to no-one and returns to Anubis in the fields. In the evening Bata sets off to sleep in his cattle stable.

In an episode illustrating the ingenuity of Anubis' wife, Bata pays a terrible price for scorning her proposition. Before Anubis returns his wife makes herself look as though she has been viciously assaulted. Instead of lighting a fire she leaves the house in darkness, perplexing Anubis on his arrival. Her normal custom is to pour water over her husband's hands when he comes home but she does not on this occasion. Instead, Anubis finds her on her bed looking distraught and in a fit of vomiting (cleverly brought on by swallowing fat and grease). Perhaps the shock of seeing his wife so distressed numbs Anubis into the inane inquiry: 'Who has been speaking with you?' His wife immediately launches into a devastating character-assassination of Bata, reversing the actual happening. She tells Anubis that his younger brother suggested that she untied her hair braids and joined him in bed for an hour. From her story it is she who protested that they were like a mother and father to him upon which he became scared at what he had proposed and beat her to stop her talking to Anubis. She challenges her husband to kill Bata, otherwise she will die.

Anubis now displays his anger. As Bata has not yet arrived home with the cattle, Anubis hides behind the stable door with his spear in hand, ready to kill him. It is the first cow in the line approaching the stable who saves Bata's life with a warning about Anubis hiding there armed with his spear. Bata catches a glimpse of his brother's feet and escapes in flight with Anubis in hot pursuit. A prayer for justice to the sun god Re-Horakhti results in the god creating an expanse of water full of crocodiles to separate the two brothers and to keep Bata safe until the following dawn. From safety, Bata vigorously protests his innocence to Anubis, describing the real sequence of events. He accuses his brother of being ready to spear him on he uncorroborated testimony of a despicable harlot. He drastically backs up his oath of truthfulness to Re-Harahkti by cutting off his phallus with a reed-knife. He throws it into the water where it becomes a morsel of food for a catfish. Gradually growing weaker through loss of blood Bata arouses the pity of his brother who stands there in tears, frustrated from reaching the bank where Bata stands because of the crocodiles.

In a last speech to Anubis, Bata asserts that he cannot remain but will go the Valley of the Pine. If this location was intended to conjure up an actual geographical region then it would be in the Lebanon. Bata states that he will take out his own heart and place it on the top of a pine flower. (How he is to survive without it is not developed in the text.) He requests that Anubis comes to search for him if the pine tree is cut down – for that will result in the death of Bata – and rescue his heart. If Anubis puts Bata's heart in a bowl of water then Bata will exact revenge on the person who killed him. The sign Anubis will receive if calamity strikes Bata will be a jug of beer suddenly fermenting in his hand. Bata departs for the Valley of the Pine while Anubis, smeared with dust to show his grief, journeys home. He kills his wife and unceremoniously throws her corpse to scavenging dogs.

Meanwhile Bata, his heart on the top of the pine flower in the Valley of the Pine, builds a villa where he lives alone. The bizarre scenario so far has merely been the platform for taking off into a flight of total fantasy. Bata encounters the Ennead of the sun god who are the governors of this region as well as of Egypt. The Ennead inform Bata that he is vindicated in his reputation and blameless of any wrongdoing. Moreover, Anubis has killed the woman who was the cause of the whole business. To relieve his loneliness Re-Harahkti instructs the god Khnum to make Bata a wife. Khnum moulds a ravishingly beautiful woman in whose body is the essence of the gods themselves. In view of the consequential disasters which she causes Bata there seems more than a fleeting similarity with the Greek legend of Pandora, fashioned by Hephaistos on the orders of Zeus to be a blight to mankind. When Khnum has finished carving Bata's wife (another nameless woman) the Seven Hathors, goddesses connected with destiny, foretell that she will come to a violent death. We cannot ignore the anomalous marital relationship now brought into being for the self-castrated Bata and a sexually attractive woman.

One day Bata gives away the secret to his wife that his heart rests on the top of a pine flower. This is to be his undoing. He tells her because he worries that if she walks on the seashore, she may be swept away. He has to admit that his vulnerability might prevent him rescuing her. Shortly after this warning, and while Bata is away hunting in the desert, the sea surges after his wife while she is out walking. She escapes into the villa but the pine next to the villa traps a scented lock of her hair on behalf of the sea which washes it upon the shore of Egypt where pharaoh's launderers carry out their work. The perfume of the hair permeates all the linen garments which are being washed and the pharaoh complains about the scent. Eventually the chief laundryman discovers the lock of hair. The meaning of the situation is interpreted by the scribes: the lock of hair imbued with the gods' essence belongs to a daughter of Re-Harakhti and has come to Egypt to encourage the pharaoh to search for her and fetch her from the Valley of the Pine. The first expedition of troops sent to bring the woman to Egypt are all slaughtered by Bata in the Valley of the Pine. The next expedition of troops and chariots is accompanied by a woman whose task is to entice Bata's wife with exquisite jewellery to leave her restricted life in Lebanon for the sophistication of the Egyptian royal court. The plan succeeds and Bata's wife comes to Egypt where she is loved by the pharaoh and given exalted status in the palace. The pharaoh learns about the heart of Bata on the pine flower and gives orders for the pine tree to be cut down. At that moment, Bata drops down dead.

The next day Anubis discovers his beer fermenting in its jug and recognises the sign of calamity about which Bata had spoken. He journeys to the Valley of the Pine and finds Bata lying dead in his villa. The search for Bata's heart takes just over three years and Anubis eventually discovers it disguised as a fruit to keep it safe. He puts it in a bowl of water and Bata's body begins to twitch. Anubis touches Bata's lips with water, Bata drinks some more, and his heart is restored to him.

Bata's metamorphoses so far have been from a virile young man to a eunuch and a corpse, but more are to come. He wants revenge on his wife and decides to travel to Egypt in the form of a strikingly coloured bull. Anubis rides on the bull's back and they both go to the royal residence. The pharaoh is captivated immediately by the beauty of the bull and rewards Anubis with gold and silver. Bata the bull is fêted and fussed over by the pharaoh. One day the bull confronts the wife of his former human self. He terrifies her when he reveals that he is Bata seeking revenge for her act of causing the pine tree to be cut down. He leaves, but his wife schemes a way of destroying this threat to her security. When the pharaoh is 'in his cups' after a delectable feast, she extracts from him a promise to let her eat the liver of Bata the bull. Later, the pharaoh regrets his promise but is as powerless to change it as Herod, captivated by Salome, was to rescind the order for John the Baptist's execution. The next day Bata the bull is slaughtered as a sacrificial offering, but as the men carry the body by the king's great gateway Bata causes two drops of blood to fall from his severed throat. During the night two huge Persea trees grow by the gateway. The pharaoh considers this propitious and a celebration is made in their honour.

A long while afterwards the pharaoh makes an official appearance at his 'Window of Appearances' – a ceremonial dais of which a well-preserved example survives as the link between the palace and mortuary temple of Rameses III at Medinet Habu on the West Bank at Thebes. Then with Bata's wife, now his principal queen, he drives in a golden chariot to inspect the Persea trees. While the royal couple are relaxing in their shade Bata reveals to his wife that he has metamorphosed from the bull into the Persea trees and is still very much alive and intent on revenge. The woman once again uses her charms and guile to get the pharaoh to agree to fell the Persea trees and make them into furniture. While she is watching the carpenters carry out the king's instructions a splinter is struck off and flies into the mouth of Bata's wife. She immediately becomes pregnant and in due course gives birth to a son who is, unbeknown to all, none other than her previous husband Bata. The pharaoh is over the moon with joy. The reborn Bata is honoured as he grows up, given the title of 'King's son of Kush', which makes him responsible for the vast gold resources of Nubia, and he is acclaimed as heir-apparent. When the pharaoh dies Bata ascends the throne and calls together the great officials of Egypt. He relates his adventures and metamorphoses. Then his 'wife-mother' is brought in and the magistrates agree in judgement upon her. Just as happens in the historical 'conspiracy papyrus' in the Turin Museum where the fate of a queen of Ramesses III, guilty of plotting to kill the king and put her son on the throne, is not specified, so the description of the judgement on Bata's wife is vague. In both cases, however, execution or invitation to suicide is certainly the sentence. Anubis becomes crown prince and when Bata, after a reign of thirty years, finally dies – without emerging in a new form in this world – it is his older brother who assumes the kingship of Egypt.

Suggestions for further reading

Reliable translations of many of the sources for the myths and legends discussed in this book can be found in J. B. Pritchard (ed.), *Ancient Near Eastern Texts relating to the Old Testament* (3rd edn with supplement, Princeton, 1969) and in M. Lichtheim, *Ancient Egyptian Literature* (3 vols covering the Old Kingdom to the Late Period, Berkeley and London, 1973, 1976, 1980). For attempts to synthesise the salient features of Egyptian religion in one book I would recommend E. Hornung, *Conceptions of God in Ancient Egypt – The One and the Many* (London, 1983), and S. Quirke, *Ancient Egyptian Religion* (London, 1992). Also as a quick reference to the essential nature of the deities figuring in these myths you can consult G. Hart, *Dictionary of Egyptian Gods and Goddesses* (London, 1986).

The chapters concerning the structure of the cosmos and the transition of the throne of Egypt from Osiris to Horus might be followed up by reading the following major sources: R. O. Faulkner, *The Ancient Egyptian Pyramid Texts* (Oxford, 1969) and R. O. Faulkner, *The Ancient Egyptian Coffin Texts* (3 vols, Warminster, 1973, 1977, 1987). The Edfu drama concerning Horus' annihilation of Seth can be found in H. W. Fairman, *The Triumph of Horus* (London, 1974). Erudite observations on the myth of kingship abound in J. Gwyn-Griffiths, *Plutarch's De Iside et Osiride* (University of Wales, 1970). For stimulating discussions both on cosmology and kingship you can turn to J. R. Allen, *Genesis in Egypt – The Philosophy of Ancient Egyptian Creation Accounts* (New Haven, Conn., 1988) and H. Frankfort, *Kingship and the Gods – A study of Near Eastern religion as the integration of society and nature* (Chicago, 1948). Two books offer penetrating analyses of the solar cults: S. Quirke, *The Cult of Ra: Sun Worship in Ancient Egypt* (London, 2001) and J. Assmann, *Egyptian Solar Religion in the New Kingdom: Re, Amun and the Crisis of Polytheism* (London and New York, 1995). For the study of Isis as supreme font of magical power the original spells are the most rewarding for initial research and are gathered in J. F. Bourghouts, *Ancient Magical Texts* (Leiden, 1978).

You should now plunge deep into the rich imagery of the Egyptian underworld, translated and lavishly illustrated in A. Piankoff, *The Tomb of Ramesses VI* (2 vols, New York, 1954). The best book to explain the complexity of the Royal Hereafter is E. Hornung, *The Ancient Egyptian Books of the Afterlife* (Cornell, Ithaca, 1999), which can be visually complemented by the survey of the Theban royal necropolis in E. Hornung, *Tal der Könige – Die Ruhestätte der Pharaonen* (Zürich, 1988). The afterlife of non-royal mortals is readily accessible in R. O. Faulkner (ed. C. A. R. Andrews), *The Ancient Egyptian Book of the Dead* (London, 1989). To pursue further some of the notable persons who became deified or entered the world of legends you can consult D. Wildung, *Egyptian Saints – Deification in Pharaonic Egypt* (New York, 1977), or his more careful and scholarly *Imhotep und Amenhotep* (Munich, 1977).

Celtic

Myths

MIRANDA GREEN

For Elisabeth

Picture credits

p. 316: Serge Ransford; *p. 321:* Corinium Museum; *p. 323:* Copenhagen, Nationalmuseet; *p. 326:* BM PRB 1847,2-8,82; *p. 329: (left)* Orléans, Musée Archéologique; *(right)* Château de Savigny, Mavilly, drawn by Paul Jenkins; *p. 332: (top)* Scunthorpe Museum; *(below)* BM PRB 1811,3-9,2; *p. 335:* Irish Post Office/Irish Tourist Board; *p. 337:* Saint-Rémy-de-Provence, Musée des Alpilles (author's photo); *p. 340:* Bonn, Rheinisches Landesmuseum (author's photo); *p. 343:* Vaduz, Liechtenstein Landesmuseum, drawn by Paul Jenkins; *p. 346:* Colchester & Essex Museum; *p. 348:* Corinium Museum (photo Betty Naggar); *p. 350:* Beaune, Musée des Beaux-Arts (author's photo); *p. 354:* Saint-Germain-en-Laye, Musée des Antiquités Nationales (author's photo); *p. 357:* BM PRB 1925,6-10,1-4, 7-9, 11-13, 16, 23; *p. 358 (left and right):* Stuttgart, Württembergisches Landesmuseum; *p. 361:* National Museum of Wales; *p. 362:* National Museums of Scotland; *p. 365:* Bonn, Rheinisches Landesmuseum (author's photo); *p. 367:* Saint-Germain-en-Laye, Musée des Antiquités Nationales (photo © Réunion des Musées Nationaux); *p. 370: (left)* BM PRB 1882,12-14,1; *(right)* Leiden, Rijksmuseum van Oudheden; *p. 373: (left)* Paris, Musée de Cluny (photo © Réunion des Musées Nationaux); *(right)* National Museum of Wales; *p. 375: (left)* BM PRB 1957,2-7,15-17; *(right)* Bath, Roman Baths Museum (photo Betty Naggar); *p. 378:* BM PRB 1984,10-2,1; *p. 379:* BM PRB 1857,7-15,1; *p. 380: (left)* Newport Museum, National Museum of Wales; *(right)* Oxford, Ashmolean Museum (photo Betty Naggar); *p. 385: (left)* Dover Archaeological Group; *(right)* BM, lithograph from *Album de la Champagne Souterraine*, by Léon Morel, 1898; *p. 387:* BM PRB 1967,2-2,1 *et seq.*; *p. 388:* Paris, Musée de Cluny (photo © Réunion des Musées Nationaux). Chapter openers by Jen Delyth.

Contents

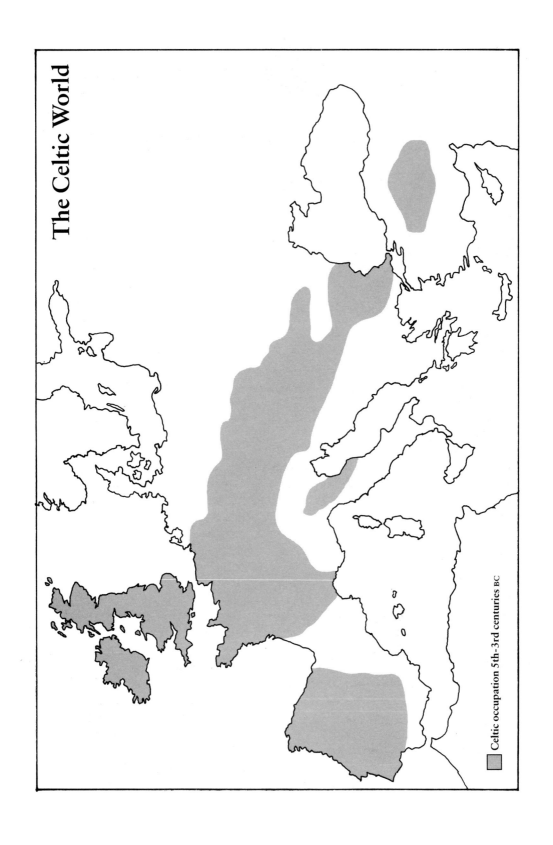

The Celtic World

Celtic occupation 5th–3rd centuries BC

How do we know about Celtic myths?

What do we mean by 'myth' and 'mythology'? These are flexible terms with a variety of meanings. For me myths are inextricably associated with religion. A useful definition involves the perception of a myth as a symbolic story, similar to a parable, a means by which human imagination can express a concept whose meaning is too complex and profound to be conveyed by simple verbal messages. In this way myths can deal with fundamental issues such as who we are, why we exist, what happens when we die: universal concerns which are unanswerable in terms of the rational explanations born of human experience. Myths can explain the phenomena of the natural world – the behaviour of the sun, weather, drought and flood – in terms of the super-natural. Thus myths exist by virtue of their link with the divine and with cult. They contain traditions of sacred beings – gods and heroes – and their association with mortals, which contribute to the framework of belief-systems. In this book the stories themselves, as they exist in the vernacular traditions of Ireland and Wales, form the fundamental core of myth in its strictest sense. But to my mind, because myths are so closely linked with religion, it is equally important to examine the other evidence for Celtic belief-systems, namely the chroniclings of the Classical writers and the archaeological material.

Time and space

Celtic Myths sets out to explore the mythology and beliefs of the pagan Celts between about 600 BC and AD 400, although some of the evidence cited in the book falls outside this range. At the period of maximum expansion (fifth–third centuries BC) the Celtic world occupied an area from Ireland and part of Spain in the west to Hungary and Czechoslovakia in the east (but including Galatia in Asia Minor), and from northern Scotland to north Italy and what was formerly Yugoslavia. Mediterranean authors first speak of *Keltoi* about 500 BC and it is then, or even earlier, that archaeologists can distinguish a certain homogeneity in material culture over much of Europe north of the Alps. From the third century BC, Celtic place-names and personal names endorse this geographical distribution of Celtic peoples.

There is no clear-cut boundary between the end of paganism and the beginning of Christianity in Celtic Europe. The old gods lingered long, but during the fourth century AD Christianity was officially adopted as the state religion by the Roman world, and in Britain and Ireland, where Celtic traditions were arguably sustained longest, the Celtic Church was established during the fifth century AD.

The problem of finding Celtic myths

The main difficulty in reaching Celtic myth and religion is that the pagan Celts were virtually non-literate and therefore did not describe their beliefs and their attitudes to the supernatural world in writing. This means that all our evidence is, in a real sense, indirect. That which exists falls into three categories, between which there are tensions and contradictions and all of which have, to a degree, to be treated separately: the chronicles of contemporary commentators from the Classical world; the later vernacular documents of Ireland and Wales; and the archaeology.

The evidence of the Classical commentators

Observers from the Greek and Roman world commented on the traditions, cults and rituals of their northern, 'barbarian' neighbours. Their testimony has the value of contemporaneity but it has inherent problems of bias, distortion, misunderstanding and omission. Unlike the Celts these observers belonged to a culture in which cities played an important role and, indeed, were regarded as the key to civilisation. Alongside rural and private cults, Mediterranean culture possessed an organised state religious system, based upon these urban centres. Thus Classical commentators on the Celts were witnesses to a set of traditions and thought-processes which were alien to them and which were based upon a less sophisticated religion. So there is the danger that Mediterranean authors selected and sensationalised aspects of cult-behaviour which they felt would fit the image of a primitive people, beyond the edge of the civilised world. Certainly the picture painted by these writers is very fragmentary. There is little information about divine beings and, where it does occur – as in the case of Caesar's chronicles – there is confusion and sometimes spurious equation between Celtic and Roman deities, and Celtic religion is frequently perceived according to the framework of the Graeco-Roman world.

Many Classical writers make some allusion to Celtic religion. A main source was Posidonius, a Greek philosopher of the Stoic School, whose first-century BC writings are lost but whose observations were quarried by a number of later commentators. Our main sources are Caesar (writing in the mid-first century BC); Strabo (late first century BC–early first century AD); Diodorus Siculus (writing c. 60–30 BC); Lucan (first century AD) and Dio Cassius (later second–early third century AD). Between them they present a large body of evidence mainly concerning ritual practices: druidism, divination, human sacrifice and head-hunting. They also comment on the Celtic attitude to death and the Otherworld (the perception of life after death as similar to that of earth).

What is missing is any clear picture of a Celtic pantheon or belief-system.

Occasionally we can discern links between these ancient documents and other sources of evidence. Thus the divinatory powers of the druids are chronicled in the early Insular (Irish) tradition. Classical writers, archaeology and the earliest Celtic stories all bear witness to the importance of water-cults; the religious significance of the human head; and a strong belief in life after death.

The vernacular sources

The earliest stories written in Irish and Welsh contain a large body of material which pertains to a Celtic mythological tradition. We use these stories, and not the early archaeological record, as our starting point for discussion since they are the sources most familiar to modern readers interested in Celtic mythology. However, this category of evidence has to be approached with caution if any attempt is made to link the myths and constant allusions to the supernatural world in this literature to the world of the pagan Celts as defined by archaeology or the Classical documents. First, the vernacular sources are late in their extant form and, moreover, they were compiled within a Christian milieu, many of them by Christian redactors, monks working within monasteries. Second, these writings relate specifically and solely to Wales and Ireland, which were on the western periphery of the Celtic world during the pagan Celtic period.

Ireland

The Irish oral tradition began first to be preserved in written form during the sixth century AD. However, the majority of the surviving manuscripts date from no earlier than the twelfth century. Their value lies in their undoubted inclusion of material which relates to a much earlier phase of Irish settlement, perhaps referring as far back as the pagan period: that is, before the fifth century AD.

There are three collections of Irish prose tales which are especially relevant to the Celtic world of the supernatural. One is the 'Mythological Cycle', which includes the *Leabhar Gabhála* or *Book of Invasions*, and the *Dinnshenchas* or *History of Places*, both compiled in the twelfth century AD. The *Book of Invasions* has its origins in much earlier compilations of monastic scholars constructing a 'History of Ireland' in the sixth and seventh centuries AD. It describes a succession of mythical invasions of Ireland from before the Flood, culminating in the coming of the Gaels or Celts. Its purpose seems to have been to establish a Myth of Creation, an explanation of the nature of Ireland and the presence of the Celts. The 'invasion' of greatest interest in the present context is that of the Tuatha Dé Danann, the divine race of Ireland, who consisted of numerous gods and goddesses, each with particular functions and concerns. The *Dinnshenchas* is less useful, but it comprises a collection of topographical lore, in which the names of places are explained in terms of myth.

The second group of tales is contained in the Ulster Cycle, of which the most important form a collection of stories known as the *Táin Bó Cuailnge* (the *Cattle Raid of Cooley*). This chronicles the great conflict between the two most northerly of the five ancient provinces of Ulster and Connacht. The *Táin* is steeped in the supernatural: Ulster is peopled by superhuman heroes, such as Cú Chulainn, and by druids, such as Cathbadh; Connacht is ruled by a euhemerised (i.e. a divine being perceived as a historical figure) queen-goddess, Medb; and the destiny of the two kingdoms rests in the hands of the great war- and death-goddesses, the Morrígán and the Badbh. The Ulster Cycle, as its name suggests, is a mythological tradition which belongs only to Ulster; there is nothing comparable for any other region of Ireland. Part of the earliest-known form of the *Táin* is contained within a flawed and fragmentary text in the oldest manuscript, called the *Leabhar na h Uidre* or *Book of the Dun Cow*. This was compiled in the twelfth century at the Monastery of Clonmacnois. In origin, however, the *Táin* is much older: the language of the earliest form of the story belongs to the eighth century, but many scholars believe some passages to be several centuries earlier still, although others challenge this view.

The third group of relevant stories is found within the 'Fionn Cycle', again compiled in the twelfth century. It contains less material of relevance to a study of myth, but it chronicles the activities of the hero Finn and his heroic war-band, the Fianna, all of whom are of supernatural status. The interest of these stories lies in their close affinity with the natural world and in the supernatural crea- tures which inhabit it. This animistic attitude to the world is a tradition for which close parallels can be found in the archaeological evidence for Celtic religion.

There is a great deal of controversy as to the value of the early Insular (Irish) sources in contributing to a construction of Celtic mythology. Not only were they compiled in the medieval period and within a Christian context, but the language used often suggests that the stories were produced no earlier than the eighth century. Indeed some of the descriptions themselves are strongly indicative of medieval Ireland. It is dangerously speculative to make close links between Irish epic literature and the pagan Celtic society chronicled by Classical writers. The gap in space and time between the Celtic Europe of the later first millennium BC and the Ireland of the early historical period is too great a gulf to ignore. But there is, nonetheless, incontrovertible evidence that some of the Irish material contains records of a Celtic tradition that is pre-Christian. This archaism is especially apparent in the Ulster Cycle, which describes a situation prior to the fifth century AD when Ulster's political position within Ireland fundamentally changed. The early, pre-Christian, political organisation encap- sulated here is explicable in terms of the function of the compilers, which was to chronicle the past. There are other factors which point to pagan origins. Chris- tianity is not apparent in these Insular legends, and a world is described whose perception of the supernatural belongs to a pre-Christian tradition.

Whatever the date the tales were compiled, they contain much that is pagan and mythological. Even so, there are genuine problems if attempts are made to link the written myths with the archaeological evidence for pagan Celtic religion, although some concepts, such as the sacred power of 'three' are prominent in both sources. While the personalities of Celtic divinities are

This Romano-Celtic stone relief from Cirencester, Gloucestershire, shows three genii cucullati (little hooded gods of fertility and well-being).

present in the literature, no allusion is made to the forms of worship or the belief-systems associated with them. With very few exceptions it is impossible to make direct identification between the gods of the Tuatha Dé Danann and the deities whose names were recorded on inscriptions in the early first millennium AD. The name of the Irish god Nuadu may be philologically linked with Nodens, whose large sanctuary on the River Severn was erected in the third century AD, and there are other examples of possible connections, but they are rare indeed. The problem with the Insular material could result from Christian 'laundering' of pagan tradition, whereby redactors who were either ignorant of or hostile to Irish paganism may have deliberately redefined or restructured the world of the supernatural in order to neutralise it. Thus Celtic religion is diluted and all that is left are superhuman heroes or gods who have been cut off from their original theological systems.

Wales

The early Welsh vernacular tradition contains elements of a rich mythology, but it is poorly documented compared to that of Ireland, and it shows evidence of greater modification from later stories. God is invoked constantly and the great array of pagan divinities seen, for example, in the Irish *Book of Invasions*, is nowhere present in the Welsh tradition. It is also possible to observe that international story-motifs are interleaved within the early Welsh material. There are links, too, between the mythological traditions of Wales and the Continental cycle of medieval Arthurian romance. The Welsh Arthur is a hero, who champions causes and braves the Otherworld in the thirteenth-century poem in the Book of Taliesin, the *Spoils of Annwn*.

Little in the extant Welsh manuscripts is demonstrably early enough for us to make direct links between the myths of Wales and the religion of the pagan Celts. So these myths can make, at best, a limited contribution to the construction of a pagan Celtic cult-system. The Welsh mythology is present but it has largely been reshaped within a different context, so that it is often barely recognisable as myth. The most relevant and the earliest material is contained within the *Pedair Ceinc y Mabinogi*, the *Four Branches of the Mabinogi* (sometimes known as the *Mabinogion*) and the *Tale of Culhwch and Olwen*, together with other material such as *The Dream of Rhonabwy* and *Peredur*. *Culhwch and Olwen* is perhaps the earliest of the mythological Welsh stories, dating to the tenth century in its original form. The *Mabinogi* was first compiled later, in the eleventh century. The early Welsh tradition is preserved in two collections: the *White Book of Rhydderch*, written in about 1300, and the *Red Book of Hergest*, which dates to the later fourteenth century. Much of the subject-matter both of *Culhwch and Olwen* and the *Four Branches* appears to relate to traditions which belong to earlier centuries than the ones in which they were compiled in their present form.

All the tales chronicle the activities of euhemerised supernatural beings whose divinity is not overt but is betrayed by their physical and moral stature. The myths of Wales abound in enchanted or magical animals; metamorphosis from human to animal form; heads with divine properties; and cauldrons capable of resurrecting the dead. There is a pagan Underworld, Annwn, presided over by Arawn, perceived as similar to life on earth and indeed very akin to the Otherworld described in the Irish tradition.

As with the Irish myths it is difficult to make other than tenuous links between Welsh myth and pagan Celtic religion as evidenced by archaeology. Occasionally Welsh beings may be directly related to Celtic divinities: Mabon the Hunter in *Culhwch and Olwen* is surely the Maponus of Romano-Celtic dedications in north Britain and Gaul. The supernatural qualities of cauldrons, human heads and animals are very close to the religious traditions which may be observed in the material culture of the pagan Celts. In addition there are some direct links between the Irish and the Welsh myths: shape-changing, animal-affinities, magical cauldrons exemplify this commonality of tradition.

The archaeological evidence

The main category of evidence which pertains directly to the pagan Celtic period is that of archaeology, the study of the material culture of Celtic religion: sanctuaries and sacred space; burial customs; ritual behaviour; epigraphy; and iconography (imagery, as portrayed in, for instance, sculpture, figurines or coins). This group of evidence has its own inherent difficulties: archaeologists can deal only with what has survived and, in addition, there are bound to be real problems associated with the interpretation of the thoughts and beliefs of communities who lived 2000 years ago solely from material remains of those beliefs. The other major problem with the archaeological evidence is that much of the iconography relating to Celtic religion dates from the time of Roman influence on Celtic lands, thereby making it difficult to disentangle Celtic symbolism and belief from the Roman tradition with which it became so closely intertwined.

The relevant archaeological evidence encompasses a period when Celts can first be distinguished by their material culture (*c.* seventh–sixth centuries

The famous gilt-silver cauldron from Gundestrup, Denmark. Second-first century BC.

BC) until the official demise of Celtic paganism, which is roughly coeval with the end of the Roman occupation of Celtic lands (around AD 400).

There is substantive archaeological evidence for pre-Roman Celtic religious space (see 'Druids, sacrifice and ritual', pp. 376–7). Built shrines did exist, although these did not conform to a formalised religious architecture. But sacred space often consisted of open-air enclosures, holy lakes, woods and springs. The Celts also dug deep pits or shafts in order to communicate with the powers of the Underworld. There is evidence, too, of repeated and formalised activity which has no apparent functional purpose and therefore may, with some confidence, be termed 'ritual behaviour'. This includes votive deposition in watery contexts, the ritual destruction of offerings, and sacrifice of living things.

In the 'free' or pre-Roman Celtic world there were relatively few stone or metal images of the gods (although the chance preservation of wooden objects leads us to believe that these may have been relatively common). Before the introduction of Graeco-Roman influences, resulting in a rich blend of intrusive and indigenous religious traditions which have left abundant material traces in the archaeological record, evidence of a Celtic belief-system is inconclusive. Celtic art was concerned more with the production of abstract design than with figural and overtly religious imagery. But there are some examples of free Celtic stone iconography in the form of reliefs and statues, the earliest dating to the sixth–fifth centuries BC, which occur in two main geographical regions: the Lower Rhône Valley (perhaps due to the influences of the Greek colony of Marseille, established in 600 BC) and central Europe. In the last two centuries BC figural imagery became more common, and bronze representations of animals, especially boars, may have had a quasi-religious function. The unique gilt-silver cult-cauldron from Gundestrup in Jutland, which probably dates to the second or first century BC, has long been accepted as important evidence for Celtic religious iconography. Its inner and outer plates are decorated with mythological scenes and deities, some of which betray exotic, eastern influences. But many features of the imagery are undoubtedly Celtic – the torc-bearing antlered god and the ram-horned serpent belong to the religious repertoire of Gaul – and the soldiers depicted bear Celtic Iron Age arms. Controversy surrounds the cauldron's place of manufacture: the best silversmiths of the period came from Thrace and Dacia in south-east Europe, and the vessel could have been made by foreign craftsmen for Celtic use. Such smiths may have heard descriptions of exotic creatures and thus included them in their art. There have been recent arguments in favour of an Indian origin for the Gundestrup Cauldron, but these conjectures overlook the close links between its religious art and that of Celtic Europe. The presence of the vessel in Denmark may be the result of looting by the Teutonic Cimbri from Gaulish territory.

Once Roman culture was established, its presence interacted on Celtic religious traditions which had previously been unexpressed in material terms. This interaction resulted in wide-scale representation of the gods, many of whom were totally alien to the Graeco-Roman pantheon. It also produced the tradition of dedicatory inscriptions which has given us names for Celtic divinities. This abundance of religious evidence, which expressed itself only under Roman influence, argues for the presence of a complex system of belief already in existence in the free Celtic period.

Archaeology and literature

Of the three groups of evidence summarised above, only archaeology and the vernacular sources contribute substantially to the construction of Celtic myth. In essence these two strands of mythological evidence have to be treated virtually as separate entities. Because of the chronological and spatial divergences already outlined, it is not possible to perceive the two as part of the same continuum of evidence. Nonetheless it is undoubtedly true that some links can be established between the material and literary sources. There are features common to both, which are too idiosyncratic to be due to chance: the sanctity of 'three'; the symbolism of cauldrons; the supernatural power of the human head; beliefs in an Otherworld similar to earthly life are a few of the traditions which bridge the gulf between the two main strands of testimony for Celtic myth.

The divine race of Ireland

The *Book of Invasions* records a series of successive mythical occupations of Ireland, beginning with an expedition led by Cesair and culminating in the coming of the Gaels (Celts). Indeed the function of this Myth of Invasions is to explain the presence of the historical Celts in Ireland. The central characters of the myth are the Tuatha Dé Danann (the 'People of the Goddess Danu'), a race of gods. A previous invader was Partholón who led the first colonisation of Ireland after the Flood. He came from Greece with his family and a large retinue, including three druids. Partholón and his people were wiped out by a plague. His character survives in modern Irish folklore as a fertility demon.

The last invaders chronicled in the *Book of Invasions* were the Gaels, the first Celts, speakers of a Goidelic language. According to mythic tradition the Gaels were descendants of the Sons of Míl, who came to Ireland from Spain. They dispossessed the Tuatha Dé, causing them to create a new kingdom beneath the earth. When the Gaels reached Ireland, they encountered three eponymous goddesses of the land, Banbha, Fódla and Ériu. Each demanded a promise from the invaders that, if they were successful in establishing themselves in Ireland, they would name the land after her. The seer or *fili* (see p. 376) Amhairghin assured Ériu that Ireland would bear her name and, in return, Ériu prophesied that the land would belond to the Gaels for all time.

The Tuatha Dé Danann

This race of divine beings, the mythical inhabitants of Ireland before the Celts, traced their beginnings back to their goddess-ancestress Danu. They brought with them to Ireland four powerful talismans: the Stone of Fál, which cried out at the touch of the rightful king; the Spear of Lugh, which guaranteed victory; the Sword of Nuadu, from which none escaped; and the Cauldron of the Daghda, from which no one departed unsatisfied. The Tuatha Dé were skilled in magic and in druid lore. Many of the gods were associated with particular functions: thus Oghma was skilled in war-craft; Lugh in arts and crafts; Goibhniu in smithing; Dian Cécht in medicine.

The most prominent gods of the Tuatha Dé Danann had special myths and stories associated with them and their skills. The Daghda (the 'Good God') was the tribal father-god, provider of plenty and regeneration. His two main attributes were a great club, of which one end killed and the other restored to

Small bronze horse-head mask, from Stanwick, Yorkshire, from the first century AD. It may have been a chariot-fitting. The artist has captured the spirit of the horse in a few simple lines.

life, and an enormous, inexhaustible cauldron. The image of the Daghda contains paradox: he is portrayed as gross and uncouth, a ridiculous, grotesque figure, who wears an indecently short tunic and eats an outrageous amount, while at the same time he is a powerful father of his tribe. This, though, is all part of his symbolism as god of fertility. Various legends concern his union with different goddesses, including Boann, goddess of the River Boyne. His coupling with the fearsome battle-fury, the Morrigán, ensures security for his people.

Goibhniu was one of a triad of craft-gods: he was the smith, Luchta the wright and Creidhne the metalworker. Together they forged magical weapons (each made a different part) for Lugh and the Tuatha Dé in their great battle against the Fomorians, local demons who pitted themselves against all invaders of Ireland. Goibhniu is the most developed character of the triad. His weapons always flew true and always killed. He had an additional role as host of the Otherworld Feast, where his special ale gave immortality. Dian Cécht, god of the craft of healing, derived his power from a combination of magic and herblore; he was at the same time a doctor and a smith. Thus he made the king Nuadu a silver arm to replace that which he lost in battle. Dian Cécht had the power to heal by magic: he restored dead members of the Tuatha Dé Danann by chanting incantations over a well in which the slain warriors were immersed. Manannán was a sea-god, and he is surrounded by marine imagery: his cloak was like the sea and the waves were his horses. He was also a magician (like his Welsh cognate Manawydan) and he provided help for the Tuatha Dé in their battles, including a boat which obeyed the thoughts of its sailor; a horse which travelled equally happily on sea and land; and a sword, Fragarach ('Answerer'), which could penetrate any armour. Manannán's magic pigs were symbols of regeneration: they could be killed and eaten one day and alive again the next, ready to be slaughtered for feasting.

Two of the best-known gods of the Tuatha Dé Danann are Nuadu and Lugh. Nuadu was king of the Tuatha Dé, but he had to relinquish his power after he lost his arm in battle: Insular rulers had to be physically perfect. During the interregnum, when Nuadu was temporarily disqualified from his leadership, a surrogate king was appointed. This was Bres ('the Beautiful'), a curious choice since he was half-Fomorian. His reign was not good: his niggardly ways caused Ireland's prosperity to fail. After the defeat of the Fomorians by the Tuatha Dé Danann, Bres was spared in return for his agreement to advise the Tuatha Dé on agricultural matters. Interestingly the Tuatha Dé were good at war and crafts but had no farming skills: for these they had to rely on the indigenous Fomorians. Nuadu was restored to the kingship after Dian Cécht made him a new arm, and he was thereafter known as Nuadu Argatlámh ('Nuadu of the Silver Arm'). But Nuadu was demoralised by the constant conflict with the Fomorians, and the young Lugh took over as leader. Nuadu may be identified with Nodens, the healer-god of Lydney in Gloucestershire: both names may mean 'Cloud-Maker', as if perhaps they were weather-gods.

Lugh ('Shining One') was related by blood both to the Tuatha Dé Danann and the Fomorians. He was a god of light, whose summer festival was Lughnasad. The Gaulish word *lugos* can mean 'raven', and there is a tenuous link between Lugh and these birds. Lugh was a warrior-hero, a sorcerer and master of crafts. He presented himself thus at the royal court of Nuadu at Tara. The association between Lugh and crafts has led some scholars to identify him with the Gaulish Mercury, whom Caesar describes as 'inventor of all the arts'. It was Lugh who exhorted Nuadu to stand up to the Fomorians, and he orchestrated the military campaigns which led to their rout. He himself slew the formidable Balor, leader of the Fomorians (and Lugh's own grandfather). In battle Lugh used both his own magic and the enchanted sword and boat of Manannán. Lugh's 'surname' was Lámfhada ('of the Long Arm'), a possible reflection of his skill with the throwing-spear or the sling (with which weapon he killed Balor).

The myths of Lugh are not confined to the *Book of Invasions*. In the Ulster Cycle the god appears as the Otherworld father of Cú Chulainn, who soothes and heals the young hero after his confrontations with the forces of Connacht.

After the dispossession of the Tuatha Dé Danann by the Gaels, the defeated gods establish a realm beneath the earth, a mirror-image of the upper world. Even though they are vanquished, they are able to deprive the Gaels of corn and milk, and they use this power to drive a bargain with them. So it is by mutual agreement that Ireland is divided into two parts, an upper and lower world. In their underworld kingdom the Tuatha Dé continue to control the supernatural by means of their magic. Each god possesses a *sīdh* (a fairy mound), which is part of the Happy Otherworld.

The battles for Ireland: the Fir Bholg and the Fomorians

In establishing themselves as lords of Ireland, the Tuatha Dé Danann had to fight two formidable groups of beings, each of whom was instrumental in shaping the 'history' of the island. The previous invaders, ousted by the Tuatha Dé, were the Fir Bholg, a mythical pre-Celtic people who probably took their name from a god, Builg. The Tuatha Dé defeated the Fir Bholg at the First Battle of Magh Tuiredh, and drove them into exile on the Aran Islands, where they are credited with building the massive fort of Dun Aonghusa on Inishmore. According to one tradition the Tuatha Dé allowed the Fir Bholg to retain the province of Connacht. It was at Magh Tuiredh that Nuadu lost his arm.

The second group the Tuatha Dé Danann had to face were the Fomorians or Fomhoire ('Under-demons'), a race of demonic beings who were permanent residents of Ireland, whom Partholón had already encountered in his earlier invasion and whom he fought in Ireland's first battle. When the Tuatha Dé occupied the land, the Fomorians caused them great trouble, pillaging their territory and imposing crippling taxes, with dreadful punishments for default-ers. The Fomorians had an awesome leader, Balor of the Baleful Eye, the gaze of whose single great eye caused instant death, and who could not be slain by any weapon. Balor dwelt on Tory Island, in constant dread of the fulfilment of a prophecy, namely his eventual destruction by his grandson. Despite his attempts to forestall this end (by keeping his daughter Eithne away from men) she became pregnant and gave birth to triplets. Balor cast them into the sea, but one survived: this was Lugh, who grew up to lead the Tuatha Dé against the Fomorians and who himself killed Balor with a slingshot through his eye.

The Fomorians are a divine race, like the Tuatha Dé Danann themselves. Balor represents the negative forces of evil whose power can only be neutralised by the light-force of Lugh, himself half-Fomorian and a relative of Balor. The Tuatha Dé and the Fomorians may represent the archetypal dualism between light and the chthonic (earthbound or underworld) forces, involving conflict but also mutual dependence. This last is demonstrated both by the ancestry of Lugh and by the Fomorians' agricultural skills which were necessary to the well-being of the Tuatha Dé Danann.

Sacral kingship

A powerful concept which underpins much of Insular myth is that of the sacral or divine king. The ruler of Ireland was inextricably linked to the fortunes and prosperity of the land itself. Thus the niggardliness of King Bres led to a blight of barrenness upon Ireland. The royal court of Tara was traditionally the sacred site of royal inauguration; here the ritual marriage was enacted between the king and the land, personified as the goddess of sovereignty. Ériu was one such personification, an eponymous goddess of Ireland who offered a golden goblet of red wine to successive mortal kings as a symbol of their union and of the florescence of the land. Medb of Connacht cohabited with nine kings, and no man could rule in Tara unless he first mated with her. A symbol of this union of divinity with mortal is the transformation of the goddess, often from an old hag to a young girl of great beauty.

The king-elect had to undergo various tests to prove the validity of his claim: the royal mantle had to fit him; the royal chariot must accept him; the Stone of Fál at Tara must shriek when touched by him. The rightful king must

This stone relief comes from a healing shrine at Mavilly, France, and is Romano-Celtic. It depicts a Celtic version of Mars, a protector against disease, with a goddess and ram-horned snake, symbol of regeneration and fertility.

Bronze stag, first century BC, from a religious hoard at Neuvy-en-Sullias, France.

be seen in a dream by the participant at the *tarbhfhess* or bull-sleep. Once elected, the king was hedged about with *geissi*, bonds or sacred rules of conduct, the betrayal of which would cause his downfall.

The Fionn Cycle

The Fionn Cycle belongs, in its developed form, to the twelfth century, although it contains earlier elements. Its central character is the supernatural hero Finn mac Cumhaill (sometimes written as Finn macCool). He is the leader of the Fianna, an élite war-band whose members are chosen by rigorous ordeals of strength and valour and whose conduct is controlled by strict rules and codes. The Fianna are pledged to support the king of Ireland against any invaders.

The divine status of Finn is demonstrated by many features of his life. He is reared by a druidess and he very early develops a strong affinity with the natural world symbolised, indeed, by his marriage to Sava, an enchanted woman, transformed to a deer by the evil force of the Black Druid. Finn's attainment of manhood is surrounded by mythological events: he acquires wisdom from Finnegas the Bard by eating the Salmon of Knowledge, for whom Finnegas has fished for seven years. When Finn arrives at Tara, his first act is to use magic to rid the court of Aillen, a malicious goblin who sets fire to the palace every year at the Celtic festival of Samhain (31 October/1 November). Throughout his life Finn has encounters with the supernatural world, hunting enchanted animals who entice him to the Otherworld, and meeting divinities such as the Morrígán, Nuadu and Oenghus. He has the gift of prophecy and is endowed with super-human battle-prowess. Finn's death is linked with a *geis* or bond that he must never drink from a horn. When the ageing hero is abandoned by the Fianna, he tries to prove his strength by leaping the Boyne, but he has broken his *geis* and perishes in the river.

In the Fionn Cycle, Finn is linked to other supernatural beings and happenings. His association with the young Diarmaid, his rival for the beautiful Gráinne's affection, shows him in a less than favourable light. His jealousy causes him to bring about Diarmaid's death by magic (see p. 349). This episode illustrates a typical aspect of Insular myth, the triangle of young lover, girl and ageing suitor, a theme with a precise parallel in the Ulster tale of Conchobar, Deirdre and Naoise (see pp. 349–50).

Finn's son Oisin ('Little Deer') is strongly associated with the Otherworld. He is bewitched by Niav of the Golden Hair, daughter of the king of Tir na n' Og (the 'Land of Forever Young'), and he goes to live with her. But he is homesick and plans to visit the upper world, against Niav's advice. She warns him never to set foot on Irish soil if he wishes to return to her. Oisin makes the journey, only to find that 300 years have passed. As he realises this, his harness breaks, he falls from his horse and, as he strikes the ground, dies instantly of extreme old age.

Myths of the Ulster Cycle

The group of epic prose tales known collectively as the Ulster Cycle concerns the activities of the Ulaid or Ulstermen, particularly their great conflict with the neighbouring province of Connacht, and the exploits of their hero, Cú Chulainn. Central to the cycle is the *Táin Bó Cuailnge*, or *Cattle Raid of Cooley*, probably first composed in the eighth century AD. The *Táin* is preserved in a number of major versions of which the earliest is in the *Leabhar na h Uidre* (the *Book of the Dun Cow*), compiled at Clonmacnois, Co. Offaly, by three monks, one of whom died in 1106. While it has generally been assumed that the Ulster Cycle was a late compilation of a much earlier oral tradition, scholars have recently put forward convincing arguments for its original composition as literature which was orally transmitted during the early historical period.

The considerable mythological content of the Ulster Cycle is very evident. Although compiled within a Christian milieu, the early monastic scribes may well have been the *filidh*, the keepers of past knowledge, who were steeped in the ancient ritual traditions and whose purpose it was to preserve myth in written form (See 'Druids, sacrifice and ritual', p. 376). There is no problem about the acceptance of some continuity of religious and ritual tradition from pagan Ireland into the Christian period.

The *Táin Bó Cuailnge (Cattle Raid of Cooley)*

The dominance of mythology in the Ulster Cycle is demonstrated dramatically by its central theme, the *Táin*, which describes the great war between Ulster and Connacht over a huge bull, the Donn ('Brown') of Cuailnge in Ulster. The story is not about cattle-rustling as a normal secular pastime, but about one fantastic and supernatural animal, around whom was woven a great quest- and battle-myth. The story begins with a foretale in which Queen Medb and her consort Ailill of Connacht boast, while in bed one night, of their respective possessions. The pair are fairly evenly matched save for one thing: Ailill owns a great white-horned bull, the Findbennach. Medb searches her land in vain for a creature of comparable splendour, but she learns of the great Brown Bull of Ulster, owned by one Daire mac Fiachniu, who agrees to lend the Donn to the queen in return for a large reward. However, on overhearing a brag made by Medb's men, to the effect that they would have taken the bull with or without his owner's consent, Daire refuses Medb and sends the Donn into hiding. Medb

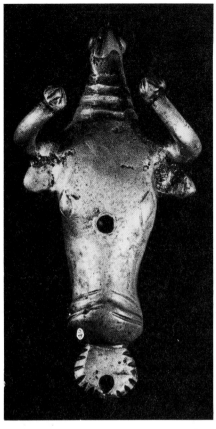

Front and side views of a bronze bucket-escutcheon in the form of a bull's head surmounted by that of an eagle, from Thealby, Lincolnshire. Late Iron Age.

Small bronze statuette of Mars with ram-horned snakes. It comes from a hoard of figurines found at Southbroom, Wiltshire and is Romano-Celtic.

decides to invade Ulster and seize the Donn by force, and there ensues a long-drawn-out war between the two provinces. On the night before the final confrontation, the Donn is sent into Connacht for safety. He bellows loudly at the scent of new territory and Ailill's Findbennach hears the intruder: no one but he before now has dared to make such a noise in his domain. Queen Medb's men appoint the mischief-maker Bricriu (a divine figure) as judge in the fight between the two bulls. The animals battle all day and night, all over Ireland. The Donn of Cuailnge eventually prevails, impaling Ailill's Findbennach on his horns, but he does not survive the conflict and dies of exhaustion.

The combat of the bulls symbolises the struggle between Ulster and Connacht: their death signals peace following the Pyrrhic victory of the Ulstermen. It is quite clear from the *Táin* that both bulls are of supernatural origin. Each is famed for his size and strength. The Donn is so big that fifty boys can ride on his back at once. The hero Ferghus comments that the two animals were sent purposely to Ireland by jealous gods, in order to cause war and bitterness among the people. He describes how the bulls are enchanted, metamorphosed creatures, who were originally swineherds and then took a succession of different forms, but had always been a source of strife and destruction. The Brown Bull is capable of human understanding: he responds immediately when Cormac exhorts him to ever greater efforts against the great bull of Connacht.

Cú Chulainn and other Ulster heroes

Three warriors stand out among the mythical heroes of Ulster: Ferghus mac Roich, Conall Cernach and – greatest champion of all – Cú Chulainn. The descriptions of all three betray their superhuman, semi-divine status. The first part of Ferghus' name is cognate with the Latin *vir* (man) and he is associated with fertility imagery: he is the first lover of Queen Medb, herself notoriously promiscuous, and mate of the nature-goddess Flidais. Ferghus is described as having a rampaging sexual appetite, requiring seven women to satisfy it. His image is that of a supernatural figure; he has the strength of 700 men; he is as tall as a giant; and at one meal he can consume seven pigs, seven deer, seven cows and seven vats of liquor. He possesses a magic sword, long as a rainbow.

Ferghus belongs to the court of King Conchobar of Ulster, and is foster-father to the young Cú Chulainn, but a particular episode causes the defection of himself and other heroes to Medb's court. This is the elopement of the lovers Deirdre and Naoise, and Conchobar's treachery (see p. 350). Some scholars are of the opinion that the Deirdre episode was added to the *Táin* specifically to explain Ferghus' defection. Once at Connacht, Ferghus liaises between Medb and Cú Chulainn. He dies at the hands of Ailill, while bathing in a pool with Medb. Some traditions credit Ferghus with authorship of the *Táin*.

Conall Cernach is the son of Amhairghin the poet and Fionnchaomh, daughter of the druid Cathbadh. 'Conall' means 'strong as a wolf'; 'Cernach' means 'victorious'. Like Ferghus, Conall has a large element of the supernatural in his imagery: he is the guardian of Ireland's boundaries and is clearly an ancestor-deity of part of the land. Again like Ferghus, he is a foster-father and tutor to Cú Chulainn. Conall is the epitome of the Irish champion: at the Feast of Bricriu (an Otherworld banquet), he boasts that he always sleeps with the severed head of a Connachtman beneath his knee. In the essentially similar tale of Mac Da Thó's Pig, he is described as wearing the head of Connacht's best warrior at his belt. Conall's status as semi-divine hero is attested by many episodes in his life; one tale relates his attack on a fort whose treasure is guarded by a great serpent. An affinity between hero and snake is displayed when the creature dives into Conall's waist-band and neither harms the other.

Cú Chulainn (the 'Hound of Culann') is the archetypal superhuman champion of epic tradition: 'Cú' is a common title for a warrior, but in this case the hound epithet has a specific meaning which relates to an episode in Cú Chulainn's childhood. When very young, he kills the hound of Culann the Smith, and pledges himself to guard the smithy in the dog's place. This dog-association continues throughout Cú Chulainn's life: he has a *geis* or bond on him not to partake of dog-flesh; he breaks the bond and thus sets the scene for his own destruction.

Cú Chulainn is destined to have a short but glorious life. He is brave, beautiful, strong, an invincible warrior. His identity may indeed derive from a warrior-cult, whence he was euhemerised into a pseudo-historical figure. His conception, life and death are closely linked with the supernatural. His father may have been the god Lugh or Conchobar, and there is incest (a mark of divinity) in his immediate ancestry. As occurs with the Welsh Pryderi, Cú Chulainn's birth is interlocked with that of horses: two foals are born at exactly the same moment as the hero, and they become his chariot-horses, the Grey of Macha and the Black of Saingliu. Cú Chulainn himself displays superhuman status from boyhood: he arrives at Conchobar's court of Emhain Macha, having routed 150 of the king's youth brigade. While still a boy, he demands arms, having heard a prophecy that whoever took up arms on a certain day should have a glorious future. Cú Chulainn breaks fifteen sets of weapons before he accepts the specially strengthened arms of Conchobar himself.

The young warrior is trained by Scáthach, a female teacher of warcraft and prophetess, who foretells Cú Chulainn's future through divination. He goes to war bearing magical weapons and armour, including the Gae Bulga, a barbed spear which inflicts only fatal wounds, and a visor, gift of Manannán the sea-god. Cú Chulainn's charioteer has the power to cast a spell of invisibility over his chariot. Cú Chulainn is the main champion of Ulster against the forces of Connacht, and of all the Ulstermen only he is exempt from Macha's curse, a weakness inflicted upon them in time of crisis. He kills huge numbers of Medb's forces single-handed. When the battle-rage is on him, he goes into 'warp-spasm', a berserk fit when he can no longer distinguish friend from foe. When berserk, he becomes a monster: his body spins within its skin; his hair stands on end, surrounded by a halo of light; his muscles swell; one eye bulges, the other sinks into his head; his howl causes all the local spirits to howl with him, driving the enemy mad with terror.

Bronze sculpture by Oliver Shepherd, 1916, now in the main Post Office, Dublin. It shows the death of Cú Chulainn, the raven-goddess Morrigán or Badbh perched on his shoulder to signify that he is dead and safe to approach. The Ulster hero bound himself to a tree in order to stay standing even in death.

The supernatural symbolism surrounding Cú Chulainn is intense: he uses magic to halt the advance of the Connachtmen; he has magical power over animals; he is linked with sacred numbers, having triple-coloured hair, seven pupils in each eye and seven digits on each hand and foot. He is closely associated with the divine: his foster-father (or natural father) is Lugh; he has many encounters with the war-goddess, the Morrigán; and he visits the Otherworld while still alive. Cú Chulainn is present at the Feast of Bricriu, a divine mischief-maker who foments strife and rivalry between warriors. At the feast Bricriu causes jealousy between the heroes Cú Chulainn, Conall Cernach and Loeghaire by offering each the champion's portion of pork.

Cú Chulainn's death at Magh Muirtheimne is surrounded with portents: when harnessed for the final battle, the Grey of Macha weeps tears of blood, and when Cú Chulainn mounts his chariot, all his weapons fall at his feet. Lastly he encounters the 'Washer at the Ford' washing his armour, a sure sign of doom in Insular myth. Cú Chulainn dies fighting, killed with a spear forged by Vulcan. The hero-light around his head dims and his death is signalled by the Badbh or the Morrigán, divine destroyers who, in raven-form, perch on his shoulder, emboldening the Connachtmen to come forward and decapitate him.

This is a chant of Cú Chulainn in his great conflict with Medb, referring to the mediator Ferghus:

My skill in arms grows great
On fine armies cowering
I let fall famous blows
On whole hosts I wage war
To crush their chief hero
and Medb and Ailill also
Who stir up wrong, red hatred

And black woman-wailing,
Who march in cruel treachery
Trampling their chief hero
And his sage, sound advice
– a fierce, right-speaking warrior
Full of noble acts.
(trans. Kinsella, 1969)

Medb and Conchobar

The opposed provinces of Ulster and Connacht are respectively ruled by Conchobar and Medb. Conchobar mac Nessa is a mythical king of Ulster, who rules from the royal court of Emhain Macha (which has been identified with Navan Fort near Armagh). Excavations have shown that the main occupation period, around 700 BC, focused on a large circular timber building standing beside a larger enclosure. In about 100 BC this 'royal' residence was replaced by a ceremonial building or sanctuary, a huge structure consisting of five circles of oak posts with, in the centre, a massive oak pillar which could be seen for miles.

Conchobar is very closely linked with war: he has a war-band known as the Red Branch Knights, of whom Cú Chulainn becomes chief. In addition Conchobar raises a youth-corps, trained as young boys in war-craft. The Ulster king's rule is steeped in myth and the supernatural. That he is a sacral king, appointed by druids, is demonstrated by an episode in the war with Connacht: when the defector Ferghus strikes the king's shield, it shrieks, as always happens when a sacred Irish ruler is in danger. Conchobar himself has prophetic powers, but most prophecy is in the hands of the royal druid Cathbadh, who repeatedly foretells the future of Ulster. He prophesies the doom to be caused by the beauty of Deirdre (see p. 350); the glorious life of Cú Chulainn; and he warns the Ulstermen against the destructive satire of the poet Aithirne. One of Cathbadh's responsibilities is to instruct young heroes in the craft of divination, the plotting of which days were lucky or unlucky for specific events or activities.

Conchobar is a complex character. He is related to Cú Chulainn as either foster-father, grandfather or natural father, and was once married to Medb before she became ruler of Connacht. His honour-code, unlike that of the archetypal hero, is flawed and his treachery to Naoise and cruelty to Deirdre bring about the defection of three prominent Ulster warriors. Conchobar meets his death by means of a brainball made from the head of the Leinster king Meas Geaghra (a brainball was made by mixing human brains with lime and allowing the mixture to harden). This curious but effective weapon was hurled at the Ulster king by Ceat mac Mághach in revenge for a wrong.

Medb ('She Who Intoxicates') is queen of Connacht, ruling variously at Tara and Cruachain, but in reality she is a euhemerised deity. Medb is a goddess of sovereignty and, in addition, she may be perceived as one of the group of Insular goddesses of war, sexuality and territory. Her rampant promiscuity symbolises Ireland's fertility, and the association of her name with alcoholic drink (specifically mead) is linked with the concept of the union between sovereignty goddess and mortal ruler, which is sanctified by the offering of a cup of liquor by the goddess to the king. Other demonstrations of Medb's divine status include her ability to change shape from hag to young girl, a characteristic of the Insular goddesses. She also shares with these deities the ability to wreak destruction: she brings about the deaths of Ferghus, Conall Cernach, her husband Ailill and Cú Chulainn. Medb's presence, driving round the battlefield in her chariot, can unman warriors; she can run with superhuman speed, and she has animal-familiars, a bird and a squirrel.

The great war between Ulster and Connacht is brought about largely by Medb's jealousy of Ailill, whose great bull she covets. She is warned by her poet and prophetess Fedelma that her enemy Cú Chulainn will destroy most of her army. Medb pits her wits against the Ulster champion, tries to bribe him with her daughter Finnebair and finally uses magic to bring about his death. Her own demise, chronicled in an eleventh-century text, occurs as a revenge-killing. She is slain by her nephew Furbaidhe whose mother, Clothra, Medb has murdered. The great queen-goddess meets an ignominious end, killed by a slingshot made of a lump of hard cheese.

The battle-furies

Three goddesses occur repeatedly in the Ulster Cycle: Macha, the Badbh and the Morrigán. They share the characteristic of possessing both single and triple form. In addition they all have a close link with animals: Macha has an affinity with horses; and like the Badbh and the Morrigán she has the ability to metamorphose from human form to that of a crow or raven. Each goddess is concerned with warfare and is, at the same time, a symbol of promiscuous sexuality.

Romano-Celtic bronze bull, triple-horned, from Glanum, southern France.

337

Macha is perceived as both one and three entities, but each of these three possesses a partially separate identity. One Macha, wife of Nemedh, a leader of the third mythical invasion of Ireland, is a prophetess who foresees the destruction of the country wrought by the *Táin* conflict. The second Macha is a warrior-ruler of Ireland. In her third identity Macha is a divine bride, the wife of a human, Crunnchu. Because Macha is a swift runner, her husband brags that she can outrun the king's horses. He has to make good his boast and, although Macha is about to give birth, she is forced to compete. She wins the race but dies giving birth to twins and with her dying breath curses the men of Ulster: at moments of crisis they will fall victim to a weakness as severe as that of a woman in childbirth, for five days and four nights.

Macha gave her name to the royal Ulster court of Emhain Macha ('Macha's Twins'). Her equine association is shown not only by her speed but also by the name of Cú Chulainn's horse, the Grey of Macha. She is a complex deity: prophet, warrior, ruler and goddess of sovereignty and fertility, closely bound up with the fortunes of the land itself.

The Badbh is essentially a goddess of battle and its destructive qualities. Her name evokes images of violence, fury and war. Like the Morrigán she may appear as woman or crow: one of her names is Badbh Catha ('Battle-Crow'). She is both a single and a triple goddess. Her power on the battlefield is psychological: her presence confounds and terrifies soldiers and she wreaks havoc, particularly among the Connachtmen. Badbh is a prophetess of doom and death. She helps Cú Chulainn, but alights in bird-form on his shoulder when he dies. She appears as a 'Washer at the Ford', rinsing the arms of a warrior who will shortly die in battle. In the story of Da Derga's Hostel, she appears to the doomed king Conaire as three black, crow-like hags: the imagery of bird and woman is merged.

The Morrigán ('Phantom Queen') strongly resembles the Badbh. She is particularly linked to Cú Chulainn: on one occasion, she appears to him as a beautiful girl but he, impatient for battle, brusquely spurns her advances. In revenge the Morrigán attacks him, changing form rapidly from eel to wolf to red heifer. Cú Chulainn wins but is exhausted. The Morrigán now appears to the hero in the form of an old woman milking a cow: she offers him milk and, in return, he blesses her, healing her wounds. Like the Badbh the Morrigán's most frequent appearance is as a death-crow, prophesying death on the battlefield. In this form she warns the Donn of Cuailnge that he will die. As a war-fury she unnerves armies and she, too, is a 'Washer at the Ford', a harbinger of death. But her prophecies are not always doom-laden: one episode in the 'Mythological Cycle' concerns her advice to the Daghda on how to deal with the Fomorians, enemies of the Tuatha Dé Danann.

In addition to her war-death role the Morrigán has powerful sexual imagery. This is seen most clearly in her mating with the tribal god, the Daghda, while astride a river. She is recalled in an Irish place-name, 'The Paps of the Morrigán'. She is a fertility-goddess, and her coupling with the god of the tribe reflects her function as a deity of sovereignty, identified with the land of Ireland.

Some early Welsh myths

Early Welsh mythology survives in recognisable form only in the *Four Branches of the Mabinogi*, the *Tale of Culhwch and Olwen* and the *Dream of Rhonabwy*, together with a few fragments, such as the poem *The Spoils of Annwn*, which has been ascribed to Taliesin.

The stories contained in these earliest vernacular Welsh compilations possess consistent supernatural elements involving god-like heroes, enchanted animals and magical happenings. Sometimes it is possible to perceive a deeper or more profound cosmogony buried within the stories, myths of creation or supernatural explanations of natural phenomena.

Pwyll, Arawn, Rhiannon and Pryderi

The First Branch of the *Mabinogi* contains the story of Pwyll, lord of Llys Arberth (Narberth), his wife Rhiannon, their son Pryderi, and the encounter between Pwyll and Arawn, lord of Annwn, the Welsh Otherworld. The meeting of Pwyll and Arawn is the first episode. It takes place when Pwyll is hunting deer and breaks his honour-code by taking another hunter's kill as his own. The hounds of this rival hunter are strange creatures, shining white with red ears (their colouring marking them as Otherworld beings – the same colours recur elsewhere in Welsh and Irish myth). The wronged huntsman is Arawn. Pwyll can redeem himself only by changing places with Arawn for a year, at the end of which he must meet, fight and kill Hafgan, Arawn's Otherworld enemy, and then return to meet Arawn at the present meeting-place, Glyn Cuch. Arawn warns Pwyll to strike Hafgan only once; if twice wounded, he will recover and be stronger than ever. An important element in the story is that both Pwyll and Arawn practise chastity in each other's households: neither ruler makes love to the wife of the other. Pwyll keeps his pledge and his year-end tryst, and thereafter the two rulers, returning to their own domains, maintain a close friendship. After Pwyll's death this relationship is preserved by his son Pryderi, to whom Arawn makes a precious gift of the first pigs in Wales. After his sojourn in Annwn, Pwyll himself is known as 'Lord of the Otherworld', a clear indication of his divine status.

This Otherworld episode is important in that it introduces a number of recurrent features of vernacular myth: the ability of certain humans to penetrate the Underworld while still alive; the need for Otherworld beings to employ full-blooded mortals to undertake certain tasks on their behalf; the use of

The horse-goddess Epona carrying fruit, on a Romano-Celtic relief from Kastel, Germany. Epona was not only a horse-deity but also had a role as a provider of plenty.

animals to facilitate encounters between the mundane and supernatural worlds.

The second significant episode in the First Branch, which is redolent with symbolism, concerns Pwyll and Rhiannon. While at Gorsedd Arberth (a magical meeting-place for the court), Pwyll sees a beautiful young woman in dazzling gold riding a large, shining-white horse and is strongly attracted to her. But although the horse is moving quite slowly, neither Pwyll nor his swiftest horsemen can catch up with it. In desperation Pwyll calls to the woman who immediately halts and speaks to him, introducing herself as Rhiannon and informing him that she has come to marry him in preference to her suitor, Gwawl. Pwyll wins Rhiannon by trickery (an act which has repercussions later in the *Mabinogi*); they marry and produce a son, Pryderi.

The character of Rhiannon herself is interesting in terms of myth. Her name may derive from that of a pagan goddess Rigantona ('Great – or Sacred – Queen'). The manner of her meeting with Pwyll has supernatural undertones, as does her consistent link with horses. After her alleged murder of her baby son (see below), it is Rhiannon's penance to sit beside the horse-block outside the gates of the court for seven years, offering to carry visitors up to the palace on her back, like a beast of burden. Rhiannon conforms to two archetypes of myth: in her generosity to the nobles of Llys Arberth when Pwyll brings her to court, which earns her the image of gracious, bountiful queen-goddess; and as the 'wronged wife', falsely accused of killing her son. Rhiannon's horse-imagery and her bounty have led scholars to equate her with the Celtic horse-goddess Epona (see p. 369).

Pryderi's birth is surrounded with supernatural mystery. When three nights old, he is stolen while his watch-women are asleep, and Rhiannon is wrongly blamed for his murder. The scene now shifts from Llys Arberth to the household of Teyrnon Twryf Liant, Lord of Gwent Is-Coed. Puzzling events take place here each May-eve, when Teyrnon's mare produces a foal which immediately disappears. At the same time that the boy Pryderi vanishes from Llys Arberth, Teyrnon keeps watch in the stable as his mare gives birth to her finest foal. Teyrnon sees a huge claw seize the foal, dragging it through the window. He hacks off the arm with his sword and saves his foal but, as he does so, he hears a scream and a commotion outside and runs out to investigate. It is too dark to see anything and he returns to the stable to find a baby boy lying on the threshold, wrapped in a silk shawl, a garment which signifies his noble rank.

Teyrnon and his wife foster the child, who grows with incredible speed and is far in advance of his age. At three years old the boy is given the foal. When he is four, his foster-parents note his uncanny resemblance to Pwyll and, knowing the story of the missing prince, realise that their boy must be Pryderi. He is restored to Pwyll and Rhiannon amid great rejoicing. The story of Pryderi contains considerable elements of myth: he disappears on the eve of 1 May, the great spring festival of Beltene (see p. 365); and his earliest life is closely associated with that of the foal, which is also taken on May-eve. (This affinity with horses is linked with that of his mother.) Finally the kidnapping of Pryderi when three nights old is precisely similar to the fate of the young Mabon, the Welsh hunter-god of *Culhwch* and *Olwen*, which is discussed later in this chapter. Celtic conception tales such as this, surrounded by curious events, may be symbolic of the transcendental meaning of birth – a child born of earthly parents but also the incarnation of supernatural essence – expressed by myth. (Similar mystery, of course, surrounds the birth of Christ.) It is clear that Pwyll, Rhiannon and Pryderi all possess elements of divinity, even though their status is never precisely defined.

Branwen and Bendigeidfran

The family ap Llyr of Harlech is the focus of the Second and Third branches of the *Mabinogi*. Their divine status is implied by their patronym 'Son of the Sea', which is cognate with the Irish god Lir. The central characters of the Second Branch are Branwen and her brother Bendigeidfran ('Brân the Blessed'), the word *brân* meaning a raven or crow. Although the Branch is named after Branwen, and therein she is described as one of the three chief ladies of the land, it is Brân whose superhuman stature dominates the story.

The tale begins with the betrothal of Branwen to Matholwch, king of Ireland. Branwen's brother Efnisien objects to the match and insults Matholwch by mutilating his horses as they stand stabled at the Harlech court. Matholwch is seemingly appeased by Bendigeidfran's gifts, greatest of which is a magical cauldron of Irish make, which can restore dead warriors to life. Matholwch and Branwen sail for Ireland, but the king's resentment smoulders and he treats his queen as a serf, sentencing her to work in the kitchens, her ears boxed each day by the butcher. Matholwch ensures that no word of this persecution can reach Wales, but Branwen herself takes a hand in her own destiny, training a starling to take word to her brother. Once Bendigeidfran hears of his sister's plight, he mobilises his army and makes war on Ireland.

Bendigeidfran, described as so large that no house can contain him, simply wades across the Irish Sea. Battle is joined and the forces of Wales win. But it is a Pyrrhic victory, and Bendigeidfran is mortally wounded by a poisoned spear. His supernatural status is displayed by his command to his men that they cut off his head and bear it with them to the White Mount in London, there to bury it facing east, so that no foreigner can invade Britain. The head of Brân has magical properties: it remains alive, conversing with his men, an uncorrupted talisman until its final interment. On their way to London with the head, Brân's men linger for seven years in Harlech and then for many more in the Happy Otherworld of Gwales, where they hear the three magical singing birds of Rhiannon. Branwen herself dies of a broken heart in Wales, at Aber Alaw, lamenting that because of her two great islands are in ruin.

Once again supernatural features run as a persistent thread through the tale: Brân's size and strength; the power of the severed head; the cauldron of resurrection; and the ability of humans to enlist the aid of animals. All these are concepts which have their parallel in Irish myth and in the symbolism expressed by pagan Celtic iconography.

Manawydan and the enchantment of Dyfed

Manawydan ap Llyr is a brother of Branwen and Brân. He is a cognate of the Irish Manannán, son of Lir, a sea-god. The marine identity of Manawydan is not developed in the Welsh myth, but the two share common features, such as the ability to conjure magic and a reputation for trickery. The Third Branch of the *Mabinogi* develops the character of Manawydan, after whom it is named. He is a magician, a trickster, a superb craftsman. Moreover, his cultivation of wheat may constitute a mythical explanation of the introduction of arable exploitation in Wales.

After Pwyll's death, Manawydan marries his widow, Rhiannon. Following a feast at Llys Arberth, the couple go up to the Gorsedd Arberth accompanied by Pryderi and Cigfa his wife. The four witness the casting of a spell over Dyfed: all settlements and inhabitants of the land vanish and the countryside itself is shrouded in a magical mist. Since nothing is left in Dyfed, the four travel to England where Manawydan and Pryderi set up as craftsmen, saddlemakers or cobblers. But wherever they go, Manawydan's skill incites the envy and malice of other artisans, who hound them out of town after town. They return to Dyfed where they survive by hunting. On one expedition Manawydan and Pryderi have a supernatural encounter with a huge boar whose coat is dazzling white, betokening his Otherworld origins. The creature lures the hounds towards a strange castle, unknown to the hunters. Despite Manawydan's prophetic warning, Pryderi follows the dogs and falls under an enchantment: in the castle he touches a beautiful golden bowl suspended from

Bronze group of hunters with boar and stag, of the third century BC, from Balzars, Liechtenstein. The men are dressed as soldiers, and the animals have exaggerated tusks and antlers.

the air by chains and sticks fast to it. His feet are rooted to the ground and he cannot speak. On hearing of his fate Rhiannon follows him and she also falls under the spell of the bowl.

Bereft of his dogs, Manawydan cannot hunt and instead he begins to cultivate wheat. The crops flourish but, just before harvest, two fields are destroyed by armies of mice. Manawydan lies in wait for them as they attack the third field; all escape but one pregnant mouse, slower than the rest. Manawydan now embarks on the bizarre process of hanging the mouse, refusing pleas for mercy from several passers-by. Finally his preparations are interrupted by a bishop who attempts to redeem the mouse. Manawydan refuses to yield unless certain demands are met: Pryderi and Rhiannon must be restored, and the seven cantrefs of Dyfed released from their enchantment. (A cantref was a group of 100 farmsteads.) Thus Manawydan recognises the bishop as a fellow magician. The terms are accepted: the bishop identifies himself as one Llwyd, explaining that he cast the spells in order to avenge the wrong done by Pwyll to Rhiannon's suitor Gwawl in robbing him of his bride. The mouse is Llwyd's metamorphosed wife, sent especially with her transformed women to destroy Manawydan's corn. Dyfed is restored and the mouse returned to human form: Manawydan's magic proves the stronger.

Math, Gwydion, Lleu and Blodeuwedd

The Fourth Branch of the *Mabinogi* concerns Gwynedd and the divine dynasty of Dôn. The story of Math, Lord of Gwynedd, may represent an early narrative, which is in fact a Myth of Creation and Fall belonging to the pre-Christian Celts. This may explain the curious description of Math himself who, unless at war, has to sit with his feet in the lap of a virgin: he depends on this contact in order to remain alive, and the virginity of the foot-holder is essential.

And at that time Math son of Mathonwy would not be alive, except while his feet were in the lap of a virgin, unless it were the disturbance of war which prevented him.
(Jones and Jones, 1976)

343

The most likely interpretation for this piece of myth is that some kind of sacral kingship is represented, whereby the life-force of the land is concentrated within the virgin, with her undissipated and undiluted sexuality. There may be a parallel with the Insular tradition of a ritual marriage between mortal king and goddess of sovereignty, the personified force of the territory, in order that the land may prosper and be fertile. If Math's contact with the virgin foot-holder does similarly signify a link with the well-being of Gwynedd, the fact that war releases him from this bond may mean that warfare is perceived to generate a life-force of its own.

In 'Math' war breaks out between Gwynedd and Dyfed, fomented by Math's nephew Gwydion, who robs Pryderi of his pigs by means of magic trickery. Gwydion's brother Gilfaethwy lusts after Math's foot-holder Goewin, and while Math is at war the two brothers conspire to rob her of her virginity. Some scholars liken the rape of Goewin to the Fall from Grace of Adam and Eve, an act which heralds trouble and sorrow for humankind. When Math returns, his fury causes him to punish the brothers, turning them for three consecutive years into pairs of different animals: a stag and hind; a boar and sow; and a wolf and she-wolf. The brothers swap sexes each time and, every year, they produce animal-offspring. These children Math restores to human form but they retain their animal-names, thus maintaining their link with wild nature:

> The three sons of false Gilfaethwy,
> Three champions true,
> Bleiddwn, Hyddwn, Hychdwn.
> (trans. Jones and Jones, 1976)

The second important episode in 'Math' concerns Arianrhod and her son. Arianrhod applies to Math for the vacant post of virgin foot-holder, but she fails the test of purity, giving birth to two sons as she steps over Math's magical staff. The main story concerns the fate of the second boy, on whom his mother places three curses: one that he shall have no name unless she agrees to name him; another that he shall bear no arms unless she equips him herself; the third that he shall have no mortal wife. The magician Gwydion tricks Arianrhod into naming the boy – Lleu Llaw Gyffes (the 'Bright One of the Skilful Hand') – and into arming him. Math and Gwydion together conjure a wife for Lleu, created from the flowers of oak, broom and meadowsweet and named Blodeuwedd.

The character of Lleu is beset with enigma and paradox from the time of his birth to a mother who is apparently virgin. His destiny imposed upon him by his hostile mother is interesting: she denies him name, weapons and a wife, the three rites of passage which are necessary for the attainment of manhood. It is only by Gwydion's magic that Lleu can reach maturity. Lleu's death is equally contradictory: he cannot be killed inside or out-of-doors, neither on land nor water, neither naked nor clothed, and only by a spear made at a time when work is forbidden. Such a 'difficult' death generally involves a woman's betrayal and it is so here. Blodeuwedd, born without roots and thus without moral sense, is faithless; she and her lover Gronw Pebyr conspire to murder Lleu by causing him to reveal to his wife the secret formula by which he can be slain. When Lleu adopts the only position in which he is vulnerable, the hidden Gronw spears him but, instead of dying, Lleu screams and, turning into an eagle, flies into an oak tree. Here Gwydion finds him, enticing him down with song and restoring him to human form. In direct contrast Blodeuwedd is punished by being turned into an owl, shunned by all other birds and condemned to hunt alone at night.

Lleu is probably an ancient British god, perhaps cognate with the Irish Lugh (see p. 327) with whom he shares a name associated with light. His birth, destiny and immortality imply his divine status, as does the care taken to protect him by the magician Gwydion. The deception, riddle and contradiction which underpin 'Math' are all devices common to myth and may be found equally in the Irish tradition and in stories of the Graeco-Roman pantheon.

Culhwch, Olwen and Twrch Trwyth

In *Culhwch and Olwen* the supernatural is ever-present; there are beings who are of indisputably divine status. Mabon ('Divine Youth'), a hunter-god, is son of Modron ('Mother'), arguably a reference to a Welsh mother-goddess cult. He resembles Pryderi in that both are stolen when three nights old. The archetypal 'Young Man' represented by Mabon has its Irish parallel in Oenghus. It is in *Culhwch and Olwen* that Gofannon, the smith-god, appears; he is cognate with the Irish Goibnhiu (see p. 326), the divine smith of the Tuatha Dé Danann.

Culhwch is of royal blood, the cousin of Arthur. Both Culhwch's birth and his name betray an affinity with animals: before he is born his mother develops a violent antipathy to pigs and, on passing a herd, gives birth in her fright and then flees, abandoning the baby. The child is found by the swineherd who names him Culhwch ('Pig-run') and restores him to his parents Cilydd and Goleuddyd. The link between Culhwch's birth and pigs betrays supernatural influence similar to that of Pryderi and the foal (see pp. 340–1).

Goleuddyd dies and Cilydd remarries: the new wife has a daughter whom she wishes Culhwch to wed, but he demurs on the grounds of his youth. The queen curses the boy, proclaiming that the only woman Culhwch will ever marry is Olwen, daughter of Ysbaddaden, Chief Giant. On hearing Olwen's name, Culhwch falls passionately in love with her and pledges himself to find her. Cilydd suggests that Culhwch go to visit Arthur, ostensibly to get his hair cut: this presumably represents a rite of passage from youth to manhood. Culhwch sets out in splendour, like a young god or hero, with a glowing aura about his face, fully armed with a battle-axe, a golden sword and a hatchet which 'can make the air bleed'. He has an ivory hunting-horn and two grey-hounds and is mounted on a great horse. As Culhwch reaches Arthur's court, his superhuman, godlike rank is revealed: the keeper of the gate refuses the unannounced Culhwch entry; the hero responds by threatening to utter three shouts that will make women barren and cause those who are pregnant to abort. The threat of barrenness probably symbolises Culhwch's ability to make Arthur's crops and herds infertile as well.

Bronze boar of the late first century BC or early first century AD, found in the Lexden Tumulus, a British chieftain's grave, at Colchester. The animal has an erect dorsal crest, symbolic of aggression and ferocity.

Culhwch persuades Arthur to help him in his search for Olwen, and the story now reveals itself as a Quest Tale. After a year Olwen is found and told of Culhwch's love. Her appearance and the heavy gold torc that she wears indicate her high rank. Olwen explains that her father will never consent to her marriage since her wedding presages Ysbaddaden's death. Nevertheless Culhwch approaches him and is given a series of 'impossible' tasks – reminiscent of the Labours of Hercules – which he must accomplish to win Olwen.

The most insuperable task forms the central core of the whole myth. This is the retrieval of the scissors, razor and comb from between the ears of one Twrch Trwyth, a huge, destructive boar who was once a king and who, together with his followers, has been transformed by God as a punishment for his evil ways. Thus we meet the concept of transmogrification being imposed upon wrong-doers, just as occurs in 'Math'. In order to track down the great boar, Culhwch and Arthur have first to enlist the help of Mabon the Hunter, who is incarcerated in Gloucester Castle and of whom there has been no trace since he was stolen from his mother Modron as an infant. By the time Mabon is released from what must be an enchanted imprisonment, he is the oldest of all living creatures, a paradox for one named 'the Youth'. In this quest-within-a-quest for Mabon, Culhwch and Arthur are aided by magical animals: the Blackbird of Kilgowry; the Eagle of Gwernabwy; the Stag of Rhedenure; the Salmon of Llyn Llaw and other enchanted beasts, the most ancient animals on earth. One of Arthur's men, Gwrhyr, is able to communicate with these creatures in their own speech. With Mabon's help, Twrch Trwyth is finally overcome, after a chase which spans south Wales, Cornwall and Ireland. The razor, scissors and comb are delivered; Culhwch and Olwen finally marry.

Elements of the supernatural manifest themselves very clearly in *Culhwch and Olwen*. Culhwch's birth-link with pigs is developed in his final struggle against the great boar. The animal-theme is strong: enchanted and metamorphosed beasts are prominent and contribute considerably to the outcome of the quest. Mabon the Hunter and Modron are overtly divine; the supernatural status of Culhwch himself is implied above all by his ability to threaten the future of Arthur's domain by imposing the curse of infertility on his people.

The divine lovers

Many Celtic myths have as their central theme the love between two supernatural beings or between god and mortal, often with destructive results. A common pattern is the triangle of young lover, girl and unsuccessful (frequently elderly) suitor, and the jealousy which thus arises has damaging effects upon the land and its community. Irish myth also contains the theme of sacral kingship, whereby the union of king and goddess promotes the prosperity of the land. Interestingly the concept of divine love and marriage has a counterpart in the archaeological evidence for pagan Celtic religion: divine couples, represented both epigraphically and in the iconography, were venerated. In these cults the partnership itself seems to be symbolically significant and to produce harmony and prosperity.

Love and jealousy in Irish myth

Midhir and Étain

The *Book of Invasions* describes Midhir as lord of the *sīdh* (Otherworld mound) of Bri Léith, one of the Tuatha Dé Danann. One story of Midhir revolves around his love for a mortal girl, Étain. This excites the jealousy of Midhir's wife Fuamnach, who casts a spell on the girl, turning her first into a pool of water and then into a purple fly. Although Étain is mortal, she has certain supernatural powers, even in her transformed state. She can hum Midhir to sleep and warn him of an enemy's approach. Fuamnach conjures a magical wind which blows Étain away, but she is rescued and harboured by Oenghus, god of love, in his palace on the River Boyne. Oenghus' power is such that he can partially cancel the curse and Étain is restored to human form from dusk to dawn. But the hapless girl is then blown away once more and this phase of her life ends when she falls into a cup of wine belonging to the wife of the Ulster hero Edar. The wine is drunk and Étain is reborn as a new child, 1000 years on.

Midhir has maintained his quest for Étain over the 1000-year period. When he eventually discovers her, she is a grown woman, married to the king of Ireland. The god wins her back to him by means of trickery, managing to contrive a kiss, which causes Étain to remember him and love him once more. Midhir escapes with his love, having first transformed both of them into swans.

The character of Étain is interesting and betrays her superhuman status. She is reborn but retains her old identity 1000 years later; she is intimately linked

Stone relief showing a genius cucullatus with an egg and a mother-goddess with fruit or bread, from Cirencester, Gloucestershire. The two deities are often associated in the Cotswold region. The egg is a powerful symbol of new life.

with two deities, Oenghus and Midhir; and, most importantly, by her marriage to the Irish king, she fulfils the function of the goddess of sovereignty, validating his rule by their union. Midhir himself is a complex god, a lord of the Otherworld and a shape-shifter, but who requires a human mate whom he can endow with a status as elevated as his own.

Oenghus and Caer

Oenghus of the Birds was an Irish god of love, one of the Tuatha Dé Danann. He is known as 'mac Oc' (the 'Young Son') because of the circumstances surrounding his birth to the Daghda and Boann. The divine pair concealed their illicit union and Boann's pregnancy by causing the sun to stand still in the heavens for nine months: so Oenghus was both conceived and born on the same day.

Oenghus' main role is as an aid to lovers in peril. Thus he intervenes in the plight of such couples as Midhir and Étain. But in 'The Dream of Oenghus' the god himself is smitten with an 'impossible' love. He dreams of a young girl whom he does not know. On waking he finds he is in love with her, and discovers her name to be Caer Ibormeith (Caer 'Yew-berry'). His search for her leads him to a lake where he finds Caer with her girl-companions. Caer is a shape-shifter: every other year, at the festival of Samhain (see p. 365), she is transformed into a swan, together with her women. Oenghus observes that each pair of girls is joined by a silver chain, but Caer has a chain of gold. Caer's father refuses Oenghus' attentions to his daughter. The only way the two can marry is for Oenghus to take Caer when she changes to swan-shape. So, at Samhain, Oenghus approaches Caer's lake and flies off with her, having changed himself also to bird-form. The pair fly three times round the lake, their magical song sending everyone to sleep for three days and nights. The couple then fly to Oenghus' palace at Brugh na Bóinne.

Like the Welsh Mabon, Oenghus is the archetypal 'Young Man' or 'Divine Youth'. Caer is also of supernatural status: her father has his own *sídh* or Otherworld dwelling-place, and she has shape-changing powers. The image of enchanted swans, linked by chains of precious metal, is not confined to this myth but recurs, for instance, in tales associated with Cú Chulainn.

Diarmaid and Gráinne

The story of Diarmaid ua Duibhne is chronicled in the Fionn Cycle. The elopement tale is first mentioned in the tenth-century *Book of Leinster*, and was incorporated into the Fionn Cycle at a later date. The tradition of Diarmaid's death occurs in compilations of the twelfth–fifteenth century. The tale of Diarmaid and Gráinne illustrates the recurrent theme of the mythic triangle: young girl, youth and jilted elderly suitor. Diarmaid is a lieutenant of Finn, ageing leader of the Fianna. Gráinne is betrothed to Finn but, at the pre-wedding feast, she sees Diarmaid and falls in love with him. Diarmaid is under a bond of loyalty to Finn and refuses Gráinne's advances, but she shames him by calling his honour as a man into question. The two flee from the royal court of Tara, and are pursued for many years by Finn. After seven years the old war-leader is apparently reconciled to the couple's union but the destructive result of the triangle is demonstrated by Finn's treachery towards Diarmaid. He invites his rival to take part in a boar-hunt, but he is aware of a prophecy that Diarmaid will meet his death in confrontation with this creature, the Boar of Boann Ghulban, who is in fact Diarmaid's enchanted foster-brother. There are two versions of the hero's death: in the first he is killed by the boar; in the second he overcomes the beast but dies when pierced by one of its poisonous bristles. Finn himself has the power to save Diarmaid by bringing him water cupped in his hands, but he hesitates and Diarmaid dies.

The fate of the couple is strongly bound up with the supernatural: the pair are aided in their trouble by Oenghus, who is Diarmaid's foster-father. He gives them advice in their wanderings, such as never to sleep two nights in one place. On their travels the couple enter the Forest of Duvnos, wherein is a Tree of Immortality, guarded by the Giant Sharvan. Though the monster is virtually immortal, Diarmaid slays him and both he and Gráinne eat the berries of the tree, thereby gaining near-immortality themselves. Diarmaid's death is only brought about by means of enchantment.

Deirdre and Naoise

The ninth-century text which chronicles the ill-fated elopement of Deirdre and Naoise was later incorporated into the Ulster Cycle as a foretale of the *Táin*. King Conchobar of Ulster has a chief storyteller, Fedlimid, the father of

Stone carving of a divine couple from Pagny-la-Ville, France. She has a patera (offering-plate) and he has a hammer and pot.

Deirdre. Before her birth the court druid, Cathbadh, prophesies that the child will grow up to be beautiful but will bring ruin to the men of Ulster. Conchobar's warriors clamour for her death, but the king decides to rear her in secret and then marry her when she comes of age. When Deirdre is a young girl, still kept cloistered away from men, she observes Conchobar skinning a calf in the snow and a raven drinking the blood. She proclaims that the man she chooses will have the same three colours: black hair, white skin and red cheeks. Deirdre's companion Leabharcham comments that there is such a man, Naoise, son of Uisnech. The girl contrives to meet him but he is mindful of the prophecy and rejects her advances. Deirdre then challenges his honour (like Gráinne) and the pair elope, in the company of Naoise's two brothers, Ainle and Ardan.

The fugitives flee to Scotland, but are recalled to Emhain Macha with a false pardon sent by Conchobar. Only Deirdre suspects treachery. They return, and the three brothers are slain by one Eoghan. After keeping her captive for a year Conchobar plans to give Deirdre to Eoghan, but she kills herself rather than marry her lover's destroyer.

There are several points of mythological interest in this story. The doom-laden love-triangle of girl, youth and spurned suitor recurs. Deirdre herself is surrounded with mystery: the pre-birth prophecy about her effect upon Ulster, and the fact that it is because of her that three great heroes desert Conchobar's court (see pages 333-6); her own prophetic gift; her personality, which is stronger than that of Naoise, all raise Deirdre above normal human status. Naoise and his brothers are interesting: of the three only Naoise has any genuine identity. The brothers are mentioned perhaps to endow the story with triadic symbolism. Many of the Welsh and Irish myths contain references to 'three' as a magical or sacred number.

The Welsh lovers

The Welsh lovers need be discussed only briefly here, since the relevant myths have been examined on pages 340-6. In the Welsh tradition two sets of lovers stand out as being of particular importance: Pwyll and Rhiannon in the First Branch of the *Mabinogi*, and Culhwch and Olwen, in the tale of that name. The story of Pwyll's wooing of Rhiannon contains elements which are comparable with those of the Irish tradition: it is Pwyll's trickery against Rhiannon's suitor Gwawl which causes the enchantment of Dyfed, chronicled in the Third Branch. The *Tale of Culhwch and Olwen* is somewhat different, but Culhwch's love causes momentous happenings and gives rise to the whole supernatural panoply of beings who appear in the myth. This love is not a herald of disaster, but it is strong enough to mobilise Arthur, Mabon and other larger-than-life individuals; and each task imposed upon Culhwch by Ysbaddaden can be accomplished only with divine help.

Divine couples in pagan Celtic religion

The pairing of male and female deities was a prominent feature of the Celtic pantheon, as expressed in the iconography and epigraphy of Romano-Celtic Europe. A certain patterning can be discerned, in that when introduced to the Celtic world, gods of Graeco-Roman origin often acquired female consorts or partners who were indigenous to the conquered territory. So inscriptions frequently allude to a god with a Classical name linked to a Celtic-named goddess, an important example of this tradition being Mercury and Rosmerta. The male deity might have a Roman name but a Celtic epithet: such is the case with Apollo Grannus and Sirona. Alternatively both deities might be called by native names: Sucellus and Nantosuelta are good examples. Some divine couples were venerated over a wide area: Mercury and Rosmerta were worshipped in Britain, Gaul and the Rhineland. Others, like Ucuetis and Bergusia at Alesia, seem to have been invoked in only one place.

The symbolism associated with all the divine pairs worshipped in pagan Celtic Europe appears to show that the couples were invoked as promoters of health, wealth or abundance. Thus Sucellus (the 'Good Striker') and his consort Nantosuelta ('Winding Brook'), named on a stone at Sarrebourg in eastern Gaul, were particularly linked with the wine-harvest, especially in Burgundy. Sucellus' hammer struck the earth to fertilise it, and the domestic aspect to their cult is displayed by Nantosuelta's emblem of a house on a pole. Rosmerta's name means 'Great Provider', and the Celtic Mercury was invoked particularly as a bringer of commercial success, symbolised by his purse (a symbol that is Classical in origin) or money-chest. In Britain, Rosmerta has a vat or bucket whose symbolism may be regenerative like that of the cauldron of renewal so prominent in Irish and Welsh myth.

A number of the divine couples represented in Celtic imagery are associated with healing and protection. Thus the 'Celtic Apollo' and his various partners are strongly linked with cults of healing springs. Apollo and Sirona were worshipped at Hochscheid in Germany and elsewhere. Apollo Moritasgus and Damona were invoked at the springs of Alesia. Interestingly there was a close affinity between healing and fertility. Sirona and Damona, consorts of Apollo, are both symbolised with ears of corn and with serpents, which combine rebirth-imagery (because of the sloughing of their skins) with that of fecundity. At Hochscheid, Sirona carries eggs, powerful emblems of both fertility and regeneration. The goddesses sometimes reveal their 'polyandrous' nature: Damona, for instance, is coupled with Apollo at Alesia, with another healing god, Borvo, at Bourbonne-les-Bains, and with a local deity Abilus at Arnay-le-Duc, all in Gaul. Ancamna was the consort of the great healer Lenus Mars at Trier, but additionally of Mars Smertrius at Möhn, also in Treveran territory. The link between the Celtic Mars and healing seems to have derived from the idea of the god as a fighter/guardian against disease, barrenness and death.

Some divine couples were strictly territorial, personifications of the land or settlement where they were invoked. Such were Luxovius and Bricta at Luxeuil-les-Bains and Bormanus and Bormana at Die in France and Veraudinus and Inciona at Widdenburg in Luxembourg. This close tie with the land has a particular interest in connection with Insular mythical traditions of sacral kingship (see pp. 328-30).

Whether or not it is sensible to attempt a link between the archaeological and vernacular evidence, what is clear from the iconography of divine couples is that the success of their cults lay, at least partly, in the marriage itself, and this may account for the popularity of divine couples throughout the Celtic world.

The sky and sun myths

For many aspects of Celtic religion and myth, the literary sources are virtually silent, and it is necessary to turn to archaeology to fill in some of the gaps. The pagan Celts perceived numinosity (the presence of spirits) in all aspects of the natural world. Archaeological evidence suggests that, of all natural phenomena, the sun was especially invoked as a life-force, as a promoter of fertility and healing and as a comfort to the dead. It is difficult to construct a mythology or theology for the sun-cult by means of archaeological data alone, but some of the iconography which expresses solar invocation is sufficiently complex to allow some insight into the belief-systems which it represents.

The vernacular tradition

In contrast with the material culture of pagan Celtic Europe, the evidence for a solar religion is sparse indeed when we turn to the Irish and Welsh vernacular myths. There are hints at a sun-cult, but they are indirect and indistinct. In Ireland the eponymous goddess Ériu possibly possessed a solar function, in her role as goddess of sovereignty, part of the ritual associated with sacral kingship. In a myth which grew up around the enactment of inaugural ritual, the sun is perceived as a golden cup full of red liquor (perhaps wine) borne by Ériu and handed to successive mortal kings of Ireland to legitimise or ratify their election and at the same time to promote the prosperity and fertility of the land. This myth is interesting for two reasons: first because the sun is associated with a goddess, in contrast to most sun-cults which are represented almost exclusively by male deities. In the pagan Celtic tradition as expressed by iconography, there is a solar goddess, represented by clay figurines, whose body is marked with sun-symbols. So there is a suggested link between the evidence of myth and of imagery. The second significant point concerns the Insular association between the sun and fecundity. This again is something which may be traced in the archaeological evidence for solar cults.

The veneration of the sun may be concerned with heat, light or both. If the light-element is emphasised, it may be difficult to distinguish between the sun and the sky as a source of cult. The Irish god Lugh ('Shining One') is clearly associated with brilliant light; he may or may not have been a sun-god, but his role as a divine young warrior, conqueror of evil, has its parallel in some of the pagan iconography considered below.

Bronze figurine of the Celtic sky-god with his solar wheel, dedicated to Jupiter and the 'numen' of the Emperor, from Landouzy, France.

The Welsh mythological tradition contains no overt evidence for a solar cult. However, there is one myth in which allusion to a god of light may be inferred. This is in 'Math', the Fourth Branch of the *Mabinogi*, which tells the story of the supernatural Lleu Llaw Gyffes (p. 343). His name means 'Bright One of the Skilful Hand', and may be cognate with Lugh. Apart from his name, details of Lleu's behaviour also imply an association with celestial imagery. When struck by the spear of his wife Blodeuwedd's lover, Lleu changes into an eagle and flies into an oak tree. In pagan Romano-Celtic symbolism both the eagle and the oak were closely linked with the cult of the sky-god, whose Roman name was Jupiter.

Sun-cults in pagan Celtic Europe

From as early as the middle of the Bronze Age, prehistoric communities in much of Europe venerated the sun and made its image in the form of the spoked wheel. The wheel-symbol was apparently chosen because of its shape and because of the element of movement common to both wheel and sun. In the early Iron Age clues as to the nature of celestial and solar religion are necessarily indirect, but certain repetitive behaviour is indicative of attitudes to the sun's power, as perceived by devotees. Warriors wore solar amulets as protection against harm in battle; people were buried in tombs accompanied by miniature sun-symbols, as if to illuminate their dark journey to the Otherworld. Worshippers offered model wheels in such shrines as that at Alesia in Burgundy, and cast them into rivers, such as the Seine, Oise and Marne, as votive offerings.

The solar wheel-god

The Romano-Celtic period in Britain and Europe saw a great burgeoning of the solar religion. The evidence is for a multi-faceted, complex cult, the powers of the sun being perceived as having many functions and concerns. In this period the image of a sun-god, associated with his wheel-emblem, displayed Celtic perceptions of a solar power in human form. This was perhaps anticipated by the late Iron Age depiction of a wheel-god on the Danish Gundestrup Cauldron, which dates to the second–first century BC. The most prominent Romano-Celtic iconography represents the solar wheel-god as conflated, to an extent, with the imagery of the Roman sky-god Jupiter. A statuette of a wheel-bearing god from Landouzy in France, dedicated to Jupiter, expresses this tradition.

Interestingly the association between the sun and war, noted in the Iron Age, continues in the Romano-Celtic phase, when a distinctive group of images displays the solar/sky-god in battle against the forces of darkness and evil. These sculptures crown tall, tree-like pillars, known as 'Jupiter-Giant columns' because of their dedication to the Roman sky-god. Although the iconography of the victor riding down the foe may have its origins in Roman art, the images on the summit of these columns nonetheless depict a Celtic religious tradition, where the god of light and life is mounted on horseback, brandishing his protective solar wheel like a shield and his thunderbolt as a weapon, riding down the chthonic forces personified as a snake-limbed giant. The link between sun and war is not confined to Jupiter-columns. The north British war-god Belatucadrus has a name meaning 'Fair Shining One'; the Gaulish Mars Loucetius, invoked with his consort Nemetona at Bath, also bears a surname evocative of light. The pottery appliqué figure of a warrior-god at Corbridge (Northumberland) is accompanied by a wheel.

The solar horse

Horses were closely linked to the solar cult. They were envisaged as animals of sufficient speed and prestige to carry the sky-god into battle, but their association with the sun is much more wide-ranging. In many Indo-European sun-myths, the solar disc was perceived as being carried across the sky in a chariot pulled by a horse-team. The chariot of the Greek god Apollo was the prototype for the reverse of many Celtic coins: Celtic artistry frequently reduced the image to a single horse, a chariot-wheel and a great spoked solar disc in the sky.

Healing and fertility

The solar properties of heat and light gave rise to cults associated with the curing of disease and the promotion of abundance. Miniature sun-wheels were cast into curative springs; the goddess who presided over the great healing sanctuary at Bath was Sulis, a solar name. The Celtic Apollo was a deity of light and healing who was equated with a number of local gods and presided over many therapeutic spring shrines. Thus Apollo Belenus ('Bright' or 'Brilliant One') was venerated at such curative shrines as Sainte Sabine in Burgundy but also far away in Noricum (Austria). The name Belenus may have philological links with Beltene, the great Insular 1 May festival at which bonfires were lit in celebration of summer and as a purification rite to protect livestock from disease. Apollo Vindonnus, worshipped at Essarois in Burgundy, had a Celtic surname indicative of pure, clear light. It is significant that his cult was especially concerned with the curing of eye-afflictions. On the pediment of his temple was an image of Vindonnus as a radiate sun-god.

Fertility was seen as an important function for the divine sun, whose heat and light were clearly perceived as life-forces. The Celtic mother-goddesses were sometimes associated with the solar cult. Little clay figurines of goddesses from central Gaul and Brittany were depicted with solar symbols on their bodies. At Netherby in Cumbria and Naix in northern Gaul a deity is represented with a solar wheel and a *cornucopia* (horn of plenty), a potent symbol of abundance.

Fire

The great fire festivals of Celtic Europe took place in acknowledgement of fire as the terrestrial counterpart of the sun in the sky. Like the sun, fire both gives and destroys life. Fire is a cleanser, a purifier, and from the ashes springs new, fertile vegetation. The fire-ceremonies were a form of sympathetic magic, enacted to persuade the sun to return after its winter desertion. Beltene on 1 May, Lughnasad on 1 August and Samhain at the end of the Celtic year (1 November) all celebrated critical times in the annual solar cycle (see 'Fertility, land and water', p. 360). The Christian midsummer festival which marked the birth of St John the Baptist derived directly from much earlier ceremonies. Both pagan and

The Felmingham Hall (Norfolk) hoard of Romano-British bronzes, including a model wheel.

Christian festivals involved rolling a flaming wooden wheel down a hillside to a river. The Christian Saint Vincent observed a ceremony in fourth-century Aquitaine where a wheel was set alight, rolled to a river and then reassembled in the temple of the sky-god. A Saint John's festival, noted as being celebrated as late as the nineteenth century, records the rolling of a great, flaming, straw-covered wheel down the Stromberg Mountain to the River Moselle. If it reached the water unimpeded and without being quenched, a good wine-harvest was predicted. Thus the pagan association with fertility and plenty has long been maintained in an ostensibly Christian ritual.

The sun and death

The supernatural power of the sun was perceived to penetrate the dark, infernal regions. During the Iron Age and Roman periods Celtic communities in Europe sometimes buried their dead with solar amulets, to comfort them in their sojourn in the Underworld. At the Dürrnberg in Austria, a deformed young girl, eight or ten years old but very stunted, was interred with a miniature bronze wheel-symbol: her burial is just one of many examples of this chthonic solar ritual. An even clearer link between death and the sun is demonstrated by a tradition which occurred in Romano-Celtic Alsace. Here tombstones were carved with solar designs which symbolically illuminated the gloom of the grave. The association between sunlight and the tomb may reflect the hope of rebirth in a happy Otherworld.

Mountain-god and thunderer

High places are appropriate foci for the veneration of sky-forces. Mountains, penetrating sacred space, raised devotees as close as possible to the sky-god's element. Local Celtic mountain deities were equated with the Roman Jupiter: Ladicus was worshipped on Mount Ladicus in Spain; Poeninus in the high

Romano-Celtic altar dedicated to Taranucnus, a derivative of Taranis the thunder god, from Böckingen, Germany.

Reconstructed Romano-Celtic Jupiter-Giant column, with horseman group at the summit, from Hausen-an-der-Zaber, Stuttgart, Germany.

Alpine passes of Gaul; Uxellinus in Austria. In the Pyrenees of south-west Gaul, a local version of Jupiter was venerated at such shrines as Le Mont Saçon and Valentine, and pilgrims dedicated small, roughly hewn altars, sometimes inscribed to Jupiter but decorated with wheels and swastikas. In this region the swastika was chosen as another sun-symbol, similar to the wheel but perhaps emphasising the concept of movement.

Mountain deities are frequently associated with weather and storms. The Syrian Jupiter Dolichenus is an example. The Celts had their own thunder-god Taranis, whose name derives from *taran*, a Celtic word for thunder. In the first century AD the Roman poet Lucan alludes in his *Pharsalia* to three terrifying Celtic gods, encountered by Caesar's army in Gaul:

> ... and those Gauls who propitiate with human sacrifices the merciless gods Teutates, Esus and Taranis – at whose altars the visitant shudders ....
> (trans. Robert Graves, Penguin, 1956)

A later glossator (commentator) on Lucan's poem links Taranis with the sacrifice of human beings in a gigantic flaming wicker man. Seven altars dedicated to this Celtic Thunderer are recorded in Romano-Celtic Europe: in Britain, at Chester; in Gaul; in the Rhineland and Dalmatia (the former Yugoslavia). On some of the dedications the god is called 'Jupiter Taranis'. Taranis is one element of celestial power, as the sun is another. But the solar wheel-god should not be perceived as the same entity as the Celtic Thunderer. Taranis represents the noisy, destructive, supernatural force of storms: his symbolism and identity are contained within the name itself.

Cult and theology

That the cult of the Celtic sun/sky-gods may have had some kind of formalised ritual is implied by certain 'liturgical' finds. The temple at Wanborough in Surrey produced two chain headdresses surmounted by wheel-symbols, perhaps worn by priests of the sun-cult. The bronze mace from Willingham Fen (Cambridgeshire) with its depiction of the wheel-god also suggests ceremonial activity. Shrines, like that of Alesia in Burgundy, with its numerous model wheels, may have been consecrated to the sun-god.

Can we speak of a theology or mythology associated with the cults of sky and sun? Clearly, in the virtual absence of documentary detail, to speak of a celestial myth *sensu stricto* is incorrect. However, certain complex iconography demonstrates the one-time presence of a fundamental belief-system which must have been underpinned by myth. The sculptures of the Jupiter-columns hint at a dualistic, seasonal myth, where forces of day and night, light and darkness, life and death are balanced in an endless power struggle. The Willingham sceptre, with its figures of sun-god, three-horned bull, eagle, dolphin and infernal monster, exhibits a complexity which again argues for the presence of myth. Finally the whole range of material evidence shows the multiplicity of concerns of the celestial powers: life, healing, fertility and the mysteries of death and rebirth.

359

Fertility, land and water

A s is the case with many polytheistic systems, the Celtic gods were everywhere: each tree, lake, river, mountain and spring possessed a spirit.
This concept of divinity in nature gave rise to many cults and myths
associated with fertility. The most important of these were concerned with the
mother-goddesses who presided over all aspects of plenty and prosperity, both
in life and after death. In Irish mythology it was the union of the mortal king
with the goddess of the land which promoted fertility in Ireland. The great
Celtic festivals were all linked to the pastoral or agricultural year and the
florescence of domestic animals and crops. Water was perceived as a life-force,
and water-cults were a prominent feature of Celtic religion. Springs were the
focus of curative cults based upon the healing and cleansing properties of pure
water.

Spirits in the landscape

The Celtic landscape was numinous (that is, possessed by spirits): the iconography and epigraphy of Romano-Celtic Europe attest to the sanctity of natural
places, which were perceived to be under the protection of local divinities. A
settlement and its god might even share the same name: thus, in southern Gaul,
Glanis was the spirit of Glanum and Nemausus was the name both of Nîmes and
of the god who presided over the sacred spring. Mountains were holy and their
spirits venerated: Vosegus was the god of the Vosges in eastern Gaul; and
Ladicus, the eponymous spirit of Mount Ladicus in north-west Spain, has been
alluded to on page 357.

Trees, groves and forests were sacred. The symbolism of trees is complex:
their roots and branches evoked an image of a link between sky and Underworld; their longevity represented continuity and wisdom; the seasonal behaviour of deciduous trees gave rise to a cyclical symbolism, an allegory of life,
death and rebirth. Trees were associated with cults of fertility and nature, partly
because of this regenerative imagery: the mother-goddesses are frequently
associated with trees; Rhenish altars to the mother-goddesses from Bonn bear
tree-symbols; the sanctuary of the mothers at Pesch (Germany) had a sacred tree
as its cult-focus. Gaulish tribal names display tree-veneration: the Eburones
were the 'Yew Tribe', the Lemovices the 'People of the Elm'. In Ireland a
sacred tree was called a *bile*; the older the tree, the greater its sanctity. All trees
in Irish myth were sacred but the oak, yew, ash and hazel were particularly

Romano-Celtic stone mother-goddess figurine with a tree, corn (or palm) branch symbol and fruit, from Caerwent, South Wales.

holy. In the *Dinnshenchas* allusion is made to trees as sources of sacred wisdom. Irish holy trees were associated with sacral kingship: the inauguration of a ruler always took place in the presence of a sacred tree, a symbol of sovereignty, tradition and wisdom. A group of trees (a grove) was equally sacred, called *fidnemed* in Ireland and *nemeton* by the Gauls and Britons.

Cults of water and curative springs

Water was perceived as both a creator and destroyer of life. Thus water in all its aspects – particularly rivers, springs, wells, lakes and marshes – was the focus of countless myths and cults which manifest themselves both in archaeology and in the western literature. The sanctity and symbolism of water continued into the Christian tradition. Rivers were regarded as a numinous life-force: from as early as the Bronze Age, people cast precious objects into them as votive offerings. In the Celtic Iron Age, rivers such as the Thames and Witham received particularly martial items: weapons, armour and shields. Rivers at their sources and confluences were especially holy. Condatis ('Watersmeet') was venerated in the Tyne-Tees region of north Britain, and 'Condate' at Lyon was the sacred site at the confluence of the great Rhône and Saône rivers. There is evidence that the *personae* of many rivers were worshipped as named spirits: Sequana of the Seine, Souconna of the Saône; Verbeia of the Wharfe are just a few examples. The Insular *Dinnshenchas* relates the myth of the River Boyne, personified as the goddess Boann, who was turned into a river as a punishment by her husband Nechtan, himself a water-spirit, for daring to visit his forbidden well (Sídh Nechtan).

Lakes and marshes were equally numinous. The Classical writer Strabo testifies to the deposition of treasure in sacred lakes, and there is archaeological evidence for this practice. At the Swiss lake-site of La Tène, wooden platforms (some dated by dendrochronology to the second century BC) were specially built to facilitate the casting of precious objects into a small bay at the eastern end of Lake Neuchâtel. Offerings included hundreds of brooches, weapons and shields, chariots and animals, thrown in over a period which centred around 100 BC. In Wales the lake of Llyn Fawr in Mid Glamorgan was the centre of cult-activity in about 600 BC, when objects including antique cauldrons and exotic material of the style known as Hallstatt (from the type-site in Austria), were deposited. Llyn Cerrig Bach on Anglesey was a watery site into which had been cast many prestige objects, including chariots, weapons and cauldrons, over a period from the second century BC to the first century AD. It is possible that Llyn Cerrig was associated with the druids, described by the Roman writer Tacitus as having an important cult-centre on the Island of Mona.

The repeated deposition of cauldrons in water is interesting. These vessels were traditionally associated with feasting and plenty, in vernacular myth. The Irish god the Daghda possessed an enormous, ever-replenishing cauldron (pp. 325-6); and the Welsh hero Brân (pp. 341-2) gave a cauldron of rebirth to the Irish king Matholwch. Their function as containers for liquid may be the reason why they were so often deposited as sacred offerings in watery contexts. The great Danish Brå and Gundestrup Cauldrons were found in marshes; the Duchcov (Czechoslovakia) Cauldron came from a Celtic spring sanctuary and held more than 2000 items of bronze jewellery. Scottish lakes, such as Carlingwark Loch and Blackburn Mill, were the focus of ritual cauldron deposition in the very late Iron Age (early first century AD).

Bogs were the centre of important cult activity, not only because of their water nature but also perhaps because of the element of danger and treachery

Late Iron Age bronze cauldron found with a second vessel inverted over it, and deposited as a votive gift in a marsh at Blackburn Mill, Scotland.

associated with them. In the Celtic Iron Age the marsh-spirits were propitiated with offerings ranging from weapons, cauldrons and wagons to human sacrifices. The Scottish Torrs Chamfrein, an elaborate item of horse-armour, came from a marsh, as did the Gundestrup Cauldron and two cult-wagons from Dejbjerg in Denmark. The most spectacular marsh-offering from Britain was found at Lindow Moss, the body of a young man who was garotted and cast naked into a marsh-pool some time during the Iron Age (see p. 378).

Springs and wells were associated with divinities and especially with cults of healing. Wells, which penetrated deep below ground, were perceived as a link between the earth and the Underworld. The goddess Coventina presided over a sacred spring and well at the Roman fort of Carrawburgh on Hadrian's Wall. A Romano-British well at Goadby, Leicestershire, contained the bodies of two people, weighted down with stones, perhaps offerings to the infernal powers. A dry well dating to the Roman period at Jordan Hill, Dorset, contained very curious and deliberately structured deposits, including stone cists filled with ironwork and sixteen pairs of tiles between each of which were the body of a crow and a coin. Sacred wells feature in Insular myths: the Fionn Cycle describes the Salmon of Knowledge which lived at the bottom of a well. The cult of the Irish goddess Brigit, who became a Christian saint, was closely associated with sacred wells. Many saints presided over holy wells: St Melor of Cornwall is an example. Saint Winifride's Well at Holywell in Clwyd is one of many in Wales. As is the case with the legend of the Welsh Saint Winifride, the severed heads of Breton saints endowed particular wells with sanctity and power.

Springs were revered in acknowledgement of their medicinal and purifying properties. In Romano-Celtic times powerful cults associated with healing springs attracted pilgrims from all over Celtic Europe. The two natural springs at Chamalières near Clermont-Ferrand possess minerals with genuine curative properties: in the first century BC and first century AD the sacred pool was visited by sick devotees who offered to the presiding spirit wooden images of themselves, displaying particularly eye-afflictions. In the same period a shrine at *Fontes Sequanae* (the Springs of Sequana) was established near Dijon, in veneration of the healing goddess of the Seine at its spring-source. More than 200 wooden models of pilgrims, or the parts of their bodies which required a cure, were dedicated to the goddess. Healing cults like this were based upon the principle of reciprocity: after bathing in the pure, sacred water of the spring, the devotee offered a model of a diseased limb or organ, in the hope that the deity would give back one that was whole and healthy.

Many other curative spring deities were worshipped in Gaul and Britain: the Celtic Apollo presided over many of these sites, sometimes with a consort (see pp. 351-2). As Apollo Belenus he was venerated at Sainte Sabine in Burgundy and elsewhere; Apollo Grannus, with his consort Sirona, was invoked at Grand (Vosges), but his shrines existed as far apart as Brittany and Hungary. Here, as in other shrines, sick suppliants bathed, offered their gifts and then slept in a special dormitory, where they hoped for a vision of the healing god. Other powerful healers included Lenus Mars, a Treveran god whose main cult-centre was associated with a stream and spring near the Moselle at Trier. The greatest British curative deity was Sulis, whose sanctuary was at Aquae Sulis, the great temple at Bath, established on a site where hot springs gush from the ground at the rate of a quarter million gallons (1,136,500 litres) a day.

Myths and cults of fertility

The Celts were an essentially rural people and, as such, were preoccupied with the seasons and with the fertility and well-being of their crops and livestock. Most of the divinities of Celtic Europe, who were associated with the natural world, had a function as providers of fertility: Cernunnos, Epona, the hunter-gods and the healers are just a few examples. Cloaked and hooded spirits, known as *Genii Cucullati*, are represented in iconography carrying such evocative symbols as eggs. Continental examples may display overt sexual symbolism: on some images the hood can be removed to expose an erect phallus. The British *Cucullati* are distinctive in their triple form and in their repeated association with depictions of the mother-goddesses.

It is the Mothers who most clearly display the concept of the personification of fertility. The earth-mother, provider of abundance, was a fundamental aspect of divinity for the European Celts (as, indeed, was the case in Classical lands and elsewhere in the ancient world). This concept bears close resemblance to that expressed in the Irish and Welsh image of goddesses such as Macha, Medb and Modron. The cult of the divine mother was popular all over Romano-Celtic Europe: she was depicted most frequently as a triad, and epigraphy too expresses this plurality, referring to the goddesses as the *Deae Matres* or *Deae Matronae*. This triplism seems to occur most frequently in the imagery of divine beings associated with prosperity and well-being. The Mothers most often appear seated in a row, with such symbols of fertility as babies, fruit or bread. A typical Burgundian image, exemplified by a relief at Vertault, shows the goddesses with a baby, a napkin or towel and a sponge and basin. The Germanic *Matronae* were topographical goddesses, with local surnames such as the *Aufaniae*. They carry fruit rather than emblems of human fertility, but are distinctive in that their images always depict two older goddesses flanking a young girl, as if the different ages of womanhood are expressed. The British mother-goddesses are depicted both with children and fruit or bread; they cluster in two geographical groups, that of the West Country and that of Hadrian's Wall.

The Celtic festivals

Four great seasonal religious festivals are recorded in Insular mythic tradition, all associated with the farming year. Imbolc, celebrated on 1–2 February, was related to the lactation of ewes. This festival was linked with the cult of Brigit, a multi-functional goddess who protected women in childbirth, presided over the

Romano-Celtic pipe-clay group of the three mother-goddesses, from Bonn, Germany. The Rhenish mothers almost invariably follow this iconographic pattern, with a young girl flanked by two older women with distinctive headdresses.

ale-harvest and was also associated with poetry and prophecy. Interestingly Brigit retained many of her pagan roles even when she had been adopted as a saint by the early Celtic Church in Ireland.

The feast of Beltene ('Bright- or Goodly-Fire') took place on 1 May; it was related to the beginning of open pasturing, and was celebrated to welcome summer and the heat of the sun which would ripen the crops. Bonfires were kindled in sympathetic magic to encourage the sun's warmth on earth. The ninth century AD glossator Cormac describes a Beltene ritual in which two fires were ignited by the druids and livestock driven between them in a magical ritual of fertility and purification.

Lughnasad was linked with the harvest. Its central date of celebration was 1 August, but the festivities lasted a month. According to Irish tradition, the fair of Lughnasad was introduced by Lugh to Ireland, either in memory of his foster-mother Tailtu or to celebrate his marriage. The festival was held at various locations, including the royal strongholds of Tara and Emhain Macha.

Samhain (31 October/1 November) is the festival about which most is known. It marked the beginning of winter and the Celtic new year. Samhain heralded the time in the pastoral year when animals were brought in from the fields, some slaughtered and others kept for breeding. Samhain is recorded on the first century BC Gaulish Coligny Calendar (see p. 374) as 'Samonios'. In Ireland during the later first millennium AD great assemblies of the five provinces took place at Samhain, occasions for pastoral rites and political debate: the festival was celebrated with markets, fairs and horse-races. Samhain was a time of ritual mourning for the death of summer and a period of great danger, a boundary between two periods, when time and space were temporarily frozen and normal laws suspended. The barriers were broken: Otherworld spirits could walk on earth and humans could visit the Underworld. The tradition of Samhain has survived into modern times as Hallow'een and All Souls' Day.

Animals in cult and myth

Animals were revered by the Celts, as by many non-Christian cultures, for their specific qualities: speed, ferocity, fecundity, valour or beauty. The behaviour of certain beasts gave rise to religious symbolism: the earthbound nature of snakes led to perceptions of links between these creatures and the Underworld; the ability of birds to fly was seen in terms of an allegory of the human spirit freed at death. An important element in sacred myth was the absence of rigid boundaries between animal and human form. This meant that, in iconography, deities could be envisaged as semi-zoomorphic. The myths of the vernacular literature abound in enchanted animals which had once been human, and divinities in human form who could shape-change to the form of an animal at will. Apart from the evidence of images and myths, the importance of animals in Celtic ritual is clearly demonstrated by the complexity and diversity of animal sacrifice.

Wild beasts and the hunt

Although wild animals were not a major food-source, hunting was a common sporting and prestige activity. The divine hunt forms an important part of vernacular myth, and the iconography of the pagan Celtic world displays a multiplicity of cults associated with hunted animals.

There existed a special and complicated relationship between the Celts and the creatures they hunted, a relationship that involved reverence and an acknowledgement of theft from the natural world, which required appropriate propitiatory ritual. The gods of the hunt protected the denizens of the wild as well as promoting the hunt itself. Sometimes this ambivalence is displayed in Celtic imagery, where the god shows tenderness toward his prey: the sculpture of the hunter-god with his stag from Le Donon (Vosges) is a good example. Many divine hunters are accompanied by dogs, just as would have been the case in real life.

The concept of the divine hunt possesses important regenerative symbolism. The spilling of the blood of the hunted means food and life for the hunters. In the Welsh and Irish mythological tradition the hunt may be the means by which contact is made between earthly life and the Otherworld. In Irish myth beings from the supernatural world lured human hunters, such as Finn, to their realm by means of enchanted animals. In the *Mabinogi*, it is a stag-hunt which brings together Pwyll and the Otherworld king, Arawn.

Stone statuette of a god wearing a torc, from Euffigneix, France. He has an eye-symbol on his side, perhaps to indicate the all-seeing power of the god, and a boar striding along his torso, dorsal bristles erect. The boar image suggests hunting or war symbolism.

Certain deities were associated with particular hunted animals. Bears were protected by Artio, a goddess worshipped near Bern in Switzerland, where a bronze statuette depicts her and her beast. Arduinna, a divine huntress of the Ardennes Forest, is portrayed on a bronze figurine astride a galloping boar, a hunting-knife in her hand. A pre-Roman carving from Euffigneix in eastern Gaul shows a god with the image of an aggressively bristled boar striding along his torso. The bellicosity suggested by the raised dorsal crest is emphasised on figurines of boars, such as that from Neuvy-en-Sullias (Loiret). Celtic helmets and shields carried boar-emblems as war-symbols, and the *carnyx* (war-trumpet) was fashioned with a snarling boar's head as its mouthpiece. The focus of the Welsh tale of *Culhwch and Olwen* is Twrch Trwyth, a huge, destructive boar (see p. 345), and similar beasts are common in Irish myth: Orc Triath is the equivalent of Twrch Trwyth.

Stags were important cult-animals, probably because of their speed, their virility and their spreading antlers, which evoked their image as lords of the

367

forest. The Iron Age rock-art of Camonica Valley in north Italy features sacred stags which are often depicted as the focus of hunting-ritual. The imagery on a seventh-century BC model bronze cult-wagon at Strettweg in Austria is of a divine stag-hunt presided over by a goddess. In later Celtic iconography the deer is the companion not only of hunter-gods but also of the god Cernunnos, who was himself antlered (see below). Supernatural stags are significant in vernacular myth. In the Fionn Cycle, Finn himself is closely associated with deer-imagery: his wife, Sava, is a metamorphosed doe and the name of their son, Oisin, means 'Little Deer'. Finn is one of the hunters enticed to the Otherworld by means of enchanted stags.

Snakes and birds

The complex symbolism of the snake arises from its physical characteristics: its habit of sloughing its skin has caused it to be perceived as a symbol of rebirth, hence its association with healer-deities such as Sirona. In Classical religion, serpents were symbols of beneficence and also of death. Snakes were linked with fertility-imagery, perhaps because of their phallic shape, the double penis of the male and the multiple young produced at one birth. The snake's earthbound nature, its carnivorous feeding-habits and its ability to kill gave it powerful chthonic symbolism. This is displayed most clearly in the iconography of the Jupiter-columns (see p. 355), where the monster of darkness is represented by a Giant with serpents replacing his legs. One distinctive form of snake-iconography consists of the ram-headed serpents: these occur particularly in Romano-Celtic Gaul. The symbolism is generally interpreted as representative of the combined imagery of fertility (the ram was symbolic of fecundity in the Classical world) and regeneration. These hybrid creatures often accompany beneficent deities of abundance or healing: Cernunnos and the Celtic equivalent of Mercury or Mars in his Gaulish role as guardian against misfortune are examples.

Snakes feature in a number of Irish myths. This itself is interesting because, since there are no snakes in Ireland, the implication must be that these snake-myths are of great antiquity. The war-fury, the Morrigán, has a son, Meiche, who is slain by Dian Cécht, the divine physician, because he has three snakes in his heart. There was a prophecy that, if the serpents were allowed to mature, they would destroy all the animals in Ireland. The Ulster champion Conall Cernach has an encounter with a great treasure-guarding snake. The Welsh cleric Giraldus Cambrensis wrote an account of a gold torc guarded by a snake in a Pembrokeshire well. The theme of a treasure-guarding serpent is widespread in European legend: it has its equivalent, for instance, in Fafnir of Norse myth.

Apart from their general symbolism associated with flight, birds possessed other, more specific, symbolism. Their distinctive 'voices' may have led to the oracular associations of ravens and doves. Water-birds may have been seen as a symbolic link between sky and water. The alert and protective character of geese led to their symbolic connection with war. In both Irish and Welsh tradition, magical birds, usually in threes, were associated with healing and rebirth in the Otherworld. The bright-plumaged birds of the Irish goddess Clíodna and the birds of the Welsh Rhiannon could lull the sick to sleep with their sweet song.

Cranes were important in Irish myth: those belonging to Midhir were birds of ill omen, whose presence robbed warriors of their courage. Ill-natured or jealous women were punished by being changed into cranes: this idea may have come about because the crane's raucous shriek was likened to the screech of a scold. The Irish sea-god Manannán possessed a bag made from the skin of a crane which had once been a jealous woman. That cranes or egrets were significant also in Gaulish religion is demonstrated by the curious iconography of Tarvostrigaranus, the 'Bull with Three Cranes', depicted on stones at Paris and Trier dating from the first century AD.

As eaters of carrion and with their black plumage, crows and ravens were particularly associated with death. Irish war-goddesses such as the Morrigán and Badbh could assume crow-form and appear on the battlefield as harbingers of disaster. In Insular myth the prophetic associations of ravens were usually related to the foretelling of evil. Ravens and crows were important symbols in pagan European iconography, but here they seem to have been linked to beneficent deities, like Nantosuelta, Epona and the healers, perhaps as prophets of good fortune. Ritual involving ravens occurred in the British Iron Age: at Danebury and Winklebury in Hampshire, bodies of ravens were deliberately buried in pits, perhaps as sacrifices to the infernal powers.

Other birds which were important in myth included eagles and swans. In iconography the eagle was associated above all with sky-symbolism. In Welsh myth the eagle is linked with Lleu Llaw Gyffes, perhaps a god of light (see p. 345). Irish myth abounds in stories of enchanted swans, which spend some time as birds and some as girls: stories about Midhir and Étain, Oenghus and Caer (see 'The divine lovers', p. 347) and Cú Chulainn all carry descriptions of magical swans wearing gold or silver chains, apparently a mark of their supernatural status. In one myth the children of Lir (a sea-god) are cursed with swan-shape for 900 years because of the jealousy of their stepmother. The particular association of swans with lovers may derive from the observation that swans mate for life.

Epona and horses

Horses were prestige animals, used for riding from at least the eighth century BC in 'barbarian' Europe. They had long been used to pull wagons, but the Celts had two-horse teams to draw light, fast chariots in battle. The horse was revered in the Celtic world for its beauty, speed, bravery and sexual vigour, and this animal became a symbol of the aristocratic warrior-élite of Celtic society, the knights. Many cults were associated with horses: warrior-gods, such as Mars Corotiacus at Martlesham in Suffolk, were depicted in iconography on

Small bronze group of Epona (above left) and two ponies, from Wiltshire. The goddess has a yoke and a dish of corn from which the animals feed. Romano-Celtic.

Large stone monument of Nehalennia (above right), shown with dog and fruit-baskets, from Colijnsplaat, Netherlands.

horseback; and there is evidence, too, that the horse was perceived as a solar animal (p. 356). Horse sacrifice was rare, but significant in its reflection of a very real loss to its owner and the community. The quartered bodies of two horses were found in a ritual deposit of the sixth century BC in the cave of Býčiskála in Czechoslovakia; and the later Iron Age chariot-burial of the King's Barrow in East Yorkshire contained the horse-team as well as the chariot and its owner.

Greatest of all the Celtic horse-deities was Epona, her very name philologically linked with *epos*, a Celtic word for horse. She was sufficiently important to have an official Roman festival, on 18 December. Epona's worshippers were drawn from all sections of society: in military areas of the Rhine and Danube she was venerated by cavalry officers of the Roman army, as a protectress of both horseman and animal. Elsewhere, especially in Burgundy, Epona was worshipped as a domestic deity, goddess of the craft of horse-breeding and, more generally, of abundance and prosperity. Her imagery is distinctive: she is always depicted in company with horses, either riding side-saddle on a mare or between two or more horses or ponies. The female sex of her mount may be important in terms of her role as promoter of fertility: Burgundian images frequently portray a sleeping or suckling foal beneath Epona's mare. The horse-goddess was essentially a Gaulish divinity, although dedications occur as far away as Plovdiv in Bulgaria. There is little evidence for Epona's cult in Britain, but a bronze statuette from Wiltshire shows the goddess with two ponies, a male and a female, whom she feeds with corn.

Irish and Welsh mythology contains a great deal of horse-symbolism: Macha, an Irish horse-goddess, outran the Ulster king's team in a race; and the Welsh Rhiannon had a close affinity with horses, and may herself have been a horse-goddess.

The symbolism of dogs

In both Classical and Celtic myth, dogs possessed the complex but symbiotic symbolism of healing, hunting and death, derived from observation of the self-healing power of a dog's lick, its scavenging habits and its role in hunting. Dogs played an important part in Welsh and Irish myth: Arawn, lord of Annwn (the Welsh Otherworld) possessed supernatural hounds, described in the *Mabinogi* as white with red ears. The 'Taliesin' poem *Cwn Annwn* (the *Hounds of Annwn*) refers to speckled, greyish-red dogs which are omens of death. The Ulster hero Cú Chulainn has a close link with dogs. Named the 'Hound of Culann', he takes the place of the smith's great hound, whom he has killed; he also has a *geis* or bond which forbids him to eat dog-flesh. Mac Da Thó, who presides over an Irish Otherworld feast, has an enormous and supernatural hound, whom he offers both to the men of Ulster and of Connacht, thus promoting their mutual hatred.

In pagan Celtic Gaul and Britain there is evidence of dog-ritual and sacrifice. At Danebury in Hampshire dogs (often in association with horses) were killed and interred in disused grain-storage pits during the Iron Age; at the pre-Roman shrine of Gournay (Oise), dogs were consumed in ritual meals. Many deities venerated in pagan Celtic Europe were associated with dogs. Hunter-gods are depicted accompanied by large hounds. Apollo Cunomaglus ('Hound Lord') was invoked at the sanctuary of Nettleton in Wiltshire. The great Romano-Celtic shrine at Lydney, Gloucestershire, was presided over by Nodens, a god who received offerings of dog-images. The marine goddess Nehalennia presided over two temples on the North Sea coast of the Netherlands, at Colijnsplaat and Domburg, both now submerged beneath the sea. More than a hundred images of the goddess have survived, nearly all of which depict her accompanied by a large, watchful hound. Nehalennia was a divinity who protected travellers across the North Sea and promoted their success in business. The baskets of fruit which accompany her suggest that she was a goddess of plenty. The dog may be a symbol of protection and fidelity.

Tarvostrigaranus and the bull myths

Bulls were venerated for their strength, their virility and roaring ferocity. Oxen were symbolic of the power of draught-animals in farming, and thus of agricultural wealth. Bull sacrifice was not uncommon: elderly oxen were ritually slaughtered at Gournay, and their bodies subjected to elaborate rites. In his

Natural History, the Roman writer Pliny refers to a druidical bull-sacrifice.

Sacred bulls are frequently represented in cult-art: figurines of the sixth century BC have been found at Hallstatt in Austria and Býčiskála. Celtic bull-images are often depicted triple-horned, thus enhancing the symbolism of the horn (which signified aggression and fertility) to the sacred power of three. Stone triple-horned bulls were dedicated at the Burgundian shrine of Beire-le-Châtel; and bronze examples occur in Gaul and in Britain. One figurine of the fourth century AD comes from a shrine at Maiden Castle, Dorset, and once was adorned with images of three women on its back. In Irish legend women were sometimes transformed into cranes, and the Maiden Castle figurine calls to mind some curious Continental iconography dating to the first century AD: one carving, from Paris, depicts a bull with three cranes perched on its back and head; the accompanying dedication reads 'Tarvostrigaranus' (the 'Bull with Three Cranes'). Almost identical imagery is present on a stone at Trier. Both stones depict the bull and birds associated with willow trees and a divine wood-cutter. The interpretation is obscure, but some scholars have advanced theories of seasonal symbolism, related to the Tree of Life, spring and fertility. This imagery may well represent a quite specific Celtic myth, the details of which have been lost.

Bull-myths are very prominent in early Irish literature. The *tarbhfhess* was a divinatory rite involving a bull sacrifice, presided over by druids (see 'Druids, sacrifice and ritual', p. 375); the bull's flesh and broth were consumed by a man who then slept and dreamed of the rightful king-elect. The most important Irish bull-myth is the *Táin Bó Cuailnge* in the Ulster Cycle (p. 331).

Zoomorphism and shape-shifting

The close religious affinity between Celts and animals manifests itself most clearly in two ways: the first concerns the representation of gods in semi-zoomorphic form; the second is metamorphosis or shape-changing, which is such a common concept in the Welsh and Irish mythological tradition.

A carving of the first century AD from Paris (part of the same monument as the Tarvostrigaranus stone) depicts the bust of an elderly man with antlers, a torc hanging from each, and the ears of a stag. The inscription above identifies him as 'Cernunnos' ('Horned One'). Similar images occur in both pre-Roman and Romano-Celtic contexts. The earliest representation is on a fourth-century BC rock-carving at Camonica Valley in north Italy. The antlered god appears on the Gundestrup Cauldron, seated cross-legged, again with two torcs, and with his stag beside him. Beneath the god is a ram-horned serpent. Most images of Cernunnos occur in north-east Gaul and date to the Roman period. He is often depicted as he is at Gundestrup, cross-legged, with torcs and a horned snake. At such sites as Sommerécourt and Étang-sur-Arroux in Gaul the snakes eat from bowls of mash on the god's lap. A rare British example, at Cirencester, portrays Cernunnos with two snakes which form his legs and rear up to eat corn or fruit by his head. Some Gaulish images have holes in the top of the head for detach-

Bronze bull-head bucket-mount (above right) from Welshpool, Wales. Late Iron Age.

Bust of a god (above left) with antlers and torcs hanging from them; above is a dedication to Cernunnos. Early first century AD, from Nôtre Dame, Paris, France.

able antlers, possibly evoking seasonal ritual. The general symbolism of Cernunnos is that of a wild god of nature, fertility and plenty. He is so close to the animal world that he actually takes on some characteristics of a beast, thus enhancing his potency as lord of Nature.

Essentially similar to Cernunnos are the horned gods, who adopt the features of bulls, rams or goats. These are especially popular among the Brigantes of north Britain, where they frequently appear as ithyphallic warrior-gods, thus linking sexual vigour with military aggression.

A strong and persistent thread running through the earliest written Celtic myths is the concept of enchanted, magical animals which may be of supernatural origin, perhaps metamorphosed gods or humans who have been changed into animals in revenge or as a punishment. This chapter has already touched upon such transmogrified beings as Twrch Trwyth, changed from a human king to a boar because of his wickedness; the various beings who change into swans; and the Irish raven-goddesses. In the *Mabinogi*, Gwydion and Gilfaethwy are transformed into a succession of animals by Math, lord of Gwynedd. Irish mythology is full of enchanted bulls, boars, stags and birds. A constant characteristic of all transmogrified creatures is that only their physical form is altered; they retain the ability to think as humans and they can often still speak. They are skin-changers, very similar to those of Norse myth.

In addition to gods or humans who can assume zoomorphic form, the western Celtic myths contain allusions to special animals with supernatural powers. Thus the Welsh Culhwch encounters magical creatures who help him in his quest. One of these is the Salmon of Llyn Llaw, a creature which bears a close resemblance to the Irish Salmon of Knowledge, chronicled in the Fionn Cycle, whose flesh imparts wisdom to the young Finn. This salmon gained its knowledge by eating the nuts of the nine hazel trees which grew beside a well at the bottom of the sea, in other words from the Otherworld.

Druids, sacrifice and ritual

his book is about myth and its prime concern is to explore stories and beliefs about the supernatural world. Nevertheless it is important also to consider the 'mechanics' of Celtic religion which underpin the myths and belief-systems themselves. This chapter therefore examines aspects of ritual behaviour, the performance of people who wished to communicate with that separate world beyond the boundaries of human perception.

Druids, seers, bards: an international Celtic priesthood?

The Druids are engaged in sacred matters, conduct the public and private sacrifices, and interpret all religious issues. To these a large number of the young men resort for the purpose of instruction, and the Druids are held in great honour among them.
(trans. Wiseman and Wiseman, *The Battle for Gaul*, Chatto and Windus, 1980)

A number of Classical writers mention the druids: Strabo, Tacitus, Lucan and Ausonius are but a few. The fullest information is given by Caesar, whose words are quoted above. He comments that the druids enjoyed high rank, being of nearly equal status with the knights. He speaks of the rigours of the druids' training, which could take twenty years and involved committing to memory oral traditions passed on through the generations. Every year, on a fixed date, the druids assembled in a sacred place in the land of the Carnutes, the official centre of Gaul. Caesar makes it clear that druidism originated in Britain whence it was disseminated to Gaul. Most Graeco-Roman sources agree that the main concern of the druids was the control of supernatural forces by means of divination. This apparently involved human sacrifice by stabbing, strangulation or other means, and the examination of the death struggles or the victim's innards in order to foretell the future.

Tacitus alludes to divinatory killing on the Island of Anglesey when it was threatened by invading Romans. This magical prediction made it possible to plan the most auspicious time for important events in the community: going to war, sowing or reaping, election of a new king and so forth. The first-century-BC Gaulish Coligny Calendar is one the earliest surviving pieces of evidence for a written (using Roman letters) Celtic language. It consists of a large bronze plate engraved with a calendar of lunar and intercalary months, each divided into lucky and unlucky halves, demarcated by the abbreviations MAT (good) and ANM (not good). It is possible that this was a calendar drawn up by the druids in order to calculate propitious times for important religious and secular

Bronze priest's crown (above left) from the Romano-Celtic temple of Hockwold-cum-Wilton, Norfolk.

Lifesize Romano-Celtic pewter mask (above right), perhaps nailed onto the door of a shrine, found in the culvert of the sacred baths of Sulis at Bath.

activities. Pliny chronicles a druidic sacrifice associated with the curing of barrenness: on the sixth day of the moon the druids climbed a sacred oak and cut off a mistletoe bough using a 'golden' (probably gilded-bronze) sickle, catching the branch in a white cloak. Two white bulls were then sacrificed. When mixed in a potion, mistletoe was believed to cure infertility.

Druids were probably very influential in religion and politics during the free Celtic period – perhaps all over the Celtic world, though we have evidence only for Gaul and Britain – but, as an active force, druidism would have gradually faded under Roman domination. Some early emperors tolerated the druids; others tried to eradicate them. The Bordeaux poet Ausonius alludes to the presence of druids in Gaul during the fourth century AD. But when the main fabric of Celtic heroic society broke down, so did most of the druids' influence. There is no archaeological evidence for druids *per se* but some liturgical regalia – headdresses and sceptres – does survive. The excavators of the Celtic sanctuary of Gournay in northern Gaul suggest the presence of a permanent staff of religious functionaries to maintain the ritual activity evidenced there. Whether these officials were druids is, of course, an open question.

Irish mythology abounds in references to druids, although they must have lost most of their power under Christianity. In the *Book of Invasions* one of the invading leaders, Partholón, arrives with three druids. The goddess Brigit was born in a druid's household; and Finn was reared by a druidess. The Ulster king Conchobar had a druid, Cathbadh, who enjoyed great influence. The druids were involved in the kingship ritual of the *tarbhfhess* (p. 372). These Irish druids had a strong divinatory role: Cathbadh's prediction of Deirdre's disastrous effect upon Ulster (p. 349) is an example. The ninth-century glossator Cormac comments on a divination ritual known as 'Himbas Forosnai', which involved chewing the raw flesh of pigs, dogs or cats. The Irish druids were also probably associated with the imposition of *geissi*, which were taboos or bonds placed upon prominent people and which they had to obey or perish.

Both Classical and Irish sources mention three religious and learned classes: the druids, bards and seers. Strabo alludes to the bards as being associated particularly with poetry; Irish bards were praise poets and involved with ceremonies related to Otherworld feasting; Finnegas the Bard was the means by which Finn gained knowledge from the Salmon of Wisdom. The seers (*vates* in Latin, *filidh* in Irish) were prominent in Ireland, where they had a function at least partly religious. They were responsible for the upkeep and transmission of sacred oral tradition. They were prophets and closely linked with divination, and they had the power to blemish or cause death by satire. Long after Ireland adopted Christianity, the *filidh* remained as seers, teachers and advisers, taking over many of the druids' functions. Indeed the *filidh* maintained a function until the seventeenth century. Brigit was the patron goddess of seers; she was perceived as expert in divination, prophecy, learning and poetry.

Sacred space: groves, sanctuaries and pits

The axe-men came on an ancient and sacred grove. Its interlacing branches enclosed a cool central space into which the sun never shone, but where an abundance of water spouted from dark springs . . . the barbaric gods worshipped here had their altars heaped with hideous offerings, and every tree was sprinkled with human blood . . . Nobody dared enter this grove except the priest; and even he kept out at midday, and between dawn and dusk – for fear that the gods might be abroad at such hours.
(Lucan, *Pharsalia*, trans. Robert Graves, Penguin, 1956)

Thus Lucan describes a sacred Celtic grove near Marseille, felled by Caesar's army in the first century BC. The Celts' perception of numinosity, the presence of spirits, in all natural things (see 'Fertility, land and water', p. 360) gave rise to the open-air worship of these beings. Groves were important partly because of the sanctity of individual trees and perhaps also because they were dark, mysterious and secret. While there can be no archaeological evidence for sacred groves or forests, there is abundant Classical literary reference to such places: Tacitus alludes to a druidic grove on Anglesey; Strabo speaks of Drunemeton, a holy grove of the Celtic Galatians in Asia Minor; and there are many more.

Some sacred space was demarcated from the profane world simply by means of a symbolic barrier which enclosed the numinous area. A piece of ground was designated as holy and thus a focus of communication with the supernatural world. The Goloring in Germany was a huge enclosure built in the sixth century BC; at its centre was an enormous wooden post, 40 feet (12 metres) high, perhaps symbolic of a sacred tree. Libeniče in Czechoslovakia, dating to the fourth century BC, was a great, sub-rectangular enclosure which contained a sunken, unroofed structure at one end. Inside this 'shrine' were the remains of two timbers associated with two bronze torcs, perhaps once crude wooden statues of deities wearing Celtic symbols of prestige. Libeniče contained sacrificial deposits of animals and the body of a woman, possibly the priestess of the sanctuary. Successive pits had been dug in the floor of the sunken structure over a period of twenty-four years, attesting the activity associated with some form of cult-ceremony.

Another group of open sacred sites were the *Viereckschanzen*, evidence of which has been found particularly in central Europe. They comprise square enclosures within which may be one or more ritual shafts. A *Viereckschanze* at Fellbach Schmiden near Stuttgart is interesting because of the discovery, inside the shaft, of oak animal-carvings, dated by dendrochronology (tree-ring dating) to the late second century BC. Ritual activity associated with pits may be interpreted as a means of associating with the infernal gods (see 'Death, rebirth and the Otherworld', p. 386). Pits are certainly a recognisable category of sacred space: the Hampshire hillfort of Danebury has yielded abundant evidence of ritual behaviour associated with grain storage pits. Bodies of animals and humans (as well as other offerings) were interred in these pits, presumably as a means of communicating with and propitiating supernatural powers.

Built shrines were used by Iron Age Celts but there seem to have been no formalised religious structures such as existed in the Classical world. It is therefore often difficult to distinguish a temple from a house, and it is necessary to look for evidence of associated ritual activity in order to identify a sacred building as such. Sometimes the religious identity of a Celtic sanctuary is implied by the presence of an overlying Roman temple. Gournay (Oise) in France, was the site of an *oppidum* (urban settlement) of the Bellovaci, which contained an important pre-Roman sanctuary with complex associated ritual. The focus of the shrine in the third century BC was a great central pit in which the sacrified bodies of elderly oxen were placed for decomposition before the bones were carefully positioned in the ditch surrounding the precinct. Young pigs and lambs were slaughtered and consumed in religious feasting; and 2000 weapons, ritually broken, were offered to the gods. The late Iron Age (first century BC) sanctuary at Hayling Island, Hampshire, consisted of a circular timber building surrounded by a courtyard which produced evidence for ritual, including ritually 'killed' weapons and the remains of sacrificed animals, with cattle apparently deliberately avoided, perhaps because of some local taboo. The identity of a rectangular porched shrine at South Cadbury hillfort in Somerset is suggested by the avenue of young animal-burials which led to it. In Ireland the great round structure at Navan (Co. Armagh) is undoubtedly a ritual monument. It had a huge central post, dendro-dated to 95/94 BC (when felled). Soon after it was built, the structure was deliberately burned down and sealed beneath a great stone cairn.

Sacrifice and votive offerings

A sacrifice is the gift of something which is of value to the giver. The Celts made offerings to the gods of precious objects: these could be inanimate (tools or weapons, for instance), animals or – occasionally – humans. The more valuable the offering, the more powerful the act of propitiation: thus one would

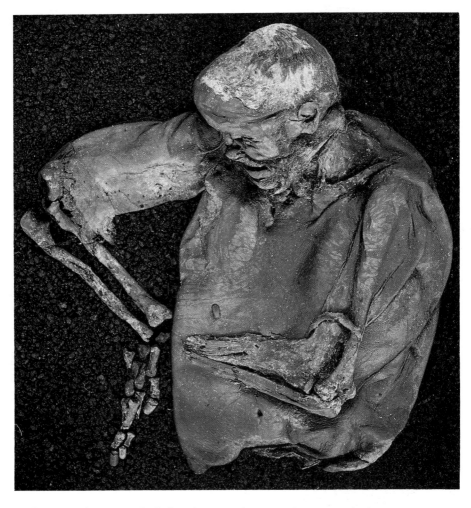

Lindow Man: the Iron Age body found in a peat-bog at Lindow Moss, Cheshire.

expect a human sacrifice to take place only at times of great need or to express great gratitude to the supernatural forces.

Although Classical sources make much of human sacrifice, there is little archaeological evidence to support the practice of ritual murder: Lucan and Tacitus tell of human remains heaped upon altars in sacred groves; there are reports of the imprisonment of malefactors for five years after which they were killed by being impaled; victims were stabbed, hanged, shot with arrows, or burned to death in huge wicker men. In examining the material evidence, care must be taken to distinguish genuine human sacrifice from bodies which were subjected to ritual after natural death. There is little unequivocal evidence for human sacrifice in the archaeological record of Celtic Europe. However, in a few instances, this manner of death does seem indicated. A clear example is Lindow Man, a young male of Iron Age date (first century AD), who suffered severe blows to his head, was garotted and had his throat cut before being thrust

Bronze ceremonial shield, deposited as a votive gift in the river Thames at Battersea, London, in the first century BC. The shield was too fragile ever to have been used in battle, and it may have been made deliberately as an offering to the gods.

face-down in a shallow pool in Lindow Moss, Cheshire. The young man was naked but for an armlet of fox-fur, and his body was painted. Just before he died, he ate what may have been a ritual meal, consisting of a wholemeal bread made of many different species of cereal grain and seed. There is very little allusion to human sacrifice in the vernacular sources, but one Irish tradition involved the ritual triple killing of a king, by burning, wounding and drowning, at the feast of Samhain.

.Although animal-sacrifice is taken for granted as endemic in antiquity, it is important to understand the different forms such activity may take. Animals were often butchered and the meat shared between the community and the gods: some parts (usually the best cuts) were consumed and the rest buried or burnt as offerings. The other main type of sacrifice, that of an entire animal which was interred or burned (a holocaust), represented a considerable economic loss to the sacrificers since it involved taking a valuable sheep, pig or ox out

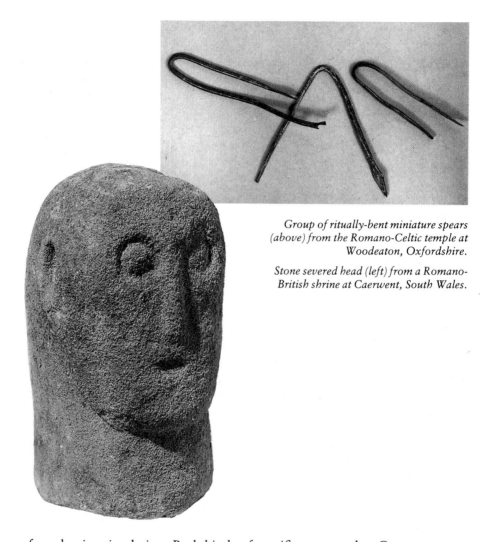

Group of ritually-bent miniature spears (above) from the Romano-Celtic temple at Woodeaton, Oxfordshire.

Stone severed head (left) from a Romano-British shrine at Caerwent, South Wales.

of productive circulation. Both kinds of sacrifice occurred at Gournay: oxen and horses were killed and left as offerings; piglets and lambs were eaten. At Danebury, Hampshire, animals were sometimes killed and interred as multiple burials in old grain storage pits. In Celtic cemeteries there is evidence both of ritual feasting on animals and of meat-offerings left to accompany the dead to the Otherworld. An interesting fact about Celtic animal sacrifice is that the vast majority of ritually slaughtered beasts belonged to domestic species.

Votive offerings

Two aspects of votive offerings of inanimate objects are of especial interest: one is deposition in watery places; the other is ritual breakage. Both rituals were practised in Europe long before the main Celtic period. Both appear to have involved the separation of votive gifts from the mundane world by ritual 'killing', rendering them inaccessible or useless to humankind and thus appropriate gifts to the supernatural powers. At Flag Fen, Cambridgeshire, ritual deposits of metalwork, much of it deliberately broken, were made in the watery fen edge over a period between 1200 and 200 BC. Bent weapons were cast into the holy lake of Llyn Cerrig Bach (Anglesey) in the first century AD. The Gaulish sanctuary of Gournay produced hundreds of destroyed weapons. The Celtic healing goddess Sulis received thousands of Roman coins as gifts, placed in the great reservoir at Bath; many of these coins had been clipped to make them worthless as money. Some of the miniature weapons which were offered in Celtic shrines were snapped or bent in half: Harlow produced a group of four model iron daggers of which two had been broken before deposition.

Rites of the human head

That head-hunting formed part of the cultic tradition of certain Celts is shown by archaeology, the Classical sources and the vernacular literature. Livy, Strabo and Diodorus all describe the decapitation of war victims, whose heads were either kept as trophies or offered in shrines. In the Celto-Ligurian area of southern Gaul, around Marseille, a distinctive group of pre-Roman sanctuaries and *oppida* attest the practice of ritual head-hunting. Most important of these is the cliff-top shrine of Roquepertuse (sixth–second century BC), the portico of which was adorned with niches containing the nailed-in skulls of young men who had died in battle. In Britain, at hillforts such as Bredon Hill (Worcestershire) heads mounted on poles guarded the entrances as symbolic protection for the strongholds. In late Romano-Celtic Britain, especially during the third and fourth centuries AD, certain individuals were decapitated after death before being interred in their tombs. Particularly curious rites took place around Kimmeridge in Dorset, where the bodies of old women were beheaded and the lower jaws removed. It is tempting to see these ladies as witches, prevented from talking and casting spells beyond the grave. That the human head was important in Celtic ritual is demonstrated by the emphasis on the head in Romano-Celtic iconography.

Heads play a prominent role in Welsh and Irish myth. The Ulster hero Cú Chulainn is said to have collected the heads of his enemies and placed them on stones. Two tales demonstrate the western Celts' perception of the magical properties of severed heads, particularly those of superhuman heroes. It was prophesied that the Ulstermen, smitten by Macha's curse of weakness, would regain their strength if they drank milk from the huge severed head of Conall Cernach. In this tale the head attains the properties of a cauldron of regeneration. Readers will recall the similar story of Bendigeidfran in the *Mabinogi*, whose severed head can speak and encourage his companions, bringing them good fortune on their long journey from Harlech to London.

Death, rebirth and the Otherworld

That the Celts had a very profound and positive attitude to death is demonstrated by both literary and archaeological evidence. Julius Caesar comments that the Gauls believed in an ancestor-god, whom he identified with Dispater, the Roman god of the dead.

The transmigration of souls

The druids attach particular importance to the belief that the soul does not perish but passes after death from one body to another.
(trans. Wiseman and Wiseman, 1980)

Caesar, commenting upon druidic doctrine, adds the acid remark that the druids promoted this idea in order that Gaulish warriors would not be afraid of death. Writing in the first century AD, Roman poet Lucan observes that the Celts regarded death merely as an interruption in a long life, as a stage between one life and another. Diodorus Siculus remarks that the Celts perceived men's souls to be immortal and that after a number of years people lived again, their souls inhabiting a new body. So there seems to have been a particular Celtic attitude to death which was discerned by contemporary observers from the Mediterranean world, an attitude which involved a kind of rebirth. The concept of souls living within a succession of bodies is similar to the picture of the Underworld painted by Virgil in the *Aeneid*.

Perceptions of the Otherworld

The mythological traditions of the vernacular literature project the image of the Celtic Otherworld, to which humans passed after death, as an ambiguous place. Much is told about the Happy Otherworld, where the dead live again in a world very much like that of earth but better. Here there is neither pain, disease, ageing nor decay; it is a world full of music, feasting and beauty, though there is still combat between heroes. The other aspect of the Otherworld presents a sharp contrast: it can be a sombre place and full of danger, especially if visited by humans before death. As we saw in an earlier chapter, the Welsh Otherworld was called Annwn or Annwfn, and was described as a court of intoxication. Pwyll, lord of Dyfed, lives in Annwn for a year:

Of all the courts he had seen on earth, that was the court best furnished with meat and drink and vessels of gold and royal jewels.
(trans. Jones and Jones, 1976)

Other documents give more detail of Annwn. The *Spoils of Annwn* describes a magical cauldron, the typical Otherworld vessel of regeneration. It is a great, diamond-studded cauldron, boiled by the breath of nine virgins – perhaps evocative of fertility because of their untapped femininity, like Math's foot-holder (p. 343). The Cauldron of Annwn refuses to cook food for a coward. The ambiguity of Annwn is expressed by the description of the Cwn Annwn (the Hounds of Annwn). In the *Mabinogi*, they are white with red ears – a colouring associated with the Otherworld. Another source speaks of the Cwn Annwn as hell-hounds, small, speckled, greyish-red beasts, chained and led by a black, horned figure. They are death-omens, sent from Annwn to seek out human souls. There is a sinister inexorability about these messengers of death which belies the carefree, happy image of the afterlife.

The Irish Otherworld is in many respects similar to Annwn. In Irish tradition the location of the supernatural world was variable: it could be perceived as on islands in the western ocean, beneath the sea or underground. Mounds called *sídhe* were the dwellings of the dispossessed Tuatha Dé Danann, allotted to each god by the Daghda: each god had his own *sídh*, his Otherworld over which he presided. Another perception of the Irish Otherworld is as the hostel or *bruidhen* which could be situated in the countryside. The supernatural world could be reached by different means: by boat across the sea, as in the *Voyage of Bran*; entry could be gained by a lake or a cave. One entrance to the Otherworld was through the Lake of Cruachain.

In Irish myth the Otherworld is a timeless, ageless, happy place, a source of all wisdom, peace, beauty, harmony and immortality. Known as Tir na n'Og (the 'Land of Forever Young'), it is a world full of magic, enchantment and music. It is a place perceived as an idealised mirror-image of the human world. A feature of each *sídh* or hostel is the feast, central to which is the inexhaustible cauldron, always full of meat. A powerful image is that of the ever-renewing pig of the feast, slaughtered each day by the presiding god, and eternally reborn to be killed afresh the next day. The divine lord of the feast is frequently represented as a man with a pig slung over his shoulder.

Earthly time has no relevance in the Otherworld. If live humans visit it, they remain young while there, but should they return home, their earthly age will catch up with them. There are horrifying stories which describe the fate of people who come back from the supernatural world: Finn's son Oisin instantly ages 300 years when he returns and the same occurrence is recorded in the seventh-century *Voyage of Bran*. Bran and his men travel to the island called the Land of Women, a manifestation of the Happy Otherworld, where they stay for a time, but then some of the men become impatient for their homeland. Like Oisin they are warned not to touch the land but, as the boat approaches the Irish shore, one man leaps into the sea and flings himself onto the beach, only to crumble to dust.

A curious feature of the Celtic Otherworld is that supernatural beings sometimes have need of humans for activities they cannot perform themselves. Thus Pwyll is required by Arawn to fight Hafgan; Cú Chulainn fights battles for Otherworld beings; Finn is lured to the Otherworld by means of enchanted stags, boars, youths or women.

The sombre aspect of the Otherworld is equally represented in myth. Samhain, at the beginning of November, is a dangerous time, a kind of limbo where the barriers between the real and supernatural worlds are temporarily dissolved, and where humans and spirits can penetrate each other's space, thus upsetting the normal balance. As a land of the dead, the Otherworld can be dark and frightening. The Irish death-god Donn is a sombre being; Arawn, too, has a dark side, and Annwn can be dangerous. Thus in the *Spoils of Annwn*, Arthur barely escapes with his life after his quest for the magical cauldron. It seems that if humans visit the Otherworld while still alive, they are in danger. Thus Cú Chulainn sees all kinds of fearsome monsters and horrific visions. The tale of Da Derga's Hostel describes the *bruidhen* of a god wherein awaits the doom of the Irish king Conaire. On his way there Conaire encounters sinister harbingers of death, three red-clothed horsemen on red horses, their colour indicating their supernatural origin. He also sees the Irish goddess of destruction, the Badbh, who appears in triadic form, as three hideous black hags, naked and bleeding, with ropes around their necks. The symbolism of death, perhaps even human sacrifice, is intense here. Derga is a god of the dead, but the word can also refer to 'red', as if reflective of blood and death. The Badbh is a black, crow-like goddess and black is death's colour.

Death

Archaeological findings suggest that the Iron Age Celts held certain beliefs associated with death and there is evidence of rituals and attempts to communicate with the infernal powers. The contents of graves may indicate a ritual which suggests the expectation of an afterlife. The placing of grave-goods with a body may imply a belief that the deceased would need them, or it might suggest rites of passage, a symbolic act of parting. Individuals of high status in early Iron Age France and Germany (seventh–sixth centuries BC) were buried under great mounds, with wagons and rich grave-furniture indicative of feasting: at Hochdorf in Germany, in the sixth century BC, a prince was laid on a bronze couch, accompanied by his cart, a vessel capable of holding 704 pints (400 litres) of mead and several drinking-horns. In later Iron Age Gaul and parts of Britain, high-ranking people were interred with two-wheeled chariots, weapons and feasting paraphernalia, including great joints of pork. Many graves demonstrate the perception of the funerary or Otherworld feast, with meat and drinking-vessels. Some very late Iron Age graves, dating from the late first century BC or early first century AD, in south-east Britain and on the Continent show the importance of feasting-rituals: amphorae, wine cups, firedogs to guard the cooking fire and meat are all present. It is tempting to link this banquet

Iron Age burial of a warrior accompanied by his dismantled chariot, weapons and other grave-goods, from Somme-Bionne, France. It may have been believed that the dead man would need his sword and spears in the next world.

Chalk figurine of an infernal deity, from what may have been an underground shrine deep in a ritual pit at Deal, Kent. Second century AD.

385

equipment with the Otherworld feast so dear to mythical perceptions of the Celtic afterlife.

While some sepulchral evidence displays the presence of formal Iron Age burial, it is clear that many people were not interred at death and, in Britain, graves are in fact relatively rare. Probably excarnation rituals were practised, whereby the body was exposed until it had decomposed and the spirit was thought to have left the body. Once the soul had departed, the bones could be disposed of without ceremony.

Communication with the infernal forces, assumed to dwell underground, was effected in various ways. At Danebury a particular ritual centred around disused corn-storage pits. Deposits of humans, parts of humans, animals or other offerings were placed at the bottom of these pits, which were then filled. These have been interpreted as thank-offerings to the Underworld gods whose space had been violated by the digging of the pits and who needed both to be placated and thanked for keeping the stored corn fresh.

Many areas of Britain and Celtic Europe show evidence of ritual pits and wells, whose main function may have been to communicate with the Underworld, propitiating the gods with sacrifices and votive gifts. At the Gournay sanctuary the focus of ritual activity was a huge central pit in which the bodies of sacrificed cattle were allowed to rot and feed the chthonic gods.

Links with the Underworld seem often to have been associated with dogs, which may have been symbols of death partly because of their hunting and scavenging imagery. The bodies of several dogs were buried in a deep pit at the shrine of Muntham Court in Sussex; five dog skulls were placed in a pit at Caerwent in Gwent. Some of the Danebury pits contained dogs, and there are many other such instances. That dogs had a mythic association with the Otherworld is demonstrated by the Cwn Annwn, the death-hounds of the Welsh Underworld.

Images of rebirth

The most powerful symbol of regeneration, as projected in both the Welsh and the Irish myths, is the 'Cauldron of Rebirth'. The *bruidhen* or Otherworld hostel, furnished with its ever-replenishing cauldron, has already been discussed. The Irish god particularly associated with this symbol is the Dagdha. In the Welsh tale of Branwen, Bendigeidfran's Irish magic cauldron is described: it can restore dead warriors to life, if they are cooked in it overnight. The soldiers rise again as strong as before, but they have lost the power of speech – a sure sign that they are still dead. This regenerative potency is paralleled by the healing well of the Irish divine leech, Dian Cécht, who restores dead warriors to life by immersing them in the water and chanting incantations over them. Interestingly one of the inner plates of the Gundestrup Cauldron perhaps displays the resurrective properties of cauldrons: it shows a large supernatural figure with a group of Celtic soldiers, one of whom the god is either dipping into or removing from a large vat of liquid.

Late Iron Age cremation grave of a British aristocrat, with equipment for the funerary feast, from Welwyn, Hertfordshire.

Clearly both the vessel and the liquid possess healing, restorative powers in the vernacular myths. Archaeological evidence supports this association between cauldrons and water-ritual: ceremonial cauldrons of sheet-bronze were used as early as the Bronze Age. In the Celtic Iron Age many great cult cauldrons are recorded: the vessels at Llyn Fawr and Llyn Cerrig in Wales; Brå, Rynkeby and Gundestrup in Denmark; Duchcov in Czechoslovakia were all associated with lakes or springs.

Rebirth could be symbolised by other vessels and liquids. In Romano-Celtic iconography, especially in Burgundy, the Gaulish hammer-god is depicted with wine barrels and goblets of red wine which seem to have been symbols of resurrection. An interesting aspect of Celtic perceptions about death and rebirth, associated with blood, is expressed in the imagery of the divine hunt, which is present in many of the myths. Since hunting required bloodshed in order to provide nourishment, the act of hunting acquired the symbolism of resurrection, and the interdependent dualism which exists between life and death. The wine-symbolism of the Burgundian iconography may likewise be linked with blood, death and rebirth.

Certain creatures are particularly symbolic of renewal: the snake was a potent image of rebirth, and the association of this reptile with both death and fertility has already been noted (p. 368). Birds, with their power to leave earth in flight, naturally became identified with the perception of the spirit rising free from the body at death, an idea which persisted into medieval Christian symbolism. Otherworld deities are often associated with birds: the Irish Clíodna had three magical birds which could heal with their song; the three singing birds of Rhiannon, alluded to in the *Mabinogi*, express the same perception of birds that symbolise life after death. Stags possessed regenerative imagery, probably because of the seasonal shedding and regrowth of their antlers, which evoked the symbolism of autumn and spring.

Trees were important symbols of rebirth. Deciduous trees apparently died in winter, their bare branches silhouetted against the sky like the bones of a skeleton, but in spring they were born again, producing new leaves and then fruit. Trees were also seen as a link between life and death, the upper and lower worlds, with their branches stretching towards the sky and their roots buried deep underground. It is interesting that trees, particularly apple trees, feature in many Otherworld myths. Clíodna's birds eat fruit from the sacred apple tree; in the *Voyage of Bran* the symbol of the Otherworld goddess is an apple branch, silver with white blossom. The Happy Otherworld of Arthurian Romance is Avalon, the Paradise of Apple Trees, a magical island in the West.

The god Esus chopping down a willow, perhaps the Tree of Life, from Nôtre Dame, Paris, France. Early first century AD.

Suggestions for further reading

A number of general reference books on the ancient Celts is available: T. G. E. Powell, *The Celts* (London, 1958, with numerous reprints); B. Cunliffe, *The Celtic World* (London, 1979, 1992), provides a well-illustrated overview; M. J. Green (ed.), *The Celtic World* (London, 1995); N. Chadwick, *The Celts* (Penguin, 1970). For those wishing to gain detailed, up-to-date information on the archaeology of the Celts, the lavishly illustrated and well-researched catalogue of the 1991 Venice Exhibition (*The Celts*, London, 1991) is good value (available in hardback and paperback).

The vernacular myths of Ireland and Wales exist in translation in various editions. One of the best collections of Welsh myths is G. and T. Jones, *The Mabinogion* (London, 1976). The Irish material is more scattered: T. Kinsella, *The Táin* (Dublin, 1969), and C. O'Rahilly, *Táin Bó Cuailnge* (Dublin, 1970), present the main Ulster Cycle myths. For the Tuatha Dé Danann see H. D'Arbois de Jubainville, *The Mythological Cycle* (Dublin, 1903); T. F. O'Rahilly, *Early Irish History and Mythology* (Dublin, 1946). Other useful sources on Ireland include P. MacCana, *Celtic Mythology* (London, 1983); D. Ó'Hógain, *The Encyclopaedia of Irish Folklore, Legend and Romance* (London, 1991); T. P. Cross and C. H. Slover, *Ancient Irish Tales* (London, 1937); M. Dillon, *Early Irish Literature* (Chicago, 1948); J. Gantz, *Early Irish Myths and Sagas* (Penguin, 1981). For discussion of Welsh and Irish myths and their relationship to archaeological evidence see M-L. Sjoestedt, *Gods and Heroes of the Celts* (Berkeley, 1982); A. and B. Rees, *Celtic Heritage* (London, 1961); M. J. Green, *Dictionary of Celtic Myth and Legend* (London, 1992); M. J. Green and R. Howell, *Celtic Wales* (Cardiff, 2000).

For general archaeological background to Iron Age Celts in Britain see B. Cunliffe, *Iron Age Communities in Britain* (London, 1991). For an examination of the relationship between Celts and Indo-Europeans, J. B. Mallory, *In Search of the Indo-Europeans* (London, 1989), is probably the most sensible source. For sanctuaries and ritual see S. Piggott, *The Druids* (London, 1968, with reprints); J-L. Brunaux, *The Celtic Gauls: Gods, Rites and Sanctuaries* (London, 1988); A. Woodward, *Shrines and Sacrifice* (London, 1992); G. A. Wait, *Ritual and Religion in Iron Age Britain* (British Archaeological Reports, Oxford, 1985); I. M. Stead, *Lindow Man: The Body in the Bog* (London, 1986). For Iron Age art see R. and V. Megaw, *Celtic Art from its beginnings to the Book of Kells* (London, 1989). For religion and the gods see H. E. Davidson, *Myths and Symbols in Pagan Europe* (Manchester, 1988), which explores the relationship between Celtic and Norse religion and myth; M. J. Green, *The Gods of the Celts* (Gloucester, 1986), *Symbol and Image in Celtic Religious Art* (London, 1989, 1992) and *Animals in Celtic Life and Myth* (London, 1992); A. Ross, *Pagan Celtic Britain* (London, 1967) and *The Pagan Celts* (London, 1986). Good surveys in French include P-M. Duval, *Les Dieux de la Gaule* (Paris, 1976); J. de Vries, *La Religion des Celtes* (Paris, 1963); E. Thevenot, *Divinités et sanctuaires de la Gaule* (Paris, 1968). More recent publications include B. Raftery, *Pagan Celtic Ireland* (London, 1994); M. J. Green, *Celtic Goddesses: Warriors, Virgins and Mothers* (London, 1995); M. Parker Pearson, *The Archaeology of Death and Burial* (Stroud, 1999); F. Lynch, S. Aldhouse-Green and J. L. Davies, *Prehistoric Wales* (Stroud, 2000).

Glossary

Achilles (*Greek*) A hero of the **Trojan War.** As a baby his mother Thetis, a **nymph**, dips him in the River **Styx**, making him immortal and virtually indestructible; but he is killed when an arrow pierces his heel, his only vulnerable spot.

Aeneas (*Roman*) Hero of a myth about the antecedents of Rome. Prince of Troy, son of a Trojan hero and **Venus.** When his city falls at the end of the **Trojan War**, he escapes and sails to Carthage. Here he falls in love with **Dido**; but **Jupiter** commands him to leave her and sail on to his destiny. After further adventures, he eventually reaches the mouth of the River Tiber where, with divine help, he defeats the local tribes and obeys Jupiter's commands to unite with them into one nation: the future Romans. Aeneas' son **Ascanius** founds a town on the future site of Rome.

Aesir (*Norse*) One of the two main groups of gods. Includes **Baldr, Bragi, Frigg, Heimdall, Hod, Idunn, Loki, Nanna, Odin, Sif, Thor** and **Tyr.**

Agamemnon (*Greek*) Leader of the Greeks in the **Trojan Wars.** King of Mycenae, elder brother of **Menelaos.**

Aillil (*Celtic*) King of Connacht, husband of **Medb.** Owns a magnificent bull, the Findbennach. Medb's quest to find its equal causes war between their kingdom and Ulster.

Amaunet (*Egyptian*) A goddess, paired with **Amun**, representing hidden power.

Amazons (*Greek*) Tribe of dangerous, warlike women, skilled riders and archers. They keep men as slaves, spending one month each year with them in order to procreate.

Amulius (*Roman*) Descendant of **Aeneas.** Usurps throne of Alba Longa from his elder brother **Numitor,** murders Numitor's sons and forces his daughter **Rhea Silvia** to become a **Vestal Virgin**, to prevent Numitor from having male heirs. When she is raped and bears **Romulus and Remus,** he unsuccessfully tries to drown them.

Amun (*Egyptian*) A god, paired with **Amaunet**, representing hidden power. Some myths say that Amun was the creator – both of himself and of all other deities.

Amun-Re (*Egyptian*) Fusion of the gods **Amun** and **Re.**

Anat (*Egyptian*) Goddess, daughter of **Re**, given with her sister **Astarte** to Seth, in consolation for his relinquishing the throne of **Osiris** to **Horus.**

Anchises (*Roman*) Hero of the **Trojan War,** father of **Aeneas.**

Andromeda (*Greek*) Wife of **Perseus**, rescued by him from a monster.

Andvari (*Norse*) **Dwarf** from whom Loki stole a magic gold ring, which eventually passed into the hands of **Fafnir** and then **Sigurd.**

Angrboda (*Norse*) A **giantess**, lover of **Loki**, by whom she gives birth to **Fenrir, Iormungand** and **Hel.**

Anna Perenna (*Roman*) Festival held on 15 March to celebrate first full moon of the New Year. Named from an old woman, later a goddess. Celebrated with picnics, copious alcohol, songs and dance.

Annwn (*Celtic*) A Welsh name for the **Otherworld.**

Anubis (*Egyptian*)
(1) God with the head of a jackal, son of **Osiris** and **Nephthys**, guardian of **Isis.** Associated with embalming and the **Underworld.**
(2) Man who, after a series of adventures with his brother **Bata** and

their treacherous wives, becomes Pharaoh of Egypt.

Apep (*Egyptian*) *See* **Apophis**.

Aphrodite (*Greek*) Goddess of love, beauty and marriage. Wife of **Hephaistos**, but courted by **Ares**. Considered to be the essence of female beauty. Equivalent to the Roman **Venus**.

Apollo (*Greek, Roman*) God of light (thus connected with the sun), reason, inspiration, arts, music, prophecy and healing. Son of **Zeus** and twin brother of **Artemis**.

Apophis (*Egyptian*) Giant snake representing chaos and destruction. As arch-enemy of the sun god (*see* **Re**), tries to block his passage through the sky and the **Underworld**. Also known as Apep.

Apples of Youth (*Norse*) Fruits which keep the gods permanently young and vigorous, guarded by **Idunn**.

Arawn (*Celtic*) Lord of **Annwyn**.

Ares (*Greek*) God of war and lover of **Aphrodite**. Equivalent to the Roman **Mars**.

Argonauts (*Greek*) Crew of a ship, the *Argo*, who sail with **Jason** on his quest to fetch the **Golden Fleece**.

Ariadne (*Greek*) Daughter of King Minos, guardian of the **Minotaur**. Falls in love with **Theseus**, helps him overcome the monster and runs away with him. He abandons her on an island, from where she is rescued by **Dionysos** who then marries her.

Artemis (*Greek*) Virgin goddess of hunting, wild beasts and childbirth. Associated with the moon. Daughter of **Zeus** and twin sister of **Apollo**.

Ascanius (*Roman*) Son of **Aeneas**, he founds the town of Alba Longa on the future site of Rome.

Asgard (*Norse*) Realm of the gods, where each deity resides in a separate magnificent hall.

Astarte (*Egyptian*) Goddess, daughter of

Re, given with her sister **Anat** to **Seth** as consolation when he relinquishes the throne of **Osiris** to **Horus**. In another myth, the sea god demands her as his wife but Seth fights in her defence.

Aten (*Egyptian*) A sun god.

Athena (*Greek*) Virgin goddess of wisdom, daughter of **Zeus**. Protects cities and heroes. Dresses in armour, yet brings peace. Patron of craftworkers, and a wise, intelligent counsellor. Equivalent to the Roman **Minerva**.

Atum (*Egyptian*) A creator god and a sun god, with both male and female qualities. Represents totality and contains the essence of every deity that he later brings into being.

Bacchus (*Roman*) God of wine, equivalent to the Greek **Dionysos**.

Badbh (*Celtic*) One of the trio of war goddesses (*see* also **Macha, Morrigan**) and a prophetess of doom and death. Appears in battle as a woman or a crow, confusing and terrifying soldiers and causing havoc.

Baldr (*Norse*) A god, known as 'the Beautiful' and 'Good'. Son of **Odin** and **Frigg**, married to **Nanna**. Dreams of his own death, so Frigg persuades all creation to take an oath not to harm him. However, **Loki** discovers mistletoe has not taken the oath and tricks **Hod** into killing Baldr with this. A giantess (possibly Loki in disguise) subsequently foils the gods' attempt to rescue Baldr from **Hel**.

Bata (*Egyptian*)
(1) God with a bull's head.
(2) A man, brother of **Anubis**.

Bellona (*Roman*) A goddess of war.

Beltene (*Celtic*) Early summer festival with bonfires, held on 1 May.

Bendigeidfran (*Celtic*) (also known as Brán the Blessed) A Welsh nobleman of gigantic size, brother of **Branwen**. When she is humiliated by the Irish, he leads an army against them but is mortally wounded. He orders his own head to be cut off and buried in London facing east, to prevent foreigners from invading Britain.

Benu (*Egyptian*) Bird, form of the sun god, said in some myths to be the first deity. Brought the first light into the darkness of chaos, and its cry was the first sound. Depicted as a heron. Sometimes identified with the Greek phoenix, which burns itself to death every 500 years, only to be reborn from its own ashes.

Blodeuwedd (*Celtic*) A 'woman' made by **Math** and **Gwydion**, from the flowers of oak, broom and meadowsweet, and given as a wife to **Lleu Llaw Gyffes**.

Bragi (*Norse*) God of eloquence and poetry, married to **Idunn**.

Brán the Blessed (*Celtic*) Another name for **Bendigeidfran**.

Branwen (*Celtic*) Welsh noblewoman, marries the Irish **Matholwch**, who treats her as a serf. She sends news of this to her brother **Bendigeidfran** via a bird. When he makes war against Ireland, she dies of a broken heart.

Brynhild (*Norse*) A **valkyrie**, who is betrayed in love by **Sigurd** and covets his magic gold ring.

Caer (*Celtic*) Beautiful Irish princess, condemned by her jealous father to turn into a swan on alternate years. **Oenghus** falls in love with her, turns into a swan himself and marries her.

Calypso (*Greek*) **Nymph** who makes **Odysseus** her lover and keeps him on her island for seven years, until he is freed by divine intervention.

Cassandra (*Greek*) Daughter of Priam, king of Troy. Prophetess who warns that the **Trojan Horse** will bring death and destruction. However, she is fated never to be believed.

Castor and Pollux (*Roman, Greek*)

Divine brothers of **Helen of Troy**, one or both the sons of **Jupiter** (**Zeus**). Protectors of sailors and cavalry.

Cathbadh (*Celtic*) Irish druid in the court of King **Conchobar**. Prophesies the doom of **Deirdre** and the triumphs of **Cú Chulainn**. Teaches young heroes the craft of divination.

cauldrons (*Celtic*) Large food vessels associated with feasting and plenty, often imbued with magic powers e.g. to constantly refill themselves or restore the dead to life.

centaur (*Greek*) Mythical creature with head and torso of a man, but the lower body of a horse. Many are violent and lecherous; a few are of noble character.

Cerberus (*Greek*) Three-headed dog guarding the entrance to the **Underworld**.

Ceres (*Roman*) Goddess of agriculture and fertility, equivalent to the Greek **Demeter**.

Circe (*Greek*) Sorceress encountered by **Odysseus**. She turns his men into pigs, but he persuades her to release them and they stay with her for a year.

Claudia Quinta (*Roman*) Noblewoman of notoriously extravagant dress and frank tongue, falsely accused of unchastity. Symbolically proves her virtue when the cult image of **Magna Mater** is first brought to Rome: the boat carrying it is stuck in mud, but Magna Mater heeds Claudia's supplications and miraculously allows her to haul it ashore.

Conall Cernach (*Celtic*) Irish semi-divine hero, grandson of **Cathbadh**, foster father and tutor to **Cú Chulainn**, guardian of Ireland's boundaries.

Conchobar (*Celtic*) Irish king of Ulster. Maintains the 'Red Branch Knights' under **Cú Chulainn**, also a band of youth warriors. A past husband of **Medb**. Plays a major role in tragic love affair of **Deirdre** and **Naoise**.

Cú Chulainn (*Celtic*) The greatest hero

of Ulster, with superhuman fighting powers from boyhood. He is brave, beautiful, strong and invincible. Closely associated with the gods, he has magic weapons and armour.

Culhwch (*Celtic*) Welsh hero, cursed to fall in love with **Olwen**, daughter of the giant **Ysbadden**. Wins her by completing a series of impossible tasks, helped by the knights of King Arthur.

Cupid (*Roman*) God of love, son of **Mercury** and **Venus**. Equivalent to the Greek **Eros**.

Cybele (*Roman*) Another name for **Magna Mater**.

cyclopes (*Greek*) Hideous, man-eating giants with a single eye in the middle of their forehead.

Daghda (*Celtic*) The most important god of the **Tuatha Dé Danann**. Provider of plenty and symbol of fertility. Owns an enormous, inexhaustible **cauldron** and a miraculous club which kills with one end and restores life with the other. Ambiguous figure, grotesque, outrageous and promiscuous, yet powerful father of his tribe.

Danu (*Celtic*) Divine ancestress of the **Tuatha Dé Danann**.

Deirdre (*Celtic*) Daughter of **Conchobar**'s story teller. **Cathbadh** predicts she will bring ruin to Ulster, so Conchobar imprisons her, but she escapes with her lover **Naoise**. When Conchobar treacherously kills him, Deirdre commits suicide.

Demeter (*Greek*) Goddess of crops and of both human and agricultural fertility.

Diana (*Roman*) Goddess of hunting and the moon, equivalent to the Greek **Artemis**.

Dian Cécht (*Celtic*) One of the **Tuatha Dé Danann**. God of healing and medicine with a smith's skills. Restores dead warriors to life by immersing them in water and chanting spells.

Diarmaid (*Celtic*) One of **Finn macCumhaill**'s warriors. Bears a 'love spot' which causes any woman who sees it to fall helplessly in love with him. **Gráinne** forces him to elope with her: Finn pursues them for many years, finally pretends to forgive Diarmaid, but treacherously has him killed by a magic boar.

Dido (*Roman*) Widowed queen of Carthage, lover of **Aeneas**. When the gods command him to leave her in order to found a new city in Italy, she curses him then kills herself. Later, when Aeneas meets her ghost during a visit to the **Underworld**, she shuns him.

Dionysos (*Greek*) God of fertility, wine and 'altered states' such as drunkenness and ecstasy. Equivalent to the Roman **Bacchus**.

Dis Pater (*Roman*) God of death and the Underworld, equivalent to the Greek **Hades**.

Djedi (*Egyptian*) Legendary magician of voracious appetite who can prophesy and repair dismembered bodies.

Djeheuty (*Egyptian*)
(1) Another name for **Thoth**.
(2) Legendary warrior of the second millennium BC.

Draupnir (*Norse*) A magic gold ring, forged by **dwarfs**. Every ninth night, it produces eight more rings, equal to it in weight.

druids (*Celtic*) Priests of extensive training and high social rank who control supernatural forces, often by human sacrifice, examining the victim's innards to foresee the future. Play an important role in many Irish myths. *See* **Cathbadh**.

Duat (*Egyptian*) The underworld through which the sun god travels overnight.

dwarfs (*Norse*) Ugly, evil creatures who live in pot-holes and caves. Exceptionally skilled as smiths, they lust after gold and women.

Ennead (*Egyptian*) A group of nine deities created by and including **Atum**. The others comprise four couples: **Shu** and **Tefnut**, **Geb** and **Nut**, **Osiris** and **Isis**, **Seth** and **Nephthys**.

Epona (*Celtic*) European goddess of abundance and prosperity, closely associated with horses.

Eros (*Greek*) God of love, son of **Hermes** and **Aphrodite**. Equivalent to the Roman **Cupid**.

Etain (*Celtic*) Mortal woman with supernatural powers, seduced by **Midhir**. His jealous wife puts various spells on her from which she is rescued by **Oenghus**. Eventually she dies but is reborn a thousand years later and marries the king of Ireland. Midhir uses trickery to win her back, turns them both into swans and escapes with her.

Eye of Re (*Egyptian*) The 'eye of the sun'. An independent entity which can take other forms, e.g. of **Re**'s daughter **Hathor**. Also *see* **Re**.

Fafnir (*Norse*) A man who turns himself into a dragon to guard a hoard of gold, including a magic gold ring. The hoard was originally paid to his father as blood-money (compensation) by **Loki**, because he had unwittingly killed Fafnir's brother Otr. His other brother, **Regin**, persuades the hero **Sigurd** to kill Fafnir, thus releasing the hoard and the ring.

Faunus (*Roman*) A god of the woodland.

Faustulus (*Roman*) The shepherd who raised **Romulus and Remus**.

Fenrir (*Norse*) A wolf, offspring of **Loki** and **Angrboda**. Alarmed by a prophecy that it will one day destroy the world, the gods commission the **dwarfs** to fashion a magic chain to bind it to a rock, with a sword in its jaws to stop it biting. Fenrir is destined to play a major role in **Ragnarok**.

Ferghus mac Roich (*Celtic*) A great hero of Ulster, serving **Conchobar** but later defecting to **Medb**'s court. Of gigantic size, strength and appetite. Owns a magic sword.

Fianna (*Celtic*) Elite band of Irish warriors, led by **Finn macCumhaill**.

Finn macCumhaill (*Celtic*) Outstanding warrior chief serving the high king of Ireland. Leader of the **Fianna** and hero of many extraordinary magical adventures.

Fir Bholg (*Celtic*) Mythical people, early inhabitants of Ireland, ousted by the **Tuatha Dé Danann**.

Fomorians (*Celtic*) Permanent inhabitants of Ireland, a divine race of evil demonic beings, opposed to the **Tuatha Dé Danann**.

Freyia (*Norse*) Beautiful goddess of love, beauty and fertility, and leader of the **valkyries**. Sister of **Freyr**.

Freyr (*Norse*) God of fertility, brother of **Freyia**. Controls the weather and owns a number of wondrous magic objects.

Frigg (*Norse*) Mother goddess who knows the fates of all people. Wife of **Odin** and mother of **Baldr**.

Gaia (*Greek*) Goddess of the earth, mother of numerous lesser deities and monsters.

Geb (*Egyptian*) The earth god, paired with **Nut**.

Geirrod (*Norse*)
(1) A **giant** who captures **Loki** but frees him in return for luring **Thor** to his hall without any weapons.
(2) A king favoured by **Odin**. When the god visits his hall in disguise, Geirrod fails to recognise him, has him tortured, and is killed in revenge.

geis (*Celtic*) Irish 'sacred bond' compelling or forbidding someone to carry out a particular act. To break this bond results in great misfortune.

genius (*Roman*) A person's protecting spirit.

Gerd (*Norse*) A beautiful **giantess**, wife of **Freyr.**

giants and giantesses (*Norse*) The original inhabitants of the world, forced out by the gods to live in **Iotunheim.** They are constantly at war with the gods. Some giants are stupid but others are cunning and wise. Many giantesses are very beautiful.

Golden Fleece (*Greek*) Fleece of a wondrous flying ram which saves two children from being sacrificed to **Zeus** by their wicked stepmother. Only one child survives the adventure: in gratitude he sacrifices the ram to Zeus and gives its fleece to King Aeetes of Kolchis. Aeetes keeps it in a sacred grove, guarded by a fierce snake, until it is stolen by **Jason.**

Gorgons (*Greek*) A trio of fierce, snake-headed female monsters. Their gaze turns people to stone. *See* **Medusa, Perseus.**

Graces (*Greek*) Three divine attendants of **Aphrodite**, daughters of **Zeus** and a sea **nymph.** Their names mean Splendour, Good Cheer and Merriment.

Gráinne (*Celtic*) Irish girl betrothed to **Finn macCumhaill**, who then falls in love with **Diarmaid** and forces him to elope with her. After Diarmaid's death she agrees to marry Finn.

Gudrun (*Norse*) Ill-fated queen, wife of **Sigurd**, friend and love rival of **Brynhild.**

Gunnlod (*Norse*) **Giantess** who guards the **Mead of Poetry** inside a mountain. **Odin** seduces her and she allows him to drink up all the mead.

Gwydion (*Celtic*) A Welsh magician who helps create **Blodeuwedd** and restores **Lleu Llaw Gyffes** to human form.

Hades (*Greek*) God of the **Underworld.**

Harakhti (*Egyptian*) An aspect of the sun god: the sun on the distant horizon, associated with a soaring hawk.

Harpies (*Greek*) Monsters with the head of an old woman and the body of a bird.

Hathor (*Egyptian*) Goddess of love and joy, daughter of **Re.** In one story, identified as the **Eye of Re**, she transforms into **Sakhmet** and tries to destroy the humans who are plotting against her father.

Hauhet (*Egyptian*) Goddess, paired with **Heh**, representing flood force.

Heh (*Egyptian*) God, paired with **Hauhet**, representing flood force.

Heimdall (*Norse*) God linked with the sea, born of nine **giantesses** in the form of waves. Knowing, tough and vigorous, and a sworn enemy of **Loki.** The watchman of **Asgard** and herald of **Ragnarok.**

Hel (*Norse*)
(1) The realm of the dead, lying amongst the roots of **Yggdrasil.**
(2) Goddess of the realm of the dead. Her face is half-human, half blank.

Helen of Troy (*Greek*) Wife of King **Menelaos** of Troy, and 'the most beautiful woman in the world'. Promised to **Paris** by **Aphrodite.** When he abducts her, this causes the **Trojan War.**

Hephaistos (*Greek*) Lame god of fire and volcanoes and a skilled smith, equivalent to the Roman **Vulcan.** Husband of **Aphrodite.**

Hera (*Greek*) Goddess of marriage and women's affairs. Sister and jealous wife of **Zeus.** Equivalent to the Roman **Juno.**

Herakles (*Greek*) Hero, son of **Zeus** and a mortal woman. Incited by the jealous **Hera** to kill his wife and children, he is punished by being sent on a mission to complete twelve seemingly impossible 'Labours', which he achieves with divine help.

Hercules (*Roman*) Roman form of **Herakles.** Centre of a cult and annual ritual feast to celebrate his destruction of an evil, fire-breathing, man-eating monster.

Hermes (*Greek*) Messenger of the gods,

who flies with the aid of winged sandals and a winged hat. Also the god of travellers and commerce. Equivalent to the Roman **Mercury**.

Hestia (*Greek*) Virgin goddess of the hearth and home.

Hod (*Norse*) Blind god, unwitting killer of **Baldr**.

Hoenir (*Norse*) A big, good-looking god who often appears as a companion to **Odin** and **Loki**.

Horus (*Egyptian*) The hawk god, son of **Isis** and **Osiris**. When his uncle **Seth** seizes his dead father's throne, Horus seeks justice from a divine tribunal. Eventually Osiris intervenes from the **Underworld** to ensure that Horus becomes king.

Hymir (*Norse*) A **giant** who takes **Thor** fishing to catch **Iormungand**, but cuts Thor's line, allowing the monster to sink safely back into the sea.

Idunn (*Norse*) Goddess of spring, keeper of the **Apples of Youth**. Married to **Bragi**.

Imhotep (*Egyptian*) Real-life architect of the third millennium BC who became revered as a cult figure embodying the wisdom of scribes and the bringer of sons. Identified as the son of **Ptah**.

Iormungand (*Norse*) The 'world snake', which lies coiled around the ocean encircling **Midgard**.

Iotunheim (*Norse*) The realm of **giants**, lying across the ocean from **Midgard**. A bleak land, dominated by storms, ice and snow.

Isis (*Egyptian*) Goddess, wife and sister of **Osiris**. Healer, magician, teacher of the skills of civilisation to women. After Osiris' death, she uses magic to restore his body to life just long enough to conceive their son **Horus**. Later she invents the technique of embalming and mummifying the body, thus giving him eternal life in the **Underworld**.

Janus (*Roman*) God of doors, arches and beginnings. His image is shown facing both ways, symbolising his link with both entrances and exits.

Jason (*Greek*) Hero who leads the **Argonauts** on a successful quest to bring the **Golden Fleece** to his uncle **Pelias**, usurper of his father's throne.

Jocasta (*Greek*) Queen of Thebes, who abandons her son **Oedipus** at birth. After being widowed, she unwittingly marries him, thus fulfilling an ill-omened prophecy. *See also* **Laios**.

Jove (*Roman*) Another name for **Jupiter**, equivalent to the Greek **Zeus**.

Juno (*Roman*) Goddess of women and motherhood, married to **Jupiter**. Equivalent to the Greek **Hera**.

Jupiter (*Roman*) Supreme god, ruler of the sky, married to **Juno**. Equivalent to the Greek **Zeus**.

ka (*Egyptian*) A person's life force or spirit, surviving physical death.

Kauket (*Egyptian*) Goddess, paired with Kek, symbolising darkness.

Kek (*Egyptian*) God, paired with **Kauket**, symbolising darkness.

Khepri (*Egyptian*) An aspect of the sun god: the rising sun, associated with the scarab beetle.

Khnum (*Egyptian*) Ram-headed god, said to have created human beings at the potter's wheel.

Labours of Herakles (*Greek*) Twelve seemingly impossible tasks, successfully completed by **Herakles**. He killed the Nemean Lion (1) and the Lernaean Hydra (2); caught the Erymanthian Boar (3) and the Keryneian Hind (4); shot the Stymphalian Birds (5); cleaned the Augean Stables (6); caught the Cretan Bull (7) and the man-eating Mares of Diomedes (8); fetched the girdle of the **Amazon** queen Hippolyte (9); killed Geryon and brought back his cattle (10);

and brought back **Cerberus** from the **Underworld** (11) and the Apples of the Hesperides (12).

Labyrinth (*Greek*) An underground maze on Crete where King Minos kept the **Minotaur.**

Laios (*Greek*) King of Thebes who abandons his infant son **Oedipus** to avoid an ill-omened prophecy, but is later unwittingly killed by him. *See* also **Jocasta.**

lares (*Roman*) Household gods.

Latinus (*Roman*) Father-in-law of **Aeneas**, ruler of the Latin people who unite with the Trojans.

Lavinia (*Roman*) Daughter of **Latinus**, wife of **Aeneas.** The city he founds, Lavinium, is named after her.

Leda (*Greek*) Queen of Sparta, raped by **Zeus** in the form of a swan. The children thus conceived are: **Helen of Troy, Castor and Pollux** and Clytemnestra, wife of **Agamemnon.**

Liber (*Roman*) Another name for **Bacchus.**

Lleu Llaw Gyffes (*Celtic*) Welsh youth, given **Blodeuwedd** for a wife. He is protected from death by a series of mystical taboos. When Blodeuwedd treacherously overcomes these, he turns into an eagle.

Loki (*Norse*) A god, an intriguing and ambiguous trickster who often gets the other deities into trouble and danger, only to save them at the last minute. Sometimes sinister, sometimes comical, he can fly and shape-change. He fathers various animals and monsters, including **Fenrir.**

Lotus Eaters (*Greek*) Inhabitants of an island visited by **Odysseus.** They live on enchanted fruits that cause memory loss.

Lugh (*Celtic*) Irish god of light, known as 'the shining one'. A warrior, sorcerer and master craftsman, related by blood to both the **Tuatha Dé Danann** (whom he leads after **Nuadu**) and the **Fomorians.**

Lupercal (*Roman*) The cave where a she-wolf finds and suckles the infants **Romulus and Remus.**

Lupercalia (*Roman*) Annual festival held on 15 February, possibly to celebrate the origin of Rome, centred on the **Lupercal.** Involved sacrifice of goats, a dog and cakes made by **Vestal Virgins**, which was followed by youths in sacrificial goatskins running a circuit and striking onlookers with goatskin thongs.

Maat (*Egyptian*) Goddess of truth, justice and orderly conduct. Depicted as a kneeling woman with an ostrich feather on her head.

Macha (*Celtic*) One of the trio of war goddesses (*see* also **Badbh, Morrigan**), linked with horses and promiscuous sexuality. Can change into a crow or raven and appears in three identities: (1) as a prophetess of Ireland's doom; (2) as a warrior-ruler of Ireland; (3) as a divine bride of the moral Crunnchu. Cruelly humiliated by him, she curses the men of Ulster to weakness in crisis.

Manannan (*Celtic*) A sea god and magician who rides the waves like horses. Helps the **Tuatha Dé Danann** in battle with his magic boat, sword and horse. Also owns magic pigs which, though killed and eaten, come alive again the next day.

Manawydan ap Llyr (*Celtic*) Brother of **Branwen** and **Bendigeidfran.** Second husband of **Rhiannon.** A magician, trickster and craftsman.

Mars (*Roman*) God of war, equivalent to the Greek **Ares.**

Mater Magna (*Roman*) The 'Great Mother', a black stone, centre of a cult introduced to Rome from Asia Minor (Turkey) in 204 BC, in an effort to improve Roman fortunes in the war against Hannibal. The cult featured eunuch priests, wild music and dancing, and a week-long festival called the Great Games. Also known as Cybele.

Math (*Celtic*) Welsh lord of Gwynedd. He can only stay alive if he sits with his feet in the lap of a virgin, except during war.

Matholwch (*Celtic*) Irish king who marries **Branwen** but treats her as a serf, causing the Welsh to make war against Ireland.

Mead of Poetry (*Norse*) A brew of honey and the blood of a wise man called Kvasir. Anyone who drinks it achieves the gift of composing eloquent poetry. Brewed by **dwarfs**, stolen by **giants**, retrieved by **Odin**, who safeguards it for posterity.

Medea (*Greek*) Daughter of King Aertes of Kolchis, guardian of the **Golden Fleece**. A powerful and malevolent sorceress, she helps **Jason** obtain the fleece then forces him to marry her, eventually destroying his reputation through her evil spells.

Medusa (*Greek*) One of the **Gorgons**, killed and beheaded by **Perseus**.

Medb (*Celtic*) Irish goddess of sovereignty, war, sexuality and territory. Also Queen of Connacht, married to **Ailill**. When her magnificent white bull defects to his herd, her quest to replace it causes war between their kingdom and Ulster. Can shape-change from hag to young girl, and runs with superhuman speed. Promiscuous: no king may rule Ireland without first mating with her. Causes death of Ailill, **Conall Cernach**, **Cú Chulainn** and **Fergus**.

Menelaos (*Greek*) King of Sparta, husband of **Helen**. When **Paris** abducts her, Menelaos summons help from all her former suitors and all the kings and noblemen of Greece, thus starting the **Trojan War**.

Mercury (*Roman*) Winged messenger of the gods and god of commerce, equivalent to the Greek **Hermes**.

Meretseger (*Egyptian*) A snake goddess. Her name means 'she who loves silence'.

Midgard (*Norse*) The realm of people; a circle of land completely surrounded by the ocean.

Midhir (*Celtic*) A divine lord of the Irish **Otherworld**, one of the **Tuatha Dé Danann**, with shape-changing powers. Married to Fuamnach, but loves **Etain** whom he chases for a thousand years and finally wins by trickery.

Mimir (*Norse*) 'The wisest of men'. During the war between the **Aesir** and **Vanir** he is sent back and forth as a hostage and finally beheaded. **Odin** pickles the head, smears it with herbs and chants spells over it. He then uses it to consult the spirit world and discover occult secrets.

Mimir's Well (*Norse*) Lying beneath a root of **Yggdrasil**, the source of all wisdom and good sense. **Odin** leaves one of his eyes in it, in exchange for some of **Mimir's** wisdom.

Minerva (*Roman*) Goddess of wisdom, equivalent to the Greek **Athena**.

Minotaur (*Greek*) A man-eating monster, half-man, half-bull, kept in the **Labyrinth** by King Minos of Crete. Killed by **Theseus**.

Miollnir (*Norse*) The hammer of **Thor**, his main weapon against the giants. When thrown, it returns to him like a boomerang.

Monad (*Egyptian*) A form of **Atum** as the sun god, the supreme being, representing totality and the quintessence of all the forces and elements of nature.

Morrigan (*Celtic*) One of the trio of war goddesses (*see also* **Badbh, Macha**). Harbinger of death, prophet, skilled shape-changer most often appearing as a death-crow. Symbol of sexuality and fertility. Plays an important role in stories of **Cú Chulainn**.

Nanna (*Norse*) A goddess, wife of **Baldr**. After his death she collapses with grief, and is burnt with him on his funeral pyre.

Naoise (*Celtic*) Lover of **Deirdre**. At first fearfully rejects her advances but is then compelled to elope with her. He and his two brothers are treacherously murdered by **Conchobar**.

Naunet (*Egyptian*) Goddess, paired with **Nu**, representing primeval waters.

Neith (*Egyptian*) 'The Great Mother', a creator goddess, also associated with war and hunting. Emerges from **Nu** to create deities and people. **Apophis** is born from her spittle. During the conflict between **Horus** and **Seth**, the other gods seek her advice.

Nephthys (*Egyptian*) Goddess, daughter of **Nut** and **Geb**, sister of **Isis, Osiris** and **Seth**. Loves Osiris and after his death joins Isis in ritual mourning.

Neptune (*Roman*) God of the sea. Equivalent to the Greek **Poseidon**.

Niav (*Celtic*) Beautiful, golden-haired daughter of the king of **Tir na n'Og**; she takes **Oisin** away to her country.

Niord (*Norse*) God of seafaring, fishing and riches who marries Skadi, a mysterious **giantess** or goddess of the far north. Their children are **Freyr** and **Freyia**. Their relationship ends because Niord wants to stay by the sea, whereas his wife longs for the mountains.

Norns (*Norse*) Three supernatural virgins who decide the fates of people and gods. They live by a sacred spring or fountain under a root of **Yggdrasil**.

Nu or **Nun** (*Egyptian*)
(1) The primeval being at the beginning of time, before the cosmos was created. A dark stretch of inert water stretching to infinity and containing the essence of all potential life. Even after the creation it continues to surround the firmament and the **Underworld**.
(2) God of the primeval waters, paired with **Naunet**.

Nuadu (*Celtic*) King of the **Tuatha Dé Danann**. Temporarily compelled to relinquish power after losing an arm in battle, until **Dian Cécht** makes him a new silver arm. Later becomes so demoralised by constant conflict with the **Fomorians** that he gives up the throne to **Lugh**.

Numitor (*Roman*) Descendant of **Aeneas** and king of Alba Longa, usurped by **Amulius**. Grandfather of **Romulus and Remus**, who later restore him to the throne.

Nun (*Egyptian*) *See* **Nu**.

Nut (*Egyptian*) Goddess of the sky. Paired with **Geb** and often depicted with her body arched over his, symbolising the sky arching over the earth. Mother of **Osiris, Isis, Seth** and **Nephthys**.

nymphs (*Greek*) Immortal female water-spirits with the gift of prophecy.

Odin (*Norse*) A major god, ruler of **Asgard** and leader of the other deities. Has over 200 names, but often known as 'All-Father'. Oversees magic, poetry, inspiration and battle. Gave away one of his eyes to **Mimir** in exchange for wisdom. Can shape-change and often wanders through **Midgard** in disguise.

Odysseus (*Greek*) Heroic king of Ithaca who deserts his kingdom to spend ten years fighting in the **Trojan Wars** and another ten years travelling home on an enchanted voyage known as the Odyssey.

Oedipus (*Greek*) Son of the king and queen of Thebes. They attempt to kill him at birth in an attempt to defy the prediction of the **Oracle at Delphi** that he will kill his father and marry his mother. However, he survives, is raised by strangers and unwittingly fulfils the prophecy. *See* also **Jocasta, Laios**.

Oenghus (*Celtic*) Irish god of love.

Ogdoad (*Egyptian*) A group of eight primordial paired gods and goddesses: **Nu** and **Naunet, Heh** and **Hauhet, Kek** and **Kauket, Amun** and **Amaunet**.

Oisin (*Celtic*) Son of **Finn macCumhaill**. Follows **Niav** to **Tir na n'Og**. Eventually he feels homesick and returns to Ireland to find that hundreds of years have passed. He breaks her **geis** not to step on Irish soil and is transformed into a decrepit old man.

Olwen (*Celtic*) Daughter of **Ysbaddaden**. Marries **Culhwch**.

Olympos (*Greek*) Home of the gods and goddesses; an actual mountain in Greece.

oracle (*Greek, Roman*) A priest or priestess inspired to give divine advice or prophecy (often obscure) to enquirers.

Oracle at Delphi (*Greek*) The **oracle** at a major religious sanctuary, regarded as 'the navel of the earth', who answers enquirers' questions with riddles.

Osiris (*Egyptian*) God, husband and brother of **Isis**, father of **Horus**. Initially rules as the first Pharaoh on earth, teaching mankind farming, civilisation and religion. Murdered by **Seth** but restored by Isis who gives him eternal life. Becomes ruler of the **Underworld** where he sits in judgement on the souls of the dead.

Otherworld (*Celtic*) A hedonistic supernatural realm, where time has no meaning, and old age and death are unknown.

Paris (*Greek*) A shepherd, and son of the king of Troy. When **Hera**, **Athena** and **Aphrodite** argue over which of them is the most beautiful, they order Paris to be the judge. He accepts Aphrodite's bribe to choose her and is rewarded with **Helen of Troy**, thus causing the **Trojan War**.

Pelias (*Greek*) Uncle of **Jason**, who usurps the throne of Iolkos and sends him on his quest to fetch the **Golden Fleece**.

penates (*Roman*) Gods of the store cupboard.

Penelope (*Greek*) Wife of **Odysseus**, who remains faithful to him during his twenty-year absence.

Persephone (*Greek*) Daughter of **Demeter**, abducted into the **Underworld** by **Hades**. Ordered by **Zeus** to stay with Hades for one-third of the year, returning to Demeter for the remaining time.

Perseus (*Greek*) Hero, son of **Zeus** and a mortal woman. Sent by the wicked King Polydektes to fetch the head of **Medusa**, he achieves the quest with divine help. On his way home he rescues **Andromeda** from a monster and marries her, then destroys Polydektes and inherits his kingdom.

Poseidon (*Greek*) God of the sea and of earthquakes, equivalent to the Roman **Neptune**.

Prometheus (*Greek*) One of the first divine beings, a Titan. Protects humankind in opposition to the gods. In revenge, **Zeus** withholds fire from humans, forcing them to live in cold and darkness; but Prometheus steals for them a flame from the forge of **Hephaistos**. Zeus punishes him by binding him to a rock where an eagle eats his liver for thousands of years. He is finally freed by **Herakles**.

Pryderi (*Celtic*) Welsh hero, son of **Rhiannon** and **Pwyll**.

Ptah (*Egyptian*) A god of creation and a master craftsman. Creates gods and kings from precious metals or by thinking of them and speaking their names aloud. Present in the hearts and mouths of all living things. Paired with **Sakhmet**.

Pwyll (*Celtic*) Welsh hero who visits **Annwn** for a year and makes a pact of friendship with **Arawn**. First husband of **Rhiannon**.

Ra (*Egyptian*) See **Re**.

Ragnarok (*Norse*) Prophetic vision of the 'end of the world', characterised by chaos, devastating natural catastrophes and a final battle between the gods and **giants**. The earth will be destroyed but eventually re-emerge, to be repopulated by the descendants of gods and mortals.

Re (*Egyptian*) The sun god, who creates humankind from his tears. Rules on earth first, but as he becomes old and decrepit he learns that people are plotting against him, so he sends his daughter **Hathor** to destroy them, but later relents and saves them. Finally moves to the sky, where he makes a dangerous daily journey through the cosmos in a ship, dying each night and passing through the **Underworld**, to be born again the following morning. Sometimes known as **Ra**.

Regin (*Norse*) Brother of **Fafnir**. Forger of the sword with which **Sigurd** kills Fafnir in his dragon shape. Sigurd then uses the same weapon to kill Regin.

Rhea Silvia (*Roman*) Daughter of **Numitor**. Forced by her wicked uncle **Amulius** to become a **Vestal Virgin** to prevent her having children, she is raped by **Mars** and bears twin sons, **Romulus and Remus**.

Rhiannon (*Celtic*) Beautiful Welsh queen, perhaps originally a goddess, linked with horses. Marries **Pwyll**, falsely accused of and punished for murdering their son **Pryderi**, but pardoned when Pryderi returns alive. After Pwyll's death she marries **Manawydan Ap Llyr**.

Rig (*Norse*) An alias of **Heimdall** when he travels through the world, fathering the three main social groups: slaves, free farmers and aristocrats.

Romulus and Remus (*Roman*) Twin sons of **Rhea Silvia** and the god **Mars**. Their mother's uncle, King **Amulius**, tries to drown them at birth, but they are found and suckled by a she-wolf, and later raised by a shepherd. As youths they operate as robbers but, after learning their true history, they kill Amulius and restore their grandfather **Numitor** to the throne. They decide to build a city (Rome) on the site where the wolf found them, but quarrel over its

exact location until Romulus kills Remus. Romulus then becomes the city's king and populates it with fugitives, criminals and the abducted **Sabine** women.

Sabines (*Roman*) Tribe neighbouring the newly founded city of Rome. **Romulus** invites them to a joint religious festival and then abducts all their marriageable women as wives for his hitherto exclusively male Roman inhabitants. The Sabines retaliate by attacking the Romans; but the women are now married and have divided loyalties, so persuade their fathers and new husbands to make peace. The two peoples thus unite.

Sakhmet (*Egyptian*) Goddess with the head of a lioness. A transformation of **Hathor**.

Samhain (*Celtic*) Festival to mark the beginning of winter and the new year, held on 31 October/1 November. Celebrated with markets, fairs and horse races. A dangerous time of ritual mourning for the end of summer, when **Otherworld** spirits walk on earth and mortals can visit the **Underworld**.

Saturn, Saturnus (*Roman*) God of sowing and seed, associated with a primitive Golden Age before agriculture was necessary.

Seth (*Egyptian*) Destructive god of chaos and confusion, brother of **Osiris**, whom he murders and then seizes his throne. His nephew **Horus** claims the throne and their dispute is taken to a tribunal of gods. Osiris intervenes from the **Underworld** to say that Horus is his rightful heir, thus forcing Seth to abdicate. Later becomes god of storms.

Shu (*Egyptian*) God of the air, paired with **Tefnut**. Son of **Atum**, father of **Geb** and **Nut**. Depicted holding up the body of Nut as she arches over Geb.

sibyls (*Roman*) Priestesses of **Apollo**, ecstatic prophetesses. Their prophecies and rules for avoiding disaster were

401

collected into a book consulted by the Romans in times of crisis. When **Aeneas** visits the **Underworld,** a sibyl acts as his guide.

sidh (*Celtic*) An **Otherworld** dwelling place of one of the **Tuatha Dé Danann,** often identified as a fairy mound.

Sif (*Norse*) A goddess, wife of **Thor.**

Sigurd (*Norse*) Heroic prince who kills **Fafnir,** thus obtaining his treasure and magic ring. He is desired by **Brynhild** but marries **Gudrun.**

Silvanus (*Roman*) God of woodlands and uncultivated land.

Sirens (*Greek*) Malevolent creatures, half-woman, half-fish. Their haunting songs lure sailors to their death.

Skylla and Charybdis (*Greek*) A pair of malevolent marine beings. Skylla is a monster with twelve feet and six heads, each with three rows of teeth; Charybdis is a whirlpool which alternately sucks down and throws up heaving water. Together they kill unwary sailors.

Sleipnir (*Norse*) **Odin**'s eight-legged horse, offspring of **Loki** when he shape-changed into a mare.

spells (*Egyptian*) Associated with **Isis,** and used for healing the sick or wounded. Common formulae combine words of magical power with a medicinal prescription, or identify a human patient with a mythological figure cured by divine intervention.

Sphinx (*Greek*) Monster with the face of a woman, the body of a lion and the wings of a bird. Torments its victims by asking an impossible riddle, destroying any who cannot answer it correctly.

Styx (*Greek*) The river surrounding the **Underworld,** across which Charon the boatman carries the souls of the dead.

Tara (*Celtic*) The sacred royal court of Irish kings, where new sovereigns ritually 'marry' their land.

Tefnut (*Egyptian*) Goddess with the head of a lioness, paired with **Shu.** Associated with moisture and dew. Daughter of **Atum,** mother of **Geb** and **Nut.**

Telemachos (*Greek*) Son of **Odysseus** and **Penelope.**

Theseus (*Greek*) Son of Aigeus, king of Athens and hero of many adventures. In the best known, he volunteers to be a victim of the **Minotaur,** which he subsequently kills with the help of **Ariadne.**

Thiazi (*Norse*) A **giant** who disguises himself as an eagle to abduct **Loki** and persuades him to lure **Idunn** into his clutches. Loki subsequently rescues her and Thiazi is killed by the other gods.

Thor (*Norse*) God of the sky, storms and thunder, protector of the common people, the law and the community. Terrifying in his strength and anger, he frequently fights **giants** and monsters but is benevolent to and loved by humankind.

Thoth (*Egyptian*) God of the moon, associated with the secret knowledge of magic. Takes the form of a baboon or an ibis, or a man with the head of an ibis. Also known as **Djeheuty.**

Thrym (*Norse*) A giant king who steals **Miollnir,** the hammer of **Thor,** and refuses to return it unless the gods give him **Freyia** as a bride. Thor disguises himself as Freyia, retrieves his hammer and kills Thrym and his cronies.

Tir na n'Og (*Celtic*) Irish **Otherworld.**

Trojan Horse (*Greek*) Huge wooden horse built by Greek warriors besieging the city of Troy. The Trojans believe it is an offering to their gods and wheel it inside their city walls. Greek warriors hiding inside it then emerge to let the rest of their army into the city, thus finally winning the **Trojan War.**

Trojan War (*Greek, Roman*) Ten-year war in which kings and heroes from all over Greece besiege Troy, after **Paris**

abducts **Helen** from her husband
Menelaos.

Tuatha Dé Danann (*Celtic*) Supernatural
descendants of the first lords of Ireland,
defeated in battle and exiled
underground and into the hills. Still
ruled by their own kings, and
practitioners of magic.

Twrch Trwyth (*Celtic*) A wicked king
transformed into a monstrous boar.
Hunted by **Culhwch** to seize the magic
scissors, razor and comb from between
its ears, in order to satisfy **Ysbaddaden**
and thus win **Olwen**'s hand in marriage.

Tyr (*Norse*) God of war. Brave and wise,
he loses his hand trying to control **Fenrir**.

Underworld
(*Greek, Roman*) Land of the Dead, lying
in the centre of the earth in a complex
of caves and rivers. After death, the
person's soul is ferried across the River
Styx into the Underworld to be judged.
The good are sent to paradise (the
Elysian Fields or the Isles of the Blessed);
but the wicked are condemned to the
dark, infernal regions of Tartarus.
(*Egyptian*) Land of rivers, islands,
deserts and lakes of fire. Dead people's
souls are taken there to be considered by
Osiris and forty-two judges. The dead
person's heart is weighed on a scale,
balanced against the feather of truth and
justice. Light hearts are judged pure and
become blessed spirits in paradise; but
heavy hearts are consumed by a monster
or condemned to eternal torment.

Utgard-Loki (*Norse*) A wise and
cunning **giant** king who outwits **Thor**
and **Loki** when they pay an unfriendly
visit to **Iotunheim**.

Valholl (*Norse*) One of **Odin**'s halls in
Asgard. Warriors killed in battle are
brought here by the **valkyries**, to spend
eternity feasting and fighting. Also
known as Valhalla.

valkyries (*Norse*) Female spirits, servants
of **Odin**. They watch over battlefields,

determining the course of war, and
choose which men should die, escorting
them to **Valholl**.

Vanir (*Norse*) One of the two main
groups of gods, including **Niord**, **Freyr**
and **Freyia**.

Venus (*Roman*) Goddess of love and
beauty, equivalent to the Greek
Aphrodite.

Vesta (*Roman*) Goddess of hearth and
home, equivalent to the Greek **Hestia**.

Vestal Virgins (*Roman*) Six females,
recruited between the ages of six and
ten, dedicated to **Vesta**. They tend the
sacred fire brought by **Aeneas** from
Troy, preserved in a sanctuary at the
Forum in Rome. Required to serve and
remain chaste for thirty years, after
which they are free to marry. Their
punishment for loss of chastity is burial
alive.

Vulcan (*Roman*) God of fire and the
forge, equivalent to the Greek
Hephaistos.

Yggdrasil (*Norse*) The World Tree, a
great tree with its roots in the realm of
the dead, its trunk passing through
Midgard and its topmost branches in
Asgard.

Ymir (*Norse*) A primeval **giant** at the
beginning of time, killed by **Odin** and
his two brothers. They make his blood
into the sea, his flesh the earth, his
bones the mountains, his teeth the rocks,
his skull the sky and his eyebrows into a
protective wall around **Midgard**.

Ysbaddaden (*Celtic*) An evil giant, father
of **Olwen**. Reluctant to let her marry,
since this will bring about his death.

Zeus (*Greek*) Ruler of the gods and
supreme power, controlling the sky,
storms, thunder and lightning. Married
to **Hera**, but has numerous liaisons with
other goddesses, mortal women and
youths. Equivalent to the Roman
Jupiter.

Index